A Few Acres
of Snow

❄

A Few Acres of Snow

Literary and Artistic Images of Canada

Edited by

PAUL SIMPSON-HOUSLEY

and

GLEN NORCLIFFE

Dundurn Press
Toronto & Oxford
1992

Editing: Judith Turnbull
Design and Production: GSN
Cover Design: Ron & Ron Design Photography
Printing and Binding: Best Gagné Book Manufacturers, Louiseville, Quebec, Canada

The writing of this manuscript and the publication of this book were made possible by support from several sources, including the Social Science and Humanities Research Council of Canada and York University. The publisher wishes to acknowledge the generous assistance and ongoing support of **The Canada Council, The Book Publishing Industry Development Programme** of the **Department of Communications, The Ontario Arts Council,** and **The Ontario Publishing Centre** of the **Ministry of Culture and Communications.**

Care has been taken to trace the ownership of copyright material used in the text (including the illustrations). Credit for each quotation is given at the end of the selection. The author and publisher welcome any information enabling them to rectify any reference or credit in subsequent editions.

J. Kirk Howard, Publisher

Canadian Cataloguing in Publication Data

Main entry under title:
A Few acres of snow

Includes bibliographical references.
ISBN 1-55002-157-5

1. Landscape in literature. 2. Landscape in art. 3. Canada in literature.
4. Canada in art. I. Simpson-Housley, Paul. II. Norcliffe, Glen.

PN3352.L35F48 1992   808.88'8   C92-093695-4

Dundurn Press Limited	Dundurn Distribution
2181 Queen Street East	73 Lime Walk
Suite 301	Headington
Toronto, Ontario	Oxford, England
M4E 1E5	OX3 7AD

To

Elona Qorri

Kelly Donoghue

Carol Davison

Carol Dorman

and to

Hilary and Brian

CONTENTS

CONTRIBUTORS

RONALD BORDESSA is a professor of geography and former dean at Atkinson College, York University, Toronto. His main interest is environmental ethics. He has recently published "The Iconic Self: Luther, Culture and Landscape in Finland" in *Sacred Spaces and Profane Places* and "Between House and Home: The Ambiguity of Sojourn" in *Terra*.

JON CAULFIELD is an assistant professor of social science at York University and author of several recent articles in academic journals, including the *Canadian Review of Sociology and Anthropology* and *Urban History Review*.

JACQUELINE GIBBONS is an assistant professor of social science and sociology at York University. Her essay entitled "Towards a Semiosis of Art Nouveau" is published in *The Socio-Semiotics of Objects*.

EDWARD GIBSON is an associate professor of geography and the director of Simon Fraser Gallery at Simon Fraser University, Burnaby, B.C. He curates exhibitions of Canadian art, has contributed to major textbooks on humanistic geography, and has recently completed a prize-winning documentary video, *Imagining Canada*.

PAULA KESTELMAN is senior technician, Department of Geography, McGill University, Montreal. Her publications include articles on Chambly, Cowansville, Granby, Magog, and La Malbaie in Quebec for *The Canadian Encyclopedia* and "Rue Saint Denis: Continuity and Change" for *Montreal Geographical Essays*.

AUDREY KOBAYASHI is an associate professor of geography at McGill University. She is co-editor (with Suzanne Mackenzie) of *Remaking Human Geography* and author of articles on racism, gender, human rights, and Japanese Canadians history.

GLEN NORCLIFFE is a professor of geography at York University. His research on industrial location and labour markets has been published in many articles and books. More recently, he has made a study of the representation of modern industry by painters in the north of England, by French impressionists, and by Canadian artists.

BRIAN OSBORNE is a professor of geography at Queen's University, Kingston, Ontario. He is co-author (with D. Swanson) of *Kingston: Building on the Past* and has published extensively in the fields of settlement history, national communication systems, and images of place in art and literature.

ALEXANDER PAUL is a professor of geography at the University of Regina. He has published articles in the *Canadian Geographer* and *Journal of Applied Meteorology* and contributed the chapter "Russian Landscape in Literature: Lermontov and Turgenev" in *Geography and Literature: A Meeting of the Disciplines,* edited by W.E. Mallory and P. Simpson-Housley.

LINDA JOAN PAUL is a lecturer, Department of Geography, at the University of Regina, Regina, Saskatchewan.

MARI PEEPRE-BORDESSA completed her Ph.D. at the University of Helsinki, Finland, and has recently published a book on Hugh MacLennan. Her interests include national literature and postmodernism.

J. DOUGLAS PORTEOUS is a professor of geography at the University of Victoria and principal of the Saturna Island Thinktank. His most recent books include *Planned to Death* and *Degrees of Freedom*.

ELLEN L. RAMSAY is an assistant professor in the Division of Humanities at York University, Toronto. She has published "Art Education: The Making or Unmaking of Artists?" in *From Orchestras to Apartheid* and has written art reviews for *Parachute, Front, Vancouver Arts Magazine, Insight,* and the *Journal of Canadian Art History*.

BRIAN ROBINSON is an associate professor in the Department of Geography at St. Mary's University, Halifax, Nova Scotia. He has published articles in books and journals, including "The Geography of a Crossroad" in *Geography and Literature* and "Literature and Everyday Life" in *Antipode*.

L. ANDERS SANDBERG is a Canadian research fellow in the Department of Geography at York University. He has published on landscape and literature in *The Canadian Geographer* and *Prairie Forum* and on Nova Scotia's forest and steel industries in *Labour/Le Travail* and *Acadiensis*.

JAMIE SCOTT is an associate professor of humanities at York University. He is co-author of *Cities of God: Faith, Politics and Pluralism in Judaism, Christianity and Islam* and *Sacred Places and Profane Spaces: Essays in Geographics of Judaism, Christianity and Islam*.

PAUL SIMPSON-HOUSLEY is an associate professor and the director of graduate geography at York University. His books include *Sacred Places and Profane Spaces: Essays in Geographics of Judaism, Christianity and Islam* (with J. Scott) and *Geography and Literature: A Meeting of the Disciplines* (with W. Mallory).

FRANCIS (GEORGE) SITWELL is an associate professor in the Department of Geography at the University of Alberta, Edmonton. Much of his research has focused on the problem of decoding the values that a people express subconsciously in the cultural landscapes they create. His two most recent publications are "The Expression of Ideology in the Cultural Landscape: A Statement of General Principles Illustrated with Examples Taken from Edmonton" in *A World of Real Places* and "A Human Geographer Looks at Religion" in *Religious Studies and Theology*.

SHELAGH J. SQUIRE is an assistant professor of geography at the University of Alberta, Edmonton. She has published on Wordsworth and Lake District tourism in the *Canadian Geographer*.

KEITH TINKLER is a professor of geography at Brock University, St. Catharine's, Ontario. His books include *History of Geomorphology: From Hutton to Hack* and *A Short History of Geomorphology*.

ELIZABETH WILTON graduated from Trent University in 1990 with a B.A. (Honours) in Canadian Studies and was the winner of the Wharry Scholarship in Canadian Studies. She has worked as a research assistant for the Canadian Studies Department of Trent University.

LIST OF ILLUSTRATIONS

ACKNOWLEDGMENTS

We wish to thank the Social Science and Humanities Research Council of Canada for financial support for a conference on "Literary and Artistic Images of Canadian Landscapes," held in 1989, that marked the first stage of this project. We also thank SSHRCC and York University for financial assistance towards the cost of publishing this book. At the 1989 conference, a number of colleagues and friends contributed incisive and informed comments on the papers: we acknowledge with thanks the contributions of Debbie Carter Park, Rosemary Donegan, Mireya Folch-Serra, Ila Goody, Ted Goosen, Jordan Paper, John Warkentin, and David Wood.

We also wish to thank Carolyn King and Carol Randall of the Cartography Laboratory, and the staff of Secretarial Services at York University. Finally, we record with gratitude our thanks to Judith Turnbull of Dundurn Press for her helpful comments and careful editing of this manuscript.

1

No Vacant Eden

Glen Norcliffe and Paul Simpson-Housley

. . . And the North was. With winter the snow came.
Whole folios of it. Yet nothing written
except one thing, a bleak expectancy –
the possible with its strenuous shade of whiteness
where an intuition almost without equipment
could trek into the faint wind of the future . . .

What are you . . . ? they ask, in wonder.
And she replies in the worst silence of all her woods:
I am Candida with the cane wind.

What are you . . . ? they ask.
And she replies: I am the wind that wants a flag.
I am the mirror of your picture
until you make me the marvel of your life.
Yes, I am one and none, pin and pine, snow and slow,
America's attic, an empty room,
a something possible, a chance, a dance
that is not danced. A cold kingdom.
— Patrick Anderson, "Poem on Canada,"
in *The White Centre* (1946)

Ces deux nations sont en guerre pour quelques arpents de neige
vers le Canada.
— Voltaire, *Candide* (1759)

*F*or several centuries the image of Canada most frequently purveyed by poets, writers, and illustrators was of a cold, hard, and unforgiving land. Voltaire's dismissive remark about a few acres of snow may lack the wonderful imagery conveyed in Patrick Anderson's verse, but they both touch upon the recurrent Canadian theme of cold, ice, and snow. Beneath the blankets of snow lies a Canadian land endowed with considerable wealth, but which yields its wealth only reluctantly. Manifold difficulties and hazards encountered in harnessing Canada's resources have deterred many of the faint-hearted or the fainéant. It requires stubbornness to survive its periodic displays of elemental fury, and patience to discover its beauty and hidden resources. The image of Canada that has been constructed by its iconographers is far from edenic.

Very different was the image often constructed of the land to the south that was to become the United States of America. There, according to some early promoters, stood an earthly paradise.[1] Vacant, but for some native people, its abundant riches lay waiting for whoever dared to claim them. Dreams of a vacant Eden occupied the minds of many a migrant to the United States. Land speculators, promoters, and frauds proceeded to gild this already voluptuous image in the brochures they wrote for their impressionable clients.[2] Migrants disappointed with what they found on the East Coast were encouraged to "go west" in search of this mythical Eden. Only much later did popular writers such as Faulkner and Steinbeck convincingly demolish this American myth.[3] Canada had no need of a Steinbeck. For several centuries it had been all too clear that this northern land was no vacant Eden.

Canadian oeuvres frequently juxtapose a motif of struggle against elemental forces with a leitmotif of hidden beauty among the hostile elements – for those who persevere in their search for it. We hear, as Mitchell (1987) observes, only fleeting chords in unison from the two opposing forces. Thus, the treatment of landscape in Canadian art and literature is far more than a turbulent eddy in the American and European mainstream. For instance, the development by the Group of Seven of a distinctive Canadian school of landscape painting was recognized internationally in the 1920s. Such works as Cornelius Krieghoff's genre paintings of habitant life in Quebec, Emily Carr's expressionist depictions of British Columbian forests and native cultures, and Paul Kane's luminous field sketches recording native life on an almost unspoiled prairie landscape add timbre to the Canadian landscape school.

In literature, likewise, a corpus of distinctly Canadian works has emerged. For example, Margaret Laurence's (1975) images and references are uniquely Canadian, with Cree legend and Canadian family tradition woven into her narratives. The sterile arid prairie, where the wind is the agent of oblivion, provides a recognizably Canadian setting for Sinclair Ross's *As for Me and My House* (1978). And the bewildering Canadian prairie ambiance is encapsulated in Gabrielle Roy's *La Route d'Altamont* (1966): "Je ne concevais pas, entre moi et ce rappel de l'énigme entière, ni collines, ni accident, passager contre lequel eût pu buter mon regard" (I did not conceive, between myself and this reminder of the whole enigma, either hills or an undulation, passing images on which my gaze might have been able to rest [editor's translation]).

Landscape studies form a common ground bordering on the fields of geography, history, literature, and art. As the following essays seek to demonstrate, crossing traditional disciplinary boundaries can be an illuminating experience. The geographical perspective, which dominates in the essays presented here, has a strong empirical basis. After all, geographers have a very long tradition, dating back to Ptolemy and Strabo, of exploring, describing, and interpreting the earth.

Impressions of landscape presented by artists, novelists, and poets are, of their very nature, more evocative and idiosyncratic; they are designed to convey to the viewer or the reader the artist's or author's particular sense of a place. In some instances they capture the essence of a place, but in other instances they may present a consciously distorted or even a contrived image.

Cultural and historical geographers have a particular interest in describing successive human impacts on landscapes by delineating the way culture has been imposed on nature. Landscapes are, however, more than an ensemble of physical and human components. They have a deeper significance, closely bound up with attitudes and values. This is the significance that writers and artists often seek; as Salter and Lloyd suggest, they are more "interested in revealing the nature of human experience . . . than in explaining and predicting human behaviour" (1976, 2).

The domain of our essays is Canadian landscape. We recognize that the term "landscape" has linguistic connotations that are particularly associated with artists belonging to the romantic movement of early nineteenth-century Europe. Here, however, we apply the term not only to essays appraising the work of artists, but also to geographical descriptions by novelists and poets. To those who view geography in strictly scientific terms, this may seem to be a bold foray. Its purpose is to show that qualitative approaches rooted in the humanities and the fine arts, and now flourishing in geography and related social sciences, present "new ways of seeing" (to use John Berger's memorable phrase) by providing us with a variety of windows through which we can look on Canadian land and society. Since most Canadian landscapes are socially constructed, such eclecticism is all to the good.

The collection of essays presented here explores diverse images of the Canadian landscape. Some authors focus on visual images, including both paintings and engravings, while others examine verbal images conjured up by novelists and poets. The perspective adopted in the essays is broadly geographical, but several of them are informed by understandings drawn from cognate disciplines. For the majority, the geographical viewpoint stems naturally from our disciplinary background, but we find resonance in the proposition made recently by Aritha van Herk (1990) in her collection *Places Far from Ellesmere,* that geography is the essential subtext of all novels. Woven into the essays are five major themes: environment, love of place (topophilia), regionalism, symbolism, and societal and economic issues.

HUMANKIND AND NATURE: WHO IS "THE MONSTER"?

The environment in Canada is frequently characterized as malevolent and implacable. To use Margaret Atwood's term, we are dealing with "Nature the monster."[4] It is futile for human beings to try to conquer nature. Those who join in this battle will find respite only in stoicism or in recognizing the hopelessness of their desires. This is the theme of environmental determinism long familiar to Canadian geographers. The most prolific of Canadian environmental determinists, Griffith Taylor, pointed to numerous instances where human activity was sternly dictated by the harsh Canadian environment. The cold of the North and the vastness of the prairies exemplify this. Attempts to dominate nature in these regions are frequently rebuffed. Indeed, Stegner (1966: 7–8) avers "eternity is a peneplain" and "nature abhors an elevation." Many Canadian authors and artists make allusion to the harsh environments that have resisted human encroachment. In Northrop Frye's interpretation (1971, 138, 142), depictions of such environments express a profound fear of nature. Indeed, he suggests (209) that in reaction to the softening of nature in picturesque images by certain nineteenth-century painters, the Group of Seven presented its harsher side in their images.

This theme is explored in this collection by Linda Paul, who describes the ruggedness of Newfoundland's outport landscape and the barrenness of the mountains of the Yukon. The prairie landscapes of Frederick Philip Grove considered by Francis Sitwell display human vulnerability to drought and blizzards as well as a sense of emptiness. Nebraskan author Willa Cather aptly summarizes the difficulty of confronting the land: "Geography is a terrible fatal thing sometimes" (1895, 8).

In antithesis, other writers and artists display the human despoliation of a perfectly indifferent nature. In this conception, human beings are "the monsters." Material success associated with mechanical and mercenary industrialization is reflected in the landscape. Degradation of the environment and impoverished townscapes are a common result. Douglas Porteous shows how Malcolm Lowry abhorred the destructive power of capitalism in British Columbia, while Anders Sandberg, in similar fashion, describes the ravages wrought by the Nova Scotia timber industry. Alma Duncan's art, appraised by Glen Norcliffe, portrays the terrestrial scars created by the Steep Rock iron mine. Is the new Leviathan a human, or does the "monster" exist in nature? Like Janus, the mythological Roman god of portals whose two faces point simultaneously in opposite directions, humankind finds it tempting to transfer the blame, but nature, with its perfect indifference, cannot be held responsible. Humans therefore cannot cope with nature without a sense of environmental ethics, a problem addressed by Ronald Bordessa in his essay. Margaret Atwood (1972b) in her book *Surfacing* has explored the same issue; immersion, for the female narrator, consists in becoming part of nature, indeed her mind's landscape is indistinguishable from nature.

In spite of the harshness of the Canadian landscape and despite twentieth- and (one anticipates) twenty-first-century demands for real issues and real characters, the tradition of romantic morality lingers, along with all its attendant values and categories. This refined tradition comes simmering from a purifying vat that permits no industrial despoliation whatsoever. Several essays probe into the realities behind romantic images. Take, for example, the sublime landscape of Lucius O'Brien's *Sunrise on the Saguenay,* the subject of Ellen Ramsay's chapter. Serenity and tranquillity are depicted in the painting. Deliberately omitted from the scene are the large blackened areas caused by forest fires and the scarred slopes resulting from the selective logging of a rapacious lumber industry. Similarly, the sheltered, even juvenile, landscapes of Lucy Maud Montgomery feature prominently in Shelagh Squire's chapter on idyllic Prince Edward Island scenery. Although Lovers' Lane, the Haunted Wood, and the Shore Road have factual counterparts, they are situated in a fantasy world devoid of industry. In *Pointe-aux-Coques,* Antonine Maillet presents a similarly romantic and nostalgic vision of a village and a region. Pointe-aux-Coques is a cherished haven from a threatening world. The forest wilderness is essentially a frame that never really intrudes on the sea, the pastures, and the farm plots that make up the world of the Acadian. The idyllic appeal of these villages is juxtaposed with the urban world, an *ensemble* captured by Maillet in her memorable phrase "an antheap of discontent."

Even in harsh environments, harmony with nature is possible. Alec Paul and Paul Simpson-Housley observe that in Ostenso's *Wild Geese,* Caleb Gare violates the earth, whereas Judith instinctively expresses her affiliation with nature by lying naked on the ground. Brian Robinson's lyrical study of Elizabeth Bishop's poetry captures several aspects of cultural harmony in Nova Scotia, while Gabrielle Roy's main character in *The Cashier,* Alexandre Chenevert, is shown by Jamie Scott to achieve internal harmony after taking a rest-cure in rural Quebec. Malcolm Lowry's demands for harmony with the environment is a form of advocacy: after all, the environment cannot defend itself. It is, however, in Inuit art that the continuity of people and nature is most fundamental. In the Far North, the separation of culture and nature is a recent phenomenon of European origin. As Jacqueline Gibbons observes, Inuit art itself brings dead objects back to life and re-creates the continuity of culture and environment.

TOPOPHILIA

An enduring theme that appears frequently in this collection is that of *place.* Place is, as Tuan (1977, 3) puts it, "security . . . : we are attached to [it] . . . There is no place like home. What is home? It is the old homestead, the old neighbourhood, hometown, or motherland." Place is contrasted with *space* or *situation:* place is an entity unto itself, but space/situation relates to other places. For example, one can look at Nanisivik or Calgary or La Mauricie as unique places, but they can also be viewed in their local, regional, and national setting. The special characteristics of places in Canada – and, indeed, of Canada as a nation – have inspired many Canadian artists. Love of place, or *topophilia,* to use the term adopted by Tuan (1977, 4), can develop at a grand scale as national identity and even as imperial patriotism, but it can also become manifest at a much more local scale as attachment to neighbourhood or home town.

The struggle to forge a nation is a recurrent theme in Canadian art and literature. Because the country was colonized by two rival and (as Voltaire laments) warring imperial nations who in the process shattered several more-ancient indigenous cultures, and has since been populated by waves of migrants whose roots lay in a kaleidoscope of different cultures, it is small wonder that nation-building has been an uphill task.[5] Brian Osborne's essay addresses the role of illustrators as fabricators of national identity. In this age of television, the importance of illustrations has been underestimated. It is clear that C.W. Jefferys and his many colleagues had a great influence, especially on children during their school years, when their identities took shape. Keith Tinkler presents an interesting variation on this tradition by making use of modern technology in the form of a Hypercard Stack attached to a desk-top computer. He proposes that the public could be more fully engaged in a nation's geography if we used these new technologies to incorporate images into the learning process and into mass communication.

Paralleling these illustrators are the writers. Edward Gibson's essay deals with Charles Mair, who in his poetry and essays developed Canadian landscape imagery in different parts of the country as he moved progressively westwards. George Grant was perhaps Canada's first literary geographer, but Mari Peepre-Bordessa nominates Hugh MacLennan as the pre-eminent literary geographer of the nation during this century. Small wonder, though, that several writers have caught on to this popular theme: as Farley Mowat and Pierre Berton discovered, it sells. Not surprisingly, the assertion of a national identity also appears in more subtle ways in these essays. Rather than simply waving the flag, there were Canadian ways of doing things. Love of the "North" or of the "wilderness" – and a literal or symbolic re-baptism in it – is part of the national culture. Canadians take a drive to see the fall colours. They have a Group of Seven painting or a native Canadian mask hanging in the living room. They boast in old age of youthful canoeing, hunting, climbing, or skiing adventures in the vast Canadian backyard. This alternation of urban living with experiences in the hinterland is part of the place rhythm of Canada. For example, in Roy's *The Cashier,* Chenevert's re-baptism in rural Quebec helps him to recover an inner equilibrium that was disturbed by the stresses of life in Montreal. In Claire Mowat's novel set in a Newfoundland outport and Aritha van Herk's set in the mountains of Yukon, there are similar themes: the personal growth of protagonists is the result of their being tested by experiences in the Canadian hinterland.

Tuan makes it clear that topophilia may also find expression at a more local scale. For most Canadians this amounts to supporting the local hockey team and reserving a special kind of skepticism for neighbouring (and therefore rival) communities. Among Canadian authors, Antonine Maillet and Lucy Maud Montgomery have perhaps most clearly articulated this zeal. At a larger geographical scale it is an undercurrent in the writing of Frederick Philip Grove and, in an artistic vein, in Adrien Hébert's paintings of Montreal and in Keith Tinkler's portrayal of the Niagara region.

Slightly different is place attachment to a particular kind of land. This distinguishes itself from local patriotism where one has to be an insider. Elizabeth Bishop was an outsider but loved life on the littoral. As Brian Robinson shows, it was being close to the marginal world of land and water that made

Nova Scotia so attractive to Bishop. For Malcolm Lowry, in contrast, the attachment was to the forested wilderness that was being mowed down by the urban-industrial juggernaut.

Place takes on a very special meaning with persons who have been *displaced*. Being uprooted means that one becomes physically an outsider. This theme is central to Kobayashi's essay. Japanese Canadians were made to feel outsiders during the war by mass internment, relocation, forced labour, and deportation. The experience of displacement led to a strong reassertion of culture and, in particular, the writing of *haiku*, a special form of Japanese poetry. A sense of displacement following Le Grand Dérangement is also central to Acadian culture; and it finds expression in Maillet's writing time and again. This sense of displacement is an undercurrent in several other essays. For example, Montgomery left her beloved Prince Edward Island when her husband's job as a clergyman took him to Ontario; for the rest of her life, this displacement coloured her image of the island.

The Regional Mosaic

Among geographers, Wreford Watson was the first to examine the regional theme in Canadian life and letters. As he notes: "Regionalism need not mean disintegration. It may mean diversification. And as long as all the diversities involved recognize their dependence upon each other, they can actually add to the idea of unity" (1965, 22). Regionalism in Canada differs from that of the Old World. It is sometimes painted with a broader brush and may lack the nuances that one finds over short distances – even from village to village – in Europe. It has involved a great deal of transplanting, whereas in Europe the character of a region seems sometimes to have been nurtured *in situ* over long centuries.

There are, of course, many strongly defined regions in Canada, particularly where an element of insularity is present. Despite its romantic interpretation, Lucy Maud Montgomery's Prince Edward Island is clearly a region apart, just as Mowat's *Baleena* records Newfoundland's very distinctive personality. Acadia is a different sort of island, a cultural rather than a physiographic one, but Maillet's writing testifies to a sense of regional insularity.

The character of Canadian regions is explored in several novels. For instance, Sitwell demonstrates that Grove was well aware of subtle regional variations within the Prairies. Of the three Grove novels selected for discussion, one is set in the Park Belt south of Winnipeg, the second further northwest near the frontier of the Park Belt and the boreal forest, and the third in the short-grass country of Saskatchewan. Each of these regions has a distinctive physiography, climate, and vegetation, which accounts for such elements in the novels as the presence (or absence) of drought, of drainage ditches, of mosquitoes, and of trees. In other novels, Maillet and Montgomery write with a certain passion of their native regions. Though Bishop, Mowat, and Ostenso were born outside their adopted regions, they too became close observers of their chosen *pays*.

Among artists, too, there are those who preferred to paint in a particular region. Perhaps the classic case is Adrien Hébert, who was labelled *un régionaliste*, but the term could apply almost as well to Marc-Aurele Fortin and Maurice Cullen, who were both drawn to the landscapes of Montreal and Quebec. This could be said equally for the Inuit and Indian art discussed by Jacqueline Gibbons, where there is a continuum between inner landscapes and the external regional landscapes that express native culture. Thus, the images are part landscape, part spiritscape. Another classic example of a regionally based artist – though not discussed in this book – is Arthur Villeneuve, whose primitivist paintings of the Chicoutimi region have a powerful regional imprint.

Other artists might be called "wanderers," since they travelled far and wide recording regional landscapes. Elizabeth Wilton examines one aspect of Marmaduke Matthews's oeuvre, his paintings of the Rockies, done at the behest of a corporate sponsor, the Canadian Pacific Railway, which had an agenda – to promote tourism and railway travel. His contemporary, Lucius O'Brien, performed a similar task in the Saguenay region. As with the novelists, these wanderers were capable of acute observation. For example, Paula Kestelman shows how Bainbrigge's paintings of Montreal captured the essence of the city in the 1840s.

Of course, regions other than provinces and *pays* are recognized in Canadian literature and art. Most essential to Canada is the dichotomy between the urban heartland and the hinterland, which is sometimes rural, but which over much of the Rockies, the Shield, and the North is simply a wilderness. Much of contemporary Canadian literature and art is urban in its focus. One thinks of Mordecai Richler, Irving Layton, Albert Franck, and Arto Yuzbasiyan. Jon Caulfield, in his essay, points to the role of paintings of city houses, some painted several decades ago, as heralds of modern taste and the wave of gentrification. Paula Kestelman, in her concern for the monumental aspect of certain paintings of Montreal, reflects upon their status as icons of urban culture. Scott notes that rural-urban contrasts form a key part of the story in Roy's *The Cashier*. As already noted, this alternation of *place* between city and hinterland is a common theme in Canadian literature.

IMAGES AND VISIONS, LITERAL AND SYMBOLIC

In fiction, geographical locations and topographical features are frequently transformed, conflated, or distorted to meet the intentions of the writer. They may thereby be given symbolic meaning. Inner logic underlies what at the surface may appear to be geographical confusion. Thus, elements with a physical form can be interpreted symbolically to satisfy emotional and spiritual needs. In *The Cashier,* Chenevert internalizes rural life in his quest for peace. Lac Vert and its environs become absorbed within him, thereby providing him with a sense of inner calm. Often such visionary associations are with one's birthplace, which, because it determines one's roots and points of reference, tends to foster a particularly strong sense of affection. Such a place may mould one's personality through intimate experiences. To lose contact with it is to lose part of one's being.

Elizabeth Bishop spent her childhood in Nova Scotia. This interior experience, combined with her later more objective outsider's view, enhanced her imagery. In Ostenso's *Wild Geese,* the harsh environment was personified in the tyrannical Caleb Gare, whose name is an anagram for rage. This vain and unlovable character produced only tension and fear in all whom he encompassed. In the end the earth avenges itself for his attempted dominance – he perishes in a muskeg. In the same novel, Judith's response to the land is one of duality; this is reflected in her name, which is an andronym (at times she appears as Jude). On the one hand, she responds negatively to Caleb and the drudgery of life on *his* land, but on the other, she finds the land in general to be profuse and romantic, and cannot violate it as Caleb does.

Lowry's symbolism is poetic. Alliteration is the device used to express the duality of capitalism and nature. A chiming of chickadees, a tintinnabulation of titmice, and a phalacrocorax of capitalists give resonance to the juxtaposed sides of Burrard Inlet.

THEMES IN SOCIETY AND ECONOMY

Creative art is, by definition, anthropocentric; being socially constructed, it revolves around humans and their culture. In consequence, art and literature commonly express the values of the cultural and political milieu, even though there are iconoclastic writers and artists who, to a degree, resist conventions and norms. Thus, although for each writer and artist there is an idiosyncratic mode of regard which has evolved during a unique formative experience, there is also a broader cultural and historical setting. As Herbert (1982, 139) observes: "Real historical analysis would tell us how Y's painting fits into his culture." He then criticizes the assumption that "forms of art, to the extent that they are not purely subjective and idiosyncratic, are related principally to one another, as distinct from the society in which they have found existence."

From an economic perspective, the single most important characteristic of the Canadian economy is that it is geared to exporting large quantities of staple products. Take, for example, Ronald Rees's delightful study of prairie landscape art entitled *Land of Earth and Sky* (1984). In the second part dealing with the art of the settlement, many of the images point to the wheat and beef economy. Most memorable are Robert Hurley's vertical grain elevators protruding from a horizontal landscape, a western equivalent of Kestelman's monumental buildings in Montreal. In this collection, the staple economy provides the interpretative theme for Norcliffe's essay on industrial landscapes. For Porteous, Ramsay, and Sandberg, forest industries are important; fishing, of course, is the *raison d'être* of Mowat's outport (Baleena); and tourism has become a by-product of the Anne of Green Gables novels. Elizabeth Wilton argues that Marmaduke Matthews's paintings of the Rockies sought to present a sympathetic vision of the symbiosis between industrial progress (in the form of railways) and the natural grandeur of the mountains. These are but some of the many instances where staples form part of the context in Canadian landscapes.

A second aspect of Canadian society, perhaps less obvious, is that it is highly urbanized. Yet a disproportionate amount of Canadian landscape art and literature is concerned with the wilderness. The Group of Seven is perhaps the best example of this trend, but Farley Mowat's stories of the North are equally to the point. Rural Canada also receives more than its fair share of attention, if population is used as a guide. The many reproductions of Krieghoff's genre paintings and of Clarence Gagnon's colourful canvases of rural Quebec (for instance, on Christmas cards), and the television serializations of Montgomery's novels point to a commodification of this romantic rural imagery. Here, we have sought to keep a balance. Jon Caulfield's essay deals explicitly with the connections between art and the urban housing market. The iconography of Kestelman's images is one of urban domination. For Roy, the city is a mixed blessing: in *The Cashier*, as in *The Tin Flute*, it is sufficiently oppressive that it drives her characters to seek relief in the Quebec countryside. Malcolm Lowry is less equivocal: ensconced in Dollarton on the very edge of Vancouver, he sees the city as a capitalistic wen that infects the surrounding region.

From these images, both pictorial and verbal, comes a sense of social relevance. Perhaps Lowry's voice is the most strident; he was twenty years ahead of the environmental movement in denouncing the rape of the earth. Though couched in more subtle terms, Ramsay's interpretation of *Sunlight on the Saguenay* focuses on the contrast between the acceptance of the sublime imagery of Cape Trinity by high-society Ottawa and the environmental reality of exploitative forestry. Lawren Harris's paintings of houses and industry likewise have a subtext linking industry with social reproduction.

Praxis and Theory

The question of theory is necessarily implicit in all of the essays, and explicit in several. Given the current debates in literature and art, this is to be expected. As editors we accept Lyotard's (1984) postmodern position that there should be no meta-narratives or privileged discourse. No approach is given dominance in this volume; we do not claim the omniscience that would allow us to choose one epistemology over another.

Structuralist ideas are evident in several essays. Strictly defined, their position is that the fundamental problem in the world is that of incoherence, and that its solution lies in the discovery of an absolute order (Folch-Serra 1988, 622). This absolute order takes the form of general structures which may not be identifiable in phenomena themselves, and hence may remain undetected in positivist research. The structures may be found by combining theory and observation. Particular versions of structuralism are the political contextualism that informs the essays of Osborne and Peepre-Bordessa, and the economic contextualism of Norcliffe.

Closely related is the approach of certain critical theorists who argue that through such things as their control of communications and of wealth, persons in positions of power manipulate the state and present information selectively so as to maintain their social domination. For example, images or literature may promote an androcentric or a bourgeois viewpoint within a society that nominally advocates (under its constitution) equality and justice. Critical analysts are particularly interested in such paradoxes. Caulfield, for instance, looks at the paradox of the bourgeoisie trying to reconcile their desires in the context of everyday life (such as housing) with the role they play in the working of industrial capital. For Ellen Ramsay, the paradox is that the bourgeois society that profited from the expansion of the forest industry was also the society which, in its preference for picturesque landscape imagery, turned a blind eye to the mess that the same forest industry was making of the Saguenay region.

Others follow the exegetical and hermeneutical approach with its focus on textual interpretation. Linda Paul exemplifies this in her use of text, and she even makes use of biblical exegesis by reference to the Book of Judges. Both of the essays by Alec Paul and Paul Simpson-Housley present a textual interpretation.

Discussion and praxis of deconstruction is provided by Gibson. Derrida's assertion that "il n'y a pas de hors-texte" encapsulates the point made by Dear that "we are never complete masters of the language we use . . . Hence, we inevitably fail in the exercise of representation" (1988, 266). In consequence we must look not just at what is said, but also at what is not said and what may be unsayable. Rather different is *Homo rimans,* the investigative man whom Sitwell introduces to the scene. *Homo rimans,* the Hercule Poirot of landscape studies, is here engaged in prying into the geography behind literature, but he does not go beyond the available evidence in the way that deconstructionists would. A more didactic approach is followed by Keith Tinkler, who urges us to go beyond our academic roots; Tinkler demonstrates that his art can inform the general public.

The ethical questions that Bordessa examines lie on a higher plane. What are human rights and responsibilities with respect to the environment, and how should they be expressed in landscape literature and landscape art? Bordessa searches for a moral environmental epistemology, which is echoed by Porteous. Thus, *in toto* we have provided an eclectic range of approaches with Canada as our parish. Unlike Byron's corsair, we hope we are married to a thousand virtues.

We conclude by admitting that despite this eclecticism, there are inevitably some gaps. The variety and sheer scale of Canadian landscapes make a comprehensive treatment an impossibility. Our topos is the landscape implications of the literary and artistic works our contributors have chosen. They examine the nation as a whole, and they traverse it, albeit with several skips and jumps, from ocean to ocean. (Places referred to in the essays are identified on the maps in Figures 1.1 and 1.2.) They explore a great variety of landscapes, from coast to tundra, from forest to prairie, and from wilderness to downtown. Moreover, the major perspectives on landscape study are represented. What we have charted may be but a small part of the artistic and literary domain that describes the Canadian landscape, but we hope that we have delineated the major dimensions, and that the domain proves sufficiently attractive that others are encouraged to explore it further.

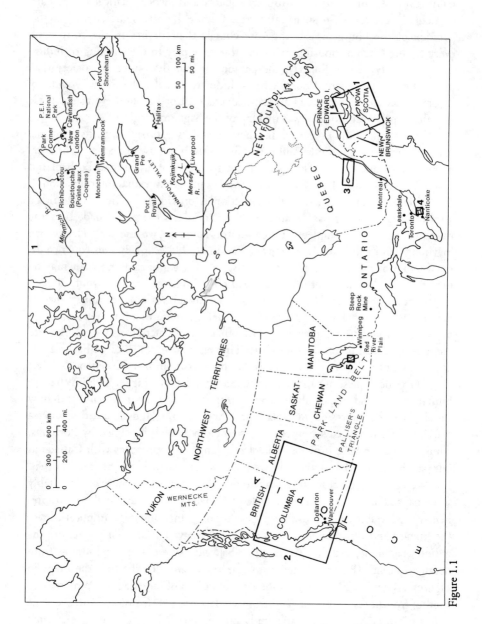

Figure 1.1

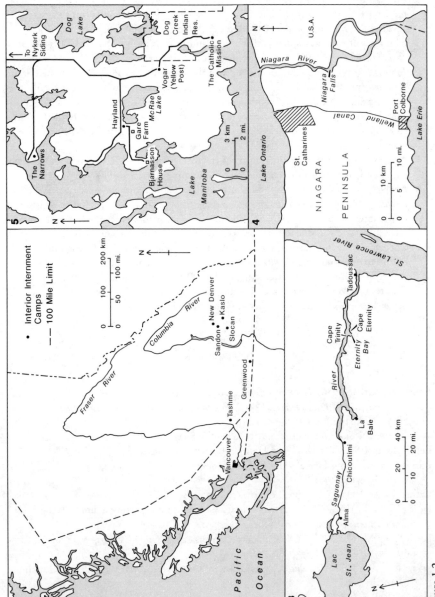

Figure 1.2

NOTES

1 An example of this can be found in nineteenth-century landscape paintings portraying the United States as a sylvan bliss. The picturesque style in fashion at this time served to enhance this romantic image (LaBudde 1958). Novak (1980) also remarks on the pastoral images of American nineteenth-century landscape painting; Thomas Cole's *Dream of Arcadia* (1838) is a good example of this style of painting.

2 Among five types of literature dealing with the physical environment of colonial South Carolina, promotional literature is identified by Merrens (1969) as the category that most assiduously cultivated the image of an earthly paradise. For instance, he cites one Samuel Wilson, who wrote, " I have here . . . described a pleasant and fertile Country, abounding in health and pleasure, and with all things necessary for the sustenance of mankind" (532).

3 Academic historians have questioned this myth for some time. A new revisionist school has recently broadened this critique. See, for example, Limerick 1987.

4 Atwood (1972a) stresses that this involves both exterior landscapes – the external natural universe – and the interior landscapes constructed in the minds of writers and artists. It is in the interior that the monstrous side of Canadian nature is featured. "Nature . . . is often . . . actively hostile to man; or, seen in its gentler spring or summer aspects, unreal. There is a sense in Canadian literature that the true and only season here is winter" (49). Not everyone would agree with this proposition; for example, Ostenso's *Wild Geese* is entirely a summer story (discussed in chapter 18).

5 As late as 1986, 16 percent of Canadians were born outside the country, and that percentage was substantially higher in Ontario and British Columbia.

REFERENCES

Anderson, Patrick. 1946. *The White Centre.* Toronto: Ryerson Press.

Atwood, Margaret. 1972a. *Survival: A Thematic Guide to Canadian Literature.* Toronto: House of Anansi Press.

———. 1972b. *Surfacing.* Toronto: McClelland & Stewart.

Berger, John. 1972. *Ways of Seeing.* Harmondsworth, Middlesex: Penguin.

Carman, Bliss, Lorne Pierce, and V.B. Rhodenizer. 1954. *Canadian Poetry in English.* Toronto: Ryerson Press.

Cather, Willa. 1895. "The Wife." *Courier,* 28 September, 8.

Dear, Michael. 1988. "The Postmodern Challenge: Reconstructing Human Geography." *Transactions, Institute of British Geographers,* n.s. 13:262–74.

Folch-Serra, Mireya. 1988. "A Postmodern Conversation." *Queen's Quarterly* 95, no. 3: 618–40.

Frye, Northrop. 1971. *The Bush Garden: Essays on the Canadian Imagination.* Toronto: House of Anansi Press.

Herbert, Robert L. 1982. "Industry in the Changing Landscape from Daubigny to Monet." In John M. Merriman, ed., *French Cities in the Nineteenth Century,* 139–64. London: Hutchinson.

LaBudde, K.J. 1958. "The Rural Earth: Sylvan Bliss." *American Quarterly* 10:142–53.

Laurence, Margaret. 1975. *The Diviners.* Toronto: Bantam Books.

Limerick, P.N. 1987. *The Legacy of Conquest: The Unbroken Past of the American West.* New York: Norton.

Lyotard, Francois. 1984. *The Postmodern Condition*. Manchester: Manchester University Press.

Merrens, H.R. 1969. "The Physical Environment of Early America: Images and Image Makers in Colonial South Carolina." *Geographical Review* 59:530–56.

Mitchell, K. 1987. "Landscape and Literature." In W. Mallory and P. Simpson-Housley, eds., *Geography and Literature: A Meeting of the Disciplines*, 23–29. Syracuse: Syracuse University Press.

Novak, Barbara. 1980. *Nature and Culture: American Landscape and Painting 1825–1875*. New York: Oxford University Press.

Rees, Ronald. 1984. *Land of Earth and Sky: Landscape Painting of Western Canada*. Saskatoon: Western Producer Prairie Books.

Ross, Sinclair. 1978. *As for Me and My House*. Lincoln, Nebr.: University of Nebraska Press.

Roy, Gabrielle. 1966. *La Route d'Altamont*. Montreal: Editions HMH.

Salter, C.L., and W.J. Lloyd. 1976. *Landscape in Literature*. Resource Papers for College Geography Series. Washington, D.C.: Association of American Geographers.

Stegner, Wallace. 1966. *Wolf Willow: A History, a Story, and a Memory at the Last Plains Frontier*. New York: Viking Press.

Tuan, Yi-Fu. 1977. *Topophilia: A Study of Environmental Perception, Attitudes and Values*. Englewood Cliffs, N.J.: Prentice-Hall.

Van Herk, Aritha. 1990. *Places Far from Ellesmere*. Red Deer, Alta.: Red Deer College Press.

Watson, Wreford. 1965. "Canadian Regionalism in Life and Letters." *Geographical Journal* 131:21–33.

2

Hugh MacLennan:
Literary Geographer of a Nation

Mari Peepre-Bordessa

Hugh MacLennan dared to name the names of my world . . . He dared
to root his story in the geography of our country . . . He was – he is –
the novelist as geographer: a man who reads rivers, who reads water . . .
the cartographer of our dreams, be they social or political or religious or
personal.

—Robert Kroetch, "Hugh MacLennan"

*S*peaking at a conference on Hugh MacLennan, well-known Canadian author
Robert Kroetch described how he had found his first role model in MacLennan's
early writings. Kroetch's words brought into focus a new perspective on Hugh
MacLennan's works, emphasizing as they did the author's contribution to Canadian literature as the "literary geographer" of the country during the 1940s and
1950s. At this time, when Canada is experiencing a renewed and profound
identity crisis, when we focus particularly on the nature of the state and wonder
whether it is to be one or two or several nations, MacLennan's writing is again of
special interest. His novels hark back to a less complicated and more geographically determined view of the country, one that, during the Second World War
and the years immediately following, had a resonance that accorded with popular sentiments of the times. The war had brought the physical realities of their
country into sharper focus for Canadians as they had followed the progress of
their soldiers across the nation on their way to Europe. Nationalist sentiment
demanded a romanticized rendering of a country which at that time was still
largely a blank waiting to be written into existence. Canadians wanted to read
more about their own country. They wanted literary images of mythic propor-
tions upon which to build a new sense of national identity. It didn't take long
before Canadian writers began to fill this need.

Hugh MacLennan was in fact one of the earliest of the Anglo-Canadian
novelists who consciously sought to portray their nation and its landscape in
fiction. In doing so, he helped Canadians to formulate the self-image upon
which their national identity is based. His first three and immensely successful
novels (*Barometer Rising*, 1941; *Two Solitudes*, 1945; and *The Precipice*, 1948)

formed a "national trilogy," presenting an entirely new vision of Canada and its landscapes for his readers.[2] Although his readers already knew Canada to be a vast and beautiful land, MacLennan's evocative images had a profound effect on how Canadians came to perceive themselves in their landscape.

The emergence of an indigenous literature is a prerequisite for national self-understanding, just as it is clear that a nation's self-perception is in turn profoundly affected by such literary expressions. Aldous Huxley makes this point well:

> Nations are to a very large extent invented by their poets and novelists
> . . . How imperfectly did mountains exist before Wordsworth! How
> dim, before Constable, was the English pastoral landscape! Yes, and
> how dim, for that matter, before the epoch-making discoveries of
> Falstaff and the wife of Bath, were even English men and women!
> (1959, 50)

A.R.M. Lower came to the same conclusion, developing the point further when he suggested that landscape and character are deterministically related and that the Canadian soul lies in the landscape of the country:

> If the Canadian people are to find their soul, they must seek for it . . . in
> the little ports of the Atlantic provinces, in the flaming autumn maples
> of the St. Lawrence Valley, in the portages and lakes of the Canadian
> Shield, in the sunsets and relentless cold of the Canadian prairies, in the
> foothill, mountain and sea of the west and in the unconquerable vast-
> ness of the north. From the land, Canada, must come the soul of
> Canada. (1946, 560)

The most successful landscape descriptions in early Canadian literature can be found in its poetry, but even the best early poems were shackled by the imitative and awkwardly transposed modes and imagery of English romantic poetry. The styles and techniques that suited the burbling brooks and daffodils of the English countryside became stilted and even ludicrous when applied to the wilderness that was the physical reality of Canada. It can be argued that Canada came into being only when a uniquely Canadian tradition of literature was developed, when its writers were able to incorporate into their language the diction and cadence of their own community and, using these, could begin to create literary landscapes that were recognizably Canadian.

This lack of suitable language was not the only problem Canadian writers faced, however. Early visions of the landscape were often unsatisfactory; land-scape descriptions ranged from the dark accounts of brutal wilderness by many early writers to the heroic hyperbole of the "our true north strong and free" school of writing engendered by the nationalist Canada First Movement.[3] The

landscape experienced by most Canadians was not the fearful, dark wilderness of
scenes such as this:

> Thick-matted woods where rank luxuriance shoots,
> Where branch entwines with branch and roots with roots;
> Where flies, in myriads, borne on flimsy wings
> Unceasing teaze, with tumefying stings.
> Where the dark adder and envenom'd snake
> In curling folds, lurk in the shelt'ring brake.
>
> (Cary 1789)

Nor could most Canadians really identify with the rhetoric favoured by nationalists in their attempt to create a myth of a superior northern breed:

> Hail! Rugged Monarch, Norther Winter, Hail!
> Come Great Physician, vitalize the gale;
> Dispense the ozone thou hast purified,
> With Frost and Fire, where Health and age reside, –
> Where Northern Lights electrify the soul
> Of Mother Earth, whose throne is near the Pole.
>
> (Taylor 1913)

Ordinary Canadians on their farms and in their cities lived in a relatively
subdued and peaceful landscape, one they could not find described in their
literature until twentieth-century writers such as Stephen Leacock, with his
nostalgia for the pine woods and northern lakes of his Ontario youth, or Frederick
Philip Grove, with his dark and realistic but evocative descriptions of the West,
began to write a Canadian landscape into being. It was Hugh MacLennan,
however, who caught something new in his writings. By sparking the imagination of his readers, he was able to assume his role as the literary geographer of his
nation. MacLennan stood at a unique point in time and space, and he made a
deliberate and self-conscious effort to penetrate that moment and to render his
geography of mind in word pictures.

MacLennan often stated that when he began to write in 1940, there was no
real body of Canadian literature to build upon, nor was there an accepted vision
of a "Canadian" landscape to use as a setting. He quickly realized that he would
have to create his own background if he wished to write about his own country.
The task was not an easy one, as he later explained:

> It seemed to me that for some years to come the Canadian novelist
> would have to pay a great deal of attention to the background in which
> he set his stories. He must describe, and if necessary define, the social
> values which dominate the Canadian scene . . . Whether he liked it or
> not, he must for a time be something of a geographer, a historian and a

sociologist, to weave a certain amount of geography, history and sociology into his novels. Unless he did so, his stories would be set in
a vacuum. (1952, 2)

MacLennan thus deliberately set out to delineate the geography of Canada for
his readers, to give voice to their perceived image of the land, and at the same
time to shape their perception of it to his own. In this he followed in the
footsteps of Canadian artists and, especially, illustrators such as C.W. Jefferys.[4]
That he was successful in his self-appointed task is attested to by the immediate
and continuing popularity of his early works.

In his first novel, *Barometer Rising* (1941), MacLennan literally wrote Canada
into existence in a series of memorable images that extended from the meticu-
lously exact geographical details of Halifax harbour, through the lyrical descriptions of Nova Scotian coasts and villages (a region he obviously knew and loved
well), to the sweepingly grand aerial portraits he drew of an entire half-conti-
nent. Copies of *Barometer Rising* were widely circulated by Canadian servicemen
overseas; in that period of heightened national awareness, many Canadians identified with the book's nationalist themes and images.

The images MacLennan created in that novel caught the essence of Canadian selfhood as no others had yet done, and in the process they changed the
self-perception of Canadian readers forever. His panoramic overviews of the
subcontinent fired the imagination of his readers and allowed them to soar
beyond the towns and villages they lived in to experience the vast sweep of
northern terrain that was their land. His railway lines tied together this limitless
space in a symbolic image that was already passing into collective memory as a
myth of nationhood.[5] His life-giving rivers flowed through prehistoric rock
formations to reach the seas and his craggy coastlines reflected the rugged character of the people who lived there.

In his next novel, *Two Solitudes* (1945), MacLennan gave Canadian readers
symbolic images of nationhood when he described for them the scarlet maple
trees of Quebec, which were "a miraculous upward rush of cool flame" (2); a
grove of sugar maple on a summer night, like "a huge net of shadows suspended
from the treetops" (179); or the Canada geese flying overhead in autumn and
spring (56). His northern winters were "a universe of snow with a terrible wind
keening over it" (4), while in his summers "the heat simmered in delicate
gossamers along the surface of the plain" (135). His third novel, *The Precipice*
(1948), brought Canadians the small Ontario town, raw and ugly to the point of
shock (13) but, still, gracious and dignified with its flower-filled gardens and its
elm-lined streets with their dark masses of leaves arched overhead "like a cathedral nave open at both ends" (5).

MacLennan's readers responded to these very Canadian images in a way that
was new to them. He gave them landscapes they could step into with a recognition of being home at last – often for the first time in their lives. They could
leave behind the European and American settings they had grown up with and

walk the streets of Halifax or Montreal, the towns and villages of Quebec and Ontario; they could rest beside a northern lake or listen to the fog bells on a cold autumn morning by the Atlantic. If literary study is really the study of "a map, a geography of the mind . . . the product of who and where we have been" (Atwood 1972, 19), then a study of MacLennan's writings is most certainly a way to discover the meaning of being Canadian.

BAROMETER RISING

In 1924 J.K. Wright declared that "some men of letters are endowed with a highly developed geographical instinct. As writers, they have trained themselves to visualize even more clearly than the professional geographer those regional elements of the earth's surface most significant to the general run of humanity."[6] These writers have trained themselves to articulate their perceptions of place and landscape more lucidly and pleasingly than most other people. A closer study of the diction, imagery, and alliterative devices used by MacLennan reveals how artists in control of their language can effectively replicate in words a scene they have observed – how they can project a literary image of the landscape into the minds of their readers. Good writers can capture the *essence* of a place and transpose it through their creative imagination and the intricate yet delicate medium of language to project it into the consciousness of their audience, enabling their readers to become part of that landscape and to share the writers' pleasure and experience of it. Language has the power to arouse pleasure of the senses; a reader caught in the verbal web of a carefully woven scene can not only see but also smell, taste, hear, and touch the environment in his or her imagination. The shapes of the words in the mouth become the shapes of the environment. The lines, the angles, the planes of a landscape can be softened to somnolence or whipped to turbulence by the alliterative and evocative quality of the words the author uses.

Several examples from MacLennan's first novel, *Barometer Rising,* illustrate this point. In a passage from the opening pages of the novel, the protagonist, Neil Macrae, who has just returned to Canada from a war-shocked Europe, has climbed to the top of Citadel Hill overlooking Halifax. He sees this familiar scene as if for the first time:[7]

> The details of Halifax were dim in the fading light but the contours were clear and he had forgotten how good they were. The Great Glacier had once packed, scraped, and riven this whole land; it had gouged out the harbour and left as a legacy three drumlins . . . the hill on which he stood and two islands in the harbour itself. Halifax covers the whole of an oval peninsula, and the Citadel is about in the centre of it. He could look south to the open Atlantic and see where the park at the end of the town thrusts its nose directly into the outer harbour. At the park the water divides, spreading around the town to either side; to the west the inlet is called the Northwest Arm, to the east it is called the Stream, and

it is here that the docks and ocean terminals are built. The Stream bends with the swell of Halifax peninsula and runs inland a distance of four miles from the park to a deep strait at the northern end of town called the Narrows. This strait opens directly into Bedford Basin, a lake-like expanse which bulges around the back of the town to the north. (3, 4)

This first scene comes to us in outline only – the fading twilight enhances the contours of the land and these contours are "good," MacLennan tells us, providing with this simple word a key to the whole passage and indeed to all the descriptions of Canadian landscapes that are to follow. These "good" lines have a strength and authenticity imparted to them by geological history: the Great Glacier itself gouged out this harbour and the consonantic arrhythmies of "packed," "scraped," and (especially) "riven" impart a harsh strength to the landscape. Next, the scene itself is described in exact detail, with geographical terms (drumlin, peninsula) lending credence to the assumption that this is exactly what the reader would see from the citadel. The landscape unfolds smoothly as the words flow in from the sea and divide to either side of the viewer, swelling inward and leaving the reader with a precise geographical setting – a word-map of a landscape that was here being described for the first time in a popular Canadian novel.

Hugh MacLennan was indeed writing Canada into being, and this caught the attention of his readers from the very first pages. Startled, they read on, eager to see more of *their* land and, in seeing, to know and assimilate it. The detailed but rather static opening scene comes to life in the novel when Neil Macrae descends down into Halifax and "the throbbing life of the city" (5). As he walks the streets of Halifax, the reader sees the city through his eyes: its crowded streets bustling with wartime traffic; girls with English faces; sailors from a British cruiser; soldiers, dock workers, civilians. This scene, one of the first cityscapes in Canadian literature, captures the vitality and the romance of a town perched on the edge of the continent, a gateway to the world but also a link to Canada's colonial past.[8]

Canadian readers were further rewarded with the following word-picture of Nova Scotia. The affection and warmth MacLennan felt for the landscape of his youth are conveyed to the reader as the lights dim and a cinematic panorama of the region unfolds:

A growing moon, pale as the inside of an oyster shell, hung over the forests and harbours of Nova Scotia, and in this nocturnal glimmer the edges of the province were bounded by a wavering flicker of greyish white, where the sea broke over the rocks of the coast. On all the solitary points thrusting out into the Atlantic, into the Fundy or the Gulf of St. Lawrence, light-houses winked or gleamed like fixed stars. Such fishing boats and small craft as still worked after dark were now black shadows rising and falling to the lift of the groundswell as they glided home to their village coves. The highways were empty and dark, and the windows of the farmhouses gave no light but that reflected from the moon. In the north of the province, around the Sydneys, pouring slag flared against the sky and turned the harbour into a pool of ruddy fire, while the blast furnaces trembled under the pressure of armament production. In all other parts of Nova Scotia, silence gripped the land like a tangible force, for in only two of its counties was there the noise of a great city or factory, or the rush of traffic over a road. (122–23)

MacLennan imposes a spatial order upon the landscape and paints it in contrasts: shades of black and white, land and sea, cold and hot, moon and slag, silence and noise. The whole picture is actually a seascape seen through a camera lens, since it is framed by the sea and the echoes of the waves wash over the forests and harbours in oyster-like colours. The author is also more meticulous with his details this time; the reader is given a real sense of the geographical setting of the province, with its peninsulas, its coves, its highways, and its two cities. A touch of romance is added by the solitary winking of lighthouses, by the small boats gliding home to rest, and by the reflection of moonlight on dark farmhouse windows. And all this is in contrast to the harsh glare of the factory pouring out the armaments that play such an important symbolic role in the story.

Perhaps MacLennan's most successful contribution as a literary geographer came when he expanded his visual territory from the Maritime region to the entire nation, giving Canadians an unforgettable landscape which became rooted in the national consciousness as part of Canadian mythology. Experiencing these landscapes, Canadians could come to a better understanding of themselves and the land that had bred them: a landscape of the mind was written into being.

In the following passage, Neil Macrae has just come to realize the scope of his Canadian heritage; the emotional excitement he feels at this moment is tremendous. What better way to illustrate for the reader the full import of what Neil has just learned than to draw a panoramic word-picture of the entire nation, from coast to coast:

He stopped at a corner to wait for a tram, and his eyes reached above the roofs to the sky. Stars were visible, and a quarter moon. The sun had rolled on beyond Nova Scotia into the west. Now it was setting over Montreal and sending the shadow of the mountain deep into the valleys of Sherbrooke Street and Peel; it was turning the frozen St. Lawrence crimson and lining it with the blue shadows of the trees and buildings along its banks, while all the time the deep water poured seaward under the ice, draining off the Great Lakes into the Atlantic. Now the prairies were endless plains of glittering, bluish snow under which the wind passed in a firm and continuous flux, packing the drifts down hard over the wheat seeds frozen into the alluvial earth. Now in the Rockies the peaks were gleaming obelisks in the mid-afternoon. The railway line, that tenuous thread which bound Canada to both the great oceans and made her a nation, lay with one end in the darkness of Nova Scotia and the other in the flush of a British Columbian noon.

Under the excitement of this idea his throat became constricted and he had a furious desire for expression. (79)

~~For readers only just becoming aware that they lived in a country that could experience simultaneously the full blaze of noon in British Columbia and darkness in Nova Scotia, this was an exciting image indeed.~~ Canada was in the process of fusing a nation out of many scattered settlements and provinces, and this kind of unifying image was one that MacLennan's readers could and did respond to.

A closer reading of this passage reveals a craftsman who has full control of his art. The picture is carefully constructed: the vast sweep of space is tied together effectively by the twin devices of time (it is *now*, and the sun is moving over the continent) and line (the thread-like railway that extends from ocean to ocean). A feeling of excitement and movement is built up throughout the passage by the use of active verbs such as *rolled, sent, turned, poured, drained, passed,* and *packed;* but the "railway line . . . *lay*" passively across the landscape – immobile, important, and effectively foregrounded.

~~The entire scene is bathed in light and colour,~~ with Neil as the spectator in a darkened theatre looking out to the "crimson" glow and "flush" of the sun, to the blue shadows it casts and the purest "bluish" white of snow. The symbolic significance of the "red-white-and-blue" does not escape the careful reader, nor do the allusions suggested by the diction so effectively employed in several places. The "alluvial" earth connotes the span of geological time which Neil will become more aware of later, and thus foreshadows his growth into the space and time of his country. The "gleaming obelisks" of the mountains create an image that suggests antiquity from a more mythological perspective.

All this is written in rolling, sonorous phrases that evoke the solemnity of the Bible and are underlined by the poetic effect given by a generous use of alliterative sound imagery. The vowels in phrases such as "sending the shadow of the mountain deep into"; the sharp glide consonants of "turning the frozen St. Lawrence crimson"; the initial plosives of "lining it with the blue shadows of the trees and buildings along its banks"; or, perhaps most effective of all, the whistling wind heard through the glides and fricatives of "snow over which the wind passed in a firm and continuous flux" (ending in a crisp consonant cluster echoing the crackle of cold snow) – all this creates for the reader a crystal-clear image of a landscape charged with movement and excitement and natural beauty.

This passage is only one of many descriptions MacLennan wrote into *Barometer Rising;* into it went the care that characterized all his attempts to create a landscape his readers could recognize and respond to. The Group of Seven had tried to paint such a landscape, poets such as E.J. Pratt and Frank Scott had caught much of its essence in their poetry, but no one had fully captured the Canadian landscape in prose until the young Hugh MacLennan took on that challenge in 1941.

The sentence that follows the passage from *Barometer Rising* quoted above becomes quite rhapsodic in its emotional response to the land:

> Under the excitement of the idea his throat became constricted and he had a furious desire for expression: this anomalous land, this sprawling waste of timber and rock and water where the only living sounds were the footfalls of animals or the fantastic laughter of a loon, this empty tract of primordial silences and winds and erosions and shifting colours, this bead-like string of crude towns and cities tied by nothing but railway tracks, this nation undiscovered by the rest of the world and unknown to itself, these people neither American nor English, nor even sure what they wanted to be, this unborn mightiness, this question-mark, this future for himself, and for God knew how many millions of mankind! (79)

"Excitement" is certainly the key word here. The same scene is painted again, this time with the emotional overtones of a man in love with his country, a man who can use his artistic skill to transform the geography of his country into images that would evoke a response in his readers. The same techniques are repeated: a "sprawling waste" and an "empty tract" tied by railway tracks and strings of cities; images of the land; the repetitive insistence of "undiscovered," "unknown," "unborn"; the sibilant alliteration; but here, above all, the compelling drum-beat rhythm of the rolling phrases as they shorten and build up to their dramatic climax of God and the "many millions of mankind!"

LATER NOVELS

MacLennan often returned to the Canadian landscape in his later novels, allowing his readers to stretch their imagination over the land and to comprehend it in all its symbolic significance. He also used these descriptive passages to impose order upon his material. By beginning many chapters with a Canadian setting, he emphasized the symbolic relationship between the land or the city and the inhabitant. His next novel, *Two Solitudes*, opens upon a broad view of the St. Lawrence pouring out to the Atlantic Ocean. MacLennan's fascination with geological time comes through clearly here, giving a new depth to his interpretation of the land:

> It is as though millions of years back in geologic time a sword had been plunged through the rock from the Atlantic to the Great Lakes and

savagely wrenched out again, and the pure water of the continental reservoir, unmuddied and almost useless to farmers, drains untouchably away. (1)

Clearly, there is an assured and imaginative control of the material here, for the passage in effect introduces the essential subject of the novel: the two "solitudes" of English and French Canada. This harsh land of solid rock drives the villages of Quebec towards the changes that provide much of the action in the novel. The reader first sees the land of millions of years ago, when that savage sword "plunged through the rock" and created the river as it now flows. A landscape as heroic as this can serve as a setting for great epics – and Canadian readers were delighted to notice here the creation of a national myth in a setting they recognized as their own.

MacLennan returned to the St. Lawrence River often in his writings. In his third novel, *The Precipice*, Lucy Cameron drives along the lakeshore highway and watches the landscape shift and flow past her. First, "the Ontario lake shore, so gentle, so immature" flows past her car window, and then her mind soars off on an imaginary voyage down the St. Lawrence, following the trail of the voyageurs, past Montreal and Quebec, to the "darkness along the empty cliffs of the Gaspé and Labrador" (133). The metaphor of the river as Canadian experience recurred throughout MacLennan's writings, appearing as the symbolic flight of Jerome Martell, that quintessential Canadian male, down the river towards self-discovery in *The Watch That Ends the Night* (1959), and finally finding its fullest expression in *The Seven Rivers of Canada* (1967).

MacLennan also tried to come to grips with the vast expanse of Canada in *The Seven Rivers of Canada*: "Space – so much of North American art and literature has been obsessed with it . . . How to proportion human beings to it, how to reveal the effects of immense land horizons on the . . . people" (vii). The space of Canada is "apparently boundless," he continued, and "on the prairies without even the suggestion of a frame." MacLennan had by now turned from his earlier railroad lines to the Canadian rivers in his search for a unifying link to tie together the incomprehensible vastness of the landscape, a link the human mind could visualize. Technological advances had made air travel possible, and indeed, common, so the aerial view he offers of the Athabaska River is quite different in tone from his earlier imaginary descriptions of the land. It is concrete and geographically exact:

The delta of the Athabaska looks like the delta of most northern rivers, and is not an excessively large one: a maze of swamps and small channels with some principal threads of broad water which are the main courses of the stream finding their way through the obstacles the river itself has deposited. Out of the flat, brownish-black mat of the delta occasional glitters struck sharply upward as the sun was reflected from water oozing through acres of scrubby bush and marsh grass. We were too high to see the birds, but the whole region seemed mysteriously alive with the energy in it. (41)

The terrain of Canada was indeed finding its way into the imagination of Canadian readers. However, it is for his lyrical descriptions of the landscape that MacLennan is best remembered. When the harsh realities of urban life become too much for his characters, they can escape to the Arcadian beauties of the Laurentian Shield. For example, at the end of *The Watch That Ends the Night*, George and Catherine Stewart find peace and meaning at their northern cottage during their last summer together, as they wait for her impending death:

> The clouds crossed the sky, country rains washed the gardens, moons shone on the lake and the hillsides, cicadas sang in the August grass, boys and girls fell in love. In the early October of that year, in the cathedral hush of a Quebec Indian summer with the lake drawing into its mirror the fire of the maples, it came to me that to be able to love the mystery surrounding us is the final and only sanction of human existence. What else is left but that, in the end? (349)

Any reader who had ever seen a northern lake in autumn could recognize and enter into this scene. Canadians had by now developed a sense of place. Other novelists and poets would later reflect other images of the land, many with more success, but by the 1960s a new generation of Canadians felt that enough had been written about the subject; a more sophisticated self-image was wanted and MacLennan's visions of the land seemed to have become old-fashioned. Hugh Kenner then wrote that "the surest way to the hearts of a Canadian audience is to inform them that their souls are to be identified with rocks, rapids, wilderness, and virgin . . . forest" (cited in Watt 1966, 249). Many people agreed with him. Canadians had developed a more comfortable rapport with their landscape. They knew it because it had been written and painted into existence for them; they could now accept it comfortably for what it was and, thanks to writers such as Hugh MacLennan, they could build new visions of their landscape upon these foundations.

NOTES

1 Gabrielle Roy was writing *The Tin Flute* at about the same time as MacLennan was at work on *Barometer Rising*. Her novels are generally considered to mark the beginning of modern French Canadian literature, and her landscapes and cityscapes served the same purpose for French Canada as MacLennan's novels did for English Canada. See Jamie Scott's discussion of *The Cashier* in this volume, chapter 14.
2 The vehement debate among Canadian academics about which writers are to stand above others as "firsts" in the country's literary history will not be settled for some time yet. In my book *Hugh MacLennan's National Trilogy*, I argue that MacLennan must be recog-

nized as having been an important explicator and formulator of Canadian national identity in the 1940s and 1950s. His novels greatly influenced a whole generation of Canadian readers, and several are still in wide circulation today.

3 The Canada First Movement was a loose grouping of Canadian nationalists who were active around the time of Confederation. Their unofficial spokesman and poet laureate was Charles Mair, whose works are discussed by Edward Gibson in this volume, chapter 4.

4 See Brian Osborne's chapter for a discussion of the how the illustrator C.W. Jefferys depicted the history and identity of Canada in pictures (chapter 3).

5 A myth which, alas, the present-day government seems bent on destroying.

6 Statement by J.K. Wright, as quoted in Salter and Lloyd 1977, 1.

7 This verbal map is necessary at the very beginning of the novel in order to help the reader make sense of the narrative that follows.

8 Many Canadians were familiar with Halifax. Not only had most immigrants entered the country through this port, but also thousands of soldiers had passed through it during both world wars. Moreover, wartime reports about troop activities in Halifax had brought the city to the attention of newspaper readers across Canada. MacLennan's novel sparked their imagination and brought Halifax and the whole region to life for them.

REFERENCES

Atwood, Margaret. 1972. *Survival.* Toronto: House of Anansi Press.

Cary, Thomas. 1789. *Quebec City.*

Huxley, Aldous. 1959. *Texts and Pretexts.* London: Chatto and Windus.

Kroetsch, Robert. 1982. "Hugh MacLennan: An Appreciation." In *Hugh MacLennan: 1982. Proceedings of the MacLennan Conference.* Toronto: University of Toronto, Canadian Studies Programme.

MacLennan, Hugh. [1941] 1969. *Barometer Rising.* New Canadian Library 8. Toronto: McClelland & Stewart.

———. *Two Solitudes.* [1945] 1967. Laurentian Library 11. Toronto: Macmillan.

———. 1948. *The Precipice.* Toronto: Collins.

———. 1952. "My First Book." *Canadian Author and Bookman* 28:2–5.

———. [1959] 1961. *The Watch That Ends the Night.* Toronto: New American Library of Canada/Signet.

———. 1967. *Seven Rivers of Canada.* Toronto: McClelland & Stewart.

Peepre-Bordessa, Mari. 1990. *Hugh MacLennan's National Identity: Mapping a Canadian Trilogy.* Helsinki: Finnish Academy Press.

Salter, Christopher L., and William J. Lloyd. 1977. *Landscape in Literature.* Resource Papers for College Geography No. 76–3.

Taylor, William Henry. 1913. *Canadian Seasons, Spring: Summer: Autumn: Winter: With a Medley of Reveries in Verse and Prose and Other Curios,* 63–64. Toronto: published by author.

Watt, Frank. 1966. "Nationalism in Canadian Literature." In Peter Russell, ed., *Nationalism in Canada.* Toronto: McGraw-Hill.

3

"The Kindling Touch of Imagination": Charles William Jefferys and Canadian Identity

Brian S. Osborne

ART AS COMMUNICATION

Throughout the late nineteenth and early twentieth century, geographic expansionism, a new Canadian political identity, and a national historiography were accompanied by a search for images appropriate for an increasingly self-confident young nation (Berger 1970; Harper 1974; Osborne 1988; Reid 1973). A post-Confederation vitality in the world of Canadian arts and letters was accompanied by several manifestations of self-conscious chauvinism: the founding of *Stewarts' Quarterly,* which published the work of Canadian writers; the "Canada First Movement," dedicated to an "Anglo-Saxon consciousness" in Canadian politics and literature; the Toronto Art Students' League calendars depicting scenes from Canadian life; the first exhibition of the Group of Seven in 1920; the Arts and Letters Club of Toronto and its publication *Lamps* (literature, architecture, music, painting, and sculpture); and the formation of the Sculptors' Society of Canada in 1928, with its declared search for subjects of Canadian significance (Coutu 1989; Davis 1986; Osborne 1988; Parker 1985).

Not surprisingly, the world of art was much influenced by such developments. Foreign renderings of the sublime and picturesque in landscape (see Ramsay and Wilton, this volume) and of the rustic and bucolic in domestic stereotypes were replaced by attempts to represent Canada's regionally distinctive physical and cultural landscapes. For some, these efforts culminated in the contribution made by the Group of Seven to a sense of unique Canadian identity. For others, the Group was but one phase and element of a process that needed to be evaluated, assessed, and critiqued.

Whatever the debate over how appropriately these images represent the Canadian identity, what cannot be questioned is the role played by such visual imagery in the development of the popular consciousness. Moreover, for this role to be effective, the concern for cultivating the nativism expressed by the various artistic practitioners had to be widespread. The images considered to be nationally charged symbols had to be physically and intellectually accessible to the general public rather than being sequestered in the drawing-rooms or galleries of the elite.

Indeed, the central premise of this chapter is that cultures are very much a product of their systems of communication. As stated by Koch:

> Communication is central to the production of culture. It is the means by which knowledge is created and shared, roles are negotiated, and social relationships are legitimized . . . Through communication, culture is both maintained and changed: behaviors and values that underlie them are accepted, questioned, or reinterpreted according to current circumstances. (1988, 6)

Clearly, visual images should also be considered as important elements of communication. While I appreciate the importance of the historical context, the power of iconographic and semiotic analysis, and the mental gymnastics possible through the imaginative exercise of deconstruction, the focus here is centred on art as message and system of communication (Barrel 1980; Daniels 1984; Rosenthal 1983, 1984).

ILLUSTRATING CANADA

Innovations in the organization and technology of the printing and publishing industries did much to further the mass circulation of the new domestic and nationalistic images. From the late nineteenth century on, the British and American domination of the Canadian book trade was challenged by several Canadian newcomers. The Methodist Book and Publishing House, Macmillan of Canada, Thomas Nelson and Sons, the Musson Book Company, and George N. Morang and Company led the field in popularizing books by Canadian authors and on Canadian themes, many of which became best sellers. Perhaps of even greater importance were their efforts in the field of textbook publishing, another segment of the industry that had hitherto been dominated not only by British and American commercial producers but also by British and American ideas. Not surprisingly, the illustrators of these new textbooks were motivated to provide appropriate visual imagery to accompany the text (Parker 1985, 151–56).

If the publishers were now in place to ensure Canadian production of the work of a growing number of Canadian literati, parallel developments in the modes of communication premitted much larger readerships. Mechanization of the printing process dramatically changed the speed, volume, and cost of output of the printed page (Parker 1985, 156–61). The new steam-powered cylinder press was well established in Canada by the 1850s. At first capable of only 1,100 impressions an hour, six-cylinder machines improved production to 6,000 impressions per hour, while ten-cylinder presses were capable of 20,000 impressions per hour.

These innovations were compatible with improvements in the production of illustrations, especially the very significant advances in cheap engraving methods.

While steel, copperplate, and wood engraving continued to be used for illustrating such volumes as N.P. Willis's *Canadian Scenery Illustrated,* the nineteenth century witnessed the rapid shift to the new technique of lithography, which was simple, inexpensive, and promised larger runs of imagery. Invented about 1796, the method had spread to the United States by 1828, and by 1831 it was in use in Canada for the production of maps, charts, cheques, banknotes, music, and pictures. A combination of nineteenth-century materialism, increased literacy, and greater affluence ensured the widespread application of this technology. In Toronto, the centre of Canadian printmaking, whereas there had only been one lithographic company in 1846, there were four by 1860, seven by 1875, ten by 1890, and sixteen by 1899 (Burant 1984; Davis 1986).

Furthermore, photography was common by the 1840s. By 1860, half-tone screen photo-engravings were achieved by using intaglio printing to transfer images to chemically treated copper plates. A redefined version of this was later patented by William Augustus Leggo as "Granulated Photography," which he further developed into his "Leggotyping" and "photolithography." Indeed, most of the modern photo-derived printing techniques used in commercial printing had been developed by the 1890s and refined to high standards of reproduction.

The application of new reproduction techniques to mass-circulated volumes was almost immediate, two fine examples being Sir Sandford Fleming's *The Intercolonial: An Historical Sketch* (1876) and George Monro Grant's *Ocean to Ocean* (1873). Two Americans, Howard and Reuben Belden, early recognizing the Canadian market for various forms of picture books, produced volumes of scenes of the countryside, county atlases, local histories, and biographies. Perhaps their most notable product, *Picturesque Canada,* was a collection of no fewer than 500 illustrations of rural and urban Canada by a team of notable artists and accompanied by a collection of essays by a no-less-distinguished team of writers. (See Ramsay, chapter 13, and Wilton, chapter 20, this volume).

While the new technology improved public access to Canadian volumes and their illustrations, of even more importance was the emergence of a new genre, the illustrated magazine. George Edouard Desbarats applied the new technology to two illustrated newspapers, *The Canadian Illustrated News* (1869–83) and *L'Opinion Publique* (1870–83). In 1888, Desbarats and his eldest son, William Amable Desbarats, began publishing *The Dominion Illustrated* (1888–93). The implications for developing a Canadian consciousness were not lost upon them. George E. Desbarats declared that his intention was to

> illustrate the Dominion of Canada, its scenery, its *industries,* its cities, its attractions and resources, its great public works . . . we are for building up a homogeneous, united, patriotic nation, and for ignoring all prejudices of race and sex; marching onward, shoulder to shoulder to the goal of prosperity that looms ahead. (Burant 1984, 121)

Eventually, the Desbarats' journals were to reproduce and circulate more than 15,000 images of places, people, and events during their fourteen years of operation. The age of the mass media had arrived, bringing with it the age of mass imagery.

Burant has argued that these developments constituted a veritable revolution in nineteenth-century visual communication that had a significant impact upon the developing consciousness of nationhood:

> Canadians in the nineteenth century learned to communicate through pictures of every kind. They emerged from a world which had very few accurate visual self-images and entered one in which for the first time most people, at little or no cost, could see life illustrated in books, newspapers, magazines, photographs, and films. Above all, Canadian cultural nationalists such as George Desbarats and the members of the Royal Canadian Academy believed that visual imagery had a unique ability to reach and influence everyone, regardless of social, cultural, or linguistic differences, for the good of the nation and the quality of social and moral life . . . The revolution in visual communication marked, for them, the beginning of a new and promising stage in the development of intellectual and social life. (Burant 1984, 121)

Artists in particular welcomed the advent of photo-engraving and photo-lithography, as their interpretations and renderings of reality were no longer subject to the distortions introduced by the intervening agencies of engraver and printer. Indeed, the contribution of the artists who were called upon to provide illustrations for mass-circulated media merits further attention. The "illustrators" of popular magazines, novels, and textbooks, for example, were powerful agents in propagating and popularizing national identity. Many of the journeyman illustrators produced what they were commissioned to produce. Others, however, were very aware of the power of their medium, and particular themes became increasingly common in the popular works of illustration.

Of all the illustrators, C.W. Jefferys (1869–1951) was undoubtedly the most prolific and certainly the most focused in his attempt to advance a distinctive image of Canada and further a national identity. In this chapter, Jefferys's works will be considered in the context of the iconography of communications and its role in creating a better understanding of the development of regional and national identity. He is commonly regarded as "Canada's foremost historical painter," the one who has "done more than any other artist to preserve for posterity the history of Canada" (Jefferys 1945). While some may question Jefferys's dominant position in the growing field of historical illustration, none can question his productivity. His oeuvre of historical paintings, murals, and line drawings constitutes a valuable body of material that allows examination of this theme of artistic imagination and national consciousness.

C.W. Jefferys: Artist and Illustrator

With the benefit of hindsight, it becomes apparent that C.W. Jefferys's career prepared him well for his role as "historical painter" and advocate of art in the service of literature and education. His qualifications as illustrator-cum-artist-cum-scholar were the essential prerequisites for his contribution to the development of Canadians' consensual image of their history — albeit an image that was to be changed in subsequent years.

Jefferys had a well-trained eye for the Canadian landscape and the distinctiveness of environmental setting. He argued that it was "inevitable that a country with such marked physical characteristics as Canada possesses should impress itself forcefully upon our artists" and that the impressionists' style was "peculiarly adapted to the expression of high keyed luminosity and the sharp clear air of mid-Canada" (Stacey 1976, 14). He and his fellow artists had been inspired by the exhibition of Scandinavian artists at the Chicago World Fair of 1893 and commented: "We perceived that their painters were grappling with a landscape and climate similar to our own, and felt a natural affinity to them . . . We became northern minded" (Stacey 1976, 13).

Jefferys's fondness for snow scenes and Ontario landscapes is revealed by his *Time, Landscape with Fence, Rail and Boulder Fence, Boulder Field,* and *Pioneer Graveyard.* With sketchbook in hand, he travelled the countryside collecting his landscape vignettes of fields, snake fences, pine trees, and the other elements of the vernacular world of rural Ontario that others considered to be unsuitable subjects for paintings. But his artist's eye ranged far beyond Ontario. His renderings of the prairies were the first important visual statements to challenge clichés of a distinctive landscape dominated by horizontal lines of land and sky. Rather, he produced images that celebrated variations in the colour of sky and foliage

C.W. Jefferys, *Time,* watercolour, 38.1 x 52.7 cm, National Gallery of Canada.

and the diversity of local topographies (Lord 1974; Rees 1984; Stacey 1985). Jefferys, therefore, was the artist of the cleared lot and settled countryside, of the prairies of the West, and the maple woods of rural Ontario. And while not sharing the Group of Seven's boreal focus, he – together with other members of the Toronto Art Students' League – certainly identified with the more famous group's concern with art as an expression of national distinctiveness. Indeed, according to A.H. Robinson, Jefferys pioneered in matters of style and subject to transform the unorthodox and mundane into the acceptable and distinctive:

> His keenly analytical mind found beauty in the stump fields, snake fences, pine trees and woodlots of old Ontario, at a time when these subjects were considered inartistic and unpaintable by the more ortho- dox artists. Wherever he paints, whether it is the Northern lakes, the St. Lawrence River, or the Western plains, his canvasses and watercol- ours have a subtlety of draughtsmanship, a deft handling of colour and a definite Canadian significance. (Stacey 1976, 16)

If Jefferys's artistic skills were honed by decades of observing Canada in the raw, his talent for narrative art started early:

> Whenever the schoolroom was to be dressed up for closing exercises and the like, I was called upon to decorate the blackboard with pictures of the landing of Julius Caesar, the Battle of Queenston Heights, or Wolfe at Quebec. My school fellows crowded me with commissions to illus- trate their books. I established a fixed scale of prices: an English history, I think, was two cents, a Canadian, one cent. My masterpiece was an illustrated Algebra, for which, as a subject that I detested, and as lying outside my legitimate field, I exacted five cents. It was a solitary *tour de force.* (Jefferys 1945)

In the 1880s, he was apprenticed to the Toronto Lithographic Company, did some illustrations for the Toronto *Globe,* became a member of the fledgling Toronto Art Students' League, and assisted in their various renderings of Cana- dian themes. Moving to the United States in 1892, Jefferys became an illustrator with the New York *Herald* until his return to Canada in 1900 to work with the ill-fated *Moon* and, subsequently, for a longer term, with the Toronto *Daily Star.* Whatever his natural talents for "narrative art," Jefferys appreciated gaining journalistic experience in the "golden age of illustration,"

> the period before the camera ousted the pen of the draughtsman. The depiction of the crowded life of the present – fires, political meetings, murder trials, society happenings, strikes, ceremonials, riots – was a startling and unwelcome change from the romantic imaginings of the past. (Jefferys 1945)

But it was not simply his penmanship that benefited. He went on to comment:

> Before long it dawned upon me that here was the very best training for the
> job that I wanted to do. I realized that yesterday was as alive as today and
> that the accurate and intensive observation of how many people acted
> now and here was the best way to understand how they acted in the past.
> (Jefferys 1945)

Certainly, he achieved some recognition in this field. On the occasion of the
publication of *The Picture Gallery of Canadian History,* the Toronto *Daily Star*
editorialized on his accomplishments: "He supplied this newspaper with some of
the loveliest drawings that have ever appeared in any Canadian daily . . . To look
through the *Star* files of that period is to be impressed with the genius of this
illustrator" (Jefferys 1942).

It was his early work as a journalistic illustrator that provided Jefferys with
both the material and style for his later activities as a historical narrative painter.

JEFFERYS AND HISTORICAL LITERATURE

Jefferys also appreciated the potential for integrating the imaginations of the
artist and storyteller. In an essay entitled "The Treatment of Landscape in the
English Novel," Jefferys reflected on the relationship between fiction and landscape art:

> Both landscape and fiction are among the younger children of art . . .
> Fiction perhaps reflects the common tastes and sentiments of mankind
> more accurately than does any other form of literature to the extent that
> the novel may be the best index of the measure and quality of the
> popular appreciation of landscape. And, since one art can sometimes
> cast an illuminating light upon another, it may not be altogether un-
> profitable in considering the use of landscape in fiction to adopt the
> point of view of the painter rather than that of the literary critic.
> Although the present essay may smell, perchance, more strongly of the
> studio than the student's lamp, the angle of vision may offer as a natural
> outcome some novelty of view. (Jefferys n.d.)

This "novelty of view" came to the fore in Jefferys's own venture into book
illustration. In 1906 he commenced a collaboration with Marjorie Pickthall to
illustrate three of her popular children's adventures: *Billy's Hero or the Valley of
Gold,* which was subtitled *A Story of Canadian Adventure; Dick's Desertion: A
Boy's Adventure in Canadian Forests,* subtitled *A Tale of the Early Settlement of
Ontario;* and *The Straight Road,* described as *Adventures in the Backwoods of
Canada.* In the same year, Jefferys illustrated D. Boyle's volume of national
doggerel for children, which was intended to capture children's imagination

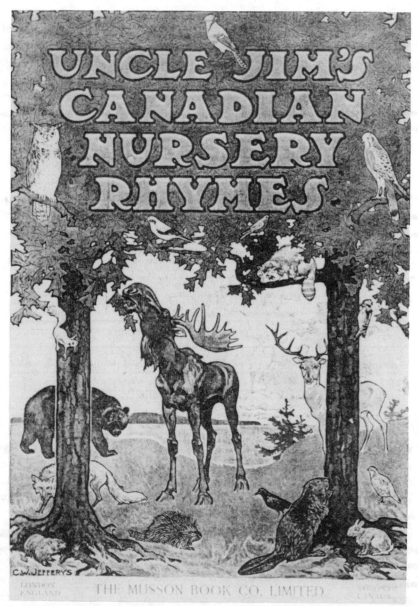

Illustration by C.W. Jefferys for the cover of David Boyle's *Uncle Jim's Canadian Nursery Rhymes.* Courtesy of the Osborne Collection of Early Children's Books, Toronto Public Library.

away from the domination of foreign-based nursery-rhyme imagery. Boyle's *Uncle Jim's Canadian Nursery Rhymes for Family and Kindergarten Use* is replete with Canadian allusions and Jefferys's beavers, bears, woodpeckers, elk, pine, waterfalls – and, of course, the ubiquitous fences (Boyle 1908). In this same period, he also provided art work for Walter Nursey's biography of Brock. In the 1920s, Jefferys continued this activity with his illustrations for such Canadian classics as Richardson's *Wacousta* and Kirby's *The Golden Dog.* One of his favourite projects, Haliburton's *The Clockmaker,* was conceptualized early but did not appear until after his death.

With the exception of *The Clockmaker,* most of these projects were limited to a frontispiece or perhaps to a small clutch of plates integrated into the storyline. They were, however, very much Canadian stories, and Jefferys's careful eye for ethnographic and landscape detail is reflected in these illustrations.

DIDACTIC ART AND HISTORY

Not content with merely dramatizing fiction and providing illustrative fillers for the works of others, Jefferys became much concerned with art as a medium for communicating history and heritage (Pierce 1950). He felt a responsibility to use his artistic talents to further a better appreciation of Canadian history and national identity and did so in over 2,000 illustrations. In a 1936 article in the *Canadian Historical Review* entitled "The Visual Reconstruction of History," Jefferys complains of the deficiencies of historical illustration:

> The critical examination of written history, the comparison of source-documents, are marked features of modern historical study. The pictorial reconstruction of history too frequently displays the lack of a corresponding degree and quality of discrimination. (Jefferys 1936, 264)

Further, he argues for an expertise that "ventures into the more perilous region of imaginative reconstruction" to rouse "popular interest in historical subjects." These were the talents he brought to bear in his several forays into interpretive historical illustration. Thus, Jefferys illustrated the *Chronicle of Canada* series (1912) and subsequently the new edition of George N. Morang's *The Makers of Canada.* This was followed by a commission to illustrate two series of American history, *The Chronicles of America* and *The Pageant of America.*

But his major concern was with Canadian history. In the 1920s, he collaborated with historian George M. Wrong in producing historical texts sponsored by the Ontario and Manitoba departments of Education and published by Ryerson. The publisher's foreword to the 1929 edition of Wrong's *The Story of Canada* asserts the central mission of the volume, so redolent of current pedagogic concerns:

> There is something radically wrong when so many students in our schools dislike Canadian history. There is sufficient romantic interest in the story of our nation to make such a state of affairs unwarrantable . . . *The Story of Canada* offers a solution. It is a course in Canadian history, and therefore a connected narrative from the earliest times to the present, stressing equally all parts of the Dominion. It is written in a simple,

vivid, narrative and dramatic style, emphasizing at all times the romance of incident and character. That is, it is a *story*. (Wrong 1929, v)

These are the key words: narrative, romance, drama. To this end, it was argued that the illustrations by "C.W. Jefferys, RCA," were central:

These illustrations are more than decorations. Mr. Jefferys is an artist and a scholar and, through years of research and artistic work, has provided a valuable commentary upon Canadian history from the earliest times to the present. The scholarly historical illustration is a comparatively new art, and Mr. Jefferys' drawings are a contribution, not only to art, but to the cause of Canadian history also. (Wrong 1929, vii)

While the sweep of the history covered by Wrong ranged from prehistoric times to the Canada of the First World War, Jefferys's thirty-two illustrations were not as comprehensive. Exploration, settlement, military exploits, and agricultural settlement are prominent, but the emphasis is certainly on a pre-Confederation Canada with little attention paid to such issues as the Canadian Pacific, mining and lumbering, towns and cities, and no immigrants – other than "les Filles du Roi" and the Loyalists! This initial collaboration with Wrong was followed by some 200 illustrations and maps for the *The Ryerson Canadian*

C.W. Jefferys, *Father Hennepin at Niagara Falls, 1678*, Imperial Oil Collection, National Archives.

History Readers, a collection that did concern itself with a more comprehensive conceptualization of Canadian history.

Jefferys's first individual application of his talents as an "artist and a scholar" was his 1930 publication *Dramatic Episodes in Canada's Story,* which consisted of sixteen essays and sixteen plates that had previously appeared in the *Toronto Star Weekly.* The author's preface repeats a now familiar refrain:

> In the selection of the episodes pictured and described herein, I have had no intention of attempting to present the most important or significant events in the history of Canada. This, in any case, would be a matter of opinion, of varying points of view. My aim has been merely to pick out from the great mine of Canadian history a few fragments that may suggest its richness in human interest and its wealth of picturesque and dramatic incident. (Jefferys 1930)

Recognizing the need for a balance between authentic sources and "artistic licence," Jefferys outlines how he approaches his renderings of the undocumented. Artists must base their images on their "own conceptions," with the aid of their subjects' actions, words, and the "probability and logic of the situation"; images are "imaginative conceptions" based on "authentic data, "minor facts," and "the spirit and larger significance of the events they depict." He concluded that "if they visualize in some degree the life of our past, and arouse an interest in the common heritage of our country's history, their main purpose will be fulfilled" (Jefferys 1930).

In 1934 Jefferys produced his second volume, *Canada's Past in Pictures.* Again his stated method is the "selection and combination of facts supplied, and such sympathetic imagination and artistic interpretation as I could bring to bear upon the subject" (Jefferys 1934). This volume was enlarged to fifty-one essays and plates, but its emphasis was still on explorers, missionaries, the military, and "other intrepid or inspiring personalities of early Canada" (*Globe* 1934). The Ryerson Press's promotion also drew attention to another distinctive feature of Jefferys's oeuvre: "Pioneer women are not neglected and stories are told of Madame de la Tour, the brides who came over from France, Marie Hebert, called the Mother of Canada, and Mère Marie d'Incarnation." Jefferys always referred to the significant role of his work in developing the minds of young boys and girls of Canada, and clearly he recognized the importance of the presence of female images for both genders.

The Queen's University Lorne Pierce Collection includes Jefferys's own copy of *Canada's Past in Pictures,* which has in it a handwritten plan for his next project. Prepared in October 1939, *A Pictorial History of Canada* was to consist of no fewer than 600 illustrations organized in three volumes as follows:

Volume I: Section 1   Indians and Eskimos
             Section 2   Discovery and settlement

C.W. Jefferys, *Samuel Hearne on His Journey to the Coppermine, 1770,* from *The Picture Gallery of Canadian History* (1945), vol. 2.

C.W. Jefferys, *Potash Boiling*, from *The Picture Gallery of Canadian History* (1945), vol. 2.

Eventually published by Ryerson as *The Picture Gallery of Canadian History*, the first volume appeared in 1942, the second in 1945, and the third in 1950. Again, the first two volumes were to be based upon Jefferys's by now distinctive methodology of historical art: "factual drawings" were to be accompanied by "a large selection from the imaginative pictures of episodes and phases of Canada's history which the author has made during the last forty years. All of these are based on authentic historical material" (Jefferys 1942). The art work was to be primary, the text being limited to "condensed introductions indicating the significant features of the life of the period and notes of such of the pictures as seen to require information additional to that supplied by the titles and explanatory lettering on them" (Jefferys 1942). It is with a tone of some regret that Jefferys recognized that the ground rules had changed for the last volume. It is almost with a lament that he comments, "Because of the nearness to our own times, and the wealth of pictorial reporting, there has been less occasion for imaginative pictorial reconstructions as in the former volumes (Jefferys 1950).

Despite the advent of photography, Jefferys made a major contribution to Canadian society in his role as interpreter and illustrator of Canadian history.

C.W. Jefferys, *Main Steet, Winnipeg, Looking South, 1902*, pen and ink, 42 x 51 cm, Jefferys Estate Archives, Toronto.

Lorne Pierce, a colleague and associate at Ryerson Press, recognized this. He comments that Jefferys had

> wearied of illustrating histories with portrait busts of the great and near great. He wanted to make these worthies step down off their plinths and live. He wanted to set them in the proper context of their time and place. He wanted to make them live again in so real a manner, that even small boys and girls at school could easily share in these experiences, and be proud of their heritage. (Pierce 1960)

This he did with considerable energy and vigour. Indeed, one of the most powerful – some would say insidious – legacies of Jefferys's illustrations of educational materials is that his work has constituted the dominant source for the development of a consensual image of Canada's history.

RECORDING FOR POSTERITY

In the preface to his three-volume study *The Picture Gallery of Canadian History,* Jefferys declares:

> The history of a country is to be read not only in its written or printed records. These, while of the greatest value and importance, do not tell us all we desire to know. Old buildings, early architecture, tools, vehicles, weapons and clothing, contemporary pictures of people, places and events must be examined to fill out the story. (Jefferys 1950)

Recognizing that "time not only works its changes but carries much away," Jefferys believed that his mission was not only to stimulate interest in history but also to record it for posterity. Stacey's evocative title "Salvage for Us These Fragments" captures another important dimension of Jefferys's oeuvre (Stacey 1978). Both the multiplicity of images and the well-informed eye serve to make the Jefferys material of particular importance in recording the development of Canadian society.

Apart from wanting to idealize the national history in his romantic representations of Champlain and Frontenac, the Loyalists and the Rebels of 1837, Jefferys felt that it was important that he also represent the ordinary and prosaic – albeit in "heroic" pose. This concern for the vernacular and ordinary, for the common experience of the majority, also resulted in his performing an important role as antiquarian, archaeologist, and – indirectly – preserver and conserver. His published illustrations and notebooks constitute a treasure trove of records of a material world long gone. His colleague and eulogist, Lorne Pierce, underscores that these works preserve

> records and minute details of buildings, tools, household utensils, farm implements, canoes, carriages, dress, weapons, and so on, which even

today are scarcely a memory. Whatever records we have of many of these are to be found in these pages, and they are correct in every detail. Jefferys would continue the hunt for years to verify a musket lock or a shoe buckle. He insisted on going over battlefields himself tracing the ruins at Louisbourg or Fort Ste. Marie on the spot, returning to old grist mills to check the machinery again, searching farm house attics for old lanterns, cradles, or carriage lamps. When he draws snowshoes they

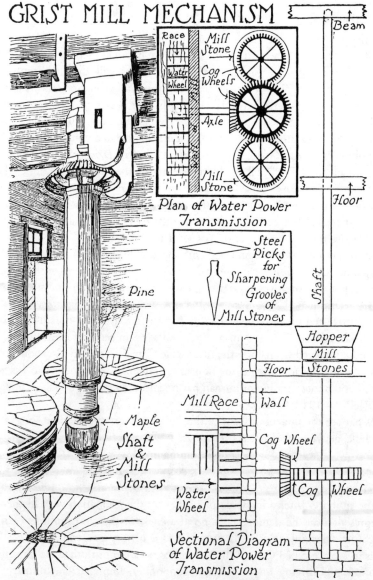

C.W. Jefferys, *Grist Mill Mechanism*, from *The Picture Gallery of Canadian History* (1945), vol. 2.

are correct for time and place and the user, whether Indian or white
man. The same is true of canoes, the dove-tailing of log-buildings, and
even wheels for cart, wagon or carriage. (Pierce 1950)

Because of this preoccupation with detail and precision, the work resulting from
Jefferys's mission "to illustrate pictorially Canada's past" came to be recognized
as a major source by museums, collections, schools, theatres, pageants, and all
concerned with knowing the details of the past.

CONCLUSION: C.W. JEFFERYS'S LEGACY

From the turn of the nineteenth century, many Canadian writers and artists were
conscious of their role in nurturing a distinctive national identity. In the 1890s,
the popular mass image of Canada for many was still that of Empire and
Canada's part in it. The advertisement for the Canadian operetta *The King's
Cadet* was certain to stir patriotic fervour in the hearts of all warm-blooded
Canadians. In the 1940s, after a half century of determined image creation by
nationally minded artists and illustrators, a mass-circulated volume on the Canadian political process, George W. Brown's *Canadian Democracy in Action*, still
turned to Norman Rockwell for his rendering of the "Four Freedoms." These
two images – *The King's Cadet* and Rockwell's *Four Freedoms* – are diagnostic of
the major threats to Canadian identity: imperialism and continentalism. More
recently these challenges have been constituted by "Dallas" and "Falconcrest"
versus "Masterpiece Theatre" and "Yes Minister"!

In his period, Jefferys countered with a veritable barrage of artistic historical
propaganda and national consciousness raising. His work progressed through
several types of initiatives and prompted a mixture of sobriquets: romantic-
historical, commercial, promotional, didactic, patriotic, and documentary. Whatever the preferred phase of his work, all demonstrate the well-honed skills of an
artist, a keen journalistic eye for a story, and a warm sense of camaraderie with
the people involved in making the distinctive Canadian society. In the words of
Lorne Pierce, "In addition to his skill as a craftsman, he brought to his work
sympathetic understanding of human nature and the kindling touch of imagination" (Jefferys 1942, flyleaf).

What are the images of Canada that Jefferys communicated? If we evaluate
his whole oeuvre, what pattern emerges? A formal content analysis would be
more precise, but at a glance we see a dominance of an Eastern Canada over the
West and of rural over urban and industrial; we see too a high representation of
French and Indian themes, of missionaries and explorers, and of war, conflict,
and the military. Interestingly, despite Jefferys's preoccupation with history and
its representation, he demonstrates no awareness of the contributions of Innis,
Creighton, Mackintosh, and Lower. His is a history of people, politics, and
events in a place called Canada, but he makes no attempt to theorize on some of
the influential driving forces of staple economies, immigration, industry, and
urbanization. However, he cannot be faulted on his sensitive awareness of the

role of three constituencies often neglected in traditional history – the native peoples, the ordinary people, and women. These are given pride of place.

His concepts and images have survived to this day – and not only in books and galleries. They are to be found as murals in the Chateau Laurier, Manoir Richelieu, and the Royal Ontario Museum; one image was reproduced as a four-cent stamp commemorating the founding of Halifax; the sculpture along the Niagara Parkway was designed by Jefferys; and his imagination was also directed to the production of the Royal Society of Canada's Tyrrel Medal and the medal struck to celebrate the Jubilee of Canada's Confederation. Not a week goes by without a modern newspaper using a Jefferys's reproduction to illustrate a historical theme. Even contemporary marketing experts recognize the allure of evocative images of patriotism – Canadian beer drinkers, for example, are urged by Jefferys's heroic nation builders to "join the Upper Canada Rebellion."

Label bearing illustration by Jefferys. Courtesy Upper Canada Brewing Company.

REFERENCES

Barrel, John. 1980. *The Dark Side of the Landscape: The Rural Poor in English Painting, 1730–1840*. Cambridge: Cambridge University Press.

Bell, Michael. 1973. *Painters in a New Land*. Toronto: McClelland & Stewart.

————. 1980. "Why look at this stuff?" *The Roles of Documentary Art in Understanding a Cultural Heritage*. Proceedings of conference held at the Art Gallery, Mount Saint Vincent University, Halifax, Nova Scotia, 31 October.

Berger, Carl. 1970. *The Sense of Power: Studies in the Ideas of Canadian Imperialism, 1867–1914*. Toronto: University of Toronto Press.

Boyle, David. 1908. *Uncle Jim's Canadian Nursery Rhymes for Family and Kindergarten Use*. Toronto: Musson.

Burant, Jim. 1984–85. "The Visual World in the Victorian Age." *Archivaria* 19:110–21.

Burgoyne, St. George. 1919a. "Some Canadian Illustrators." *Canadian Bookman*, January, 21–25.

————. 1919b. "Some Canadian Illustrators." *Canadian Bookman*, April, 27–30.

Coutu, Joan-Michele. 1989. "Design and Patronage: The Architecture of the Niagara Parks, 1935–1941." M.A. thesis, Queen's University, Kingston, Ont.

Daniels, Stephen. 1984. "Human Geography and the Art of David Cox." *Landscape Research* 9, no. 3: 14–19.

Davis, E. Angela. 1986. "Business, Art and Labour: Brigden's and the Growth of the Canadian Graphic Arts Industry." Ph.D thesis, University of Manitoba, Winnipeg, Man.

————. 1988. "The Hothouse of Canadian Art." *The Beaver*, February/March, 37–47.

Duffy, Dennis. 1976. "Art-History: Charles William Jefferys as Canada's Curator." *Journal of Canadian Studies* 11, no. 4: 3–18.

Duval, Paul. 1961. "The Story of Illustration in Canada." *Provincial's Paper/Word and Picture* 26, no. 2.

Harper, J.R. 1974. *Painting in Canada: A History*. Toronto: University of Toronto Press.

————. 1974. *A People's Art: Primitive, Naive, and Folk Painting in Canada*. Toronto: University of Toronto Press.

Jefferys, C.W. 1930. *Dramatic Episodes in Canada's Story*. Toronto: Ryerson Press.

————. 1934. *Canada's Past in Pictures*. Toronto: Ryerson Press.

————. 1936. "The Visual Reconstruction of History." *Canadian Historical Review* 17: 249–65.

————. 1942, 1945, 1950. *The Picture Gallery of Canadian History*. 3 vols. Toronto: Ryerson Press.

————. 1956. *Sam Slick in Pictures: The Best of the Humour of Thomas Chandler Haliburton*. Toronto: Ryerson Press.

Kirby, William. 1925. *The Golden Dog: A Romance of Old Quebec*. Toronto: Musson.

Koch, Susan. 1988. "Communication and the Production of Culture." In *Communication Systems for an Information Age*, Communication and Technology Program, Office of Technological Assessment, U.S. Congress, Washington, D.C.

Lord, B. 1974. *The History of Painting in Canada*. Toronto: NC Press.

Osborne, Brian S. 1983–84. "The Artist as Historical Commentator: Thomas Burrowes and the Rideau Canal." *Archivaria* 17: 41–59.

————. 1983. "Art and the Historical Geography of Nineteenth Century Ontario: An Humanistic Approach." In F. Helleiner, ed., *Cultural Dimensions of Canada's Geography": Proceedings of the German-Canadian Symposium, August 18–September 11*, Occasional Paper 10, Department of Geography, Trent University, Peterborough, Ont.

————. 1988. "Images of People, Place, and Nation in Canadian Art." In Dennis Cosgrove and Stephen Daniels, eds., *The Iconography of the Past.* Cambridge: Cambridge University Press.

Pantazzi, Sybille. 1966. "Book Illustration and Design by Canadian Artists, 1890–1940." *National Gallery of Canada Bulletin* 4, no. 1: 6–9.

Parker, George L. 1985. *The Beginnings of the Book Trade in Canada.* Toronto, University of Toronto Press.

Pickthall, Marjorie L.C. 1906. *Dick's Desertion: A Boy's Adventure in Canadian Forests, a Tale of the Early Settlement of Ontario.* Toronto: Musson.

————. 1908a. *The Straight Road: Adventures in the Backwoods of Canada.* Toronto, Musson.

————. 1908b. *Billy's Hero, or the Valley of Gold.* Toronto: Musson.

Pierce, Lorne. 1960. "Eulogy at Unveiling of Plaque Commemorating C.S. Jefferys," 30 August.

Rees, Ronald. 1976. "Images of the Prairie: Landscape Painting and Perception in Canadian Art." *Canadian Geographer* 20: 259–78.

————. 1978. "Landscapes in Art." In K. Butzer, ed., *Dimensions of Human Geography.* Chicago: University of Chicago Press.

————. 1984. *Land of Earth and Sky: Landscape Painting of Western Canada.* Saskatoon: Western Producer Prairie Books.

Reid, D. 1973. *A Concise History of Canadian Painting.* Toronto: Oxford University Press.

Richardson, John. 1906. *Wacousta: A Tale of the Pontiac Conspiracy.* Chicago: A.C. McClurg.

Rosenthal, Michael. 1984. "Approaches to Landscape Painting." *Landscape Research* 9:2–13.

Spurgeon, Greg. 1983–84. "Pictures and History: The Art Museum and Visual Arts Archives." *Archivaria* 17:60–74.

Stacey, R. 1976. *Charles William Jefferys, 1869–1951.* Kingston: Queen's University.

————. 1978. "'Salvage for Us These Fragments': C.W. Jefferys and Ontario's Historic Architecture." *Ontario History* 70:147–70.

————. 1985. *C.W. Jefferys.* Ottawa: National Gallery of Canada.

Sutherland, Fraser. 1989. *The Monthly Epic: A History of Canadian Magazines.* Markham, Ont.: Fitzhenry & Whiteside.

Symons, Harry. 1958. *Fences.* Toronto: McGraw-Hill Ryerson.

Wrong, George. 1929. *The Story of Canada.* Toronto: Ryerson Press.

————. 1950. "A Biographical Introduction" to C.W. Jefferys, *The Picture Gallery of Canadian History*, vol. 3.

4

Theory in Literary Geography: The Poetry of Charles Mair

E.M. Gibson

INTRODUCTION

Only twenty-five years ago, literary geography was a new phase in Canadian letters. Wreford Watson's essay "Canadian Regionalism in Life and Letters" (Watson 1965) was sharp enough to cut some of the ice in literary nationalism and to anticipate the high modernist interpretations of Canadian literature – Northrop Frye's *The Bush Garden* (1971) and Margaret Atwood's *Survival* (1972). More recently, the theme of landscape and literature shows some sign of becoming less reductionist. Indeed, as the *Canadian Geographer*'s published proceedings of a 1988 workshop on the topic show (Sandberg and Marsh 1988), literary geography has acquired the shiny new vocabulary of contemporary critical theory and will no doubt become strategic in establishing geographic research in life after modernism. My reaction after reading "Focus: Literary Landscapes – Geography and Literature" was one of delight. First, I was delighted to find the records rich in references to geographers who are newly published on the topic. Second, I was delighted to discern both a willingness to linger with approaches to literary geography that were conventional two decades ago and a willingness to explore new approaches in light of developing methodologies in neighbouring disciplines. All too often we seem stalled in acrimony because we draw unnecessary lines between older and new models of interpretation.

Underlying the endorsement for new models is the assumed value of what Richard Morrill, writing about geography in general, calls the "theoretical imperative":

> If there is not a convincing theory of why and how humans create places and imbue them with meaning, then it is time to develop that theory – or someone else will do it for us. I think that a lot of fine cultural and historical geography does just that, perhaps through historical and ethnographic methods, rather than statistical, but via a disciplined inquiry that is capable of duplication and verification. (Morrill 1987)

That quotation is typical of the predominantly liberal tone of Richard Morrill's plea for theory. But the tone, as liberal as it is, excludes any direct reference to the critical theorists deployed in Brian Osborne's gentle argument for the application of the interpretive procedures of semiotics, structuralism, and deconstructionism, and a more theoretically informed critique of social communications and cultural formations (Sandberg and Marsh 1988, 268).

The appeal to theory, critical theory at least, surrounds us. There is a virtual Niagara of Canadian essays, dissertations, books, new societies, new journals, new courses, conferences, institutes, and workshops, all of which rest on a corpus of critical theory. The citations of Benjamin, Barthes, Ricoeur, and de Man, of Derrida, Habermas, Foucault, Gadamer, and Jameson, are numerous in the humanities and social sciences. Below the surface of this urgent quest for theory is a suspicion, a suspicion that should be crucial for our generation: that theory may not be an authoritative entity; theory may not lie before us awaiting our intellectual constructions that will explain the features of a poem or the features of the environment in which a poem is created.

This essay attempts to dispel absolute faith in the capacity of theory to furnish explanations in literary geography. It will do this by assessing what is at risk in assuming the theoretical basis of structuralism, semiotics, post-structuralism, hermeneutics, and deconstructionism, and by showing the instability of these models of inquiry in relation to three poems written by Charles Mair.

THEORY IN LITERARY GEOGRAPHY

In an initial step to destabilize the faith we hold towards theory, we might keep before us the fact that even those who denounce theory utilize it despite their protestations to the contrary. Those early examples of literary geography that followed the humanist interpretations of Wreford Watson rely on common sense and the shared values of a common culture in interpreting the literature of Canada. They treated literature as autonomous aesthetic works that record familiar concerns. In a sense even these early studies are theoretical, since to claim they are not is already a theoretical position. Thus, even those not devoted to critical theory demonstrate a theoretical basis to their work at one level. But what about those who are self-claimed devotees of critical theory? Within the baffling, but no doubt productive, literature of critical theory, a geographer is bound to complain about the clouded distinctions and the overlapping of meanings associated with structuralism and post-structuralism. A reading of Jonathon Culler's introduction to his 1982 text, *On Deconstruction, Theory and Criticism after Structuralism* (1982), helps to clear the confusion, but certainly not entirely. Culler neglects to place in context the works of Roland Barthes, Jurgen Habermas, and Fredric Jameson. Structuralism, according to Culler, is most crucially distinguished from its opposing field, post-structuralism, by its abiding faith in rationality and its use of linguistic models in a series of scientific projects that account for literary forms and meanings based on "grammars" or systematic inventories of linguistic elements (Culler 1982, 22). Levi-Strauss's *Structured Anthropology*

(1963) and the early work of Roland Barthes (e.g., 1966) are examples of structuralism, but some would also add the positivistic interpretations of Northrop Frye (1957). Post-structuralism investigates the way these projects are subverted by the text itself or by the context of economic, social, and political inequalities. Thus, for our purpose of interpreting texts, the critical theories of Habermas (McCarthy 1978) and Jameson (1971) are included in the post-structural genre. Geographers' familiarity with Marxism (Harvey 1973) and with Anthony Giddens's (1981) theory of "structuration" would tend to suggest that these latter two critical theorists should be included as champions of structuralism. When we read from literary criticism that lays claim to either structuralism or Marxist post-structuralism, we feel that something complex and authoritative is going on, something scientific, something that is canny, duplicatable, and verifiable. To the degree that this is true, structuralist and Marxist post-structuralist studies would seem to meet the requirements Morrill sets for geography.

But the more we read in critical theory, the more accurately we are able to discriminate in the meanings the word "theory" attains in different contexts. In his 1982 argument for theory, the distinguished deconstructionist Paul de Man (1982) laments the resistance to the use of theory that is developed outside the literary arts to interpret literature. However, in seeming contradiction, de Man also argues that resistance to theory is integral to the use of theory. On another level, both de Man and Jacques Derrida, perhaps the most "pains-taking" of the post-structuralists, formulate their theory from existing works of creative writing. Neither has written a book that is pure theory. In Derrida's 1974 text, *Of Grammatology,* the operating definitions of analytical procedures ("arch-writing," "temporal experience," "trace," and "hinge") are developed from established texts such as those of Rousseau; they are not drawn from idealized abstract schematics.

The distinction between theory and practice collapses in the theories of even the most orthodox deconstructionists, such as the American scholar Harold Bloom (1973) and Culler (1982, 228). If we know anything about deconstruction theory, we would expect that works derived from founding authorities would, by their nature, deconstruct theories of the founding authorities. There can be no stable and universal deconstruction theory in the sense that there is a stable central place theory.

Hillis Miller (1976), the American deconstructionist, goes so far as to label the systematic linguistical procedures developed by de Man and Derrida as Dionysian, tragic, and uncanny because no matter how ordered and logical their procedures, the threads of logic of these post-structuralists lead to regions of the absurd and illogical or they lead to impasses. Unlike the measurable results of structuralists like Claude Levi-Strauss (e.g., 1976) and of the semiologists like Roland Barthes (1966, 74–124), the interpretations of the deconstructionists are not completely brought out into the sunlight of happy reason and theory.

We may in a like manner, but at a different level, dispel the notion that hermeneutics is a theory-oriented method of analysing meaning in literary work, a method that is devoid of practical experience, of life in the "real world."

Hermeneutic theorists such as Hans Georg Gadamer (1977) and Paul Ricoeur (1976) are closer to the humanist critics who informed earlier works of literary geography, the geographers whom Douglas Porteous took aim at in his insightful critique "Literature and Humanist Geography" (1985). Hermeneutic interpretations sidestep the question of rhetoric, grammar, and linguistic functions entirely. They rely on the assumption of a monolithic, stable, common-sense meaning of the text, a meaning that is controlled by the intentions of the author and by narrative references to the "real world" of history and geography. Hermeneutic interpretations are conspicuously bloated with the jargon of science and the complex schematics of Heidegger and Hegel, but ultimately these interpretations are a rejection of scientific theory. Gadamer leaves no doubt that the scientific method is not the way to knowledge and truth. He replaces it with participatory involvement in dialectics and the so-called hermeneutic circle. Based on human or lived experience, the interpretations of Gadamer are an antidote to all the doubting of the deconstructionists – they tend to tell us that the world is very much as it appears.

This brief deconstruction of theory with a view to its use in literary geography shows that the genre of literary theory is heterogeneous. The critical theories we have introduced as of use in literary geography are those that have the power to make strange what is now familiar to us, and to make us conceive of our analysis in new ways. But now that we have shown the risks of applying theory to literary geography, suppose we see how it works in practice.

CHARLES MAIR AND LITERARY GEOGRAPHY

While there are very good reasons for a geographer to be interested in the work of literary nationalist Charles Mair, the aesthetic appeal of these works is not among them. Even his champion biographer, Norman Shrive (1965), and more recent critics (Woodcock 1975) are unsparing in their criticism of Mair's plodding imitation of British romantics and his inability to control language. There are several reasons why the writing of Charles Mair appeals to contemporary students of literary geography: his work enjoyed widespread popularity in Canada towards the end of the nineteenth century; Mair wrote from lived experience in every region of the country excepting Quebec and the Atlantic region; there is documented evidence that he intended to write as a political ideologue and with a "native style"; and the context of his writing varied with respect to his relative economic, social, and political power.

The occasion of this chapter is not the first time I have read from Charles Mair. There was an initial selective reading in Karl Klinck's undergraduate course on Canadian literature at the University of Western Ontario. There was a second, more systematic, reading from Norman Shrive's well-received *Charles Mair: Literary Nationalist*, at the time of the Canadian centennial. The most recent and detailed reading I have undertaken was subsequent to my having read the work introduced in the beginning sections.

The important question that surfaced during my last reading was this: Did place of residence have any association with the imagery of Mair? Or is the imagery of Mair a consequence not so much of where he was living when he wrote (Southern Ontario, Portage la Prairie, Prince Albert, the Okanagan Valley, or the West Coast) as it is a function of the place to which he returned and the direction to which his mental compass frequently pointed (Southern Ontario) (Mandel 1977)? Had this question come to mind prior to my having read critical theory my inquiry would have taken the form of Shrive's biography. I would have been attracted to the most aesthetic images in his work, I would have tried to determine the geographic references – all this in the interest of under-standing the universal as opposed to understanding the particularistic references to the "objective" geography of Mair's changing residence and of Southern Ontario. In fact, I no doubt would have proceeded the way Wreford Watson did in "Canadian Regionalism in Life and Letters." Such an inquiry would have been worthwhile. I never thought of Watson's essay as being unsystematic or "light" when reading it in 1965. Indeed, I found it exciting, illuminating, and intellectual in feeling.

Yet in contrast to Watson's humanist criticism, and from the perspective of deconstruction, a more systematic inquiry is possible, one that separates every element of what Mair said from what his text might mean in an ideological sense. We would begin such an analysis by organizing his text into categories of literary types – poetry, novels, dramas, reports, and so on; then we would determine which types were written in the various parts of Canada Mair lived. This procedure establishes that Mair's poetic verse offers the best text for exami-nation – in particular the utopian poem "Dreamland" (written in southeastern Ontario during 1868) and the poems "Absence" (a love verse) and "Kanata" (a patriotic verse), both written in Prince Albert during 1888.

At this point a special reference to Derrida's *Of Grammatology* is made. It becomes critical to stress that from a deconstructive perspective, a reference to Derrida is only an iteration. Derrida's procedures are not a pure set of instruc-tions to copy blindly. The followers of Derrida and de Man do not necessarily copy procedures in the way that those using central place theory copy the procedures established by Walter Christaller. They respect them, imitate them, but also deviate from them and parody them according to the needs of their inquiries. It is important in this illustration that before detailed analysis gets under way there be confirmation of the existence of particular records. There needs to be evidence of what Derrida calls "trace" (records of the conditions of social, economical, and political settings in which Mair wrote in both these places and times). There are such records (Shrive 1965). It is also important to establish if in these cases of changed residence there are what Derrida calls a "hinge," or a fundamental shift in the social, economical, and political condi-tions in which Mair wrote poetry. And there is.

Mair was a bachelor in his thirties during the time he wrote "Dreamland." He had the modest but comfortable support of his merchant family's estate and spent his time in Ottawa, Perth, Kingston, and his home town, Lanark. In the months before and during 1868 he was also a medical student and worked at his family business; during the final editing of "Dreamland," he held an appointment in the Parliamentary Library, one partly obtained through his association with the Conservative Party. These were times of rich promise for Charles Mair: his poetic and political aspirations were supported by his involvement in the Canada First group and his first lyrics were read before public bodies and published in provincial presses.

What emerges from the life he led twenty years later and finds expression in "Absence" and "Kanata" is startlingly different. Mair had married and lost one son. He was earning a reasonable living, if uneven, from trade and land development, had lived in Manitoba and the Northwest Territories, but returned to Southern Ontario for extended visits to write his drama "Tecumseh" (Shrive 1965, 157–95). His political position and loyalties to the Conservative Party had shifted: he had become unhappy with the National Policy because it benefited Central Canada at the cost of Western Canada. This shift in loyalty to Western Canada is striking, particularly since he and his family had been prisoners of Riel's insurgent forces and that rebellion had led to the loss of his library and working manuscripts. While there is no doubt about his political compass swinging westward during these twenty years, what, we may ask, happened to his poetic imagery?

In response to this query, an inventory was made of imagery contained in the three poems cited. The source of these poems was the 1926 publication *Master-works of Canadian Authors,* edited by John Gavin and introduced by Robert Horwood. It is appropriate to note that the twenty-five volumes of this series were printed the year Charles Mair died in Victoria, British Columbia. The inventory comprised the 180 lines from "Dreamland," 24 lines from "Absence," and 80 lines from "Kanata." The imagery was divided into metaphors, similes, and allegories on one axis, and on another axis, into landscape references (with subcategories of vegetation, water, and landforms) and animal references (with subcategories of birds, mammals, and other creatures). On the second axis, a third category was designated for sources of imagery other than landscape and animal – for instance, weather and climate.

"DREAMLAND" AND THE IDEOLOGY OF NATIONALISM

The predominant imagery in "Dreamland" employs fragments of landscape. Regardless of whether the form of imagery is metaphorical, mimetic, or allegorical, the referent is vegetation, a body of water, or a landform; it is rarely a human being, an animal, or a cosmological force. True to romantic intent, Mair dismembers the scientific geography of his ambient environment with archaeological enterprise. He clears away the ground cover and digs around the foundations for his new utopian home(land). Mair deduces his utopia not so much from the present as from the anterior past, from the dead. In so doing, he creates verse that imitates the pattern of imagery deployed by Percy Bysshe Shelley in "The Triumph of Life" (Shelley 1949, 358–78). In Mair's dream, water and flora imagery is pivotal. The night "is noon-tide" (I.20), the "paleface spirits" who populate the dream rise "from ancient rivers and the sea" (I.135), and "the melancholy waste of wave [is] dead" (I.85). The references to vegetation are universal, particular neither to Southern Ontario nor to Western Canada, whose geographic details Mair knew second-hand as a result of his research tasks in the Parliamentary Library. The one exception to the universality of floral imagery is perhaps the attention Mair gives to seasonality: "See now 'tis like the firstling of spring. Which / win their fragrance in the snow's despite" (I.23–24). But even here there are the precedents of the British romantics. The marked seasonality may have as much to do with the attention writers have given the appearance of spring in the United Kingdom as it has to do with Canada. When the dreamer sees the land, there are few details of flora. There are only "beamless forests" (I.56), not pine or maple forests, and there are only "snowy flowers" (I.77), not daffodils or snowdrops.

Universal references also predominate in the case of landform imagery. There are "wide plains" (I.49), "Aerial mountains" (I.55), and "Marmorean hills." Dreamland scenery is not native to Southern Ontario, nor is it native to the new nation of Canada, whose reality the poem advances.

Mair's view of Canada was integral to the moral privilege he gave to British imperialism. British imperialism was the model for his nationalism, a nationalism that in practice was colonialism, contrary to what Mair and other members of the Canada First Movement believed. The mental compass by which Mair found his way through his Dreamland did not point to Southern Ontario or to the emerging nation of Canada; it swung to British cultural models and to the United Kingdom.

KANATA AND THE IDEOLOGY OF REGIONALISM

There are differences between "Dreamland" and "Kanata." So far as literary geography is concerned, a main difference is that the subject of "Kanata" is a region, Western Canada, while that of "Dreamland" is Canada. A second difference, one of imagery, rests on the contrasting contexts in which the two poems were written. These contrasts between Mair's life when he wrote "Dreamland" in 1868 and his life when he wrote "Kanata" in 1888 are described in the paragraphs above. Much is invested in landscape imagery in "Kanata," a short patriotic verse expressing the promise of a prairie region in the West. And as in "Dreamland," the verse is an archaeological puzzle: it establishes a relationship between the ancient inhabitants of the region and the destiny of the region. Attention to the remote past is given in several metaphors of landscape: "In undiscovered woods wast born" (I.12), and, "o'er the vacant rivers glide / With ghostly paddle and canoe" (II.34–35), then, "With phantom forests on each side – " (I.36), or, "Nor bitter storm, nor ancient night" (I.40).

Similes and metaphors referring to flora and to landforms are also copies of the images Mair fashioned for "Dreamland." They are universal images: "And supple forms from forests wide" (I.16), and, "Thy plains are whispered of afar, / Thy gleaming prairies rich increase" (II.49–50).

These passages hardly justify the claim that the contextual differences of Mair's life in 1868 and in 1888 subverted the language and meaning in "Kanata." But we do begin to get an idea of prairie subversion when we see so many references to the sky: "Kanata! Sylph of northern skies! / Maid of the tender lip and hand, / And dark yet hospitable, eyes" (II.6–8), and, "Where spirit-wildings roamed afield, / And spirit-pinions swept the skies" (II.31–32), or, "Alas! for equal life and laws, / And Freedom 'neath the Western sun" (II.69–70).

If the absence of sky imagery in "Dreamland" and the presence of such imagery in "Kanata" suggest the capacity of Western Canada to subvert language, then the presence of mountain imagery in "Dreamland" and its absence in "Kanata" add to the suggestion. There are three references to mountains in "Dreamland." There is not one in "Kanata."

A short love verse, "Absence," was composed by Mair in Prince Albert during the same year that he finished "Kanata." If this love verse is representative of poetry Mair completed during the years he spent in Western Canada, as I believe it to be, then the role of a Western Canadian context in subverting language is further documented.

It is impossible to say how the polarity of the landscape images matches the mood of the narrator. Trees "cast their spectral shadows down upon a spectral / land" (I.8). The landscape is in harmony with the narrator's loneliness without his loved one. And yet a similar number of landscape metaphors are the opposite of spectral: "A dream of fragrance fills the air, the moon-flower's cup o'erflows" (I.11).

On close examination, it seems the narrator identifies with "The burning rose [that] turns to the moon its folded heart, / dew-fed" (I.17) as much as he identifies with "The perfect womanhood, which gave a meaning to them / all" (I.16). The poem suggests a strong attachment to the landscape through the particularism of its landscape imagery; this particularism is in contrast to the universality of images deployed to describe the narrator's loved one. The parkland surrounds of Prince Albert are described: "Without, assembled here and there, the trees like phantoms stand" (I.7). There are not only flowers but examples of flora native to the prairies, the rose and the lily. The flower imagery is intimate: the lily "shrinks" and has a "stainless head" (I.18).

Like the first prairie poem, "Kanata," the love poem "Absence" is embellished with both universal landscape imagery and imagery particular to Western Canada. Both poems are therefore distinctly different from "Dreamland." The differences are associated with shifts in Mair's deepest expectations of life. His growing political independence from the Conservative Party of Canada and his economic dependence on a developing prairie culture produced subtle but noticeable transformations in landscape imagery. Mair's poetics, his "house of being," as Heidegger would say, became more Western Canadian.

CONCLUSION

Is a theoretically based literary geography urgently needed? Is it possible to create such a discipline? This essay has suggested the panoply of current literary theory to be wide, indeed very wide. Only some genres of this theory have procedures that reproduce even the liberal notions of theory called for by geographers of our generation so far. Other genres of literary theory place less faith in the authority of modern physical and social sciences. An example of these "uncanny" theories is deconstructionism. In this chapter, a derivation of Derridian deconstruction procedures was applied to the poetry of Charles Mair and was demonstrated to be of value in pursuing problems in literary geography. Whether or not these procedures are more economical and accurate than an orthodox humanist critique with a geographic perspective remains to be seen. One is easily impressed by the potential of Norman Shrive's biography of Mair. If this biography were to find its way into the hands of a dedicated geographer with a bias against theory, who can tell what kind of literary geography might be the result? One begs to ask if there is all that much difference between the value of deconstructionism and the value of good humanist criticism. One is tempted in this context of uncertainty to take a cue from Mackenzie King: yes, theory in literary geography, if necessary; but not necessarily theory!

Author's Note: The author wishes to thank Gayle Bertrand and Lydia Harris for their assistance in the research reported here.

REFERENCES

Atwood, M. 1972. *Survival.* Toronto: House of Anansi Press.

Barthes, R. 1966. "Introduction à l'analyse structurale des recits." *Communications* 8:1–27.

Bloom, H. 1973. *The Anxiety of Influence: A Theory of Poetry.* New York: Oxford University Press.

Culler, J. 1982. *On Deconstruction, Theory and Criticism after Structrualism.* Ithaca, N.Y.: Cornell University Press.

de Man, P. 1982. "The Resistance to Literary Theory." *Yale Studies* 63:3–20.

Derrida, J. 1974. *Of Grammatology.* Baltimore and London: Johns Hopkins University Press.

Frye, N. 1957. *The Anatomy of Criticism.* Princeton, N.J.: Princeton University Press.

———. 1971. *The Bush Garden.* Toronto: House of Anansi Press.

Gadamer, H. 1977. "Truth and Method." In F. Dallmayr and T. McCarthy, eds., *Understanding and Social Inquiry.* Notre Dame: University of Notre Dame Press.

Garvin, J.W., ed. 1926. *Master-Works of Canadian Authors.* Vol. 14. Toronto: Radisson Society of Canada.

Giddens, A. 1977. *Studies in Social and Political Theory.* London: Hutchinson.

Harvey, D. 1973. *Social Justice and the City.* London: Edward Arnold.

Jameson, F. 1971. *Marxism and Form: Twentieth Century Dialectical Theories of Literature.* Princeton, N.J.: Princeton University Press.

Levi-Strauss, C. 1963. *Structural Anthropology.* New York: Basic Books.

Mandel, E. 1977. "Writing West." *Canadian Forum* 57:25–29

McCarthy, T. 1978. *The Critical Theory of Jurgen Habermas.* Cambridge, Mass.: MIT Press.

Miller, H. 1976. "Stevens' Rock and Criticism as Cure." *Georgia Review* 30:5–31, 330–48.

Morrill, R.L. 1987. "A Theoretical Imperative." *Annals of the Association of American Geographers* 77:535–41.

Porteous, J.D. 1985. "Literature and Humanist Geography." *Area.* 17:117–22.

Ricoeur, P. 1976. "History and Hermeneutics." *Journal of Philosophy* 73:691–95.

Sandberg, L.A., and J. Marsh, eds. 1988. "Focus: Literary Landscapes – Geography and Literature." *Canadian Geographer* 32:266–76.

Shelley, P.B. 1949. "The Triumph of Life." In M. Elwin, ed., *The Poetic Works of Shelley,* 358–78. London: MacDonald.

Shrive, N. 1965. *Charles Mair: Literary Nationalist.* Toronto: University of Toronto Press.

Watson, J.W. 1965. "Canadian Regionalism in Life and Letters." *Geographical Journal* 131:21–33.

Woodcock, G. 1975. "Poet and Poetaster." *Canadian Literature* 63:85–89.

5

Moral Frames for Landscape in Canadian Literature

Ronald Bordessa

Land and landscape are major themes in Canadian literature. As Grace notes, "our major writers create out of a profound and pervasive awareness of the natural landscape – prairie, Northern Shield, mountain, seashore" (1984, 193). The argument developed in this chapter is that these writers also create out of a sense of what the world is, how we all came to be here, and what constitutes morally justifiable ways of living. The answers to these questions, then, form the ground on which creative literary constructions are erected. This claim to a general connection between conceptions of reality and literature will be narrowed in the current essay to a consideration of the specific connection between morality and treatments of landscape in Canadian literature.

Three incompatible conceptual views of the world are sketched: those from religion, those from science, and those from aesthetics. In the first two views, universals, absolutes, necessities, and stabilities underwrite notions of knowledge and truth, the means to achieve them, and the uses to which they should be put. Religious and scientific conceptions of the world posit a particular foundational belief with respect to truth, which necessitates a particular moral orientation to nature. The aesthetic view, in contrast, is particular, relative, contingent and changeable, and contemplates knowledge and truth quite differently. And although it is associated with a moral orientation to nature, its internal logic authorizes *choice*, not *necessity*.

THREE CONCEPTIONS OF THE WORLD

Religion: A World of Differences of Kind

The puzzle of what the world is and why we are here found its most ubiquitous and comforting answer millennia ago – God made the world, and us to be his servants in it. From this deterministic solution easily follows the conviction that morals are, like mathematical truths, necessary, universal, and unchangeable elements of the world. Moral justification – for example, of human use of the environment – must refer to the conditions of morality contained in God's creation. If God created moral form, we have been left to fill in the moral content that conforms to it.

Descartes's meditations led him to a moral content in which human exploitation of nature was legitimized by a conception of God's plan that set humans, as unique possessors of an immaterial soul, above and against the rest of creation. By the end of the seventeenth century, "a new philosophy of nature based on particles of inert, dead matter moved by external forces was adopted by elites working in France, England, and Germany . . . The new philosophy was consistent with an environmental ethic that nature was dead and could be exploited for human progress" (Merchant 1989, 127).

Science: A World of Differences of Degree

Empirical science rejects the argument for categorical human differentiation and places humans on a continuum of life. Dawkins is clear about this point: "More, I want to persuade the reader, not just that the Darwinian world-view *happens* to be true, but that it is the only known theory that *could*, in principle, solve the mystery of our existence" (1986, x). Humans are reconceived as evolved creatures competing against others in a functioning system. In principle, natural selection accounts for the current condition of the system, and the degree to which biological entities succeed is governed only by their ability to compete. The Darwinian world view is a biocentric one that gives an account of an operating system containing biological entities with claims to moral consideration. Nature is no longer beyond moral questioning.

Within this framework, morality is depicted as simply another question for biology. Ruse argues that Darwinism contains the basis of both objective and subjective orientations to morality: "The Darwinian argues that morality simply does not work (from a biological perspective), unless we believe that it is objective. Darwinian theory shows that, in fact, morality is a function of (subjective) feelings; but it shows also that we have (and must have) the illusion of objectivity" (1986, 253). The Darwinian conception of reality thus necessarily sets up a series of tensions: between objective and subjective foundations of morality, between humans as subjects and humans as objects, and between the claims of an inner mental life and those of an outer connective life.

Aesthetics: A World of Dissolved Differences

The universality represented by both religion and science has been rejected by a third construction of reality, one that denies foundations, order, certainty, closure, systemic unity, coherence, and all forms of privileged discourse. In their place is a world that is disclosed individually as a series of fragments, unfolding in response to contingencies, displaying no necessary meanings and yet a multiplicity of meaning, granting no warrants that privilege anyone's knowledge, explanations, truth, or morality. Nietzsche relocates the question of morality *entirely* within the conscious self, and at the same time despairs at the state of morality and the values it was founded upon, which had been produced by idealism – whether of the Christian or Darwinian sort.

Nietzsche opens up morality to plural interpretation by conceiving, as Megill points out, "of the world as aesthetically self-creating," thereby initiating "the aesthetic metacritique of "truth," wherein "the work of art" or the text or "language" is seen as establishing the grounds for truth's possibility" (1985, 33). Relocation of the possibility of grasping reality in such reflections of life itself dissolves the differences worried over by religion and science. Morality is re-situated outside these totalizing systems as a socially constructed, historically variable issue.

Heidegger, taking up Nietzsche's torch, determined that the ordinary human being did not constitute the world as subject relating to objects. Rather Heidegger thinks of us only as "being in the world" and goes on to give a descriptive account of existence which dispenses with the Cartesian problematic. Indeed as Barrett (1962, 218) points out, Heidegger's analysis of existence is conducted "without using either 'man' or 'consciousness.'" In doing so, "Enlightenment rationality, with its ruthlessly dominative, instrumental attitude towards Nature, must be rejected for a humble listening to the stars, skies and forests" (Eagleton 1983, 63–64). The human being is dethroned and decentred to become a "field of care": "He secretly hears his own name called whenever he hears any region of Being named with which he is vitally involved" (Barrett 1962, 219).

Neither Heidegger's focus on being nor Nietzsche's focus on aesthetics contains a logically necessary moral imperative. On the contrary, they are under-pinnings for moral relativism and postmodern literary discourse, which can be seen, respectively, as practical and theoretical explorations of the possibilities inherent in the revolt of their thought against foundationalism.

THREE LITERATURES OF CANADIAN LANDSCAPES

There is a danger of seeking out three treatments of landscape in Canadian literature simply to supply evidence in support of the three independently dis-cerned conceptual worldviews summarized above. Identification of literature which fits neatly with these conceptions is satisfying but is no ground, in itself, for claiming that this particular classification of literature reflects and captures shifting conceptual orientations. The charge that the literary treatments of land-scape recorded in Figure 5.1 are wedged into place only to bring symmetry to the general argument can be defended using independent categorizations of Canadian literature constructed for quite different purposes. Specifically, Malcolm Ross's 1986 inaugural address on the essential characteristics of Canadian litera-ture, delivered at Edinburgh University's Centre for Canadian Studies, precisely replicates the categories of Figure 5.1:

> In our concern with the land and the landscape, we followed in turn the
> neo-classical and Romantic fashions, responded to Darwinism and even-
> tually arrived . . . at psychological expressionism in which the interior
> landscape shapes rock and stone and tree into figures of the mind and
> those phantasms that lurk beneath the mind's floor. (1988, 191–92)

Figure 5.1

Conceptual Views and Literary Treatments of Landscape

Conceptual Worldview	Environmental View	Moral View		Literary Treatment of Landscape			
		Ontology	Epistemology	Ontology	Epistemology	Style	Mode
Religious	Man against Nature anthrocentric ethic	objective	rationalist	landscape as design	positivist[2]	conformist	realist[1]
Scientific	Man in Nature biocentric ethic	objective/subjective	empiricist	landscape as context	structural/ humanistic	connective	realistic/ symbolic
Existential	Man as Nature ecocentric view	subjective	experiential	landscape as condition	humanistic	contingent	symbolic

1 This term has different uses in philosophical and literary discourses. "In modern philosophy, however, it [realism] is used for the view that material objects exist externally to us and independently of our sense experience. Realism is thus opposed to idealism, which holds that no such material objects or external realities exist apart from our knowledge or consciousness of them, the whole universe thus being dependent on the mind or in some sense mental" (Edwards 1967, 77). In literary discourse, realism accepts the idealism inherent to a conception of reality that treats the human mind as autonomously authoritative. Authenticity is to be found in representation of the world as it is understood by the mind, for the contents of the mind are held to be real (though not necessarily accurate) simply by virtue of being housed there (that is, by virtue of idealism).

2 Auguste Comte's claim that only observable phenomena can form the foundation for knowledge construed as causally connected relationships within such phenomena, would seem to rule out a positivist approach to literature that owes its entire perspective to a religion-based conception of the world. Such a perspective, by definition, contains a metaphysics antithetical to positivism. To overcome this contradiction, it is necessary to recognize that the positivism associated with the quantitative revolution in geography in the 1960s and the positivism of realist literature that adheres to a God-given world of dualities both share an unbending acceptance of rationalism. That the metaphysics of the realist writer of this sort would be rejected by the geographer of the logical positivist persuasion is of no consequence, for each is governed by the rationalist argument. In both instances, the contents of the mind are regarded as data of precisely the sort that can be subjected to positivist treatment.

Canadian cultural history also provides a parallel context for our indigenous literature. Northrop Frye says of this history: "It has its own themes of exploration, settlement, and development, but these themes relate to a social *imagination* that explores and settles and develops, and the imagination has its own rhythms of growth as well as its own modes of expression" (1976, 334).

Realist writing, both neoclassical and romantic, imagines Canada as a land to be explored – a rough, hard land where nature is opposed to human endeavour, but also a land of dignity and beauty. These discoveries are associated with the certainties of religious convictions that set an agenda for the conquest of nature and for writing about Canada.

Waves of settlement in territories that had been explored wrested from nature the means to construct a better life in the "Bush Garden." In the struggle, with survival often in question, Canadians made their contracts with nature and themselves, and these contracts are written down as the mainstream of Canadian literature, chronicling life as it is lived on the seashore and Shield, in the prairies and the city. As protagonists in this literature search within themselves for the symbols that make sense of their lives, and look outside themselves to the natural and human landscapes that are their context, we observe the essential interplay of individuality and community (both social and natural).

Only when the survival of settlement ceases to become questionable is the mind freed to reflect on the condition it finds itself in. Only when that question is removed are we able to interrogate ourselves about the deepest meanings of existence, searching for them not on the surfaces of nature, but deep down inside ourselves. Current Canadian literature, taking up postmodern concerns, reflects a country that already has been explored and settled. Development, to continue the line of Frye's thought, is represented by imaginations in postmodern Canadian writing that replace the expressive realism of a world of certainty with "psychological expressionism," "inner fiction," or "mental mappings" in which denial destroys affirmation. It is part of the conditionality of postmodernism that all certainty must be denied, including that of the writer's privilege to represent anything. All that can be achieved is fragmentary, discontinuous, and ambiguous discourse open to equally uncertain "readings."

In such reflexive writing, the role of landscape becomes uncertain, but it cannot be obliterated, for it is an enduring category. Geography is beyond denial. Here we find a general clue to why geography, understood to include land and landscape, has been so central to Canadian writing. To chase down this clue is to provide an interpretation of Canadian literature in which geography is an integral part of the constitution of that literature. Geography inheres in literature in the Canadian case, and this cannot be said for other national literatures. This forces an examination of why geography and literature are so intertwined in Canada.

In their attempt to distinguish their new society from a cultured Europe they had left behind, European settlers in North America recognized that time-dependent marks of civilized values belonged to Europe and could not become their own. To make them so, to copy, would be to deny the freedoms many had ventured over the seas to find. In Canada, there were of course settlers who sought only to live as colonists. Nevertheless, Canadian history is better understood as one of value creation, rather than as one of transported values, at least at the more abstracted level.

If time was the settlers' enemy, space was their friend. Abundant space and as splendidly spectacular as anything Europe had to offer – here was the means to establish the basis of a new society. Northrop Frye's well-known statement that the "Canadian sensibility . . . is less perplexed by the question 'Who am I?' than by some such riddle as 'Where is here?'" (1976, 220) is taken by Cook to indicate a shift in the search for a Canadian identity "away from the subjective question of identity to the spatial question of location" (1985, 87).

Canadian literature has greatly concerned itself with questions of identity. It is hardly surprising (if Frye has correctly specified the peculiarly Canadian riddle) that it has elaborated these questions in spatial terms. Identity is referential: in the European case, to time (geneology, heritage, and inheritance); in the Canadian case, to space (exploring, settling, and transforming). The land and the landscape are metaphor for Canada and central preoccupations of its writers.

In that preoccupation, writers have detected the moral tone in Frye's putatively geographical question. As Malcolm Ross says: "We are what we are because we are where we are" (1986, 141). What we are, including our moral selves, and how that is entwined with where we are – with the landscapes of our lives – set an important agenda for Canadian literature. Before discussing some of the work issuing from that agenda, it is instructive to examine how Frye went about answering his own question, for that answer reinforces the centrality of the human relationship to land and landscape in both the Canadian experience and its expression in Canadian literature.

Ironically Frye gains access to "where is here" *via* a piece of primitive American art, Edward Hicks's *The Peaceable Kingdom,* painted about 1830. It depicts a scene in which some native people and Quaker settlers under Penn sign a treaty in the presence of a group of animals – lions, tigers, bears, and oxen – "The reconciliation of man with man and of man with nature" (Frye 1965, 360). This scene, Frye intimates, moves towards "the haunting vision of a serenity that is both human and natural which we have been struggling to identify in the Canadian tradition. If we had to characterize a distinct emphasis in that tradition, we might call it the quest for the peaceable Kingdom" (1965, 360).

The Canadian quest is thus essentially a moral one. Only by confronting and reconciling moral values with "the vast unconsciousness of nature" can we overcome the garrison mentality that "a huge, unthinking, menacing, and formidable physical setting" creates (Frye 1965, 342). It is this confrontation of conscious mind and unconscious nature, of mind inclining towards serene reconciliation and a peaceable kingdom and often inhospitable natural conditions, that is adumbrated in our literature. Human encroachments upon nature are at the heart of Canadian experience and guarantee the creation of a Canadian literature that is penetrated through and through by geography.

Landscape as Design: Literature as Representation

Are there any moral structures in the very fabric of the world? Is there anything ontologically real that functions as the reference of the moral component of our moral judgements? Are there any irreducibly moral facts? (Puolimatka 1989, 18)

Often in Saskatchewan a man awakens of a winter night hearing a great wind, and his heart sinks at the prospect of more shut-in days, more cold, difficulty, discomfort and danger. (Stegner 1973, 74)

An affirmative answer to Puolimatka's questions means that morality is objective. An objective morality can spring from sources other than a purposively created world, but in the Western tradition, moral objectivity and creator design have in practice gone hand in hand. Implicitly, if not always explicitly, foundational notions of this sort and privileged claims to represent them underpin realist writing. Landscape viewed as part of the very fabric of the world becomes implicated in the design that encompasses the moral conditions of human presence in the world.

In the Saskatchewan prairie (and many other places in Canada), the design pits humans against hostile nature. Yet, as Stegner continues, sometimes there is the chinook. Nature can revive the spirit as well as destroy the body. Thus is set up an opposition that contains a hint of reconciliation. But it is only a hint, as Margaret Atwood demonstrates in her examination of "the types of landscape that prevail in Canadian literature and the kinds of attitude they mirror" (1972a, 49). She concludes: "Nature seen as dead, or alive but indifferent, or alive and actively hostile towards man is a common image in Canadian literature. The result of a dead or indifferent Nature is an isolated or 'alienated' man; the result of an actively hostile Nature is usually a dead man, and certainly a threatened one" (1972a, 54).

Literature grounded in the opposition of humankind and nature, in the rationality of humankind and the availability of nature for its betterment, is confident of its foundations and ultimately didactic in its intent. Expressive realism is the literary (and artistic) form that best describes writing requiring secure foundations of this type. Ruskin believed that it was the responsibility of landscape painters to, first, (re)present landscape and, second, to express the feelings landscape evoked in them so as to instruct and ennoble the spectator. This view of literature or art requires a reality that can be known and represented and the belief that only high-minded individuals are capable of adequate expression. But when it is achieved, "as in the hands of a master like Turner, landscape became in Ruskin's eyes a suitable subject for examining the deepest moral and artistic truths" (Daniels and Cosgrove 1988, 5). In place then is an idealist belief in certain knowledge, a claim to privilege in expressing it, and a connection between landscape and the morals associated with the ground of such certain knowledge.

Charles Sangster's (1856) early description of the landscape he viewed as he voyaged from Kingston past Quebec and "up the Saguenay that was already famous for its wild beauty" (Keith 1985, 28) was conditioned by his view that "the wilderness is automatically, or so it would seem, associated with God and religious certitude" (1985, 28). God's hand in nature is everywhere in Sangster's poetry, and Keith notes that "one begins to doubt whether Sangster would dare consider the possibility of a natural world outside divine control" (1985, 28).

Clear traces of a straightforward role for nature and particularly landscape, namely to be available for the propagation of one's own projects, are to be found in MacLennan (see Peepre-Bordessa, this volume, chapter 2), who constantly invokes landscape images to express his vision of Canada and to infuse his readers with the same sense of attachments. Landscapes for MacLennan are a useful commodity for his own declared project, the task of inculcating into the Canadian people the same sense of nationhood that he himself, as a high-minded artist possessing the sensibilities Ruskin spoke of, already had. MacLennan's landscapes of Canada are splendidly evocative, but that is testimony only to MacLennan's skill. For all that, they remain rock, river, and seashore – products of creation – and commodified as beauty, diversity, danger, and all the other characteristics of the Canada MacLennan holds in his mind. And it is his mind that matters, for in it he is morally certain of his own understanding of Canada and of the project he has for its people. Indeed, the source of his certainty is none other than God's guiding hand (see Mandel 1986, 117).

The opposition of humans and nature is also assumed by Canadian industrial landscape painting (Norcliffe, this volume, chapter 6), Charles Mair's poetry (Gibson, this volume, chapter 4), Nova Scotia's foresters (Sandberg, this volume, chapter 9), and Newfoundland settlers (Paul, this volume, chapter 7). Those chapters are replete with descriptions of the power of nature and the struggle of humans against it. And as Sandberg notes, Keefer sees in the struggle one avenue to identity for people who "derive dignity and even moral stature from their mastery of elemental forces in the wild."

Landscape as Context: Literature as Reportage

As Darwinian creatures, humans look both inwards reflexively and outwards to the natural and cultural environments of which they are a part. Margaret Atwood recognizes this duality of mind, tuned to inner emotions and outer realities.

Poems which contain descriptions of landscapes and natural objects are often dismissed as being mere Nature poetry. But Nature poetry is seldom just about Nature; it is usually about the poet's *attitude* towards the external universe. That is landscapes in poems are often interior landscapes; they are maps of a state of mind. Sometimes the poem conceals this fact and purports to be objective description, sometimes the poem acknowledges and explores the interior landscape it presents. (1972a, 49)

Atwood is here recognizing that lives are lived by reference to two maps, the first being our representation of an objective external reality and the second our representation of a subjective internal reality. The second map is partly derivative from the first but is enormously enriched by the construction of meaning and by creative imagination. Such mapping of the mind parallels the subjective/objective illusion of the basis of morality. Construction of a world with an imaginative inside and an outside that contains modernistic scientific foundations underlies the mainstream of literature in Canada. This literature implicitly accepts the Darwinian view of things and sets about examining everyday life. Landscape is clearly context for a literature that reports on the state of life as lived both in the private world of each mind's eye and in the public world of relationships with nature, people, landscape, region, and country.

A few examples will establish the force of relational literature of this sort. Over the course of roughly a decade (1941–52), Sinclair Ross's *As for Me and My House* (1941), W.O. Mitchell's *Who Has Seen the Wind* (1947), and Ernest Buckler's *The Mountain and the Valley* (1952) established this mode of writing. Ross explores a narrow slice of life in a small prairie town, Horizon, over a period of a year. Kroetsch notes, "The name of the town, Horizon, suggests a no-place that is tantalizingly visible but always out of reach: a version of namelessness" (1989, 114). Perhaps this is why Kroetsch also sees the novel as "the paradigmatic text in Canadian writing" (1989, 44): it is metaphor for Canada. Everything is modestly drawn but portrays an existence that is generally readily appreciated. The physical conditions are depicted for themselves and as metaphor – the prairie drought dries up the soul as well as the land.

Mitchell's developmental novel stays with the prairie, of which Mitchell says in his opening sentence, "Here was the least common denominator of nature, the skeleton requirements simply of land and sky – Saskatchewan prairie." But in these minimal conditions Mitchell was able to find "the complex interaction of delicacy and crudeness, beauty and ugliness, good and evil, that makes up the background of human life on earth" (Keith 1985, 146). And the landscapes of the prairie are constantly represented as a foreground for life, not just a place where life is lived but at times the only bearable place to be, as it was for Brian at the death of his father: "He walked on with the tall prairie grass hissing against his legs, out into the prairie's stillness and loneliness that seemed to flow around him, to meet itself behind him, ringing him and separating him from the town" (238). Of Buckler's *The Mountain and the Valley*, Moss says it is "an almost perfect fusion of regions of the imagination with regions of actuality" (1981, 43). By this he means we are given a sense of the landscape of the Annapolis Valley as well as of the contours of mind of those drawn together by rural family life.

Darwinism's doctrine of "survival of the fittest" has, as Horkheimer points out, "become the prime axiom of conduct and ethics" (1974, 124). The doctrine's depiction of the harsh realities of the competition for survival is tempered by its support for the revolt of nature against reason. Three essays in the current collection reflect a Darwinian undercurrent. In various ways, but all of them directly related to landscape, the essays highlight the importance of home, civilization's domestication of niche.

In this volume, Squire's analysis of Montgomery's *Anne of Green Gables* (chapter 11) stresses Anne Shirley's spiritual attachment and sense of belonging to Prince Edward Island – her point of origin and instinctual referent. Paul's analysis of Mowat's *The Outport People* (chapter 7) chronicles an attempt to create a home in a chosen niche, a destination for a new beginning far removed from the Toronto that was left behind. Finally, Scott's focus in Roy's *The Cashier* (chapter 14) is on the journey itself, necessitated by Chenevert's origins and terminated in a deathbed vision that makes sense of his journey – a vision of a heaven on earth. To arrive at this vision, Chenevert has to pass through the experience of not feeling at home in either the city or the country; nature eventually revitalizes and changes him, and he feels comfortable both in himself and in his world.

Landscape as Condition: Literature as Experience

In their self-reflexivity, Canadian postmodern novels offer yet another example of the self-conscious or "meta"-sensibility of our times, that is, of the awareness that all our systems of understanding are deliberate and historically specific human constructs (not natural and eternal givens). (Hutcheon 1988, x)

The public face of the act of self-reflexivity appears as an unveiling of subjective experience; experiential literature is its catharsis. Such literature denies all authority and claims only the authenticity of experience. Postmodern writing cannot be about the world because there is no one world. It can only be about the experience of being in the world. Only insofar as landscape is part of that experience will it become part of literature. In Canada, landscape is an inescapable part of experience not by virtue of its mere existence, but because space and geography are at the very heart of our understanding of what Canada is and who we are as moral and social beings.

Postmodern writing in Canada thus faces a peculiar contradiction: only experience matters and there are no necessary externals to which authority is granted, yet landscape is an inexpungible ground (and therefore necessary referent) of the postmodernist modality. The escape from this contradiction is found in the internalizing of landscape in Canada. Landscape is not an external objective reality to be written about, but a defining ingredient of the constitution of the Canadian experience. It is a condition of being, and postmodern literature consciously elaborating the experience of being can be expected therefore to be writing *from* landscape – rather than *about* landscape – because it is *in* our being.

I have argued that landscape has been internalized in Canada. This is consistent with a definition of human that eliminates boundaries and stresses connections. In the creation of one world in which everything is ultimately connected, morality becomes self-referential, because self is all-inclusive. Similarly, self-reflexive postmodern writing can now be understood to be about the human imagination reflecting on the experience of an inclusively understood self. Current environmental concerns and the emergence of an environmental ethic that collapses the entire world into one indivisible moral realm, universally confer (at the extreme) the status of moral subject on all there is. In doing so, it de-centres humans and completely destroys the idea of centre and margin.

Postmodern writing, which typically employs double vision, does the same. Just as it sets up these two categories as its targets, it tears them down. Hutcheon notes postmodernism's "challenging of all kinds of '-centrism' (andro-, hetero-, Euro-, etc.)" (1988, 11), and its fascination with "the margin or the border [is] the postmodern space *par excellence*, the place where new possibilities exist" (1988, 4). Aritha van Herk's *The Tent Peg* (see Paul, this volume, chapter 7) can be read in part as a conscription of nature, "woman as mother earth," to the female challenge of male centralized power in a survey camp. The project of much postmodern writing in Canada is to marginalize the centre by radical critique and to "centrize" the margin by using its resources to construct a more "humane" ecumene. The project is to eliminate margins and centres in order to eliminate distinctions and privileges – to create one world, one moral domain admitting a plurality of moralities. It is against this background that postmodern writing in Canada can be read – as traces of experience imaginatively left to us.

The literary destruction of distinctions and privileges also brings nature and women to the fore. Nature and women are seen, from the postmodern perspective, to have shared a marginalized fate. They are now separately, and jointly because of their conjunction in "woman as mother earth," reclaimed in the revolt against realism and installed as essential to a visioning of a better world.

Women writers and commentators (see Godard 1986, Neuman and Kamboureli 1986), in asking "How can 'nature' be represented more as a *process* than as a landscape to be penetrated, named, raped or claimed?" (New 1990, 106), are also asking about their own lives. In closing her review of the Canadian novel from 1972 to 1974, Hutcheon (1988, 27), quoting Iser, notes that the consequence of a number of novels all sharing postmodern characteristics, notably a search for solidity and voice, is that they challenge the assumption "that fiction is an antonym of reality." Landscapes – real, imagined, and half-remembered – are incorporated into the process of life-making itself; and with deliberate detailing or by neglecting to make anything meaningful of them, landscapes express the essential ambivalences of reality.

In Kroetsch's *Studhorse Man,* for example, Hazard Lepage moves "through an identifiable landscape; from the information provided we could trace his peregrinations on the map of Alberta" (Stratford 1986, 72). But the landscape is incidental in his life. It is incidental because the postmodern condition is integrative rather than oppositional. The realism of landscapes is not denied, it is just not critical to the referencing of life (as it is for MacLennan). This does not mean that landscape is irrelevant for life or that it does not appear in postmodern literature. On the contrary, landscape is so much a part of Canadian life that its presence is taken for granted. It is an integral part of self, felt but not paraded.

Porteous (this volume, chapter 22) recognizes Malcolm Lowry as an early exponent of current environmental sensibilities. It may also be argued that Lowry merged his identity with landscape. Lowry's fragmented work is often interpreted in terms of his fragmented life, but as Porteous shows, both his writing and his life possess a coherent moral dimension. Nature is within his "field of care," part of the conditionality of his life and of his sense of self. Lowry can claim to speak for wild nature only because he lives in the same "uncivilized" space: he is not an advocate for the mute, but a voice from his own wilderness. Nature, land, landscape, and wildscape are an inescapable part of Lowry's self-description of his condition. We see in his tortured writing, as Porteous intimates, his tortured self as "civilization" attempts to tame him – in all his parts.

In contrast to Lowry, Margaret Atwood confronts "civilization" head-on, often by interrogating its dualities, most notably male/female and nature/culture. She has, arguably, developed the inward experience of life most consistently. For example, in *Surfacing* (1972b), Atwood internalizes landscape as a means to recover her protagonist's capacity to cope.

Robert Kroetsch interprets *Surfacing* as an example of attempts by Canadian fiction writers to "resolve the paradox – the painful tension between appearance and authenticity – by the radical process of demythologizing the systems that threaten to define them. Or more comprehensively, they uninvent the world" (1989, 58). In *Surfacing*, it is the threat of Americanization that disturbs the narrator and sends her on her journey to find herself. It is a Canadian journey into self that discovers in landscape the means to reinvent self authentically and find sanity by uninventing the world she had lived in.

In his own writing, Kroetsch, once persuaded that MacLennan had named our reality (see Peepre-Bordessa, this volume, chapter 2), later "realize[d] that under MacLennan's controlled surface is the dark 'if' of the Canadian unconscious, Do we exist?" (1989, 57). Kroetsch's voluminous writings can be seen in part as an exploration of this question, plumbing our "reluctance to venture out of the snow; into the technology," out, that is, of our natural landscapes where "in our very invisibility lies our chance for survival" and into the world of the American machine. Again, to be Canadian is to be landscape. Thus, if we wish to find a distinctively Canadian answer to Frye's distinctively Canadian question, we must first make visible all the resources that have created the quest for the peaceable kingdom – and central among them is the internalization of landscape through the reconciliation of humans and nature.

REFERENCES

Atwood, M. 1972a. *Survival: A Thematic Guide to Canadian Literature*. Toronto: House of Anansi Press.

———. 1972b. *Surfacing*. Toronto: McClelland & Stewart.

Barrett, W. 1962. *Irrational Man*. Garden City: Doubleday/Anchor.

Buckler, E. 1952. *The Mountain and the Valley*. New York: Holt.

Cook, D. 1985. *Northrop Frye: A Vision of the New World*. Montreal: New World Perspectives.

Daniels, S., and D. Cosgrove, eds. 1988. *The Iconography of Landscape*. Cambridge: Cambridge University Press.

Dawkins, R. 1986. *The Blind Watchmaker*. London: Longman.

Eagleton, T. 1983. *Literary Theory: An Introduction*. Minneapolis: University of Minnesota Press.

Edwards, P., ed. 1967. *The Encyclopaedia of Philosophy*. Vol. 7. Toronto: Macmillan/Free Press.

Frye, N. 1976. *The Bush Garden*. Toronto: House of Anansi Press, originally published as the conclusion to Carl F. Klinck, ed., *Literary History of Canada* (Toronto: University of Toronto Press, 1965).

Godard, B., ed. 1986. *Gynocritics*. Toronto: ECW Press.

Grace, S. 1984. "Quest for the Peaceable Kingdom: Urban/Rural Codes in Roy, Laurence, and Atwood." In S.M. Squier, ed., *Women Writers and the City: Essays in Feminist Literary Criticism*. Knoxville: University of Tennessee Press.

Horkheimer, M. 1947. *Eclipse of Reason*. New York: Oxford University Press; New York: Seabury Press, 1974.

Hutcheon, L. 1988. *The Canadian Postmodern*. Toronto: Oxford University Press.

Keith, W.J. 1985. *Canadian Literature in English*. London: Longman.

Kroetsch, R. 1969. *The Studhorse Man*. Toronto: Macmillan.

———. 1989. *The Lovely Treachery of Words*. Toronto: Oxford University Press.

Mandel, E. 1986. *The Family Romance*. Winnipeg: Turnstone Press.

Megill, A. 1985. *Prophets of Extremity: Nietzche, Heidegger, Foucault, Derrida*. Berkeley: University of California Press.

Merchant, C. 1989. *Ecological Revolutions: Nature, Gender and Science in New England*. Chapel Hill: University of North Carolina Press.

Mitchell, W.O. 1947. *Who Has Seen the Wind*. Toronto: Macmillan; Toronto: Seal, 1982.

Moss, J. 1981. *A Reader's Guide to the Canadian Novel*. Toronto: McClelland & Stewart.

Neuman, S., and S. Kamboureli, eds. 1986. *Amazing Space: Writing Canadian Women Writing*. Edmonton: Longspoon NeWest.

New, W.H. 1990. "Studies of English Canadian Literature." *International Journal of Canadian Studies* 1, no. 2: 97–114.

Puolimatka, T. 1989. *Moral Realism and Justification*. Helsinki: Suomalainen Tiedeakatemia.

Ross, M. 1986. *The Impossible Sum of Our Traditions: Reflections on Canadian Literature*. Toronto: McClelland & Stewart.

Ross, S. 1941. *As for Me and My House*. New York: Reynal; Toronto: McClelland & Stewart, 1970.

Ruse, M. 1986. *Taking Darwin Seriously*. Oxford: Basil Blackwell.

Sangster, C. 1856. *The St. Lawrence and the Saguenay*. Kingston: Creighton and Duff.

Stegner, W. 1973. "Carrion Spring." In B. Littlejohn and J. Pierce, eds., *Marked by the Wild*. Toronto: McClelland & Stewart.

Stratford, P. 1986. *All the Polarities*. Toronto: ECW Press.

6

In a Hard Land:
The Geographical Context of
Canadian Industrial Landscape Painting

Glen Norcliffe

*I*f one compares the industrial landscape paintings of Britain, France, and Canada, one finds unmistakable differences in their iconography. Northern England was the cradle of the Industrial Revolution, the region that pioneered the steam engine, the railway, the factory system with its textile mills, tall chimneys, and terraced workers' housing, and many other facets of industrial capitalism. Industry is depicted by many artists as *dominating* the landscape; indeed, it is often shown to hold sway over the workforce as well. Human activity is no longer in harmony with nature. The skies are black with smoke or milky white with pollution. The skylines, no longer natural, are composed of barrack-like mills, chimneys, pitheads, and viaducts. Natural forms such as twisting pathways and shaded streams have been supplanted by the geometrical lines of roads, canals, and railways. Factories commonly occupy the foreground, emphasizing that industry was the *raison d'être* of many towns. This ensemble has been captured by the most famous of industrial landscape painters, L.S. Lowry, in many of his composite landscape paintings.

France, in contrast, was touched lightly and late by the Industrial Revolution. Moreover, pockets of heavy industry such as the Saint-Etienne basin and Lille were shunned by most artists. By the time that French landscape painting was being transformed by the Barbizon school and the early impressionists into realist art, Baron Haussman was reshaping central Paris as a living space for the haute bourgeoisie; industry was obliged to locate outside the city in the newly annexed *grandes banlieues* (especially La Villette) and surrounding small towns such as Asnières, Argenteuil, and Louveciennes, towns which up until then had been small market centres. In consequence, one finds many paintings that juxtapose images of industry with leafy suburbs, regattas, sleepy ports, racecourses, and the countryside (Clark 1984; Herbert 1988). These images therefore *balance* industry with other elements of the French landscape. The factories are often placed in the middle ground or even the background.[1] Thus, in his provocative essay on French industrial images, Robert Herbert suggests that in several paintings "industry is peacefully absorbed into the landscape" (1982, 155). Indeed,

Herbert points to Daubigny's *Les deux rivages* as a painting that explicitly captures this ambiguity.[2]

Canada, in contrast, is a storehouse of raw materials, a land of mines and sawmills, oil derricks, canneries, and grain elevators. The iconography is different yet again. No vacant Eden, the dominant image is of the *struggle* to harness resources in a harsh country. As Osborne puts it, "The natural environment was being doggedly transformed into a cultural landscape" (1988, 165). Be it hard rock, a hard climate, or hard work, the land has only reluctantly yielded its riches.

Harold Innis's writings on Canadian staple exports capture the essence of Canadian economic history. It has involved the transport of a series of primary and processed commodities – fish, fur, wood, wheat, metals, and minerals – along a network of railways, rivers, and lakes to the great ports through which Canadian commerce is funnelled for export.[3] Canadian industrial landscape painting records many elements of this system. Of course, there are some paintings of Canadian factories that bear a likeness to those found in Europe and the United States, but even a brief glance at Rosemary Donegan's pioneering exhibition of Canadian industrial images confirms that their main focus is on various manifestations of the staple export economy (Donegan 1988).

The economic rationale for such a focus was provided long ago by the economist David Ricardo. Production, he suggested, required a combination of three factors: labour, capital, and resources. A country will make intensive use of its best endowment. Since Canada's 984 million hectares are sparsely populated, few activities can afford to make intensive use of labour. And since a great deal of capital is required to harness resources and build the infrastructure to export them, Canada has throughout its history been an economic colony, a net importer of capital. British, American, and Japanese capital have in turn played a major role in the staple industries. It is the abundance of resources that distinguishes the Canadian economy. But the exploitation of these resources and their exportation in the face of competition from rival foreign producers have increasingly required the adoption of technologies suited to mass production using a limited workforce. In many staple industries this has meant progressively larger-scale production using huge machines with fewer and fewer operators and, because of the capital costs involved, increasingly oligopolistic ownership.

The canvasses discussed in this essay depict the extraction, processing, and manufacturing of materials and goods that are then either exported to the United States, Europe, and, more recently, the Pacific Rim or are used in Canada as part of the staple infrastructure. Many artists have captured the unusual orientation of the Canadian economy: whereas most wealthy nations have built up an industrial economy based on high value added industries and services, Canada has invested above all else in staple industries. There is a modest concentration of high value added industries between Windsor and Quebec City, but in comparison with other advanced industrial countries, industry in this area is feebly developed and, moreover, dominated by foreign interests (Britton and Gilmour

1978). Given this truncated industrial structure, it is not surprising that Canadian industrial landscape images are distinctive.

In this essay I will focus on the industrial landscapes of Lawren Harris, Alma Duncan, and Adrien Hébert. Their works represent a broad range of the industrial landscape genre – they painted in somewhat different styles, their work belongs to different (though overlapping) periods, and they worked in different parts of Canada. But the main reason I selected these three artists is that they interested themselves in different elements of the Canadian economic system. Harris travelled widely, his style evolved quite dramatically, and he painted an unusual range of subjects, which included forestry and mining activities in the interior. Alma Duncan's oeuvre deals with Quebec and Ontario, and her industrial images focus particularly on the system of production that begins with iron ore mining in the North and ends with the production of steel in large mills. Hébert was the Albert Marquet of Canada, the observer of the great port of Montreal, which at that time served much of Canada's vast hinterland.

LAWREN HARRIS (1885–1970)

Lawren Harris painted a wide range of Canadian subjects, geographically spread from coast to coast. As a leading light in the Group of Seven, he is best known for his landscape painting. Nevertheless, it is difficult to categorize Harris because he made several stylistic changes during the sixty years he was active. He began in the early 1900s by adopting a misty and somewhat impressionistic style notably similar to that used in Maurice Cullen's paintings of Montreal and J.E.H. MacDonald's of Toronto during the same period. He then moved through an expressionist phase (Donegan 1988, 4), after which he began experimenting with a simplification of form that ended in an almost geometrical rendition of the landscape. There are indeed some parallels between what Picasso did for portraiture and what Harris did for landscape painting.

Lawren Harris was born to a wealthy family of Brantford manufacturers whose business amalgamated with that of another well-known Canadian family in 1891 to form Massey-Harris, in due course one of the world's largest manufacturers of agricultural machinery. After a brief enrolment at the University of Toronto, it became evident that his talents lay in art, and he left in 1904 to study art in Berlin for three years, spending two summers sketching and walking in the Austrian Tyrol. He travelled widely, visiting many exhibitions at a time of ferment in European art, before returning to Canada in 1908. From that year onward, a series of painting and sketching trips, beginning in the Laurentians and extending, as the years went by, to Haliburton, the Ottawa Valley, Minden, Algoma, the North Shore of Lake Superior, and finally the Rockies, resulted in a remarkable series of Canadian landscape paintings. But, as Caulfield notes in his essay, urban scenes were also an important part of his work, particularly in the earlier "representational" period. As Harris put it: "My whole interest was in the Canadian scene. Any paintings, drawings or sketches I saw with a Canadian tang in them excited me more than anything I had seen in Europe" (Adamson 1978).

Harris's early canvas *The Eaton Manufacturing Building from the Ward* (1911)
was painted during his impressionist period. Though it does not depict the staple
economy directly, there are some connections. By this time the Timothy Eaton
Company had established itself as the Hudson Bay's Company's main rival in
Canadian retailing. Both had flagship stores in big cities, but whereas the Bay's
special niche was its trading posts scattered across northern Canada, Eaton's took
advantage of low postal rates to become Canada's number-one catalogue merchant (Kerr 1987, 73). This in itself is an interesting commentary on the dispersed and rural character of Canada's staple hinterland, where the catalogue was
often the only way of purchasing higher-order goods. A large number of Canadians on farms, in mining, lumbering, and fishing communities, and in small
country towns made great use of the Eaton's catalogue. This in turn made
Eaton's one of Canada's leading companies, and not just as a retailer: Eaton's
had large distribution warehouses and at this time was also engaged in manufac-

Lawren S. Harris, *The Eaton Manufacturing Building from the Ward*, 1911, oil on canvas, 76 x
75 cm, T. Eaton Company Limited.

turing. The painting of Eaton's No. 4 factory shows a clothing factory of some twelve storeys (for that time a truly dominating structure) on what appears to be a mild winter day. Sunlight or diffused smoke all but mask the top four storeys of the building. It was located just west of Eaton's current complex on Yonge Street, Toronto. The small houses in the foreground were probably occupied by immigrant Jewish workers, who also provided much of the workforce in the Spadina-Bathurst clothing quarter a little further to the west (Lord 1974, 140). It is significant that the first exhibition of this painting coincided with a strike by women garment workers employed at this factory that lasted four months and broke their fledgling union (Frager 1986). As Northrop Frye suggests, this canvas exemplifies the first and most important of Harris's bridges, the bridge between art and society (Harris and Colgrove 1969, xii).

By the 1920s Harris's interest in German expressionist art had led to a change in his style.[4] His images were now greatly simplified, and he frequently used backlighting to bring out the stark structure of features in the landscape. Two of his paintings from this period that show a strong similarity of style are *Elevator Court, Halifax* (1921) and *Miners' Houses, Glace Bay* (1925). *Elevator Court* depicts workers' housing in the port of Halifax and an elevator used in winter to export Western Canadian grain. As in most of his industrial scenes,

Lawren S. Harris, *Miners' Houses, Glace Bay*, c. 1925, oil on canvas, 107 x 127 cm, Art Gallery of Ontario.

industry (represented here by a tall red chimney) is located immediately adjacent to the clapboard houses. The scene is backlit on a winter's afternoon, and not a soul is in sight. Glace Bay, in contrast, was part of an industrial complex of national importance that was developed principally in the 1890s and 1900s. Sir William C. Van Horne's remarkable painting *The Steel Mills, Sydney, Cape Breton* (1907), with its series of blast furnaces pouring flames and smoke into the night sky (reminiscent of J.M.W. Turner's study of Westminster Palace on fire), reflects on the scale and importance of Sydney at this time. But whereas Van Horne gloried in this scene (in which he had a big financial interest), Harris chose to paint the barren and regimented landscape of the nearby company town of Glace Bay. The scene, which is dominated by rows of workers' houses looking like coffins on end, points to the social relations of the mining industry.[5]

Between 1891 and 1911 the population of Sydney grew sevenfold, while that of Glace Bay grew almost as fast. Workers migrated there from elsewhere in the Maritimes, but above all it was immigration from Scotland that provided the workforce (Wynn 1987). In short, this was a veritable boom town at the turn of the century, the result of growth triggered particularly by railway construction on the Prairies, which in turn was a prerequisite for the wheat export trade. Sydney's relatively low-quality steel was (and still is) much used for rails. The First World War created big demands for coal, iron, and steel, and again this was a boom period in Cape Breton. However, Harris's first visit there in 1921 was during the postwar recession marked here and elsewhere by wage cuts, layoffs, high unemployment, mine closures, reductions in coal and steel production, and widespread social deprivation.

Graeme Wynn (1987, 228–32) reviews Cape Breton's industrial history: the appalling working conditions, mine and industrial accidents, labour unrest, and the forging of a working class during this period. Conditions were sufficiently bad that in 1925 (the year Harris probably painted this landscape) a royal commission was established to examine the mining industry.

Van Horne and Harris captured two aspects of the same reality. For Van Horne in 1907 it was the physical scale of mass iron and steel production that caught his imagination. For Harris in 1925 it was the regimented barracks-like housing provided for an industrial workforce. His painting makes a statement about living conditions in Glace Bay at a time of heightened public awareness of the issue. The absence of vegetation and people from the landscape emphasizes the intensity of his statement.

ALMA DUNCAN

Alma Duncan's work has been widely seen by Canadians because her paintings have been selected for several stamp series.[6] Her interests, which are diverse, include portraiture, still life, scenes from nature, landscape, and film animation. She has worked mostly in charcoal, chalk, pastel, and watercolour. Although not widely known for her industrial art until recently, she has focused on the industrial scene during three phases of her career: 1943–47, 1956 and 1958, and 1985–86 (Murray 1987).

Born in Paris, Ontario, in 1917, she lived in Pennsylvania between the ages of four and nine, before returning to live first in the steel town of Hamilton and then in Montreal. From 1936 to 1943, she was a part-time student as McGill University (studying political economy and anatomy) while working part-time in an advertising studio. During this period, she studied life drawing with Ernst Neumann at his studio and with Goodridge Roberts at the school of the Montreal Museum of Fine Art.

Along with Frederick B. Taylor, Alex Colville, Caven Atkins, Fritz Brandtner, and Karl Shaeffer, she became a painter of industrial scenes because of the Second World War. She had sought acceptance as one of the group of official war artists, but it was not until after the war that the armed forces recognized women artists. So instead, she began to record scenes from the "home front," including oil refineries, munitions factories, and other war facilities. All of her industrial drawings in the 1943–47 period are in black chalk or charcoal on paper – a munitions factory, a Vickers naval shipyard, the Imperial Oil and Shell refineries (all located in Montreal), a nickel mine in the Sudbury Basin, a rubber plant in Sarnia, a coal terminal at Sault Ste. Marie, and a pulp and paper plant in Hull, Quebec. This is a revealing list of Canada's staple industries and of the transportation infrastructure needed to store and move bulky primary materials to processing plants and ultimately to foreign markets. These subjects also underline Canada's status as a supplier of materials for the European war effort.

Duncan's drawings of factory interiors usually juxtapose human forms with the much more geometrical forms of machines and products. Typically, the machines loom large and dominate the workforce; indeed, in some images the workers look antlike. Two images of particular interest from this early period are *Industrial Hamlet* (1947), which depicts the town of Coniston, a little east of Sudbury, and *Interior with Pulpwood* (1947), a scene in the now demolished E.B. Eddy pulpwood plant in Hull, opposite the federal Parliament Buildings.

Until the 1960s, logs were floated down the Ottawa River to the Eddy plant where they were pulped or made into matchsticks. Duncan chose to sketch a pulping room in which a classic example of Fordist (production-line) technology is used to begin the conversion of cord-length logs into paper. In this drawing, logs are being fed into large washers. The scene predates the development of automated technology, and the process depicted thus requires substantial inputs of labour. Men are working laboriously at machines that are belching steam into the high roof of the building. This is the classic Canadian scene of a raw material being processed in bulk into an intermediate product, mainly for export. The high value added activities that create the end-product, be it a newspaper, a book, or a cardboard box, are located close to final demand, usually outside Canada.

Painted in 1947, Duncan's *Industrial Hamlet* presents a disturbing picture. In the background stands the *raison d'être* of the scene, a metal smelter near Sudbury; as in so much of Canada's hinterland, the economy is dominated by a few big producers. But the housing in the foreground seems to fall below the

Alma Duncan, *Industrial Hamlet,* 1947, charcoal on paper, 44x 59 cm, artist's collection.

status even of company housing. It consists of a series of shacks, distributed higgeldy-piggeldy in what is almost a shanty town. The hamlet is surrounded by a lunar landscape of spoil heaps and bare rocks (thanks to massive air pollution from the smelters, no vegetation can be seen). In the midst of this desolation, a small child is at play. Thus, this image also records a common problem with Canada's staple industries: negative externalities (traffic congestion, noise, waste heaps, and air and water pollution) are inflicted on those unfortunate enough to live nearby.[7]

During the 1956–58 period, Duncan made a series of drawings of the open cast mine and iron ore processing plant at Steep Rock Lake near Dryden, northwest of Lake Superior. These were done in pastel on paper for the good reason that the various reds and purples of the iron ore are superbly rendered in this medium. She made a series of drawings exploring this theme; the recurring image is of a vast scar in the side of the earth, the result of excavations by mine equipment and trucks which, though huge, are nevertheless dwarfed by the mining operation, as in *Giant Machines Look Small* (1956). The large scale of activity is also seen in *Truck Carrying Ore to Crusher* (1956): several layers of the mine workings are visible, and in the background what appear to be forested slopes rise above the mining scene. Mining operations such as this are scattered across the Canadian hinterland, and their size is most obvious in open cast operations such as Steep Rock. The scale of operations reflects the concentrating effect that modern technology has had on Canadian industrial capital.

Alma Duncan, *Truck Carrying Ore to Crusher*, 1956, pastel on paper, 50 x 71 cm, artist's collection.

Duncan's *Sunlight and Steel* (1956) moves along the sequence of production from iron ore mining and crushing in the north to Stelco's huge steelworks in Hamilton. It is noteworthy that Stelco, then Canada's largest steel maker, is located in the heartland of Canada, close to the main markets. Given the polluted atmosphere of the works, Duncan adds black chalk to pastels to achieve the required sooty effect. The scene is drawn from a vantage point beneath a large black bridge-like structure. Centre-left, a huge chimney rises through the scene and continues up out of sight. Behind is a massive shed, reflecting the scale of operations in Hamilton.

When Duncan returned to industrial art thirty years later, she focused on two plants, Stelco's steel plant at Nanticoke on Lake Erie and Maclaren Industries' pulp and paper operations at Thurso (near Hull) in Quebec. Stelco's geographical development makes an interesting story. For nearly a century the company has succeeded in growing "in situ" on the south shore of Hamilton Harbour by purchasing and then demolishing neighbouring housing and factories on the landward side and by purchasing water lots on the other side from a compliant Hamilton Harbour Commission and filling them with slag. During this long drawn-out process, the two big steel makers, Stelco and Dofasco, have purchased and infilled water lots that cover one third of Hamilton's original harbour. Having run out of space in Hamilton, in the 1960s Stelco purchased a large greenfield site at Nanticoke, some fifty kilometres to the south on Lake Erie. This site allows Stelco to avoid Welland Canal tolls on inputs delivered via the Upper Great Lakes. *Steam, Clouds and Blast Furnace* (1985) shows the huge

Alma Duncan, *Steam, Clouds and Blast Furnace,* 1985, pastel on paper, 50 x 71 cm, artist's collection.

modern blast furnace Stelco constructed at Nanticoke. This high-technology installation looks rather like a rocket launching pad. To the left, stockpiles of coal and ore are connected to the top of the furnace by a large overhead conveyor system. No employees are in sight; a plant using such highly automated technologies has a surprisingly small workforce. Almost all the coal and iron ore inputs to the plant are transported by lakers to the nearby dock facility. From there, a large covered conveyor belt carries the raw materials to huge stockpiles adjacent to the plant. *Conveyor from Ship to Stockpile I* (1985) shows part of this system. A large, partly covered conveyor crosses a green wasteland and in the middle distance links up with a massive stockpile of coal. In the midst of this coal heap is a huge revolving crane that builds stockpiles of coal to supply the blast furnace.

Duncan's contribution to Canadian industrial art is therefore a series of exteriors and interiors, usually drawn in a realist style. Some of her works are in black and white, some are in pastel. All of them are topographically accurate. While they seem fairly neutral on an ideological plane, they point to several important aspects of Canada's staple industries, including their progressive mechanization, the growing scale of operations, and the environmental consequences.

ADRIEN HÉBERT

Adrien Hébert lived from 1890 to 1967, which makes him a close contemporary of Lawren Harris. He was, as Ostiguy (1986, 38) stresses, "un régionaliste."

Although his style evolved out of a series of long visits to France, it was Quebec, and Montreal in particular, that he chose to paint. Portraits and, to a lesser extent, genre painting are represented in his oeuvre, but he was above all else a recorder of the urban landscape.

Prior to 1919, Hébert's style was somewhat decorative and even fanciful. Thereafter, he focused more and more on realist scenes, particularly following a fifteen-month sojourn in France in 1922–23 when he was clearly influenced by Cézanne's painting. He also began to adopt some cubist mannerisms, albeit in a realist form.[8] In recording the port scene in Montreal, then a vital component of the Canadian economy, Hébert visually linked Canada's interior with its foreign markets. For Canada to be an exporter of staples, a storehouse providing advanced industrial nations with the bulky materials needed for their industries, there had to be big ports. In the 1920s Montreal was both the largest city and the largest port in Canada.[9] Although Toronto was beginning to challenge Montreal's financial dominance, in most other respects it was Montreal that still remained in first place (Kerr 1987, 102–4). At this stage of history, Canada's trade with Europe and the U.S. East Coast states was much more important than it is today: the West Coast Pacific orientation has grown strongly only since the Second World War.

Hébert's *Loading Grain, Montreal Harbour* (1924) is arguably, the most expressionist of all his works.[10] The perspective looks towards the harbour from Île Ste-Helène, and in the middle ground is a cargo vessel loading grain from an adjacent elevator. A tug smokes in the harbour, while a second vessel is moored on the opposite quay, above which a conveyor connects to a large grain elevator. In the background, and partly hidden, are four of the turrets of Elevator No. 2, one of the monumental buildings discussed in Kestelman's essay (chapter 15). With a capacity of 2.6 million bushels, it was at that time among the largest man-made structures on earth (Donegan 1988, 34). A scale model of this elevator was built for the Canadian exhibit at the 1936 Paris Exposition as part of a campaign to promote the export of durum (hard) wheat (used to make French bread), hence the structure was both in reality and symbolically part of Canada's staple export trade. The whole scene is side-lit to give it a dramatic effect and to accentuate the geometrical forms of the port scene.

Equally geometrical are the shapes in *Le Port de Montréal* (1925), but this time the same scene is observed from the opposite direction. Two ships with black and white topsides and red and black funnels are moored side by side on the far quay. These are the colours of the Cunard Line and the grain being loaded is almost certainly destined for Birkenhead (near Liverpool), where at this time and through to the 1950s the world's largest flour mill was to be found. This provides a fascinating link between the industries of Canada and northern England in the latter days of Empire. Canada was the granary, and Montreal the main port exporting wheat to feed the army of workers employed in Britain's industries, which in turn clothed, armed, furnished, and otherwise equipped an

Empire close to its zenith. Canada's role in this system was therefore as a
somewhat peripheral supplier of staple materials, a role that is illustrated by
many Canadian industrial landscape paintings. Significantly, the final product –
flour – was manufactured outside Canada.

Adrien Hébert, *Loading Grain, Montréal Harbour,* 1924, oil on canvas, 104 x 74 cm, Art
Gallery of Hamilton.

Art in a Geographical Context

Robert Herbert (1982) has insisted that art history should be a contextual history. It is not just a procession of styles and a succession of preferred subjects. Art history has a social and historical setting. Paul Hayes Tucker (1982) illustrates this thesis in his writings on Claude Monet's experiences at Argenteuil, in the 1870s a booming satellite of Paris. Upset by the intrusion of industry into his rural idyll, Monet experienced a painter's block that he eventually resolved by moving to Giverny, deep in the Normandy countryside. What is implicit with Herbert and Tucker, and explicit here, is that landscape art also has a geographical context.[11] And though in some cases there is little to be gained from considering matters geographical, in paintings of Canada's industrial landscapes the geographical, social, and economic contexts are all clearly of importance.

Canada's resource dependence is depicted in many industrial landscapes. But these resources are not located in a land flowing with milk and honey. The resources have to be cut down, dug up, harvested, caught, or trapped, frequently under difficult conditions. The staple is then processed either locally or somewhere along the main transportation arteries before passing through the handful of major ports en route to overseas markets. Lacking a massive industrial workforce, Canadian staple producers have substituted technology: large machines requiring commensurately large investments make the system work. Big is usually ugly, but in the Canadian economy this seems to be the norm. Thus, ever-larger farms, bigger deep-sea trawlers, deeper mines, faster mechanical tree harvesters, and vaster quarries, which are increasingly automated, increasingly dominated by a few oligopolistic producers, and increasingly controlled by foreign interests, have come to be the current reality of Canadian industry. These technological, social, and geographical contexts have not gone unnoticed by Canadian landscape artists. Lawren Harris, Alma Duncan, and Adrien Hébert are but three among several dozen artists who have, in their own manner, painted the Canadian industrial scene. Far from Edenic, their art depicts in different ways Canadian adaptations to local possibilities and constraints. It frequently pits people *against* nature. And because the staples are typically bulky, that struggle involves vast projects that stand out, obtrusively, from the landscape. As in so many other aspects of Canadian life, the hand of geography can be seen to play a powerful role in the way artists have painted Canada's industrial landscape.

Notes

1 To give just a few examples that illustrate this point: Georges Braque's *L'Estaque* (1906); Paul Cézanne's *Usines près du mont du Cengle* (c. 1869–70); Edgar Dégas's *Jockeys at the Tribune* (1879); Vincent van Gogh's *Le Verger en Fleurs* (1888); Emile Loubon's *Vue des Aygalades* (1853); Claude Monet's *Vue de Sannois* (1872); Henri Rousseau's *La Fabrique de Chaises à Alfortville* (1897); and Maurice Utrillo's *Lavoir Champeau* (n.d.).

2 Based on a poem by Pierre Lachambeaudie, this painting juxtaposes, on opposite sides of a stream, a tranquil verdant setting and a scarred and angular industrial landscape.

3 These are discussed in Innis's books. An accessible summary of staple theory is presented in Watkins 1963, while the implications for metropoles are considered in Careless 1989.

4 German expressionism is particularly suited to the industrial scene. See, for instance, the recent paintings of Eisler (1987). It was the Norwegian expressionist, Edvard Munch, who most influenced Harris (Lord 1974, 141).

5 Harris's woodcut *Glace Bay* (1921) is more explicit about the suffering of miners' families; it shows a distressed mother and two children and in the background a miner trudging up a road past the same miners' houses towards the mine.

6 One of her watercolours for the Maple in Four Seasons stamp series was chosen by an American philatelic journal as the best 1971 stamp in the world.

7 In the case of Sudbury, it was some twenty years later that mining companies were required to install scrubbers in their chimneys to reduce the discharge of pollutants. Thereafter, vegetation began to re-establish itself quite quickly.

8 Hébert in some ways anticipated the American cubist-realist (precisionist) school. See Boyanoski 1989.

9 As Ostiguy puts it: "Adrien Hébert brings us a moving and unique testimony to the reality of one of the few great Canadian cities of the twenties and thirties." (1971, 9).

10 Hébert returned to the same scenes many times. For example, his *Le chargement du blé dans le port de Montréal* (1927) is painted from the same spot as his 1924 scene. To add confusion, he sometimes changed the title of his paintings.

11 It is, indeed, explicit in Herbert 1988; he includes maps of Paris on the inside cover and several other maps in his text, while chapter titles such as "Paris Transformed," "Parks, Racetracks, and Gardens," "Suburban Leisure," and "At the Seaside" all have a geographical connotation.

REFERENCES

Adamson, J. 1978. *Lawren S. Harris: Urban Scenes and Wilderness Landscapes 1906–1930.* Toronto: Art Gallery of Ontario.

Boyanoski, C. 1989. *Permeable Border: Art of Canada and the United States 1920–1940.* Toronto: Art Gallery of Ontario.

Britton, J.N.H., and J.M. Gilmour. 1978. *The Weakest Link.* Ottawa: Science Council of Canada.

Careless, J.M.S. 1989. *Frontier and Metropolis: Regions, Cities and Identities in Canada before 1914.* Toronto: University of Toronto Press.

Clark, T.J. 1984. *The Painting of Modern Life: Paris in the Art of Manet and His Followers.* London: Thames and Hudson.

Donegan, R. 1988. *Industrial Images.* Hamilton, Ont.: Art Gallery of Hamilton.

Eisler, G. 1987. *Landscapes of Exile.* Vienna and Frankfort: Europaverlag.

Frager, R. 1986. "Sewing Solidarity: The Eaton's Strike of 1912." *Canadian Women's Studies* 7:96–98.

Harris, B., and R.P.G. Colgrove. 1969. *Lawren Harris.* Toronto: Macmillan.

Herbert, R.L. 1982. "Industry in the Changing Landscape from Daubigny to Monet." In J.M. Merriman, ed., *French Cities in the Nineteenth Century,* 139–64. London: Hutchinson.

———. 1988 *Impressionism: Art, Leisure, and Parisian Society.* New Haven, Conn.: Yale University Press.

Kerr, D. 1987. "The Emergence of the Industrial Heartland c. 1759–1950." In L.D. McCann, ed., *Heartland and Hinterland,* 70–107. Scarborough, Ont.: Prentice-Hall Canada.

Lord, B. 1974. *The History of Painting in Canada.* Toronto: NC Press.

Mellen, P. 1970. *The Group of Seven.* Toronto: McClelland & Stewart.

Murray, J. 1987. *Alma Duncan and Men at Work.* Oshawa: Robert McLaughlin Gallery.

Osborne, B. 1988. "The Iconography of Nationhood in Canadian Art." In D. Cosgrove and S. Daniels, eds., *The Iconography of Landscape,* 162–78. Cambridge: Cambridge University Press.

Ostiguy, J-R. 1971. *Adrien Hébert: trente ans de son oeuvre, 1923–1953.* Ottawa: la Galerie nationale du Canada.

———. 1986. *Adrien Hébert: premier interprète de la modernité Québécoise.* Saint-Laurent, Que.: Editions du Trécarré.

Tucker, P.H. 1982. *Monet at Argenteuil.* New Haven, Conn.: Yale University Press.

Watkins, M.H. 1963. "A Staple Theory of Economic Growth." *Canadian Journal of Economics and Political Science* 28:141–58.

Wynn, G. 1987. "The Maritimes: The Geography of Fragmentation and Underdevelopment?" In L.D. McCann, ed., *Heartland and Hinterland,* 174–245. Scarborough, Ont.: Prentice-Hall Canada.

7

Human Encroachments on a Domineering Physical Landscape

Linda Joan Paul

$\mathcal{M}$any contributors to this book have chosen to review writers or artists who describe regional rather than national landscapes. In selecting Claire Mowat and Aritha van Herk for study in this chapter, I am no exception. Similarly, Squire's discussion of Lucy Maud Montgomery's writings, Alec Paul and Paul Simpson-Housley's description of Martha Ostenso's *Wild Geese,* Scott's commentary on Gabrielle Roy's *The Cashier,* Sitwell's examination of Grove's novels, and even some of Peepre-Bordessa's comments on Hugh MacLennan's earlier books focus on the regional landscapes portrayed by their authors.

However, the portrayals of these landscapes vary. Van Herk's Wernecke Mountains, Mowat's Newfoundland outports, and Ostenso's interlake prairie landscape are harsh, relatively unyielding. Norcliffe extends this theme to Canadian industrial landscape painting. He comments in chapter 6, "The resources have to be cut down, dug up, harvested, caught, or trapped, frequently under difficult conditions."

In direct contrast, Scott suggests the rural landscape represented "paradise" to Chenevert, the cashier. Squire depicts Montgomery's representation of Prince Edward Island as a "rural idyll," and Ramsay describes how Lucius O'Brien's *Sunrise on the Saguenay* paints a sublime landscape, serene and tranquil. Undoubtedly, significant regional contrasts occur among Canada's multifaceted landscapes.

To a geographer, the geographical overtones of Claire Mowat's *The Outport People* (*OP* in text page citations) and Aritha van Herk's *The Tent Peg* (*TP* in text page citations) are immediate. Both novels are introduced through the use of a map. The maps help to set the atmosphere of the books and also suggest the characters' anticipated relationship with the environment. In addition, they introduce the region the characters are about to confront. These environments, although similar in many ways, are viewed differently by the authors. While Mowat has fallen in love with the map of Newfoundland and all that it is anticipated to represent (*OP*, 1), to van Herk, the map suggests a foreboding, dangerous, deceptive, and powerful landscape.

J.L., the female protagonist in *The Tent Peg*, watches Mackenzie, the leader of the summer geologists' camp, trace the flight route with his finger on the map. We soon learn that "the lakes below are an impelled deception; if you raise your eyes for one moment, you become instantly lost," that the land is "an unending hesitation of sameness . . . and yet ever-changing . . . Skull teeth gleam through an invitation; the tundra can both restore and maim. No man lives to presume its power" (*TP*, 1987, 7). On the other hand, Mowat holds a romantic preconception of what Newfoundland will be like: "I used to stare at the Newfoundland map, entranced by the icon of that distant island of cool winds surrounded by the blue Atlantic . . . I could feel the salt spray on my face and hear the foghorns bleating." Like Lucy Maud Montgomery's Anne's House of Dreams, Mowat has her windblown island of her dreams.

For geographers, vivid and detailed descriptions of physical, cultural, and regional landscapes expand our comprehension of place. Mowat and van Herk paint detailed pictures of the Newfoundland and Yukon environments, certainly through the prism of their own experiences and visions, but also through the perceptions of their characters as well.

Setting often is not as important as other elements of a story – plot, character, and theme. A setting's importance depends on the purpose of the story. If the author wants his or her story to be universal, elements of the story will not be so strongly localized or obvious. Sometimes, however, authors want to stress local rather than universal themes. In this essay, local elements of setting will assume importance (Berlinguette 1989). *The Outport People* and *The Tent Peg* are regional novels that constantly refer to regional settings.

Interestingly, the novels have many elements in common. The protagonists, both female, decide to leave a mundane urban environment for isolated and more simple locations. For J.L., the particular destination was not important. "I did it deliberately. I wanted this job, I wanted to head for nowhere and look at everything in my narrow world from a detached distance" (*TP*, 23). On the other hand, the Mowats chose a specific locale:

> We decided, irrationally and passionately, to live there . . . it was going to be so much cheaper to live in an outport where houses were half the price they were in Ontario, and without roads we wouldn't need a car. We planned to eat a lot of fresh fish and wild berries. I would make my own bread and my own clothes. We would be as far away as possible from the vexations of the urban, managed world. (*OP*, 3)

Both protagonists left regional capitals: J.L. escaped from Edmonton, while Claire Mowat's flight was from Toronto. Both chose hinterland locations as their end-points. Within these hinterlands, they chose locales so isolated they could not be reached by road. For Mowat's Newfoundland outport Baleena, a weekly scheduled supply ship was the umbilicus that linked "forty isolated coastal communities with the rest of the world" (*OP*, 2). In *The Tent Peg*, what eventually becomes known as Fort Chaos can only be reached by air. "I'm the pilot that [*sic*] flies them fuel, food and mail once a week, Wednesdays. It's a long flight from Mayo, but I don't mind, it's beautiful country" (*TP*, 78). The frail transportation connections suggest there are human encroachments in these isolated spots but that the natural environments of both regions make these inroads difficult.

To many, their environments are considered harsh. The situation in the Arctic is considerably more extreme than in Newfoundland. In *The Tent Peg*, the first planned geological survey site was in the Northwest Territories. "Nothing but tundra and lakes, lakes and tundra. Once you're out there, in amongst the moss and the occasional outcrop, you melt right down in the barrens. Not a dot of anyone anywhere" (*TP*, 10). But Mackenzie liked it that way. J.L.'s thoughts follow similar patterns, ". . . thinking of the barrenlands, that shivering silence stretched out over the pale flatness, treeless and unashamed."

Preparations for a summer camp at this first site are abandoned when company headquarters anticipate a uranium find in the Wernecke Mountains of the eastern Yukon.

> The cold surface of the water reflects inlaid turquoise against a dull overhang of mountains. You might believe that the ice has melted but it's only sunk, green and congealed, to the bottom of the lake where it will hover all summer, chilling the water. That damn lake will never be warm enough to swim in.
>
> The snow too lies scattered and torn in patches on the moss . . . We're here . . . in an alpine valley that never feels summer, just varying shades of winter. Nothing to break the angry gusts coming off those mountains. We're above the tree line, above everything. (*TP*, 42)

Mowat describes grey granite outcrops, steep, rocky slopes, marsh, the barrens, and the North Atlantic, stormy and cold. The force of the wind is so strong that even trees adapt, stunted and bending, to its onslaught. These scenes contrast sharply with Squire's depiction of Montgomery's Prince Edward Island as a pastoral idyll and Lucius O'Brien's portrayal of landscape in *Sunrise on the Saguenay* as sublime.

Within a lazy day's sail from Baleena, Mowat waxes poetic as the entrance to Rosey (Enragee) River, a fjord, comes into view.

> The cover . . . was spectacular. We were surrounded on three sides by a deep evergreen forest, that rose almost straight up the side of a steep cliff. Far above us we could see a fresh-water stream, the seemingly weightless drops splattering and sparkling as they fell down to the sea. North of us a landscape of glacier-worn rocks marched into the distance, and below us the water was so clear. (*OP*, 168)

At times, then, both authors describe the majesty of their surroundings. Straying from their campsite, only a few miles downstream, Mackenzie, in *The Tent Peg*, guides Thompson to a new world, surprisingly different for its proximity. The air is hot and thick, and they leave the stony bare landscape for trees, almost forgotten, and the steady whine of mosquitoes! After a walk, they hear

> a long, far-away roar that grows larger as we walk, louder and stronger until it overtakes and conceals the sounds of the forest.
>
> And then, without warning, we are standing at the edge of a narrow gorge that is creased hundreds of feet deep into the rock. Over it roars a mountain stream that, in its fall, unleashes itself to brilliant life. (*TP*, 197).

In both books, there are elements of danger. For Mowat danger appears sporadically. For van Herk it is omnipresent. Mowat writes:

> One day we decided to climb to the top of the cliff that loomed above our little hideaway. It was our intention to find the source of the waterfall. We climbed, with considerable difficulty, for nearly two hours, up over the vertical rocks and slippery boulders, clinging to feeble little spruce trees as we went. When we reached the crest of this isthmus which divided the inland waterway from the sea, we could once again see the Atlantic Ocean stretching into infinity to the south of us. We were ecstatic – the way Cortes must have felt where no men, and certainly no woman, had ever stood before . . .
>
> Then we started to consider our trip back down, and wondered what would happen if one of us fell and broke a leg amid the jagged crevices of this landscape that was more suited to eagles than to people. (*OP*, 169–70).

Interestingly, aboriginal people undoubtedly inhabited the environments portrayed by both authors long before Europeans arrived on the scene. Yet these possible intrusions are scarcely alluded to by either writer.

In *The Tent Peg*, foreshadowing keeps the elements of the environment in the mind of the reader. Both Mackenzie and J.L. hear the mountain beginning to shift. But when the massive overhang finally lets go, only J.L. is awake to sense it:

> I felt the mountain rumble, I felt it stir and I was instantly awake, listening with every bone arched . . . I'm clear of the camp, moving up the valley. The cirque rests at the neck of the mountain, it creeps upward, lifts itself against the moment of upthrust time that left it there to wait . . . I hear the splash of a pebble bouncing from a cliff. The sound seems to fade but then it's joined by the smaller chinks and spatters of stones, a trickle that gradually cascades . . . begins to sing, to surge, to roar, and finally to rumble . . . the whole side

of the mountain caught in a torrent of itself . . . The east side has let go and
slid down into our valley. Where once was an even slope rises a raw gap.
(*TP*, 120–21)

The camp crew, who are a hundred yards from being hammered to death by
boulders, are stunned. Danger is imminently present, although no deaths occur.
The foreboding results of the rock slide lie adjacent to the camp for the rest of
the summer, constantly reminding the team of nature's engulfing power.

The harsh environment extends beyond the inanimate. On more than one
occasion, J.L. confronts a grizzly bear, which again spooks the men. References
to and sightings of grizzlies foreshadow the possible event. J.L. and Ivan spot a
grizzly and her two cubs from the helicopter. Jerome carries his Magnum and
brags about what he will do if he encounters it. Cap says he's horny, and J.L.
tells him to find a grizzly bear. Eventually a grizzly lumbers into the camp. Cap
reports, "I have to blink to focus on what I see. And then I cannot move, I am
absolutely pillared in place" (*TP*, 108). The bear roars, J.L. confronts it and
stares it down. Both the she-bear and J.L. turn and move in opposite directions.
The bear and the rock slide are such powerful symbols it is hard, at one level, to
take these events at face value; both of them represent the formidable danger of
the Yukon.

In the two novels, the descriptions of and feelings for the landscape vary
with the perceptions of the characters. Natural environments can induce or
reflect mood. Weather is an obvious barometer of characters' moods. Sometimes
they react to it mentally, sometimes they describe it dispassionately. It is, however, a regional force to be reckoned with.

One of Claire Mowat's objectives in writing her book was to explain, describe, and interpret Newfoundland's outports and all their intricacies to the rest
of Canada. The reader is guided with humour, and warmth, on a laywoman's
geographical tour of the region. The weather, always different from Toronto's
scorching and humid summer heat, became a fascination for Mowat, a significant regional contrast. (Similarly, Squire, in chapter 11, notes Montgomery's
juxtaposition of the idyllic P.E.I rural landscape and Toronto's dingy streets.)

Indeed, for Mowat, weather was a marker of the passing days. Changeable,
penetrating, it was often a domineering physical force in the natural landscape.
Most noticeable were the storms.

Rain turned to snow and back to rain again and at night the glass in our
bedroom window rattled ominously. Almost every week a gale blew
with such ferocity that in the more popular places of this world it would
have made headline news. Winds of fifty, sixty and seventy knots were
commonplace, and gusts reaching a hundred knots were not infrequent.
At the railway terminal at Port-aux-Basques, empty freight cars were
blown right off the track at least once every winter.

Fortunately these hurricane winds didn't come without warning.

We watched the southern sky gradually turn from pale grey to the colour of school blackboards. We bolted our doors against it and waited. It was known locally as a "blow" – surely one of the greatest understatements in the English language. (*OP*, 18–19)

She later comments that wind, rather than cold, was the chief peril of winter. Often the temperature hovered around the freezing point, and freezing rain, known locally as "glitter storms" (*OP*, 19) was a common occurrence.

Perils extended beyond the land. Obvious were the dangers for fishermen caught at sea in a storm. More obscure dangers existed as well, such as ships being crushed in the ice. On sunny winter days, the sea, often a deep indigo blue, deceptively resembled the inviting Caribbean, giving no hint that it could freeze a person to death within minutes. However,

whatever kind of weather we got, it didn't last very long. Mingled with those tempestuous winter days . . . we had plenty of "civil" days. They dawned sunny and unexpectedly serene and mocked the calendar that told us it was December. On such sunny days in March, every clothesline in Dog Cove was laden with undulating sheets. (*OP*, 72)

These sunny days are interspersed with endless days of drizzle and fog. "It was June, the month of everlasting fog. Fog is no one's friend. It doesn't water the garden, it doesn't fill up the well and you can't skate or ski on it. It is the bane of all seafaring men" (*OP*, 123).

Weather was a less prominent aspect of the geology crew's life, undoubtedly because their season in the Arctic was for the short summer months only. Still, when arriving in the Territories, J.L. was fascinated by sun dogs.

Dramatically, the dangers of the spring break-up were brought to the fore. Mackenzie, his airplane having previously landed on weakening ice, takes a running leap from the lake shore to the Cessna and falls partially through the ice. His leg and clothing instantly freeze.

Although winter storms are over for the season, rain, especially, affects the morale of the survey crew.

It's been raining for a week. Cold rain that chills you right through. Puts everybody in a foul temper. When I fly the men out, the helicopter is full of curses and the smell of steamy rain suits. And the mist. It obscures the mountains . . . At night everyone's wet and muddy and snarling. They drink more. In the morning they're late getting up. (*TP*, 131)

The pilot is bitchy as hell; they don't like flying in break up. Use skis and you'll need floats; use floats and you'll need skis. Who can tell? It's that kind of country, changes her mind the minute your back is turned. (*TP*, 11)

As with the Newfoundland outport, a shift in the weather can brighten spirits: "The crew is pleased as can be . . . the rain has stopped, it looks like a good day, sunshine and a breeze. Every one of them feels good, you can tell by the way they stomp around" (*TP*, 144). Hearne, a photographer, reiterates this enthusiasm during a clear day when he feels he can capture the texture of rocks which form the massive landslide.

Environmental perception also varies with the outlook and mood of the characters, as does the sense of isolation, similarly described by Paul and Simpson-Housley with regard to Ostenso's *Wild Geese*. Mackenzie, the party chief and veteran Arctic surveyor, remarks of the Northwest Territories, "I like it out there alone. Alone with nothing around but tundra and quiet, the two of them holding each other down against the sky at their own expense" (*TP*, 12). Later, at the Yukon site, J.L. comments of Mackenzie, "He's glad to be out here, away from town, the transition accomplished. This is his world, he moves effortlessly, the moss under his feet natural and yielding."

Milton, the Mennonite, has ambivalent feelings towards this mountainous, isolated environment: "I figured you could get closer to God up here, but He feels farther away" (*TP*, 63). Later he comments of the mountains, "They are an example of God's glory" (*TP*, 66). In contrast, Hudson, the upper-class Englishman, finds the isolation anything but glorious: "God's glory. They look murderous to me" (*TP*, 67). To him, the remote, pressing mountains were like glinting teeth.

Milton also compares the Yukon to his permanent home: "Every night now we have a fire, we gather sticks and burn them . . . It's eerie, the sparks against the solid darkness. The mountains lie uneasy after the slide, they're not peaceful and far like the prairie is. I miss the prairie, the unrolling land" (*TP*, 148).

Roy, the pilot, feels that three months of isolation in the Yukon mountains would drive a saint mad. Yet by the summer's end, most of the crew have come to terms with the campsite and the foreboding mountains. Their perceptions change and this environment becomes part of an accepted way of life. Drying tundra moss on her tent floor, J.L. summarizes this eventual feeling of acceptance, suggesting the summer was worth the stay, just for the scent of the moss.

"Maps are seductive" (*OP*, 1). In this first sentence of her novel, Clair Mowat suggests how she perceives Newfoundland's isolated outports. Later, however, as Mowat's sojourn in Baleena lengthened, she was willing to admit that if they hadn't lingered until it was too late to move on, they might never have become infatuated with the place. In general, the Mowats like the isolation. Yet they seemed surprised when others, as urbane as themselves, chose a similar lifestyle. Of the fish plant owners, the Drakes, Mowat was to inquire, rhetorically, why a couple who kept an impressive wine cellar and read magazines like *Gourmet* and *Vogue* should choose to live in this remote outport. Later she answered part of the question herself. Freeman Drake seemed content when hunting and fishing in the back country. The Mowats also liked hiking into the back country and taking long walks in varying weather: "One brave little boy ventured to tell me that there were t'ousands blueberries up t'river. We eventually discovered that up the river was the source of a lot of things that made for a pretty nice life – salmon, trout, moose, caribou, ptarmigan, wild berries and firewood" (*OP*, 161).

Although domineering, both physical environments allow human encroachments. In neither place, however, is it easy to carve out a permanent cultural niche. Mowat describes her first impression of her home-to-be in Baleena.

> We rounded a small island of grey granite topped with a pelt of tawny grass, and suddenly there it was, lonely as a lighthouse, the house we had impulsively bought . . . Our new home stood apart from its neighbours, its clapboard walls painted a pristine white in contrast to the turquoise, yellow and green of the other houses. Behind it was a steep rocky slope, with a marsh below, and beyond that only the cold and stormy North Atlantic. (*OP*, 5)

> There wasn't a single passenger car for two hundred miles. Nor was there a foot of pavement.
> Baleena appeared to be a haphazard scattering of small tidy houses connected by pathways and bumpy trails. Houses seemed to grow together in clusters in those places where massive boulders and rocks did not. (*OP*, 3)

Similarly, van Herk paints a scene of a physical environment unwilling to yield to human encroachment easily: "The snow too lies scattered and torn in patches on the moss. In between, our boxes and bags, our summer's survival, seems lost, inadequate" (*TP*, 42). There are perpetual reminders of their transient visit. The wind carries the voices of the crew, who are setting up the Storm Haven tents, clustered close together so as to ward off the chill. As the helicopter appears, Mackenzie states,

> I wave my arms in a circle to signal a flat landing spot . . . The machine needles closer and closer to the ground, dust and dry winter moss blowing up from the cushion of air under the skids, when suddenly the Storm Havens billow and lift, struggle olive and canvas and alive against their puny ropes and pegs . . . Huge crippled kites, they green the chilly air like blossoming sails for one wild escaped moment, only to hesitate and then collapse in heaps of inert canvas on the gray moss. (*TP*, 42–43)

Jerome, another surveyor, does not like the scattered layout of the tent village: "The Jutland's set up facing the lake so the wind will hit that tent square every night. The Storm Havens aren't in a row, they're just any old way . . . The garbage pit's too close and the shitter is too far away. Somebody's decided to build a shower" (*TP*, 54).

In both these rugged environments, settlements are scattered insignificantly, yet are colourful and bold, perhaps to announce that humans do exist there.

Human imprints in the survey camp are minor, impermanent adaptations to the environment – radio antenna hung with bright flagging, paths worn to the garbage dump and latrines, or two dozen brown bottles cooling at the edge of the lake. The day the campsite is established, Thompson is already discussing the anticipated sadness the crew will feel at the end of the summer when they leave their temporary home. The only significant landmarks, after the crew has left, will be the stakes, testament to the Yukon's two-post system for staking mine claims for mineral rights. After their discovery of gold, regulations allowed each person to stake eight claims. Thus, a total of eighty claims would be staked, an initial and end post, 1,500 feet apart, indicating the length of each claim. Each person was required to strike his or her own claims, which they did by hammering posts into the ground and heaping stones around the base to give more support.

But little human evidence exists to indicate the intense activity of a summer's work. Frequent comments show the crew's awareness of their stay's impermanence. At the close of the season, the campers dismember their cultural landscape, everything from worn or torn clothing to the table used for food preparation. As they do this, J.L. still feels the mountains hover above them, awaiting their departure.

In Baleena, human encroachments on the natural landscape were somewhat more permanent, since Euro-Canadians had inhabited the area for a longer period of time than in the Yukon, aboriginal people even longer. Nine hundred people lived in this outport, which, though officially one community, was in fact really five. A government wharf, a freight shed, a few old trucks (though not a single passenger car), two churches, a few stores, and a post office created an artificial environment. The only industry was the fish plant, "a series of plain wooden buildings that sprawled along the shore of the deep harbour of The Gut" (OP, 21). In addition, transient vessels, such as those carrying fish to ports in New England, anchored at Baleena. A few prominent buildings could be found, such as the doctor's Edwardian mansion and the Anglican church constructed like an inverted ship.

Though not designed as such, one boat became a temporary home. "Frank . . . lived in the tiny forepeak of his trap boat, which he had rigged out with a narrow bunk and a small coal stove" (OP, 8). Other boats were put to new uses as well. The refrigerator ship carrying fish products south had been a minesweeper in the Second World War. Change of form, function, and environment did occur. But in general, most people believed a good life was possible without continual change. These outports did not rush headlong into the twentieth century, grabbing and transforming, adapting to the continually changing technology that was so evident in Central Canada.

Interestingly, Baleena and Fort Chaos shared some common cultural features – worn pathways and territorial claims. Fishing was territorial, as were claims staked for gold. And as with the surveyors' camp, supposedly pristine water bodies around Baleena collected the garbage of higher civilization.

> The end of winter is the best season for beachcombing. As the ice and snow melt, the bounty that has been hurled ashore by months of storms begins to appear. Driftwood and sea shells were everywhere, along with the occasional fragment of whale bone, the skeletons of birds and a lot of other mysterious jetsam . . . Less intriguing were the hundreds of fragmented plastic bottles and bags that were altogether too easy to identify. (*OP*, 83)

Transience was evident in Baleena too. Stretched out "like an aerial photograph . . . were the long-deserted settlements of Outer Island and Offer Land, with only the collapsing stick fences of their cemeteries as barely visible reminders of the human lives they once harboured" (*OP*, 82-83). In 1919, the families of Outer Island decided to abandon their island homes to move to less remote outports like Baleena. Some had dismantled their houses, board by board, and then rebuilt them at Round Harbour. Near the end of the Mowats' stay at Baleena, the nearby outport of Grand Anse was to be relocated and two hundred people would be moving to Baleena. Dismantling came in other forms too. The house of the Roses, the Mowats' neighbours, typified an alteration commonly resorted to by elderly couples whose children had grown up and left home. To reduce heating costs and housework, the house was decapitated of its second floor.

Eventually even Baleena could not hold the twentieth century at bay. A television transmitter was under construction, and surveyors were planning the route of the eventual Trans-Canada Highway. The isolation, their simple lifestyle that had so attracted the Mowats to Newfoundland, was quietly slipping away (*OP*, 236–37). Thus, the Mowats bid farewell to that windswept rock which they had called home.

Before we turn to the final theme of this chapter, one other symbolic geographical feature should be discussed, an occurrence found in *The Tent Peg*. Some of the characters are named after early Canadian explorers – Mackenzie, Franklin, Hearne, Hudson, and Thompson. Their importance to the geographical discovery of Canada has long been recognized. Mackenzie, Thompson, and Hudson have great Canadian rivers or water bodies named after them. Place names are an integral part of the cultural geography of languages. In a novel representing the gigantic physical forces and spaces of Canada's northern regional hinterland, their quests into unknown regions cannot be overlooked. In her book, these five characters all symbolize exploration in the physical and spatial sense. The search for minerals in the Wernecke Mountains is a major theme of the book. However, exploration can be sensed at more than one level.

J.L. describes Mackenzie as an explorer who loved his work and who loved rocks and maps and the way the earth had given birth to herself. Thompson was still deciding, still on the edge. Franklin analysed everything. Hearne was a photographer who liked colour and textures (*TP*, 138). Hudson, the Englishman, was incongruent, a smooth diamond in a rough world. For the most part he hated the isolation. Yet he was willing to take a risk, to confront the unknown, difficult as it was. None of these men had stopped questioning, exploring, discovering. Thus, new worlds and spaces, physical and mental, were opened to them.

One significant difference between the two books concerns the symbolic literary landscape. While van Herk uses the landscape very symbolically, Mowat responds to the Newfoundland landscape much more matter-of-factly, with no hidden symbolic agenda. Her purpose is to describe the outport life from her point of view, but nonetheless as accurately as possible. She knows that a unique lifestyle may soon disappear. The final subject to be examined in this chapter, then, centres on the major symbolic theme of *The Tent Peg* – the confrontation of stereotypes and the ties that bind (women especially, but also men), those conventions in society that inhibit freedom. This is not a new phenomenon. In fact, the original story of Deborah, a prophetess and judge, and Jael, wife of Heber the Kenite, is found in the Book of Judges in the Old Testament.

First written in prose (chapter 4) and then in poetry (chapter 5), these chapters from the Book of Judges recount a story of conquest, ultimately under the direction of and then at the hand of women.

The people of Israel, at the time, were facing a long and difficult struggle to gain possession of the promised land. In *The Tent Peg*, van Herk symbolically asks whether there is a promised land for women. Judges were chosen by God to lead the Israelites. Deborah was one of these charismatic leaders, gifted with wisdom and prophetic insights (Duncan 1989). Judging Israel at the time, she called Barak, leader of the Israelites' army, saying God commanded him to gather his army at Mount Tabor, traditionally the mountain of the transfiguration. God, she continued, would also draw Sisera, captain of the Canaanite army, with his chariots and men, and would ultimately "deliver him into thine hand" (Judges 4:6, 7). "And she said, I will surely go with you: nonetheless, the road on which you are going will not lead to your glory, for the Lord will sell Sisera into the hand of a woman" (Judges 4:9). This story of conquest relates directly to the force of two women – Deborah, who prophesied the battle, and Jael, who killed Sisera, the Canaanite general. Indeed, *The Interpreter's Bible* describes the first ten verses of chapter 4 as "The Power of Women" (1953, 711). The two armies fight. Sisera and the Canaanites are routed. Sisera escapes to the tent of Jael. As peace had previously existed between Jabin, his king, and the house of Heber, Sisera trusted Jael. She promised him refuge, gave him milk, covered him with a rug so he could sleep. "For Jael the wife of Heber took a tent peg, and took a hammer in her hand, and went softly to him and drove the peg into his temple, till it went down into the ground, as he was lying fast asleep from weariness. So he died" (Judges 4:21).

Chapter 5 recounts the deeds of Deborah, Barak, and Jael in a long poem known as "The Song of Deborah" (Nunnally-Cox 1981, 49). "Most blessed of women be Jael, the wife of Heber the Kenite, of tent-dwelling women most blessed" (Judges 5:24). And the land had peace for forty years (Judges 5:31).

Throughout *The Tent Peg*, the symbolism of this episode is referred to constantly, continually reminding the reader of the analogy. J.L. lives in a tent. The men in the survey crew, weary from a day's work, sleep in their tents through the catastrophic event of the rock slide. At various times, they come to J.L.'s tent for comfort and counsel. Nails are driven into the ground (temple of the earth) as tent pegs or as stakes in the gold claim. Men's visions are pierced without their being aware of the change in their perceptions. This leads to their freedom, but more importantly perhaps, to J.L.'s, to her emancipation as a woman. As a result, new geographical relationships and a new spatial organization can be forged. J.L.'s struggle for and final acceptance in the new territory of a male-dominated survey camp in the Yukon is a prime example of this.

At one point, Cap summarizes the major symbols of the novel:

This summer gets stranger and stranger. First she, J.L., hits right in the middle of that target, even though she's never shot a gun before. And if I hadn't seen her talking to that bear with my own eyes, I wouldn't have believed it . . . Then she sees a rockslide that stops just short of camp. Even worse, the rest of us don't hear a thing, just sleep right through tons of falling rock that practically roll right over us. (*TP*, 125)

Hitting the bull's eye symbolizes J.L.'s recognition of the problems of stereotyping she must face. In confronting the she-bear, a grizzly, J.L. gains the initiative and strength to remain in the wilderness, to confront and challenge the men who do not want her to overstep conventional women's bounds within society. J.L. interprets the grizzly as her friend, Deborah, acting out the role of a prophetess in the twentieth century. And finally there was the rock slide, massive and terrifying. Only J.L. was awake at the time. Only she witnessed it. The men were asleep in their tents, their temples to the ground. This event was to mark a turning-point in the novel. Their temples had been pierced. Gradually, all but Jerome accepted J.L. and her position within the camp, and thus her new equal position within society. As they accepted her, J.L. also changed, willing to see men and her relationship to them in a new light.

At the close of the book, as J.L. dances above the fire, her last night in camp, she summarizes her perceptions of the summer. She alludes to the symbol of Mount Tabor, traditionally the mountain of the transfiguration, as she refers to her and the men's transfiguration: "For a moment I can pretend I am Deborah celebrating myself, victory, peace regained. And in their faces I see my transfiguration, themselves transformed, each one with the tent peg through the temple cherishing the knowledge garnered in sleep, in unwitting trust" (*TP*, 226).

And so, "I leap free," at face value, *of the fire;* on another level, *of society's bonds.* Her last words are, "They can rest now, we can all rest." Men and women are free to choose new directions in time and space.

Two novels, Claire Mowat's *The Outport People* and Aritha van Herk's *The Tent Peg*, describe domineering, harsh physical landscapes in Canada, isolated regions that have been ignored by and to a large extent have been unknown to the majority of Canadians. They are powerful, rugged, unyielding. In both books, the encroaching cultural landscape has a tenuous hold at best. All traces of van Herk's temporary summer camp could evaporate if the site is neglected for a few years. The outports could last longer, but through relocation, many of these could gradually disintegrate, transforming into a non-human environment once more. Often Claire Mowat regards her isolated outport region with affection. However, the towering mountain and its massive landslide thundering to the tip of the tarn where the geology camp is situated symbolize the respect the Yukon always demands of its human encroachers. Juxtaposed in this essay are two dominating landscapes. Their authors' perceptions and the reactions of their human intruders show diverging responses to their power.

REFERENCES

Berlinguette, Lorna. 1989. Personal comment, October.

Biblical references. 1952. *Revised Standard Version*. Toronto: William Collins and Sons.

Duncan, Reverend Mary. 1989. "Women of Faith: Deborah." Unpublished sermon, Wesley United Church, Regina.

Eliade, Mircea. 1961. *The Sacred and the Profane*. Translated by Willard R. Trask. New York: Harper Torchbooks.

The Interpreter's Bible. Vol. 11. 1953. Nashville: Abingdon Press.

Montgomery, Lucy M. 1922. *Anne's House of Dreams*. Toronto: Seal Books.

Mowat, Claire. 1983. *The Outport People*. Toronto: Seal Books.

Nunnally-Cox, Janice. 1981. *Foremothers: Women of the Bible*. New York: Seabury Press.

van Herk, Aritha. 1987. *The Tent Peg*. Toronto: McClelland & Stewart, New Canadian Library. (First published by McClelland & Stewart/Bantam, 1981).

8

The North and Native Symbols: Landscape as Universe

Jacqueline A. Gibbons

The Canadian North has attracted people's curiosity and inspired explorers to chart its vast tracts of quintessential coldness. European travellers and explorers sailed to our northern boundaries first to catch the then abundant fish and whales, and later to engage in the fur trade. This sense of adventure was also manifest in Arctic exploration that initially involved a search for the North West Passage and then the race to be first to achieve the most northern "tip" of the planet. There was a magic about the Far North. A land of extreme cold with but one long day and an equally long night each year, it fascinated and lured explorers wishing to conquer and stake their claims. Yet this Arctic "other world," which represented the antithesis of home for European explorers, also represented centrality and haven, and provided home and sustenance for its indigenous communities. The Inuit had arrived from across the Bering Strait some two thousand years earlier. They had carved, in every sense of this word, a homeland; they had given shape to a culture that, rather than defying the elements, embodied a symbiosis with nature. The land, its snow, the ice-clad earth, and the waters were not to be conquered but were seen as part of an indigenous whole. Hunting and fishing were done with sensitivity, respect, and reverence for this totality. The search for animals and fish was essential to human survival. These activities, in this cold and often stark environment, provided sustenance – meat to eat; skins to provide warmth; oils for light and cooking; stone and bone for tool making, utensils, toys, small magic objects; and bone, ivory, and leather for ornament and adornment.[1]

Families, villages, and whole tribes thrived in conditions under which Europeans died like flies. The natives' human presence in this vast region was part of the natural cycle of birth, life, and death that encompassed earth, sky, ice, snow, water, and living nature. This totality was a "Gaia" that evoked creation myths, tales of morality, animal magic, and an omnipresent spiritual power.

The Inuit moved across the land as the seasons altered, their lives integrally connected with the animals they depended on. Nature and culture were entwined.[2]

A particular manifestation of the magical component that unites earth with the other-worldly was the shaman or *angakoq*. Historically, within tribes this person cured illnesses and injury, solved problems, mediated between social and psychic states, and generally acted as a facilitator for members of the community in their connection with the spirit world. The first shamans "arose specifically to help man, to cure him in his sickness, and to aid him in procuring food" (Blodgett 1978, 28). Among the Iglulik Eskimos,

> a man became the first shaman when he suddenly went behind the skins hanging at the back of the sleeping platform and dived down into the earth . . . it was the spirits who had contacted him out in the solitude. But he dived down to the Mother of the Sea Beasts and brought back game to mankind, thus ending the famine. (Blodgett 1978, 28)

Not only could the shaman solve human problems, he could also interweave the worlds of humans and animals, breaking down traditional boundaries – promoting a sense of oneness with nature. Thus, "a person could become an animal, and an animal could become a human being. There were wolves, bears, humans and foxes but as soon as they turned to humans they were all the same. They may have had different habits, but all spoke the same tongue, lived in the same of kind of house, and spoke and hunted in the same way" (Blodgett 1978, 75).

The transformation of the shaman into another guise was further facilitated by his use of special clothes and masks. He might also adorn himself with claws on his fingers or in his mouth. In fact, contemporary artists today still appropriate tusks or large teeth in depicting human beings (Blodgett 1978, 76).

Commerce, industrialization, and "development" were later to split the related concepts of nature and culture into separate compartments, thereby creating a culture that has become increasingly separated and fragmented – one that many would regard as alienated and, certainly, transformed. Nature and culture in the North were first severed, irrevocably, during the Second World War. War defence strategies and employment of local people led to an industrial technological awakening in the North and to the introduction of a cash economy. The Inuit tradition of barter and exchange was replaced by the pay-cheque (Swinton 1968). The seasonal movements of the Inuit began to be replaced by communities that stayed in one place and whose inhabitants trapped and hunted from one base. The end of the war created a vacuum for many local people who were now dependent on the comfort of a pay-cheque. This colonial-type withdrawal had become a national concern by the late 1940s. This was when the first Eskimo cooperatives were created to make work for local communities. Intriguingly, these cooperatives were patterned after a Japanese teamwork model. Local people were taught how to make stone-cut prints for an art market being developed in the South (Swinton 1968). Crucially, they learned to enlarge upon their carving skills; the small objects of utilitarian or religious use of the past were transformed into sculpture for the present and the future.

Kenojuak, of Cape Dorset, discusses – with remarkable insight – how she goes about depicting her subjects:

I don't start off and pick a subject matter as such; that's not my way of addressing a drawing. My way of doing it is to start without a pre-conceived plan of exactly what I am going to execute in full, and so I came up with a small part of it which is pleasing to me and I use that as a starting point to wander through the drawing. I may start off at one end of a form not even knowing what the entirety of the form is going to be; just drawing as I am thinking, thinking as I am drawing. And that's how I developed my images. (Blodgett 1980, 36)

Kenojuak is known for her drawings of animals and, especially, birds. She draws "owls, seagulls, geese, and other birds, but also people and animals, in-cluding the fox, dog, bear, walrus, seal, muskox, fish and hare" (Blodgett 1980, 34). Her imagery derives from a life that for her has spanned half a century and from a sense of the land that harks back to the old days of hunting and curing skins.[3]

These "art objects" of the Inuit embodied the myths and legends of the past and depicted scenes of people and animals that combined past with present. The stone used in the carvings was cut from the Arctic bedrock and fashioned in accordance with a certain sense of the spirituality of Inuit culture. While art and artifact had been inseparably one in the past, art now became separated from the old culture to be wedded to an elite notion of fine art that emanated from the more "modern" Euro-Canadian culture of the South and elsewhere.[4] Yet despite this split between nature and culture, there was embodied in this new cultural artifact/art object an iconography that was rooted in the old way of life, even though it also encoded new images and ideas from the "modernization" process that was going on in the local communities.

Until the 1970s, the visual depictions had been of traditional life and legend – hunting scenes, animals, igloos, and mythic creatures. Then there crept into this old iconography a rare aeroplane (one such drawing was made into a Cana-dian stamp in 1978) or helicopter or square modern house. One unusual depic-tion was a visual metaphor – Inuit artist Pudlo's high-rise igloo. (This picture of stacked igloos was the artist's humorous response to the high-rises he saw on a visit south.) These are two examples of an "ethnoaesthetic" showing displace-ment/reformulation/transformation as art and artist played with depiction of material, edifice, and mixed urban geography. Where some have argued that native art represents a "marginalization" of culture, it seems more reasonable to claim that this is not mere peripheralization or fragmentation, but rather incor-porated transformation, which is the sign of culture changing, emerging, and altering course.

The new media the Inuit have worked in since the Second World War (sculpture, print-making, stencils, and appliqué) contain the idea of "memory"

(Benjamin 1968) alive and well, yet at the same time there is an appropriation of the "imaginary landscape" (Appudarai 1990). The Inuit speak of carving as freeing the image from stone and releasing the "soul" from the material. The rock from the landscape becomes animal, human, mythic spirit, ocean, and goddess.[5] The usage and appropriation of whalebone, hair, antler, fox teeth, ivory, driftwood, and animal skins are part of this landscape reformulation and textual shake-up. Visual representations in sculptural works form another layer of meaning, one that relates to the natural universe.

One shape in the North that attracts special attention is the *inukshuk*. This has been a particularly intriguing signifier and sign in the architecture of the northern landscape. It comprises a pile of stones that points the way to a special place and that can offer a hunter shelter or a hiding place. The *inukshuk* has a human outline and, in the vast tracts of rock, snow, and open space, it is like a primordial signpost. There are no trees in these regions, and a rocky signpost built by humans alters the contours of the land, making a startling, powerful, and special writ-in-stone statement.

With regard to artistic "perspective," landscape in northern art has its own uniqueness in the proportioning and appropriation of space. As we see in *Camp Scene* or in *Walrus Hunter*, people, animals, and objects are strategically placed in a space that is meaningful to the artist and requires an alternative aesthetic that is in sharp contrast to classic training in European notions of "perspective." Landscape and objects have new relationships that are not of photographic derivation. There is an organization of spatiality that moves sign, signifier, and signification into a visual code that makes sense in this northern universe.

The meaning of the petroglyphs that are found on large rocks in a number of parts of Canada has been the subject of much speculation. The most extensive occurrences are along Alberta's Milk River (Dickason 1972, 32). Generally, these depictions are along the edges of water. They were drawn or carved and were produced until very recently. They address spiritual and material wants or needs and suggest a process of "shaping" the land in relief or painted form, connecting human life with the eternity the rock embodies.

The depiction of land and people as holistic, mythic, and connected with birth, life, and death is also common in much of the Indian art by natives across the nation. The visual interweavings and renderings of sun, rivers, birth, rebirth, and the circle (a symbol of fundamental importance) can be found in many Indian works.

The art of an Indian artist such as Norval Morrisseau draws upon totemic imagery but also upon biblical sources, because of the immense influence of Christian imagery that was thrust upon the natives until relatively recently. One stylistic characteristic Morrisseau has developed is the weaving of inner body landscape with cultural symbols of community and the spiritual source. In a picture of a woman, the inner parts of her body may be displayed – her heart, breasts filled with milk, or womb. Lines of movement in his depictions of people may represent the beating of the heart, and a line emerging from the mouth may

Inukshuk: This is an example of the pointers/landmarks/signposts that are built around and about the rockscape of the North. Photograph by Alistair Macduff, Repulse Bay.

represent a special kind of communication, such as shaman talk/speaking in tongues (Sinclair and Pollock 1979). The circle, which represents the female body form (breasts/vagina/hips), also means, in Morrisseau's work, good and evil, day and night, heaven and earth. Body insides and surfaces are thus intrinsically connected with the motions and bodies of planets, sun, and universe. A

Kananginak, *Camp Scene*, 1968, engraving, courtesy West Baffin Eskimo Co-operative Limited. The *inukshuk* on the hill signifies a special area. The knife carried by the person indicates that work is still in progress (igloo making/cutting of meat). Snow is depicted as "space," and track of dogs and sled are deemed important markers in this snowy landscape. The Caribou antler are indicative of food, hunting, and magic.

number of these images embody a fair amount of what we may call abstract art (where this means that symbols rather than traditional realistic images are employed). One is also struck by similarities between Canadian and Australian aboriginal artistic depiction.

The native peoples' concern about contemporary ecological issues is illustrated by Bill Reid, of Haida origin. Reid, a master carver and jewellery maker with a strong awareness of his West Coast heritage, has stood for the preservation of the forests in South Moresby, where Haida and loggers had confronted one another with their different principles and values. Reid

> makes it clear he is not mounting an attack on logging, loggers, or the lumber industry, but pleading for the institution of "true multi-use of the forest with due regard for its own regeneration, the wildlife it nurtures and, most neglected, its aesthetic values – that is the nurture it affords human life." (Shadbolt 1986, 176)

These trees in South Moresby, some of which have flourished in the natural environment for up to 800–900 years, are now threatened by commercial ex-

Keeleemeomee, *Walrus Hunter,* Cape Dorset, 1972, stone-cut, courtesy West Baffin Eskimo Co-operative Limited. By juxtaposing one unusually small hunter beside three large walrus, the artist creates a sense of spiritual reverence through unexpected contrast of scale. There is, too, the suggestion of "transformation" between human and animal that is imposed by ancient beliefs and legends.

ploitation. Reid makes his plea as a Haida who has been educated by and lived with Europeans and Euro-Canadians. He breaks down the boundaries between white urban culture and the culture of his ancient ancestors, bringing to his art a deep awareness of spiritual past and present.

Reid has recounted some of the old legends in story form (Reid and Bringhurst 1984) so that a larger Canadian and international public can appreciate their sacredness and wisdom. In telling how earth became lit by the rays of the sun, he explains how Raven

> had recently stolen the light from the old man who kept it hidden in a box in his house in the middle of darkness, and had scattered it through the sky. The new light spattered the night with stars and waxed and waned the shape of the moon. And it dazzled the day with a single bright shining which lit up the long beach that curved from the spit beneath the Raven's feet westward as far as Tao hill. (Reid and Bringhurst 1984, 26)

Reid tells how, before the light had been stolen, the "whole world was dark. Inky, pitchy, all consuming dark, blacker than a thousand stormy winter midnights, blacker than anything anywhere has been since" (Reid and Bringhurst, 12). This sense of complete night and of the contrast with the illumination of sunshine is a native-originated Genesis that turns to the bird for its primordial origins. Tales about the Raven are numerous. In the story of the Eagle and the Frog, the Raven himself, in one of his many incarnations, fell deeply in love one day. He fell in love with the mainland stream, a sonorous, cool, sundappled, clear-running creek whom he happened to meet when she was dallying on her private mainland beach in the form of a beautiful young woman.

Her nails were pure, solid copper. A living hummingbird nuzzled her hair, and she carried a stick adorned with another fine creature, the one the Haidas called the forest crab: a frog. (Reid and Bringhurst 1984, 76)

Here is the marriage of supernatural with natural, and the sense of land and water as bountiful nurturer.

The connection between heavenly bodies and earth, between heavenscape and land, may be found in the artistic depictions of stars and sky in Inuit and Indian art. In Indian art these stars may be flowers because meaning systems become fused; examples are nineteenth-century East Coast beaded bags, Ojibway beadwork, and in the tales of the Raven, which employ Haida symbolism of celestial mapping/navigation. In the late nineteenth century, the Plains Indians depicted stars in their representations of the ghost dance, and the Tlingit of Alaska have been known to incorporate heavenly stars with the stars, stripes, and eagle of our American neighbours. (It should be recalled that the Canada/U.S. border does not separate the native cultures of North America.)

Today, the older Inuit recall the days when they travelled by kayak, sometimes turned into sailboats:

The only boats we used in those days were kayaks. We used to make our own boats from sealskins and mustache sealskins. If we used sealskins we used about twenty four skins, and if we used mustache sealskins we would only use five or six. For sails we used the long intestines of the mustache seals. We cut them up and sewed them together. In those days we didn't have the fabric to make things with, but we always had skins. (Hodgson 1976, 19)

In Inuit art the Aurora Borealis is most spectacularly illustrated by Baker Lake artists Tom Peryouar and Marjorie Esce. Their picture *Swept Away by Northern Lights* (1976) shows a woman carried along by these lights and straining against the power/stream of these forces. She holds her hands up against her ears. The artist says that "the sound of the Northern Lights is like the shaking of dry skin and the lights can reach out and pick you up" (Baker Lake 1976). The picture shows this women against a whirling series of coloured striations (turquoise, pink, yellow, blue, mauve, and green) that encompass the globe like the ring of Venus. It is said among the Inuit that the northern lights can decapitate a person who whistles at them and that it is dangerous to stand up in them.

Native people have used products of the land, such as animals, in making clothing, footwear, hunting gear, and other items. The Assiniboine made moccasins of buckskin and decorated them with porcupine quills dyed different colours (Dickason 1972, 52). Wampum belts were often decorated with white beads made from the lining of conch shells and purple or black beads from the insides of quahog clam shells. These belts could be used as personal ornament, as currency, and for ceremonial or diplomatic purposes. In fact, "the belt which was used to seal the pact of the Five Nations (later to become the Six Nations when the Tuscora joined in 1713) is now at the National Museum . . . [of Civilization] in Ottawa" (Dickason 1972, 46).

Buckskin could be black, when tanned with balsam smoke, or white, when bleached. Snowshoes, too, were not necessarily or merely utilitarian in design; snowshoe makers could incorporate intricate *babiche* webbing in varied woven and geometrical designs and use colours such as pink, black, grey, brown, or beige. These intricate and artistic variations allowed a certain personalization in both production and imprint, as native people traversed the land in the depths of winter, "patterning" the earth through the journeys made, the land traversed, and the creatures hunted.

Birch-bark could be decorated with natural or geometric shapes. The "bitten birch-bark" pattern was made by elaborately folding the bark and imprinting it with bites; when unfolded, the bark revealed a symmetrical pattern, not unlike that of Japanese paper ornamentation.

Haida of the nineteenth century made a rainproof hat out of woven spruce root, often decorating it with painted animal motifs (Dickason 1972).

I have argued here that the connection between culture and the land-in-its-naturalness embodies holism and a strong sense of empathy and continuity between earth and its creatures. Clearly there is a sensuality in the stone carvings of the Inuit and in the way they use natural materials in their representations of symbolic worlds. The tusks and carcasses of animals are intriguingly recycled and reborn as they are whittled[6] from death to life by these northern artisans and crafts-artists.[7] This is clearly a weaving of life force into art/artifact, as nature and culture are intertwined.

Northern natives' symbols contain natural and cultural images – from the inner workings of the body to the movements of the planets and the shaping of the heavens. Physical and symbolic notions of landscape in these more remote parts of our nation emerged from the lifestyle, culture, and imagination of our native precursors. While our Euro-Canadian perceptions are a product of our post-industrial, super-technological times, the visible expression of the culture described here manifest the continuity of people and nature, past and present. This vision of continuity would serve us well in our attempts to solve many contemporary environmental problems.

Notes

1 Relevant aspects of the fur trade in Canada are discussed by Dickason 1984.
2 For discussion of the problems and dilemmas that arise in definitions of "nature" and "culture," see Ortner 1974.
3 Anaittuq, of Pelly Bay, is known to use "whalebone, often for a base area; antler, which . . . can create a landscape base setting; and stone both for bases and for carved elements, such as the heads of birds . . . sinew is used for container handles, hanging rope, fishing line, fish drying line, harpoon line, and bow line" (Blodgett 1985, 5).
4 Art and craft were entwined in Western Europe up to the medieval period. The development of the guilds raised the standards of crafts to the level of art form in many enterprises. However, it was with the advent and "celebration" of solo artists, many of whom attracted patrons, in the sixteenth century onwards that fine art became separated from whence it came; it was now treated in elite terms and contrasted with "craft," its more "lowly" sister – thus the "art versus craft" distinction.
5 An important mythic woman figure is the sea goddess Sedna, whose tail is sometimes that of a dolphin, a whale, or a fish. She is sometimes described as living in an icy temple below the ocean, and she holds together aspects of the universe as she metes out justice and manifests compassion. She thus spans land and ocean and represents, in a semiotic sense, morality rooted in natural form.
6 The Inuit carvings of old were actually called "whittles."
7 We here combine the terms craft and art, since the other distinctions, in light of the context of the argument here, are artificial and ideological.

References

Appadurai, Arjun. 1990. "Disjuncture and Difference in the Global Culture Economy." *Public Culture, Bulletin of the Centre for Transnational Cultural Studies* 2, no. 2: 1–24.

Baker Lake Prints Catalogue. 1976. Ottawa.

Benjamin, Walter. 1968. *Illuminations.* New York: Schocken Books.

Blodgett, Jean. 1978. *The Coming and Going of the Shaman.* Exhibition catalogue. Manitoba: Winnipeg Art Gallery.

———. 1985a. *Augustin Anaittuq.* Exhibition catalogue. Toronto: Art Gallery of Ontario,

———. 1985b. *Kenojuak.* Toronto: Firefly Books.

Dickason, Olive. 1972. *Indian Arts in Canada.* Ottawa: Indian and Northern Affairs.

———. 1984. *The Myth of the Savage.* Edmonton: University of Alberta Press.

Hodgson, Stewart. 1976. *Stories from Pangnirtung.* Edmonton: Hurtig.

Ortner, Sherry. 1974. "Is female to male as nature is to culture." In Z. Rosaldo and L. Lamphere, eds., *Women, Culture and Society.* Stanford: Stanford University Press.

Reid, Bill, and Robert Bringhurst. 1984. *The Raven Steals the Light.* Vancouver: Douglas & McIntyre.

Shadbolt, Doris. 1986. *Bill Reid.* Vancouver: Douglas & McIntyre.

Sinclair, Lister, and J. Pollock. 1979. *The Art of Norval Morrisseau.* New York: Methuen.

Swinton, George. 1968. *Sculpture of the Eskimo.* Toronto: McClelland & Stewart.

9

The Forest Landscape in Maritime Canadian and Swedish Literature: A Comparative Analysis

L. Anders Sandberg

> The novel accentuates reality by elevating it to fiction.
> —Jan Myrdal, *Karriär*

> [A] national character does not emerge as the result of a general historical process; it is the result of a people's fight for their interests. Our lyrical tradition is a social heritage.
> —Jan Myrdal, "On This Question of Sweden"

*L*arge areas of the Maritimes and Sweden are forested, and many regional novels are set in the forests or in forestry-based communities. This paper explores the description and use of the forest in Maritime Canadian and Swedish literature. My hypotheses are that there are substantial differences between the literary use of the forest in Maritime and Swedish literature and that these differences stem from the historical reality of forest use and work.[1]

Traditionally, the forest in both the Canadian Maritimes and Sweden was a communal storehouse for game, food, firewood, and construction material, as well as a place of fear – the home of wild animals, trolls, and fairies. It was also an obstacle to settlement and agriculture, a source of industrial raw material, and a hunting, fishing, and recreation preserve for wealthy urban elites.

There are, however, some crucial differences. The treatment of the Maritime forest has been more consistently colonial and dominated by the principles of possessive individualism and the sanctity of private property rights (MacPherson 1962). The forest has been raped successively, with little effort at conservation or regeneration. The market in forest products has been dominated by a few large pulp and paper companies that have set the terms of trade in wood and labour with small woodlot owners and forest workers.

Forest use in Sweden, by contrast, has been more varied and less exploitative and exclusive. Rapacious exploitation has been tempered by conservation measures. Some access to the forest has been ensured for all, even the poor, and the forest is considered a refuge from both the communal and national perspective.

The common rights of farmers and workers to the forest as a source of income have been widely recognized. Common property notions and the right of universal access to the forest still prevail.

THE FOREST AS RAW MATERIAL AND REFUGE

Successive stages of selective logging have yielded the present industrial pulpwood forest, characterized by monoculture and chemical treatment, in the Canadian Maritimes. Literature offers poignant descriptions. Thomas Raddall provides one illustration of the sawmill industry in nineteenth-century Nova Scotia:

> The big pine was there to be raped, just as the moose and caribou were there to butcher for their logging camps in the winters. The great slabs they cut off the logs with their wasteful old-fashioned saws in the mills were just something to burn or dump into the river with the sawdust; and if all this trash fouling the clean water and cluttering the river bottom had a bad effect on the salmon run, who cared about that either? . . . Tomorrow? That's somebody else's day. Come on, boys, let the daylight into this clump. Get the big stuff and hustle off to the next before Tom, Dick, or Harry gets an axe on it. Timberrrr! Never mind the slash. Let it lie. Who cares about dead brush? Fire's just a nuisance anyway. Let the next rain put it out. Plenty more pine further up the river. Get a move on. (1961, 70)

By the turn of the nineteenth century, Paine described this forest as "bleak, unsightly, unproductive, mangled and distorted out of all shape and form of loveliness" (1982, 29). Such literary descriptions were also applicable to Swedish forest development at the time. The forest companies bought and exploited the northern forests, and the process was justified by the prevailing laissez-faire ideology, ably described by novelist Martin Koch:

> This is not theft, it's the development of the concept of right of possession, it is high culture. This is a clearing in the wilderness, the plow moves in untouched earth and throws worms and hidden wretches to the side, gold is sown and gold is harvested, and gold is needed for man to live. It is pitiful to see the small farms – this is all the old peasants managed to get out of the riches of the earth. They barely survive, and here thousands could gain their livelihood. The valley of the Timber is an industrial landscape and not an agricultural land, even the blind can see that. Here gold shall grow to the blessing of all people. (1946, 49)

The turn of the twentieth century marked a divergence of forest use in the two regions. By the 1950s, the Maritime forest had been exploited to the point where it was no more than a scrappy pulpwood stand: " . . . tall, skeletal trees growing so close together that their roots suck the life out of one another, and each one is prevented by its neighbours from gaining access to the trees. Good-for-nothing-trees. Grotesquely overgrown weeds" (Nowlan 1973, 4).

In describing his native Miramichi River in northern New Brunswick, David Adams Richards provides the literary picture of the ultimate result of the sense-less exploitation: "You know, I've lived to see long rafts on this river – I've lived to see long logs on this river – I've lived to see pulp drives on this river – and now I've lived to see nothing on this river" (1976, 256).

In Sweden, by contrast, the exploitation was an interlude tempered by the combined pressures of a social dialectic. On the one hand, the industrial state did not intervene when the sawmill industry acquired large areas of forest lands in the nineteenth century.[2] On the other hand, the ruthless exploitation of forest lands by oligopolistic forest companies raised state concern and led to legislation prohibiting company purchases of forest land in the north in 1906, a law extended nationwide by the 1920s (Stridsberg and Mattsson 1980). The owner-ship pattern in forest lands has since been frozen, with over a 50 percent share owned by small woodlot owners. Irresponsible exploitation of the forest also led to mandatory forestry legislation on public as well as private forest lands (Stjernquist 1973).

The government established large forest reserves in the north, and many farmers held on to their forest for future use. Eyvind Johnson states:

> The most clever farmers said, oh no, stop, we will get more money in twenty years, in fifty, I'll let you stand Forest. They were more careful, cutting one tree here, one there and did not bow humbly or happily saying, be my guest, Company, but presented the stick first after they had money in their mitten . . . When the state put up its finger in the air and felt that the winds were getting colder in Sweden after all the unrestricted cutting, it declared: now we say stop. This is a fine forest, we'll let it grow, it is placed under the protection of the law. (1974, 92–93)

The adventures of the wealthy in the forest, as described by Charles G.D. Roberts, S.W. Mitchell, and Albert Bigelow Paine, provide another literary rep-resentation of the colonial use of the Maritime forest. With these writers, one finds a reaction to the rapacious exploitation of the forest and a distaste for "all the useful, ugly attributes of mankind"(Paine 1982, 147). Paine's New Englanders – on a trout fishing trip to Lake Kejimkujik in interior Nova Scotia – marvel at the "open grove of whispering pines that through all the years had somehow escaped the conflagration of the axe. Tall colonnades they formed – a sort of Grove of Dodona which because of some oracle, perhaps, the gods had spared and the conquering vandals had not swept away" (Paine 1982, 174). One can also feel "that delirious odour of the spruce, richest after rain, which to smell in the winter, amid the roar of the city, brings to the wood-farer the homesickness of the distant forest" (Mitchell 1894, 10).

The forest does not constitute a popular refuge so much as an escape for wealthy British and American fishermen, hunters, and nature-lovers, who flee their "starched collars" for the freedom of the wilderness. In the forest "the vagrant blood that lurks within our race springs up and refuses to be still" (Roberts 1896, 1). In the forest "the chase of the trout grips body and soul and nothing else matters – nothing else exists" (Paine 1982, 40). The escape is coloured by the stamp of the wealthy adventurers of Wall Street (to whom Paine appealed; 1982, 106) who compare themselves to Canadian voyageurs threading a network of unknown waters, pioneers in a desolate spot, Stanley and Livingstone in the African jungles with their native guides, Charles the Strong and Del the Stout, portaging canoes, the general outfit, and the stores while the "colonizers" carry the "sporting paraphernalia" (62). For the colonizers, "what Nova Scotia most needs is money, and the fishermen and the hunter, once through the custom house, become a greater source of revenue than any tax that could be laid on their modest, not to say paltry, baggage" (17). The conception of the forest in these accounts is colonial. The forest, its resources, and its natives were there to receive and be used by the foreign fisherman, hunter, and recreation seeker who were temporarily fleeing the ugly but inevitable consequences of urban industrialization.[3]

During the nineteenth-century era of romanticism and bourgeois realism, some Swedish literature was also characterized by "a kind of literary tourist propaganda from an exotic country on the periphery of the western world" (Algulin 1989, 100). But in contrast to Maritime Canadian literature, Swedish literature also consistently harbours the forest as a popular refuge to all, even the poor and vulnerable. The so-called public access prerogative or Everyman's Right (allemansrätten), a right of custom, entitles every individual to make use of somebody else's land (Paulsson 1978). The support of the common access prerogative has found expression in literature. As Jan Myrdal puts it: "It is impossible to understand why the Swedes at every given opportunity express themselves in the form of nature poetry if it is not related to allemansrätten, that is, the public's right of access to and use of all uninhabited land" (1979, 142). The forest as a source of spiritual refuge figures prominently in Swedish literature. To Vilhelm Moberg, "the nature in Sweden . . . is primarily the forest. It remains unchanged as it awaits me under all seasons, and any changes in weather. During the winter the lakes are frozen and shut under the lid of ice, but the forest remains open and accessible. It shines greener and smells fresher in winter than summer" (1971, 138).

To Sven Delblanc, the forest is a "stronghold for dreams and hope . . . and healing solitude, a place for young love encounters and a source of mushrooms and berries" (Sörlin 1983, 16).[4] Eyvind Johnson writes of the centrality of the forest in the life of one of his characters:

The forest was connected with his whole existence, with an old thought that his life was a path through the forest. There was the fright, the happiness and the peace. When one wandered within oneself one wandered in a forest which was at once hall of pillars and brushwood: life on earth was the same way. The forest figured in his whole existence, and the lives of his people were bound up with the forest. (Sörlin 1983, 108)

The forest is also seen as a last bastion and potential saviour of a polluted and alienated world. Selander likens the treetops to an untouched and longing world not yet spoiled by humanity (Sörlin 1983, 69). Fries feels we must learn "to soften our voices, to tread silently, and, first and last, not only to walk and walk but stop and wait, and be in the forest." It is only then that we can "once again feel the freedom of poverty that we have sacrificed for welfare and security" (Sörlin 1983, 14).[5]

In all these accounts, the forest remains a public domain, and the public's concern for the forest is almost as strong as its concern for private space (Mead 1981, 292). That the forest is a source of communal escape is as self-evident as the common access prerogative (Sörlin 1983, 53).

FOREST AS PLACE OF WORK AND MEANS OF LIVELIHOOD

Hard Work, Despair, and Marginality

The forest and the forest community as a workplace does not find a pleasant or proud place in Maritime history. In the past, farmers worked seasonally in the forest; today, the occupation is one of last resort. The large pulp and paper companies use subcontractors in their harvesting operations. The competition is intense, indebtedness high, wages low, working conditions harsh, and labour organizations nearly non-existent.

Small woodlot owners have shared the poor lot of the forest workers. Forest land has accumulated in the hands of the pulp and paper companies as freeholds or cheap crown leases. The price of pulpwood is notoriously low. Small woodlot organizations date from the 1960s, but they remain weak and divided.

In one genre of Maritime literature, forest people and lumberjacks are portrayed as "sizable men, men of sinew and bulk, and women tall and ruddy" (Roberts 1921, 147) who "derive dignity and even moral stature from their mastery of elemental forces in the wild" (Keefer 1987, 66). In the lumber camps, natural hazards threaten both humans and domesticated beasts. Yet every unmarried man in the lumber camp willingly responds to a call to clear a log jam (Roberts 1921, 135). A lumberjack wanders off, "perchance to gather sprucegum . . . and he is found, days afterwards, half-eaten by bears and foxes . . . A solitary chopper throws down his axe and leans against a tree to rest and dream, and a panther drops from the branches above and tears him" (Roberts 1896, 80). Such anecdotes are indeed comical in this day and age, when occupational hazards are a far more likely cause of death than wild animals.

Roberts's writings are stripped of class considerations, portraying instead man's struggle against nature. Social conflict is attributed to the faults of individuals – for example, the two "hands," "surly and mutinous all winter [who] at last, by some special brutality, enraged the 'boss' and their mates beyond all pardon [and were thereby] hooted and beaten from the camp" (Roberts 1900, 137). The picture of the forest worker is a picture executed by a literary colonizer, distorting and romanticizing the life and work in the forest.

Novelists of the postwar generation demythologize the earlier romantic era (Oliver 1976, 214). In Charles Bruce's *The Channel Shore* (1984) – set in the Port Shoreham area of Guysborough County, Nova Scotia – the story centres on a farmer and his son and their efforts to establish a sawmill. The focus on the individual small producer (not the collective of small producers) as an emergent local capitalist (Kristiansen 1988, 31–33), however, creates a new mythology that suggests that hard work and personal integrity lead to success. By contrast, the marginalized farmers and workers at the sawmill are described less favourably. Anse Gordon, the black sheep of the community, represents one example:

> On either side of the track lay small clearings here four years ago; in the last winter before his enlistment, he and Stewart had cut box-logs. Fallen tops and old brush made a scattered tangle and through these skeleton branches young raspberry canes were pushing up. For a moment, as he remembered, Anse's mood darkened. Four cents for a seven-foot stick, five inches across the small end. Work, from cold sunrise to raw dark, and after. Night and morning the barn to tend. Work, and nothing else, except for hanging around at Katen's and once in a while a dance at Forester's Pond. (Bruce 1984, 15)

The communities of poor farmers and sawmill workers were mere "place[s] to be born in, to grow your teeth in, and to get the hell away from"(205).[6] The structural confines of personal destiny, the monopolization of land by pulp companies, the low price of pulpwood, and the politics of wood are absent issues. Such structural limits were clearly enormous. The political hegemony of pulp made popular struggles difficult, and they are therefore absent in the text of novels.

The despair of small woodlot owners and forest workers in Lockhartville, a fictitious lumber town on the fringe of the Annapolis Valley, Nova Scotia, is more realistically treated by Alden Nowlan (1973, 1988; Robinson 1988). For Nowlan's Kevin O'Brien, servility is almost instinctive and the habit of obedience is in the blood (Nowlan 1973, 119). Judd O'Brien, Kevin's father works in the sawmill every summer and in the winter,

> he cuts long lumber if he's lucky and subcontracts [from a contractor who is almost as poor] to cut pulpwood if he isn't. He prefers the mill, because there he's "sure of his pay," which means he's certain that come payday he'll be handed a cheque and the cheque will be good. "Always try to find a job where you're sure of your pay," he used to say to me, he

having learned from bitter experience that this was the most he dared ask of fate: a job where he knew that he was going to be paid. (Nowlan 1973, 48)

Kevin protests in his fantasies until the protest wears off and work becomes part of life. In another Nowlan story, a foreman instructs his boy "to start actin' like a man . . . There ain't no room for kids in the pulp woods" (1968, 53). The boy, in turn, reflects on "the millions of trees he would have to fell before he died. For as long as he lived, he would kneel beside a tree, a slave to the monotonous rhythm of the pulpsaw" (56). In the total submission, Nowlan describes an aging sawmill worker who sees death approaching but still has a burning longing for the mill "like a boy's desperate need for a girl . . . Checking the water level, checking the water gauge. Grabbing armfuls of slabs and shovelfuls of boardends. He had done these things for so long that they had become part of his very being: doing them over and over again was no more monotonous than was the act of breathing" (1968, 98–99, 105).

It is very seldom that the pulp and paper industry is identified as a cause of the poverty of small producers and workers, and of the decline of rural communities. We find here that the industrial ideology holds a firm grip on communities, even the Maritime literary tradition. This is the case in a novel where the pulp and paper industry figures prominently, Thomas Raddall's *The Wings of Night*. One of the central characters, Sam Quarrender, operates a pulp mill in a small community in the Liverpool area, on the Mersey River, Queen's County, Nova Scotia. The pulp mill is neglected, "Quarrender's workmen makin' a bare livin' and gittin' rheumatics and TB in that dam' wet wooden cave he calls a mill" (Raddall 1961, 45). The mill is not kept up-to-date because Quarrender is "all tied up in timberland . . . picking up timberland whenever the mill gets a few thousand dollars ahead of the game" (47).

Quarrender's official motive for assembling forest land is conservation, something that earns him a Senate seat in Ottawa, but his real motive is to cash in on the sale of profitable pulpwood stands in the future. In the meantime, Sam feeds "his mill with pulpwood bought cheaply from farmers along the main railway line" (78). In this situation, the novel's main character asks:

Why hasn't Oak Falls or this town right now got a paper mill as big as a couple of city blocks, with six or seven hundred papermakers drawing two dollars or so an hour and driving up and down Main Street in Buicks and such, and an army of other well-paid characters working in the bush? Figure that one out my dear Watson? (1961, 151)

Quarrender eventually sells his land and a pulp and paper mill of the above sort is established. Raddall's novel is based on real events and rightfully critical of Sam Quarrender (based on the pulp mill promoter, conservationist, and politician Frank Barnjum). In the coming of the modern pulp mill, however, the novelist reveals more about himself than the reality of the pulp and paper industry. Raddall was for a long time employed by the Mersey Paper Company, one of the three large pulp and paper companies in Nova Scotia. His picture of Mersey fits the corporate image but not the reality of forest workers and small woodlot owners. The small number of mill workers may be a relatively well-paid group protected by a national union, but they work in an export enclave economy that is still subsidized by poorly paid forest workers and small woodlot owners.

The "modern" pulp and paper industry receives a more damning assessment in David Adams Richards's writings. Richards shows in microcosm the destruction of a way of life rooted in farming, fishing, and forestry by the coming of foreign pulp and paper mills to his native northern New Brunswick.[7] We once again confront the life of the colonized and subjugated, a life reflected in the monotonous work of the crews at the pulp and paper mill:

> It was the mill again, the grinding smell. He was in the bin and the pulpy mass kept shooting out, he standing knee high and resting on the shovel every so often. Big shovelfuls, he kept thinking. He would cut at the soft mess of it with his spade, watching the shovel blade slide so easily into it and then lifting and throwing, his hands sweating on the handle. His hair in knots itching and sweating. But as soon as he had the pile half depleted again the shriek of the shoot opening, the whine of a mechanical mouth regurgitating something sickly and again the pile would be where it was before. (Richards 1982, 167)

The routine and monotony of the mill is transferred into the life of the community where all the amenities of modern civilization exist – pornography, drugs, a disco, a shopping mall, and a McDonald's. In Richards's pulp town a moral vacuum prevails where pointless violence and thoughtless cruelty are commonplace and where the characters are victims of foreign capitalist forces they do not understand and cannot control (French, in Stamp 1983, 34). Protest is nevertheless present in Richards's writings, although it is symbolic (Connor 1984), based on the individual rather than the collective and therefore not rooted in past or potential future social action.

Hard Work, Hope, and Modest Returns

In Swedish literature you find a similar picture of the difficult lives and work experiences of forest workers, small woodlot owners, and sawmill and pulp mill workers. Roberts's "backwoodsmen" have their equivalent in Swedish literature, in the writings of, for example, Almqvist, Bremer, Runeberg, Heidenstam, and Karlfeldt (Algulin 1989, 90, 99–100, 104–5, 140, 149*ff*). Yet a further literary dimension is added by the popular struggles and relative successes obtained by the "backwoodsmen." This literary heritage is rooted in the legislation prohibiting companies from buying forest land, aiding the formation of small woodlot organizations and cooperatively owned sawmills and pulp and paper mills, and enabling forest industry workers to obtain the same standard of wages and job security as other workers (although mechanization and automation have reduced their num-ber substantially).

Typically, literature whose subject is the forest industry is about workers and physical labour, is written by authors of a working-class background, and is directed towards a working-class audience (in Lönnroth and Delblanc 1988, 234). The conflict, compromise, and growth of mutual respect between capital and labour form the central themes in such literature, celebrating the rise to power of a national labour movement and social democracy. Less common, but by no means insignificant, is the literature that covers the dark sides of social democracy and the continuing ill-effects of capitalism.

Albert Viksten's *Timmer* (1949) provides one of many representative cases romanticizing social democracy and calling for actions in its support (see also Karl-Oskarsson 1949, 1951; Lind 1943; Matthis 1947; Viksten 1954). The revolutionary argues against piecemeal progress in living and working conditions, claiming that such acts only disarm the working class and delay the revolution.[8] The new form of capitalist, a mere cog in a wheel, rebels against the old tyrannical woods subcontractor and the dishonest storeowner. The "sensible" men promote gradualism and the cooperation of the forest workers and the farmers who drive the timber to the lakes and rivers with their horses.[9]

Gustav Hedenvind-Eriksson captures the collective spirit of resistance of farmers and forest workers:

> A strong opinion against the exploitation of the forest began to emerge among the farmers. Even the forest workers began to mumble and shake their heads. Should this state of affairs remain for ever? Were they predestined to exchange their heavy and life-threatening labour for a meagre existence on pork and bread, a smoky cottage and a drink at Christmas? (Hedenvind-Eriksson 1910, 8)

Such reasoning resulted in the prototypes who started the movement of enlightenment. The Kevin O'Briens and the Anse Gordons, the lumpen-proletarians and the black sheep, become awakening slaves who strive for human dignity and a place in the sun (Jonasson 1980, 31). Otto Karl-Oskarsson, like Alden Nowlan, tells a story of a young forest worker whose father considers him a puppy who should shut up and work hard. But as the young man grows up, he becomes a treasurer in the forest workers' union and learns to speak up to the employers:

> Just like the old forest workers, he could look over the markings [of the trees to be cut] and see whether the price would yield a fair wage. And against the employer he could almost speak the language of the lean brush spruces and scrawny pines when they marched over the bogs and plains, and on occasion he was instrumental in increasing the flexible pay scale [tied to the nature of the forest and the conditions of the cut] to ease the back pains of the workers. (1977, 28)

Parling documents the coming of the chain saw into a small woods camp in the 1950s, its potential use in easing the work of the forest workers, and its threat to their independence in that it could be seen as a capitalist tool of domination. In the end, the workers buy a chain saw cooperatively and manage to increase their earnings. It was not the technology per se that determined the outcome, but political and economic power:

> Well, you see, the forest people are no longer part of society's stepchildren, it is a long time ago that they awoke and made their will known, nowadays no capitalists can sit down and shit on their noses, there are too many of them, they are too defiant and too freedom-loving. They cannot be forced. Their freedom they hold high. (1953, 199)

Another genre of Swedish working-class literature is more critical of the achievement of the labour movement and social democracy. Birger Vikström, for example, describes the migrant forest workers in the north who welcomed union bureaucracies, rules, and regulations with mixed feelings. Collective agreements become employer vehicles for "keeping wages down," workers need a university degree to interpret paragraphs and tables, and union representatives become detached from the rank-and-file worker. Many workers did not join "the movement" but guarded their rights to strike or leave a work site without notice:

> Perhaps we should have been scolded for our lack of solidarity, our short-sightedness, our lack of understanding for the larger societal context which all showed up in the fact that we were not organized. But we had always thought of the unions as agents of class struggle and we couldn't see the Forest Workers' Union as such. We looked at the immediate and left the talk of societal balance to the higher-ups who understood these matters better. The daily bread was for us more important than the grand ideas, the neat plans, and the beautiful congressional resolutions. (Vikström 1976, 117)

Other problems of forest work – mechanization, job loss, and migration to urban centres – are covered in Hans Peterson's *Pelle Jansson: En kille med tur*. Pelle moves from a forest-based community in Norrland to Gothenburg. His father, a forest worker displaced by machines, holds a new job with Volvo, and his wife works at a department store. The family's adjustment is difficult and the longing for home is strong (Peterson 1970).

Swedish literature on forest work contains powerfully engaged texts, dealing with moral, political, ethical, and existential issues in the lives of the common people (Lönnroth and Delblanc 1988, 246–47). The literature also reflects a world of hard work, hope, and modest returns. The novelists are of working-class background and their themes are strongly influenced by the greatest of all poems: "Life" (Hedenvind-Eriksson 1910, 15).

CONCLUSION

A basic premise in this paper is that literature provides insights into the character of the forest landscape of Maritime Canada and Sweden. The forest of Maritime Canadian literature is often described as an exploited colonial staple, from the inception of the timber trade in pine for masts and spars to the recent exploitation of the ubiquitous pulpwood stand. The forest is also described as a hunting, fishing, and recreational summer resort for the wealthy that in winter is only remembered through the scent of the Christmas tree (Mitchell 1894, 10). In Sweden, the picture is different. Hedenvind-Eriksson's description (1981) of a wealthy nobleman from Germany constructing a hunting cottage for a pending moose hunt is instructive. The party arrives with lackeys and their own cooks and, after mistaking a floating tree root for moose antlers, leaves never to come back. The cottage becomes a place to extract the seeds from cones for forest plantations: "The first seeds were literally sown for the regeneration of future forests" (1981, 35). The literary forest evolves to become something communal; it is a more powerful escape in winter when it shines greener and smells fresher than it is in summer (Moberg 1971, 138).

The literary images of forest work are also radically different in Maritime Canada and Sweden. In the former, forest work is romanticized and reduced to the heroic struggle between people and a harsh environment, the individual struggle of small producers trying to get ahead in a marginal world, and the benign efforts of a modern multinational corporation in the face of the opposition of a local pulp mill baron. Another genre of literature describes the disparaging position of forest, sawmill, and pulp mill workers. The actions of industry and government are seldom identified as the cause of the plight of these workers. Literature is seldom a reflection or catalyst for social action other than in the symbolic sense. In Swedish literature dealing with the forest industry, the confrontation between small farmers, forest workers, and sawmill and pulp mill workers is central to the plot, either celebrating or questioning the achievement of a national labour movement and social democratic rule. Much of this literature is part of the common people; its authors are of proletarian stock, and the text carries an element of realism, a message of modest achievement, as well as a call for social action.

NOTES

1 The basic theoretical premise in this chapter is that literature and art are products of the society in which they are a part, a premise based loosely on the principles of historical materialism (Coser 1972). In this volume, a similar premise is assumed by Caulfield (chapter 16) and Ramsay (chapter 13).

2 The forest companies own about 25 percent of forest lands in Sweden. Most of the lands are concentrated in the northern part of the country.

3 Ramsay, chapter 13 in this volume, provides a similar example, by pointing to how Lucius O'Brien's painting *Sunrise on the Saguenay* was distorted and "colonized" to suit

the tastes of the wealthy; Squire, chapter 11 in this volume, shows how Lucy Maud Montgomery's literature has been commodified to attract wealthy tourists to Prince Edward Island.

4 Born in Manitoba, Sven Delblanc has also written an interesting novel series about his family's experiences on the prairies. I have written on this elsewhere (Sandberg 1988).

5 Compare with the ecotopia of Malcolm Lowry in British Columbia. See J.D. Porteous, "A Loving Nature: Malcolm Lowry in British Columbia," chapter 22 in this volume.

6 On the common Maritime practice of "going down the road," see B. Robinson, "Elizabeth Bishop from Nova Scotia," chapter 10 in this volume.

7 Richards's critical stance against capitalism and its pollution and destruction of the environment has parallels in the writings of Malcolm Lowry (Keefer 1987, 171); the environmentalist position of Lowry is treated in J.D. Porteous, "A Loving Nature," in this volume.

8 This man is affected by a bad cough and in his dying feverish moments decides to kill his boss. While standing in the forest waiting for his prey, he falls dead from his illness. The scene symbolizes the author's lack of support for the Swedish Communists.

9 This description represents the author's sympathetic view of the rise to power of Swedish social democracy.

References

Algulin, I. 1989. *A History of Swedish Literature*. Stockholm: Swedish Institute.

Bruce, Ch. [1954] 1984. *The Channel Shore*. Toronto: McClelland & Stewart.

Connor, H.W. 1984. "Coming of Winter, Coming of Age: The Autumnal Vision of David Adams Rishards' First Novel." *Studies in Canadian Literature* 9, no. 1: 31–40.

Coser, L. ed. 1972. *Sociology through Literature*. Englewood Cliffs, N.J.: Prentice-Hall.

Davies, B. 1986. "Dulce vs. Utile: The Kevin O'Brien Syndrome in New Brunswick Literature." *Studies in Canadian Literature* 11, no. 2 (Fall): 161–67.

Hedenvind-Eriksson, G. 1910. *Ur en Fallen Skog*. Stockholm: Folket i Bild.

———. [1957] 1981. *Snöskottning i Paradiset*. Kungsbacka: Litteraturfrämjandet.

Johnson, E. [1935] 1974. *Här har du ditt liv!* Stockholm: Bonniers.

Jonasson, B. 1980. *Den Hårda Vintern*. Stockholm: Författarförlaget.

Karl-Oskarsson, O. 1949. *Alla Ävens Timmer*. Stockholm: Bonniers.

———. 1951. *Kall Blåst Över Oxnäset*. Stockholm: Bonniers.

———. 1977. *Fingret som Pekar*. Halmstad: Settern.

Keefer, J.K. 1987. *Under Eastern Eyes: A Critical Reading of Maritime Fiction*. Toronto: University of Toronto Press.

Koch, M. 1946. *Timmerdalen*. Stockholm: Bonniers.

Kristiansen, E. 1988. "Considerations on Maritime Literature: Janice Kulyk Keefer and the Search for an Ideal Community." *New Maritimes* 7, no. 1: 29–33.

Lind, A. 1943. *Skogen Brinner*. Stockholm: Folket i Bild.

Lönnroth, L., and S. Delblanc, eds. 1989. *Den Svenska Litteraturen: Den Storsvenska Generationen, 1890–1920*. Stockholm: Bonniers.

MacPherson, C.B. 1962. *The Political Theory of Possessive Individualism: Hobbes to Locke*. Toronto: Oxford University Press.

Matthis, H.P. [1928] 1947. *Älven Kommer*. Stockholm: Bonniers.

Mead, W.R. 1981. *An Historical Geography of Scandinavia*. London: Academic Press.

Mitchell, S.W. 1894. *When All the Woods Are Green*. New York: Century.

Moberg, V. [1970] 1972. *A History of the Swedish People: From Prehistory to the Renaissance.* New York: Pantheon Books.

———. 1971. *Min Svenska Historia: Från Engelbrekt till och med Dacke.* Stockholm: P.A. Norstedt & Söners Förlag.

Myrdal, J. 1979. "On This Question of Sweden." In P. Wästberg, ed., *An Anthology of Modern Swedish Literature,* 142–44. Merrick, N.Y.: Cross-Cultural Communications.

———. [1975] 1986. *Karriär.* Suffolk: Legenda.

Nowlan, A. 1968. *Miracle at Indian River/Stories by Alden Nowlan.* Toronto: Clarke Irwin.

———. 1973. *Various Persons Named Kevin O'Brien.* Toronto: Clarke Irwin.

———. 1988. *The Wanton Troopers.* Fredericton: Goose Lane Editions.

Oliver, M.B. 1976. "The Presence of Ice: The Early Poetry of Alden Nowlan." *Studies in Canadian Literature* 1 (Summer): 210–22.

Paine, A.B. [1908] 1982. *The Tent Dwellers.* Halifax: Cranberrie.

Parling, N. 1953. *Motorsågen.* Stockholm: Tidens Förlag.

Paulsson, V. 1978. "Allemansrätten." *Skogs-och Lantbruks-akademiens Tidskrift* 117:95–103.

Peterson, H. 1970. *Pelle Jansson: En Kille med Tur.* Stockholm: Rabén & Sjögren.

Raddall, T. 1961. *The Wings of Night.* London: Pan Books.

Richards, D.A. 1976. *Blood Ties.* Ottawa: Oberon Press.

———. [1974] 1982. *The Coming of Winter.* Toronto: McClelland & Stewart.

Roberts, C.G.D. 1896. *Around the Camp-fire.* Toronto: Musson.

———. 1900. *The Heart of the Ancient Wood.* Toronto: Copp Clark.

———. 1921. *The Backwoodsmen.* New York: Macmillan.

Robinson, P. 1988. "Alden Nowlan and the Maritime Literary Renaissance." *New Maritimes* 7, no. 1: 25–26.

Sandberg, L.A. 1988. "Literature As Social History: A Swedish Novelist in Manitoba." *Prairie Forum* 13, no. 1: 83–98.

Sörlin, S., ed. 1983. *Sinnenas Skog.* Umeå: Prisma.

Stamp, R.M. 1983. "Where Does Geography End and Literature Begin?" *Operational Geographer* 1:33–35.

Stjernquist, P. 1973. *Laws in the Forest.* Lund: Gleerup.

Stridsberg, E., and L. Mattsson. 1980. *Skogen Genom Tiderna.* Stockholm: LTs Förlag.

Viksten, A. 1949. *Timmer.* Stockholm: Folket i Bild.

———. 1954. *Blå Gryning.* Stockholm: Folket i Bild.

Vikström, B. [1949] 1976. *Att Vara Dräng.* Stockholm: Rabén & Sjögren.

10

Elizabeth Bishop from Nova Scotia: "Half Nova Scotian, Half New Englander, Wholly Atlantic"*

Brian Robinson

*E*lizabeth Bishop (1911–79) grew up in Great Village, Nova Scotia, as a virtual orphan. Her father had died, her mother was to spend the rest of her life in an institution, and Elizabeth was placed in the care of relatives. It was an experience she never tried to put behind her either in her poetry or in her adult life, which was spent almost entirely outside Nova Scotia (she lived in Brazil from 1951 to 1967).[1]

But despite her almost permanent absence from the province, we know from her letters that Nova Scotia was a continuing source. For example, when she visited Cape Breton in 1947 her description had the seeming casualness of her poetry:

> . . . just a few houses and fish houses scattered about in the fields, beautiful mountainous scenery and the ocean. I like the people particularly, they are all Scotch [*sic*] and still speak Gaelic, or English with a strange rather cross-sounding accent. Offshore are two "bird islands" with high red cliffs.

Her observations are ornithological, mingling general naturalist comments (puffins, "last on the continent, or so they say") with astute details (ravens, "rough black beards under their beaks").[2] Indeed, birds were a leitmotif throughout her life. For example (but to continue with another Nova Scotian island, another leitmotif), on a visit to Sable Island in 1951 she combined a personal mythology of roots with an interest in local bird life, particularly the indigenous Ipswich sparrow. Her personal curiosity stemmed from how this "cheerfully named graveyard of the Atlantic" had been where her "great-grandfather and his schooner and all hands were lost." The coincidence that her aunt had a Sable Island pony

---

*Robert Lowell, draft: cited in David Kalstone, *Becoming a Poet* (New York: Farrar, Strauss, Giroux, 1989), 182.

added to her naturalist cum personal interest. As Sable Island is 200 kilometres offshore, she was obviously prepared to go considerably out of her way in search of a genealogical source for, "if I'm not fulfilling my destiny and get wrecked, too . . . maybe a poem or two."[3]

More tenuous was her interest in the legendary abandoned ship, *Mary* [sic] *Celeste.* She knew it had been built in Nova Scotia, but she hoped to discover that it was from her mother's village. She realized the looseness of the connection and admitted that she was surprised it meant so much to her.[4] For an orphan, "the graveyard of the Atlantic" and a mysteriously abandoned ship are obvious enough poetic soundings. But what is perhaps characteristic of Bishop is the deliberate and persistent search for sources that points to her abilities as a poet, a search involving not merely roots or regional sources but also carefully considered *resources.*[5] These were correlative resources that contributed to her ability to understand the past even though she knew that parts of it were irremediable. In that sense her poetry involved a lifetime of researched resourcefulness.

She maintained as many links as possible with Nova Scotia. In her Brazil home she kept a Nova Scotian "array" of preserves and jellies (risking the obvious misunderstanding), a kind of poetry of homemaking.[6] Letters between Nova Scotia and Brazil reminded her of northern seasons.[7] Photographs of relatives were sent by her aunts. These included some childhood pictures of her uncle, who, she thought, looked like her.[8] Included in the communications was a naive local history of Great Village that gave her some clues. Here she noted details of both people and buildings. Her aunt's house was lined with birch-bark and her grandfather's place had been a wayside inn of ill repute. She generalized from these particulars to observe that "the dying out of local cultures seems to me one of the most tragic things in this century."[9] Notably the loss was not just Nova Scotia's but Brazil's, and it was not idiosyncratically or self-pityingly hers.

And so on. Somewhat speculative return visits home, forced hunches concerning the past, and real artifacts kept her in touch, or rather, she kept them, observed them, in the several senses of the word, as touches of Nova Scotia – and we are in danger of the merest cliché, namely, of reducing Elizabeth Bishop's poetic journey to an exploration of her roots. Empirically derived connections will elucidate much and are indeed rewarding because they provide an inherent resistance to ideology, but they cannot speak to us of the language, the particular kind of care taken, in the poetry. As Terry Eagleton has claimed, it is not just experience, but language, that takes a writer away from home because "there is something curiously rootless about writing itself which is writing only to the degree to which it can survive transplantation from one context to another" (1983–84, 77). This is not to go to the other extreme and assert that Bishop's poetry is "about" survival and transplantation. Given the empirical basis of the approach taken in this chapter, the question is rather, to what extent could Bishop combine the irremediable mark of her Nova Scotian past with the reiterable cunning of poetry and exile? We have to be concerned with both exile and roots, with what Lowell means by, in sum, "wholly Atlantic."

PLACE: "BY THE SEA"

Initially, the trauma that clichéd notions of loss of place implies may not have been severe for Bishop, since as the Robert Lowell epigraph suggests, her preferred poetic environment was by the sea. In this continuously transplanted Atlantic context, the coastline extends beyond Canada's "Maritimes," north to Newfoundland and Labrador, south to Boston, Cape Cod, and Florida – eventually taking us to the South Atlantic of Brazil. For example, when fishing in Brazil, she often made the Brazil, Florida, Maine, Nova Scotia connection: "(strange the way one's life goes in little cycles)," she adds (Eagleton 1983–84, 77). It is fitting then that the titles of her books are so geographical: *North and South, Questions of Travel,* and *Geography III.*[10] She also participated in a popularized geography of Brazil (1962) for Time-Life Books.[11] Of course, Bishop's intent is not so literally littoral, otherwise her poetry would be merely descriptive. But she could be disarmingly literal. For example, when she received an award in Oklahoma, in her acceptance speech she couldn't help observing that it was strange to be honoured such a long way from the ocean (Bishop 1977, 12). As late as 1968, despite much continent hopping, she had never been to Chicago. Her response to this remote interior is telling: "I had never been to Chicago before or believed in Nevada, Utah and so on. Utah exactly like HELL."[12] Land-locked? too far inland? At first this seems like whimsy until we begin to think of her out of her element, away from the milieu where she belonged, which should be, as she puts it in her "Sandpiper" poem, "where (no detail too small) the Atlantic drains / rapidly backwards and downwards."

Yes, Elizabeth Bishop was focused on, preoccupied by, obsessed by this to-and-fro marginal world that fringes continents: thus her sandpiper darts frantically (south) in and out of focus, "a road clambers along the brink of the coast," or "a small bus comes along, in up-and-down rushes," and in another poem (another clinging coast),

> through late afternoon
> a bus journeys west,
> the windshield flashing pink
> pink glancing off of metal
> brushing the dented flank
> of blue, beat-up enamel
> down hollows, up rises

Yes, but she was not sea-locked. Her coasts double with interiors in ways that cast light on the darkness that interiority normally suggests. Elizabeth Bishop's coastlines illuminate continents even when, as is the case with the interior of Cape Breton's Highlands,

> . . . we cannot see,
> where deep lakes are reputed to be
> and disused trails and mountains of rock

> and miles of burnt forests standing in gray scratches
> like the admirable scriptures made on stones by stones –
> and these regions now have little to say for themselves.

She works her way from what she knows to regions and *limes* of which it is more difficult to speak. In part this accounts for the peculiar relationship between direct observation and the underlying menace. Imagine then, doubling these two seemingly incongruous interiors, Nova Scotia's Cape Breton and Brazil's Amazonia, in order to see the perspective that distance allows us, each from the other.

TIME: "FLOWING, AND FLOWN"

We have to fold in another dimension, namely, the distance that is created by time. As has been suggested, this can be shown in a simple biographical way.

Elizabeth Bishop was not born in the Maritimes, nor did she die there. Although born a New Englander, she lived for many years outside the United States, especially in Brazil. Her earliest "geographies" are not about "the Maritimes" and her great poems of the region were written relatively late (although they obviously took a lifetime to write). Even precisely observed events had to wait a lifetime before they could be reclaimed in poetry. In tandem with the great distances that separate her places, we have childhood and poem being separated by an abyss of years.

There is no mystification here. She does not try to evoke or dredge up from the depths of childhood, and if there is repression, it is linked "to capacity for discovering and, almost by reflex, for pleasure in the present" (Kalstone 1989, 218). "I do not even have to try to remember, or reconstruct; it is always right there, clear and complete," she says (Bishop 1984, 4). Anecdotal evidence supports this assertion. For example, she told Robert Lowell how, when once asked by Marianne Moore to say grace at a meal, after "a minute's dreadful blackout . . . something out of the remote Baptist past mercifully came to me in perfect condition."[13] The events are not psychologized retrospectively. For instance, she calls one of her "memory" poems simply "Poem." The title seems vague compared to her explicit "geographical" titles ("The Map," "Santerem," "Cape Breton") until we realize that "Poem" means "picture this in a poem." What is being described *is* a picture of which this poem is not simply the vehicle, it is an equivalent event. Like coastline and interior, "Poem" doubles and is juxtaposed along with "picture." It is also Nova Scotia from the distance of where she happens to be, which is Brazil, where she received the picture.

The poem begins with a description that is seemingly naive and simple. The first nine lines treat "this little painting" as "a minor family relic" of no artistic value to which not even her family members paid much attention.

Next she describes the painting. "It must be Nova Scotia" and we imagine Elizabeth examining it as a generic naive link with the past. However, the tone remains, or appears to remain, casual:

> In the foreground
> a water meadow with some tiny cows,
> two brushstrokes each, but confidently cows,
> two miniscule white geese in the blue water,
> back to back, feeding, and a slanting stick.

Even the questions, typical of her poetry, are indeterminate: "Elm trees, low hills, a thin church steeple / – that gray-blue wisp – or is it?" And again, "A specklike bird is flying to the left. / Or is it a flyspeck looking like a bird?" – her humour seems offhand too.

Then suddenly, "Heavens, I recognise the place, I know it!" It isn't just folkart Nova Scotia, it's the place where she lived! Bishop expresses the thought as if she has, *has,* caught her breath in the act of recognition: "It's behind – I can almost remember the farmer's name. / His barn backed on that meadow. There it is, titanium / white, one dab." There it is – the act of recognition and the deft stroke are one, that special place, "Miss Gillespie's house." Now the juxtaposition of genres is truly mixed up and the dialectic of "Poem" and "Painting" is being dissolved in the art of poet and painter. Recognition has now become the artist's "vision," except that, as always with Elizabeth Bishop, she feels that "vision" is too strong a word.[14] She disarms us again when she says that she prefers "our looks, two looks" to the too serious "visions." She says:

> Our visions coincided – "visions" is
> too serious a word – our looks, two looks:
> art "copying from life" and life itself,
> life and the memory of it so compressed
> they're fused into each other. Which is which?
>
> Life and the memory of it cramped,
> but how live, how touching in detail
> – the little that we get for free,
> the little of our earthly trust. Not much.
> About the size of our abidance
> along with theirs: the munching cows,
> the iris, crisp and shivering, the water
> still standing from spring freshets,
> the yet-to-be-dismantled elms, the geese.

And so she ends with a description of what has been naively given to her, but it doesn't resemble what she first saw when she casually looked at the picture, before poem and painting and life and memory unexpectedly coincided. Distances have become cramped and what must have been a journey through time as disjointed as a journey through a dark landscape has become an instant, clear and childlike. But this "Elsewhere" of recognition is not a privileged place, since

"Geography" is less a milieu than a medium, namely, the journey towards remoteness and insecurity. "Geographies" cannot be lived in, hence the clarity, the initiating shocks, the poetry they may provide. A journey to a distant place has the same effect as a journey into childhood. A distant place arrives as childhood! It is not accidental that she begins her geography of Brazil with the story of a kidnapped child who is eventually found.[15] A lost child who has been found has been born to its parents twice; recovered and rediscovered, there is an awakening, a new awareness. But what of the period before recovery?

QUESTIONS: "WHICH IS WHICH?"

At first glance the question "Which is which?" seems too precious. But it is context that counts, which is why it is necessary at this stage to relate space and time to the more readily assimilable milieus of landscape and people.

THE ELEMENTS: "TOPOGRAPHY DISPLAYS NO FAVOURITES"

Questions inform Elizabeth Bishop's poetry. This is because her questions create a controlled yet imagined examination of observation itself (the "too serious" received word being meditation). Bishop's landscape descriptions never hint at what can be wrung from myth making. Instead the elements have not yet returned our look.

> It is like what we imagine knowledge to be:
> dark, salt, clear, moving, utterly free,
> drawn from the cold hard mouth
> of the world, derived from the rocky breasts
> forever, flowing and drawn, and since
> our knowledge is historical, flowing, and flown.

Only nature comes ready-made in this landscape and there are no overbearingly culturized places pointing the way. On the contrary, Bishop's dispossessive questions take us to what can be coherently imagined of what is other than ourselves. The movement is between objective description and guarded subjectivity.

> Land lies in water; it is shadowed green.
> Shadows, or are they shallows, at its edges
> showing the line of long sea-weeded ledges
> where weeds hang to the simple blue from green.
> Or does the land lean down to lift the sea from under,
> drawing it unperturbed around itself?
> Along the fine tan sandy shelf
> is the land tugging at the sea from under?

Water meeting land, thereby creating a coastline, becomes a gentle unhurried investigation, each of the other – elements scribing their innocent logics on which we must suspend judgment.

> The water seems suspended
> above the rounded gray and blue-gray stones.
> I have seen it over and over, the same sea, the same,
> slightly, indifferently, swinging above the stones,
> icily free above the stones
> above the stones and then the world.

Simply by being surfaces, things suggest an above or a below, a borderline.

> Absorbing, rather than being absorbed,
> the water in the bight doesn't wet anything,
> the colour of the gas flame turned as low as possible.
> One can smell it turning to gas; if one were Baudelaire
> one could probably hear it turning to marimba music.

The question lies in correspondences and conjunction: what if things were "only connected by 'and' and 'and'"? And, of course, "What if . . ?" is both question and imagination. This question would be an excuse for a more whimsical vein, and in part, this explains Bishop's seeming weakness for the fanciful and the surreal. But Elizabeth Bishop is the most responsible of surrealists because her artifice is controlling moving within.

> The islands haven't shifted since last summer,
> even if I like to pretend they have
> – drifting, in a dreamy sort of way,
> a little north, a little south or sidewise,
> and that they're free within the blue frontiers of sky.

Geography cannot be ambushed; and poetry cannot arrange or rearrange without an injurious price. Some things have been presumed.

PEOPLE: "WE LIVE BY THE SEA"

It may only be someone getting on or off a bus; or it may be a simple conversation, either directly or indirectly reported; or there may be just sounds of human activity – engines, work noises, and so on ("all the untidy activity continues, awful but cheerful") – no matter which, people have a presence in Bishop's landscapes in ways that are artifactually mundane yet illuminating ("homely and fantastic") (Moss 1977, 29). But aren't most landscapes (most lives) seemingly disorganized (Wilson 1989)? "The bight is littered with old correspondences," she says, but she does not present a setting in the historical references of Robert Lowell. Her "activities" are too untidy for an entangling mythology. However, her economical descriptions are not stark and nostalgia is not altogether derided. Thus, the seminal opening of "The Moose" ("From narrow provinces / of fish and bread and tea / home of the long tides . . . ") implicates a logic of mappable shapes with provincialism and intimacy, which is associated with conversation, unpretentious meals, a living to be made and talked over, the ocean nearby, the tide playfully "taking the herrings long rides." A setting to be sure; the heart of something, certainly; but not the very centre. There are, instead, fleeting moments whose meaning we cannot know outside the chronicle of a bus journey through a landscape made out of brief indications.

> One stop at Bass River,
> Then the Economies –
> Lower, Middle, Upper:
> Five Islands, Five Houses,
> where a woman shakes a tablecloth
> out after supper.
> A pale flickering. Gone.

Places and houses, houses and people, are linked in the journey that adventitiously threads them all together in chronological literalness.[16] Her inventorial device has the happy effect of not making one aspect seem more valuable than another. Mere connection and noteworthy detail have their own power, like a child's address (name, home, province, planet), which links "individuals to families, families to villages, villages to a whole rural Nova Scotia, part dependent on part" (Gunn 1990, 792). Several commentators have noted that the coastline linearity of the poem is a form which, as details accumulate, has both an ordering presence and a capacity to leave traces behind (Schwartz and Estees 1983). However, it is also literally true that we do leave behind the landscape of elements of the opening, eventually entering childhood and the lives of the people, a journey that ends with the haunting animality of the moose. To this sequence I would add the observation that although sight dominates initially, the other senses – hearing and, finally, smell – take over as darkness draws around.

> In the creaking and noises,
> an old conversation
> – not concerning us,
> but recognizable, somewhere,
> back in the bus:
> Grandparents' voices

The first way we inhabit a place is through conversation . . .

> what he said, what she said,
> who got pensioned . . .
> the year he remarried . . .
> she died in childbirth . . .
> He took to drink. Yes . . .

> . . . that peculiar
> affirmative. "Yes . . . "
> A sharp, indrawn breath,
> half groan, half acceptance,
> that means, "Life's like that
> We know *it* (also death)."

Even in this condensed version, the marvelous meandering of conversation ("a dreamy divagation") takes us through time in the same way that the bus takes us through the countryside. And at this point we know we have reached the heart of something that has the beat of memory. But – "Suddenly the bus driver / stops with a jolt, / turns off his lights . . ." and we are beyond knowledge because

> A moose has come out of
> the impenetrable wood
> and stands there, looms, rather,
> in the middle of the road.
> It approaches; it sniffs at
> the bus' hot hood.

This is impenetrable knowledge, the weakest of the human senses because we can rarely reduce it to use. The passengers are reduced to unmeditated exclamations: "Sure are big creatures" / "It's awful plain" / "Look! It's a she!" A kind of childlike physiognomical gaze, the little we know, as we are confronted by a questioning of conception.

> Taking her time,
> she looks the bus over,
> grand, otherworldly,
> Why, why do we feel
> (we all feel) this sweet
> sensation of joy?

A moment of enduring recognition nevertheless, after which the poem ends with a codalike mingling of loose ends:

> by craning backward,
> the moose can be seen
> on the moonlit macadam;
> then there's a dim
> smell of moose, an acrid
> smell of gasoline.

A hint of unravelling that literally leaves things in the air as opposites meet. "The Moose" is presence as speechless form. "She" is never described and is beyond inquisitiveness. So, while it is understandable why Eleanor Cook (1988) has drawn our attention to "the voice" of the Maritimes in this poem, both Bishop's natural reticence and the homely voices of the people in the bus implicate an environing silence as much as a local "cross-sounding" accent. Although Cook does not give her reasons, Canadians and Maritimers can be grateful to Elizabeth Bishop for "The Moose," for they will find "a voice" which, in Costello's words, "belongs to them as their heritage" (1983, 131). (Indeed, Bishop [1983b, 309] has said that it was one of the few poems her Canadian relatives liked.) However, this is not a gentrified heritage and Bishop's understanding "Yes" is not an unqualified affirmation. Resignation is also implied because "Yes . . . life's like that" stoically admits the ups and downs that are nature's way. *Limes* are limitations, and, like her, village Nova Scotians knew theirs was a good place to start from (even if many may lose it).

Similarly, "The Moose" is structured in such a way that nostalgia is not a time capsule: thus, although voices on the bus do suggest a form of closure, it is provisional. And while the meeting with the she-moose is a (felt) presence, that feeling is presented interrogatively. The ending is not a coherently harmonized epiphany. Instead it is understated, leaving loose ends, and it is that which we may have to live with. Even as we leave, the moose's scent is already dispersed among the bus fumes and we are left wondering what that less than homely memory can maintain. All we can be certain of is that we have to learn how to let be. In other words, discovering isn't just learning how to approach something, there is also an art in withdrawing and, ultimately, losing. The traces left behind are the promise that we will find, in Kalstone's words, "a confirming external response from a mysterious enduring, independent other world" (1989, 239). Or, to put it more mundanely, this is why this Nova Scotia poem took a lifetime to write. It had to wait for what heritage and nostalgia obscure.

Conclusions: "Here, or there"

Nearly all the quotations in this essay have come from works with maritime connections (either in the regional or littoral sense of the word). I have therefore maintained a moveable context. Northrop Frye's provocative inclusion of "expatriates" in a list of American "regions" is well taken (1976, 1). It is not necessary to place Bishop in some regional canon. As her surreal city poems attest, her poetry resists being tied down, even by the "geographies" she has become famous for. Obviously it would be inappropriate to enlist her in a Canadian cosmology. While she derided deracinated angst, it is noteworthy that, unlike the equally peripatetic Malcolm Lowry, she never immersed herself in Canada by default.[17] Default brought her to Brazil, but care had brought her to Canada, and this is why she wrote about both, each "answering" the other (Kalstone 1989, 221). As we thread our way through all of these possibilities, what is needed is a way of showing the relationship between the many "elsewheres" of Bishop's poetry, not just the Maritimes.

One "answer" is to be found in Bishop's use of objects as (one hesitates to say) mnemonic devices. We have already noted her use of a painting, which took her travelling. Another example is an old photograph of a Nova Scotia uncle that was sent to her in Brazil. Characteristically, it is not a Proustian involuntary recall to conjure with: "Although there are more, these are all the memories I want to keep on remembering – I couldn't forget them if I tried, probably – and remembering clearly, as if they had just happened or were still happening."[18] No, what she notes in the end is that the photograph has been, like her, uprooted and it is that shock that has brought about her quite voluntary observations. Memory in Elizabeth Bishop is always observable, so that she can begin again, renewing her resources.

Places have the same effect as objects. As "elsewheres," they create distance alongside the time that separates her from "home, wherever that may be." Wherever and whenever home may be, it is not so much that she does not belong and that the questions follow, rather places "question" each other:

> Is it lack of imagination that makes us come
> to imagined places, not just stay at home?
> Or could Pascal have been not entirely right
> about just sitting quietly in one's room?
>
> Continent, city, country, society:
> the choice is never wide and never free.
> And here, or there. . . . No.
> Should we have stayed at home,
> wherever that may be?

The word "home" does not seem to rest easy among the more abstract categories "continent, city, country, society." But it half-rhymes with Pascal's room. Perhaps this can be "answered" in the way she imagines Robinson Crusoe's "exile" from his island when he is back in England. She imagines him on his island when he is drunk on home brew:

> and so I made home-brew. I'd drink
> the awful, fizzy, stinging stuff
> that went straight to my head
> and play my home-made flute
> (I think it had the weirdest scale on earth)
> and, dizzy, whoop and dance among the goats.
> Home-made, home-made! But aren't we all?
> I felt a deep affection for
> the smallest of my island industries.
> No, not exactly, since the smallest was
> a miserable philosophy.

Philosophy is homesickness, yet we are all home-made! It is the making that counts and it is what we make of it that tells in the long run. This is why Bishop also admires primitive painters – their steady love of detail, individual (though lonesome) industriousness, and their fanatical need to put together a world from anything that comes to hand (1984, 51–59). Poetry is handiwork too.

She survived in the same way that she addressed the split between New England and the Maritimes via the two sides of her family. As she is taken into exile from Halifax to Boston through a black night, locked up with her grandparents on a train, she observes that her American grandfather (who she felt was kidnapping her) was wall-eyed: "At least, one eye turned the wrong way, which made him endlessly interesting to me. The walleye seemed only right and natural, because my grandmother on the other side in Canada had a glass eye" (1984, 13). It is not enough to say that she should try to equate and balance the two. Loss is not the poetry's burden: it's one's own and separately so. It has to be mediated rather than confessed. Robert Lowell therefore speaks of the "harmonious exercise of one's faculties" (1983, 187), John Hollander of "guarded mythologizing" (1983, 248), and Howard Moss of "factual illumination" as being characteristics of Elizabeth Bishop's poetry (1977, 30).

Once again it is best to refine how distance in time and space are structured in Bishop's poetry so that there is a threshold that has to be crossed. One notes how crossing from Nova Scotia to New England might become mythologized as in a rite of passage, but it would be paranoia to assume that every change can be a sea change. For the most part life goes on, "awful but cheerful." There are inconsequential "questions of travel" in which "and" and "and" seem to be the only connections. Besides, things being what they are, haphazard "geography," more often than not, might remain as handy but carefully wrought reportage. Moreover, there are predictable touristic seductions of instant rapport and initiation, the sentimental other side of estrangement. Here description might fend off experience. Begin with, say, a map and explore it as a cool contained model; or with the sandpiper's frantic, narrowly focused look (only connected by look! and look!); or with a depopulated landscape where the elements are beyond our ken. In each case, something other, "not concerning us," has been addressed and that sometimes-impossible task places humanisms in parenthesis (risking cordoning them off, turning history into geography). Here Bishop had to find a way to name an already-existing reality without rearranging it. And there was always Nova Scotia, fortuitously suspended, containing trauma, but controlled via geographies.

In an extreme form, this might mean a disconnected surrealism, meaning elsewheres without echoes. What was different in Bishop's case was that, as Thom Gunn points out, she was able to move from the contained Cornell box to "the discomforting . . . implications of the excluded" (1990, 792).[19] Without resorting to confession, existentialist experience and so on, her work conveys the echo of a scream. It is the impossible cleansing North in Brazil's "tired sweat-polluted sea."[20] For example, the short story "In the Village" seems so contained that it is understandable why it has been described by Hardwick (1984, 34) and Kalstone (1989, 119) as "woven." But "the skein of voices" does not so much have a frame as a fringe or "surround."[21] It is true that there is much that is indelible and that *in* the village there are things locked up by other things – shoes in shoe boxes, gifts in postal packages, a ring inside a fish, even the fire (can it be contained?) in the blacksmith's – but each, like a bell-buoy out at sea, has an accompanying "elsewhere." And although each of these is part of the shadow and silhouette catena of the others, to be "caught in the skein of voices" is not a seamless experience (anymore than a skein is woven material). Instead the story is an inventory that postpones rather than denies exhaustiveness. Containing over time rather than contained in time, description "questions" nature's indifference and human innocence. Even the "sure-as-a-hymn" northerly completeness of the opening paragraph (so solid, seemingly it wouldn't break if dropped) has a questioning "or" that opens up the frame of human frailties ("those pure blue skies . . . too dark, too blue, so that they seem to keep on darkening a little more around the horizon – or is it around the rims of the eyes?").[22] Literally, "In the Village" denotes what is not in the village, without which the story could not have been written. It is the same separation that can be taken from nature to art and back again. Bishop's geographic literalness both refers to and effaces human frailties. From the point of view of psychologizing the poetry, it suggests a necessary schizophrenia that removes even as it pays attention. From that of a life lived, it points to what may be "all to the good" and what calls for "determination," "patience," and, as Bishop added, "ignorance."[23] In time, in Bishop's work, Nova Scotian down-homeness became part of the sustained hyphenated tension between elsewheres (past–present, interior–margin), clarifying observation, in order not to forget, in order to be able to go on.

NOTES

Author's Note: Excerpts from Elizabeth Bishop's letters to Robert Lowell are reprinted by permission of the Houghton Library, Harvard University.

1   Brief biographies of Bishop are found in Robert Giroux 1984, vii–xxii; Kalstone 1989; and Peter Sanger 1985.
2   Elizabeth Bishop to Robert Lowell, 14 August 1947, address Breton Cove, Cape Breton. The puffins are still there, despite competition from Kittiwakes (9 August 1991).
3   Bishop to Lowell, 11 July, 19 August 1951.
4   Bishop to Lowell, early January 1949. Actually the ship was built quite close to Great Village at Spenser's Island in 1861. Its original name had been *The Amazon*. Charles Dickens in 1863 wrote about an emigrant ship called *The Amazon* in the poem "Bound for the Great Salt Lake," in *The Uncommercial Traveller* (1868). Thanks are due to the Nova Scotia Maritime Museum.
5   In a solicitous observation concerning whether Robert Lowell's daughter could swim or not, Bishop remarked, "I believe in swimming, flying and crawling and burrowing" (Bishop to Lowell, 29 June 1960). The other side of these activities would be, as Parker

(1988, 32) suggests, "to reduce yourself to your own resources, the most powerful of which is often dream." Parker accordingly de-emphasizes the significance of Bishop's famous empirical descriptions. A geographer may be forgiven for only occasionally hinting at the uncertainties inherent in relying on one's own resources.

6 Bishop to Lowell, 25 January 1957.

7 "My aunt writes me long descriptions of the 'fall colours' in Nova Scotia and I wonder if that's where I shouldn't be after all" (Bishop to Lowell, 30 October 1958).

8 The photographs were of "Gertie" aged eight and "Artie" aged twelve. "How strange to see them in Brazil" (Bishop to Lowell, 11 December 1957). In the same letter, she asks, "When does one begin to write the *real* poems?" She often refers to the difficulty she had with articulating her marginality: "I feel that I could write . . . about my Uncle Artie, say – but what would be the significance. He became a drunkard. Well maybe it's not too late!" (Bishop to Lowell, 14 December 1957). The poet has to find what her own resources are. There is more uncertainty here than the empirically minded geographer may allow.

9 Bishop to Lowell, 4 and 5 April 1962. See, Great Village Women's Institute 1960.

10 All references to Bishop's poetry are to *The Complete Poems* (1983a).

11 One of Bishop's copies of this book deposited in the Houghton Library, Harvard, is "corrected" in green ink. Nearly all the chapter headings have been amended. However, Bishop's interests are readily discernable, as are the Time-Life popularizations. She says that *Life* was nervous about the inclusion of naturalists and jungle (Bishop to Lowell, 20 August 1961).

12 Bishop to Lowell, 15 August 1968.

13 Bishop to Lowell, 30 June 1948.

14 See Schultz 1989. The naive but calculated simplicity of the title is part of look-vision relation. Look, naive painting, "Poem" together establish Bishop's mediation between art and life. For some notes on the painter of the picture, see Sanger 1985.

15 Bishop (1962, 9–10). As Peter Szondi has said of Walter Benjamin, "This earliest image, which is a promise, comes to the adult not only from early childhood, but also from . . . the shelter of foreign lands" (1988, 22–23).

16 The road taken was the former main highway (no. 2) before the Trans-Canada Highway diverted traffic away from Great Village. The sequence of places – Bass River, the Economies, and Five Islands – is in the order that would be taken by a bus *leaving* the peninsula of Nova Scotia. As Parker (1988, 122) points out, "this bus takes people away from their homes."

17 Cf. Moss 1974, 17, and Porteous 1975, 117–22. She regretted Lowell's willingness to mine his own and others' (including Bishop's) experience (Bishop to Lowell, 11 December 1957). She had less regard for the confessional poetry of Anne Sexton.

18 See Bishop 1984, 249. However, awareness in Bishop is Proustian in its reliance on awakening.

19 Parker (1988) suggests that Bishop's work was always open. The sequence I suggest has the same conclusion as Parker's has.

20 Bishop to Lowell, 8 January 1963.

21 Here I am trying to write around what is within and what is beyond the seeming containment of "In the Village." See Krauss 1985, 21, on materialist and symbolist aspects of within and without.

22 See Bishop 1984, 251. "Sure-as-a-hymn" is a phrase she used to describe the "northern music" of Robert Lowell's "Skunk Hour" (Bishop to Lowell, 17 June 1963).

23 Bishop to Lowell, 29 January 1958.

REFERENCES

Bishop, E. 1962. *Brazil*. New York: Times Inc.

———. 1977. "Laureate's Words of Acceptance." *World Literature Today* 51, no. 1: 12.

———. 1983a. *The Complete Poems*. New York: Farrar, Strauss & Giroux.

———. 1983b. "Interview." In L. Schwartz and S.P. Estees, eds., *Elizabeth Bishop and Her Art*. Ann Arbor: University of Michigan.

———. 1984. *The Collected Prose*. New York: Farrar, Strauss & Giroux.

Cook, E. 1988. "A Seeing and Unseeing in the Eye: Canadian Literature and the Sense of Place." *Daedalus* 117:214–35.

Costello, B. 1983. "The Impersonal and the Interrogative in the Poetry of Elizabeth Bishop." In L. Schwartz and S.P. Estees, eds., *Elizabeth Bishop and Her Art*. Ann Arbor: University of Michigan.

Eagleton, T. 1983–84. "New Poetry." *Stand Magazine* 25:77.

Frye, N. 1971. *The Bush Garden*. Toronto: House of Anansi Press.

Giroux, R. 1984. "Introduction" to Elizabeth Bishop, *The Collected Prose*. New York: Farrar, Strauss & Giroux.

Great Village Women's Institute. 1960. *Great Village History*. Great Village, Nova Scotia.

Gunn, T. 1990. "In and Out of the Box." *Times Literary Supplement*, 27 July–2 August, 792.

Hardwick, E. 1984. "The Perfectionist." *New Republic* 190 (19 March): 34.

Hollander, J. 1983. "Elizabeth Bishop's Mappings of Life." In L. Schwartz and S.P. Estees, eds., *Elizabeth Bishop and Her Art*. Ann Arbor: University of Michigan Press.

Kalstone, D. 1989. *Becoming a Poet*. New York: Farrar, Strauss & Giroux.

Krauss, R. 1985. *The Originality of the Avant-Garde and Other Modernist Myths*. Cambridge, Mass.: MIT Press.

Lowell, R. 1983. "Thomas, Bishop, and Williams." In L. Schwartz and S.P. Estees, eds., *Elizabeth Bishop and Her Art*. Ann Arbour: University of Michigan Press.

Moss, H. 1977. "The Canada-Brazil Connection." *World Literature Today* 51, no. 1:29–30.

Moss, J. 1977. *Patterns of Isolation*. Toronto: McClelland & Stewart.

Parker, R.D. 1988. *The Unbeliever*. Urbana and Chicago: University of Illinois Press.

Porteous, D. 1975. "Literature and Humanist Geography." *Area* 7:117–22.

Sanger, P. 1985. "Elizabeth Bishop and Nova Scotia." *Antigonish Review* 60:15–27.

Schultz, S. 1989. "Marianne Moore and Elizabeth Bishop." *Wilson Quarterly* 12:128–38.

Schwartz, L., and S.P. Estees, eds. 1983. *Elizabeth Bishop and Her Art*, 26 (D. Kalstone), 47 (H. Vendler), 132 (Costello), and 203 (J.Ashberry). Ann Arbor, University of Michigan.

Szondi, P. 1988. "Walter Benjamin's City Portraits." In Gary Smith, ed., *On Walter Benjamin*. Cambridge, Mass.: MIT Press.

Wilson, D.S. 1989. "The Rhetoric and Esthetics of Haphazard Landscapes." *Landscape* 30: 29–33.

11

Ways of Seeing, Ways of Being: Literature, Place, and Tourism in L.M. Montgomery's Prince Edward Island

Shelagh J. Squire

There are beautiful landscapes elsewhere, all over Canada, but
they lack the indescribable charm that haunts [Prince Edward
Island]. It is too elusive . . . too subtle . . . for definition . . .
Lands have personalities just as human beings have, and the
spirit of one land is not the spirit of another nor ever can be.
—L.M. Montgomery,
"Prince Edward Island" (1939)

*L*ucy Maud Montgomery (1874–1942) is one of the most regionally based
and popular Canadian writers. All but one of her twenty novels were set in her native Prince Edward Island, and her red-headed heroine, "Anne of Green Gables,"
is intrinsically linked with P.E.I.'s identity and, in a broad sense, with Canadian
culture. Montgomery's literary landscapes are more than part of a regional geographic mosaic. Landscape may be read in different ways, and although in her
fiction, Montgomery immortalized Prince Edward Island, her impressions of
that landscape were coloured by emotion and nostalgia. Subsequently, the literary landscape has been transformed – through television dramatizations, tourist
brochures, and, today, through the growing phenomenon of mass tourism. Just
as Montgomery found literary inspiration in the "real" landscapes with which
she was familiar, her imagined world has today been appropriated for other
purposes, thereby shaping new cultural patterns.

Montgomery's fiction resonates with her personal attachment to place. Readers
in different places and at different times will respond to this vision of place in
different ways. Much work on literature and geography has been concerned with
writers and their responses to place (Lanegran and Toth 1976; Pocock 1981,
1988; Mallory and Simpson-Housley 1987). Similarly, tourism research has
tended to focus on the economic aspects of tourist growth and the development
of tourist areas, with scant concern for questions of qualitative meaning (compare reviews by Dann, Nash, and Pearce 1988 and Pearce 1979 with Cohen

1988 and MacCannell 1973). Literary tourism (or the intersection between literature, place, and tourism as manifested by tourist travel to areas made famous by literary associations) yields fertile ground for a qualitative analysis of cultural meaning – how it may be both created and interpreted over space and time (Butler 1986; Squire 1988a, 1988b). In Montgomery's novels and in the contemporary tourist settings for these novels, landscape is a fluid construct, a text that reflects not only the author's emotive feelings, but also a sphere of cultural processes involving the reader as much as they do the writer.

In this chapter, I want to explore Montgomery's impressions of Prince Edward Island in terms of both their explicitly humanistic and broader cultural contexts. From a humanistic perspective, Montgomery's work, and the portrait of Prince Edward Island that it encompasses, reflects the author's childhood experiences and love of place. Yet, in a larger sense, Montgomery's novels reveal much about Canadian landscape preferences and, in particular, about the rural myth that still pervades the Canadian cultural consciousness. Montgomery's novels are the medium that other media – tourism and television, for example – have reinterpreted. The author experienced Prince Edward Island in a particular way, shaped by late nineteenth- and turn-of-the-century circumstances. Today, not only have those experiences been preserved in a literary context, but also, over time and through different media, literary meaning has been appropriated and transformed into a much broader cultural framework.

LANDSCAPES AND PLACES

Montgomery was born at Clifton (New London), P.E.I., in 1874. After her mother's death in 1876 and her father's subsequent decision to emigrate to Saskatchewan, the young Lucy Maud was sent to live with her maternal grandparents at Cavendish (see Figure 11, map 1, page 12). Here she spent her youth, and as she later commented, "were it not for those Cavendish years, I do not think that 'Anne of Green Gables' would ever have been written" (Montgomery 1917, 52). A self-described "indefatigable little scribbler" (Montgomery 1917, 52), Montgomery used words to conceptualize aspects of her everyday experiences. Personal catharsis thereby became the basis of a successful literary career.

Montgomery's first and most famous novel, *Anne of Green Gables*, was published in 1908. This engaging tale of a red-headed orphan, Anne Shirley, who was adopted by Matthew and Marilla Cuthbert at Green Gables, a Prince Edward Island farm, soon became a best seller. Montgomery's realization of childhood, no less than her idyllic descriptions of life in a late nineteenth-century Prince Edward Island village, appealed to public sentiment, both in Canada and abroad.

Montgomery drew on landscape in different ways. She later acknowledged that the fictional community of Avonlea, setting for many of the Anne books, was loosely based on Cavendish. Certainly it is possible to draw parallels between the author's fictional world and autobiography. Lover's Lane, the Haunted Wood, and the Shore Road, for instance, all had factual counterparts. Matching of fact with fiction, however, has serious limitations. Just as Montgomery drew inspiration from her own childhood surroundings and experiences, she also juxtaposed this environment with a landscape of the imagination.

In all of her novels, Montgomery's depiction of Prince Edward Island was as much the reflection of her intense love of place as it was the result of any conscious attempt of hers to replicate a particular regional geography. The author found the wellspring of her creativity in a "harbour shore and . . . a cluster of weather-grey fishing huts," in a "saffron sky," and "in the tang of the sea in the strong, fresh air" (Montgomery 1968, 246, 251). Her landscapes were rich in evocative sensory imagery, and Green Gables is a prototype of the late nineteenth-century Canadian pastoral idyll.

> A huge cherry-tree grew outside, so close that its boughs tapped against the house, and it was so thick-set with blossoms that hardly a leaf was to be seen. On both sides of the house was a big orchard, one of apple trees and one of cherry trees, also showered with blossoms . . . In the garden below were lilac trees purple with flowers, and their dizzily sweet fragrance drifted up to the window on the morning wind.
>
> Below the garden a green field lush with clover sloped down to the hollow where the brook ran and where scores of white birches grew, upspringing airily out of an undergrowth suggestive of delightful possibilities in ferns and mosses and woodsy things generally. (Montgomery 1968, 33–34)

Montgomery revelled in pastoral nature, and throughout *Anne of Green Gables* she attempted to put into prose the intangible aspects of landscape and place that Prince Edward Island evoked for her. Her journals and letters are replete with references to this spiritual attachment to "home." In 1891, on a visit to her father in Saskatchewan, she wrote to a Cavendish friend: "I wish I were home this spring . . . Often in my dreams I see the dear old shore with its brown rock and pebbled coves and the blue waters of the sparkling gulf" (Montgomery to MacNeill, 22 April 1891; Bolger 1974, 124). Love of home was synonymous with love of the Prince Edward Island countryside, an attachment that shaped all of her fiction.

After the success of *Anne of Green Gables*, Montgomery published numerous sequels to the book, while also writing about other young heroines. In her later novels, her descriptions of Prince Edward Island became increasingly mystical. Marriage in 1911 and a move to Leaskdale, Ontario, meant her exile from the island. Thereafter, Montgomery's visits were infrequent, and in conjunction with a troubled marriage, ill-health, and the unceasing and unwelcome demands made upon her as a minister's wife, her nostalgia for home intensified. Each trip brought

> a little shock of amazement . . . There is nothing like it in smug, opulent Ontario. Such fields of daisies and clover! Such sunsets and

twilights and fir woods, such blue majestic oceans, such provocative
alluring landscapes . . . I felt that I *belonged* there – that I had done some
violence to my soul when I left it. (Weber Collection, 17 October 1923)

Writing enabled her to retreat into an ideal world of childhood memory. As
she once commented: "It is possible to create our own world and live in it
happily. If it were not I do not think I could exist at all" (MacMillan Collection,
3 December 1905; Bolger and Epperly 1980, 15–17). Like Elizabeth Bishop
(Robinson, this volume), Montgomery too suffered from a loss of place.

Anne's House of Dreams (1917) was one of Montgomery's many sequels to
Anne of Green Gables. Although the love story of Anne and Gilbert Blythe
provides narrative structure, romantic sentimentality is as integral to landscape
description as it is to plot and dialogue. The story is set at "Four Winds Harbour," and as Montgomery later claimed, "New London harbour was in my
mind, though I altered the geography to suit my requirements" (Rubio and
Waterston 1987, entry for 21 July 1917, 222). Images of "golden mists and
purple hazes," "red, winding harbour roads," "velvety green hill[s] . . . yellow
harvest fields . . . and bits of blue sea" resonate throughout the novel, conveying
the author's acute environmental sensitivity (Montgomery 1981, 59, 60, 39).
Such lyrical descriptions echo cadences that appeared in her only published
volume of verse, but where this technique failed her in conventional poetry,
poetic lyricism in prose form, as in *Anne's House of Dreams,* contributed to an
idyllic image of place (Epperly 1985, 45). The halcyon landscape that Montgomery
had evoked in *Anne of Green Gables* recurred here, most notably in descriptions
of Four Winds Harbour.

> . . . before (Anne) lay Four Winds Harbour like a great, shining mirror
> of rose and silver. Far down, she saw its entrance between the bar of
> sand dunes on one side and a steep, high, grim, red-sandstone cliff on
> the other. Beyond the bar the sea, calm and austere dreamed in the
> afterlight. The little fishing village, nestled in the cove where the sand-
> dunes met the harbour shore, looked like a great opal in the haze . . .
> the whole landscape was infused with the subtleties of a sea evening.
> (Montgomery 1981, 37)

Rich in romantic imagery, this portrait of place supersedes conventional geographic description.

This pastoral motif is particularly explicit in *Pat of Silver Bush* (1932) and
Mistress Pat (1935). Environmental imagery from previous novels recurs: "a long
red road that wandered on until it reached the sea" (Montgomery 1988c, 146),
and "the velvety green of the hill field" (Montgomery 1988b, 254). To her
friend MacMillan, Montgomery had written: "It seems somehow pleasant to
revisit the past and forget the present" (MacMillan Collection, 22 January 1905).
Her fiction had come to serve as a vehicle for this kind of nostalgic introspection.

Only in her last major novel, *Jane of Lantern Hill* (1937), did Montgomery synthesize all these notions of landscape into a coherent whole. Jane's story is a fairy tale – good triumphs over evil and a family is reconciled. Plot and narrative are paralleled in landscape description. Toronto, with its "dark and dingy . . . forbidding, old-fashioned brick houses, grimy with age" (Montgomery 1988a, 1–2), is repeatedly contrasted with an idyllic Prince Edward Island:

> . . . a glimpse of far-off hills that seemed made of opal dust . . . a whiff of wind that had been blowing over a clover field . . . brooks that . . . ran off into green shadowy woods where long branches of spicy fir hung over the lacy water . . . Everything seemed just on the point of whispering a secret of happiness. (65–66)

When Jane returned to Toronto after a summer in Prince Edward Island, she "was re-entering prison" (144). Henceforth, her spirit's home was at Lantern Hill: "a little house looking seaward . . . a white gull . . . ships going up and down . . . spruce woods . . . misty barrens" (149). Landscape as setting was but tenuously linked to the lineaments of regional geography. Montgomery's juxtaposition of Prince Edward Island and Toronto, a utopian-dystopian polarity that has no parallel elsewhere in her fiction, enabled her to make her most explicit statement about Prince Edward Island. For her, it was a place of the soul.

Culture and Context

A humanistic approach to geographic analysis argues that art and literature, among other forms of cultural expression, may foster a more acute sense of place and region than conventional geographic description (Pocock 1981; Salter and Lloyd 1976). Certainly, Montgomery is one writer whose vivid prose offers a more subjective and emotionally tinged appreciation of place than could be garnered from other, purely descriptive material. In Montgomery's work, the real Prince Edward Island countryside is integrated with a landscape of the mind, coloured by the author's intense emotional attachment to her native province. The way that she conceptualizes landscape in her fiction to some extent reflects stages and aspects of her own life experiences, a process that may be documented in excerpts from her journals and letters. What must be recognized, however, is that such an explicitly humanistic perspective offers but one way of approaching Montgomery's fiction. Although it is neither possible nor desirable to divorce the writer and the writer's life experiences from his or her literary work, as some structuralist critics have argued (Selden 1985, 52), it is necessary to move beyond a purely humanistic appraisal to set both writer and work within a wider contextual schema. Montgomery was writing at a particular time and within particular literary conventions and cultural constraints. The continued popularity of her work and its contemporary representations in other media raise questions that lead beyond the humanistic agenda.

Montgomery's novels belong with a much larger body of regional fiction that predominated at the turn of the century in Canadian literature. If Hugh MacLennan's writings offer "a way to discover the meaning of being Canadian" (Peepre-Bordessa, this volume), his work was not without precedent. The regional idyll celebrated the virtues of rural life and small communities, and its "appearance . . . had a major effect on [the] embryonic [Canadian] literary tradition, marking an important step towards the use of local settings and local themes as the basis for literature" (MacLulich 1983, 491). The works of Ralph Connor, Marian Keith, and Nellie McClung were also part of this tradition, while even Stephen Leacock's *Sunshine Sketches of a Little Town* acknowledges the conventional regional idyll in order to satirize it.

Many early writers, Montgomery included, immortalized rural areas in their fiction, and small towns are a recurring motif in Canadian literature. Those who subscribed to the tenets of the regional idyll looked "to their own childhood[s], not to an historical era outside their own experience" for literary material (MacLulich 1983, 492). By drawing upon elements of their own uniquely Canadian experiences, and "despite the sentimentality of most of their books, the authors of regional idylls helped to create a sense that their new nation did have a cultural identity of its own" (MacLulich 1983, 492). At a more complex level, and suggesting the pervasiveness of this genre, these themes reappear in the work of more recent Canadian writers, most notably Margaret Laurence, W.O. Mitchell, and Alice Munro.

Linked to this body of rural fiction, and to its concomitant relationship to Canadian literary identity, is the subtheme of topophilia, or romantic love of place, which characterizes both the regional idyll and Maritime literature in particular (Thompson 1985; Paul and Simpson-Housley, "La Mer, La Patrie," this volume). While images of wilderness and settlement transcend not only Maritime fiction (Sandberg, this volume), but Canadian literature as a whole, humans-versus-environment conflict is virtually absent in the idyllic rural communities created by Montgomery and her contemporaries. Today, Montgomery's Prince Edward Island fiction evokes nostalgia for a small-town rural Canada that surmounts time and space. Canadian identity is not so much an intrinsic part of the books; indeed, Canadian nationalism is frequently subsumed in vibrant regionalism and the belief in a strong island identity. Yet Montgomery, as a Canadian author, and "Anne of Green Gables," as a potent symbol of Canadian childhood, have become important parts of the Canadian cultural consciousness. As one critic observed: "To denigrate the literary qualities of *Anne of Green Gables* is as useless an exercise as carping about the architecture of the National War Memorial. Anne arrived and she has stayed" (Egoff 1967, 252).

Such far-reaching cultural dimensions of Montgomery's work, and of *Anne of Green Gables* in particular, suggest that the books carry a variety of contextual meanings. One aspect of their literary identity and of their links to nascent Canadian literature may be theorized in terms of the regional idyll. Yet this rosy view of village life as depicted in Montgomery's work is rich in mythic connotations that today still impinge on the Canadian cultural consciousness.

Montgomery's impressions of Prince Edward Island have been abstracted from the literary texts, transformed into symbols of Canadian cultural identity, and represented in other forms, in particular, through tourist development.

LITERARY TOURISM

The popularity of Montgomery's novels transformed tourism in the part of Prince Edward Island that she wrote about. Although the north shore of the province was already attracting summer visitors at the time Montgomery was writing, in several instances even providing her with literary material, Cavendish was still a "farming community" (MacMillan Collection, 9 November 1904). The success of *Anne of Green Gables* irrevocably altered the fabric of that community, as tourists, in search of Green Gables, created a demand for vacation amenities that continues to the present.

Literary heritage is given tangible expression at "Green Gables" in Prince Edward Island National Park, established in 1937. The choice of the park site was influenced by the fact that "Cavendish was already a sort of shrine on account of the ['Anne'] books" (MacMillan Collection, 27 December 1936). Although Montgomery insisted that Green Gables was practically imaginary, the house that by virtue of its setting and style came to be known as "Green Gables" is a vehicle sustaining the myth of place that the author wove into her fiction.

Parks Canada's interpretive policy at Green Gables recognizes that historical authenticity must sometimes be compromised with literary accuracy. Site redevelopment has been guided by details from the novels, and only if these sources proved inconclusive would "information about the actual farm that existed on the site" or a comparable nineteenth-century farmstead be used (Parks Canada 1981, 30).

Such policies, designed to convey "the essence of L.M. Montgomery's writings of Prince Edward Island" (Parks Canada site interpretive material), represent one way that literary heritage has been appropriated from its original context and given new meaning. Outside the National Park, in both Cavendish and the surrounding area, this process has taken a different form. Many local businesses boast Montgomery-inspired names: the Anne Shirley Motel and Marilla's Pizza Restaurant are two examples. At French River, "Anne's House of Dreams" depicts the home of the fictional characters in the novel of the same name. Less contrived, in terms of literary and family heritage, are the Montgomery birthplace museum at New London and the Anne of Green Gables Museum at Silver Bush, Park Corner.

Although the appropriateness of some of these attractions may be debated, each of these sites has drawn inspiration from literary heritage to create a tourist setting. While Montgomery transferred elements of the Prince Edward Island landscape into her fiction, tourist development has inverted this process, giving that which was fictional a factual identity through a number of tourist attractions.

While it is impossible to separate the lure of the literary theme from the popularity of other area attractions, such as the beaches, Prince Edward Island

Tourism (the government's tourism agency) recognizes the significance of the Anne theme to regional development. Package tour holidays and contests centred around the theme of "Prince Edward Island Seen through the Eyes of Anne of Green Gables" are perhaps the most important of recent national marketing initiatives. In the international market, the Anne theme has special appeal for young Japanese women. Montgomery's evocative landscape descriptions, no less than her independent, though family-oriented, heroine, have attracted a cult following (Gaudet 1987; Katsura 1984). To cater to this interest, the tourism department uses the theme "Green Gables . . . My Dream" to promote the province (*Highlights of the 1987 Marketing/Media Plan,* 12). In both the international and domestic markets, however, tourism works on the Anne dream, creating an industry out of literary heritage and giving what were once purely literary experiences tangible form.

As much as they are shaped by literary associations, images of Prince Edward Island may today be drawn from many sources. The television films directed by Kevin Sullivan and based on *Anne of Green Gables* and its sequels have generated enormous interest, a phenomenon evident in Parks Canada's visitation statistics at Green Gables. The first film was aired in December 1985, and between 1985 and 1986 visitor numbers rose from 165,124 to 217,292, a 52 percent increase (Parks Canada 1987). Television has appropriated the literary texts and transformed them into different contexts, adding new layers of meaning. Some visitors, for example, are disappointed upon finding that Parks Canada's Green Gables differs from that portrayed in the television dramas, the latter filmed largely in Ontario.

WAYS OF SEEING, WAYS OF BEING

In cultural geography, much landscape research has been concerned with describing the meanings and values associated with particular environments. What has tended to go unrecognized is that culture and the cultural landscape must be interpreted as active human constructs and, as Osborne (this volume) argues, as systems of communication. Individual authors work within comprehensive cultural frameworks, and the landscape imagery and cultural meanings expressed in literature, later transformed in diverse ways, require new approaches to the study of literary landscapes.

Montgomery's depictions of Prince Edward Island do reflect her "idiosyncratic mode of regard" or personal perceptual filter (Hardy 1928, 225; Simpson-Housley 1988). Today, however, her novels are being read in contexts different from those within which they were originally written; tourist development in particular has seized upon the Montgomery heritage and reinterpreted it in various ways. A humanistic approach to Montgomery's work must therefore be tempered with the recognition that, given its emphasis on the primacy of the individual, such an approach cannot adequately account for broader social and contextual elements.

The tension between wilderness and settlement, the rural and the urban, is integral to the history of Canadian literature and cultural expression (Scott, this volume). Typically, these concepts have been seen as irreconcilable. Influenced by English notions of the picturesque and pastoral, the Canadian relationship with land was rooted in the urge to control and "civilize" it (MacLaren 1989). Yet, as Williams (1973) has emphasized in the context of English cultural values, the country and the city are interdependent. Much of the appeal of the rural idyll lies in its nostalgic look at small communities, reminders of a supposedly simpler way of life in an increasingly urban and industrialized nation. The continued popularity of Montgomery's novels reflects the pervasiveness of this wider cultural discourse, one that is inseparable from entrenched environmental attitudes.

Much of the tourist development in Cavendish can be seen as exploitative, and commercialization of the Montgomery heritage is of concern. If visitors are seeking the pastoral landscape that Montgomery wrote about, yet tourist development is allowed to destroy the vestiges of that landscape, the future of literary tourism may be jeopardized. All of the literary attractions are part of the evolving cultural landscape, however, and as tourism represents a means through which to experience a particular interpretation of the past, it is also dynamic, shaping new patterns of cultural experience.

If landscape constitutes a "way of seeing," literary landscapes are a rich source of textual meaning (Cosgrove 1984, 15). Although the present study is concerned with aspects of environmental imagery, the folkloric aspects of Montgomery's fiction offer a vivid temporal portrait of a particular society. This relationship between society/space and literature/place/culture thus suggests other possible areas of inquiry.

Correspondingly, if "place is to be understood as the level at which social processes are experienced," it may be argued that "landscapes become places through the meanings that they have for different human subjects" (Jackson 1986, 119–20). As a "way of seeing," landscape is perceived from the outside, while place is perhaps best interpreted as a "way of being." Montgomery's Prince Edward Island novels (and the tourist development resulting from the popularity of those novels) reflects the intersection between place and landscape that lies at the heart of cultural geography. Literary geography has largely been concerned with the relationship between writers and their places. Yet, if literature has a role to play in the formation of environmental attitudes and is an integral part of a country's cultural sensibility, the engagement between the reader, the text, and the place is equally significant.

REFERENCES

Bolger, F.W.P. 1974. *The Years Before 'Anne.'* Charlottetown: Prince Edward Island Heritage Foundation.

Bolger, F.W.P., and Elizabeth R. Epperly, eds. 1980. *My Dear Mr. M: Letters to G.B. MacMillan from L.M. Montgomery.* Toronto: McGraw-Hill Ryerson.

Butler, R.W. 1986. "Literature as an Influence in Shaping the Image of Tourist Destinations: A Review and Case Study." In J.S. Marsh, ed., *Canadian Studies of Parks, Recreation and Tourism in Foreign Lands*, 112–32. Peterborough: Department of Geography, Trent University.

Cohen, E. 1988. "Authenticity and Commoditization in Tourism." *Annals of Tourism Research* 15:371–86.

Cosgrove, D. 1984. *Social Formation and Symbolic Landscape*. London: Croom Helm.

Dann, G., D. Nash, and P. Pearce. 1988. "Methodology in Tourism Research." *Annals of Tourism Research* 15:1–28.

Department of Tourism and Parks. *Prince Edward Island Canada: Highlights of the 1987 Marketing/Media Plan and Three Year Marketing Strategy (1987–1989)*. Charlottetown.

Egoff, S. 1967. *The Republic of Childhood: A Critical Guide to Canadian Children's Literature in English*. Toronto: Oxford University Press.

Epperly, E. 1985. "L.M. Montgomery's *Anne's House of Dreams:* Reworking Poetry." *Canadian Children's Literature* 37:40–46.

Gaudet, C. 1987. "Why the Japanese Love Our *Anne of Green Gables*." *Canadian Geographic* 107:8–15.

Hardy, F.E. 1928. *The Life of Thomas Hardy: 1840–1928*. London: Macmillan.

Jackson, P. 1986. "Social Geography: The Rediscovery of Place." *Progress in Human Geography* 10:118–24.

Katsura, Y. 1984. "Red-Haired Anne in Japan." *Canadian Children's Literature* 34:57–60.

Lanegran, D.A., and S.A. Toth. 1976. "Geography through Literature." *Places* 3:5–12.

MacCannell, D. 1973. *The Tourist: A New Theory of the Leisure Class*. London: Macmillan.

MacLaren, I.S. 1989. "The Pastoral and the Wilderness in Early Canada." *Landscape Research* 14:15–19.

MacLulich, T.D. 1983. "Anne of Green Gables and the Regional Idyll." *Dalhousie Review* 63:488–501.

MacMillan Collection (George Boyd MacMillan Collection). National Archives of Canada, MG30D185, vols. 1, 2.

MacNeill Letter Collection (Penzie MacNeill Letter Collection). "Letters from L.M. Montgomery to Penzie Maria MacNeill, Circa 1886–1894." Robertson Memorial Library, University of Prince Edward Island, Charlottetown.

Mallory, W.E., and P. Simpson-Housley, eds. 1987. *Geography and Literature: A Meeting of the Disciplines*. Syracuse: Syracuse University Press.

Montgomery, L.M. 1917. *The Alpine Path: The Story of My Career*. Don Mills: Fitzhenry & Whiteside.

———. 1939. "Prince Edward Island." In *The Spirit of Canada, Dominion and Provinces*. Toronto: Canadian Pacific Railway/McClelland & Stewart.

———. 1968. *Anne of Green Gables*. Toronto: McGraw-Hill Ryerson.

———. 1981. *Anne's House of Dreams*. London: Puffin Books.

———. 1988a. *Jane of Lantern Hill*. Toronto: Seal Books.

———. 1988b. *Mistress Pat*. Toronto: Seal Books.

———. 1988c. *Pat of Silver Bush*. Toronto: Seal Books.

Parks Canada. 1981. *Green Gables Area Plan Concept*.

———. 1987. Prince Edward Island National Park, unpublished data.

Pearce, D.G. 1979. "Towards a Geography of Tourism." *Annals of Tourism Research* 6: 245–72.

Pocock, D.C.D., ed. 1981. *Humanistic Geography and Literature: Essays on the Experience of Place*. Totowa, N.J.: Barnes and Noble.

————. 1988. "Interface: Geography and Literature." *Progress in Human Geography* 12: 87–102.

Rubio, Mary, and Elizabeth Waterston, eds. 1985. *The Selected Journals of L.M. Montgomery.* Vol. 1: *1889–1910.* Toronto: Oxford University Press.

————. 1987. *The Selected Journals of L.M. Montgomery.* Vol. 2: *1910–1931.* Toronto: Oxford University Press.

Salter, C.L., and W.J. Lloyd. 1976. *Landscape in Literature.* Washington, D.C.: Association of American Geographers.

Selden, R. 1985. *A Reader's Guide to Contemporary Literary Theory.* Brighton: Harvester Press.

Simpson-Housley, P. 1988. "The Idiosyncratic Mode of Regard." *Canadian Geographer* 32: 269–70.

Squire, S.J. 1988a. "Wordsworth and Lake District Tourism: Romantic Reshaping of Landscape." *Canadian Geographer* 32:237–47.

————. 1988b. "L.M. Montgomery's Prince Edward Island: A Study of Literary Landscapes and Tourist Development." Unpublished M.A. thesis, Carleton University, Ottawa.

Thompson, H. 1985. "Topophilia: The Love of Place in Maritime Literature." *Canadian Children's Literature* 39/40:45–54.

Weber Collection (Ephraim Weber Collection). National Archives of Canada, MG30D53.

Williams, R. 1973. *The Country and the City.* London: Chatto and Windus.

12

La Mer, La Patrie:
Pointe-aux-Coques by Antonine Maillet

Alec Paul and Paul Simpson-Housley

The French-speaking Acadians of Canada's Maritime provinces, in the region they call Acadia, trace their history in the New World back to 1605. In that year Champlain and de Monts established the first year-round settlement at Port Royal in southwestern Nova Scotia (see Figure 1.1, page 12), two years before the founding of Jamestown, three before the founding of Quebec City.

By the early 1750s about eight thousand Acadian French were spread over a number of settlements in southern and western Nova Scotia. Continued warfare between the French and the English, however, placed them in a precarious position. They pursued a neutral course, withstanding pressure to swear an oath of allegiance to the English Crown. Their steadfast refusal angered Lawrence, the English governor of Nova Scotia, who ordered in 1755 that the Acadians be rounded up and deported. The deportation order was carried out, and this traumatic event, often called by the Acadians Le Grand Dérangement, still looms large in their collective memory.[1]

A decade later, it was becoming clear to the victorious English that the Acadians no longer posed a significant threat to the English hold on northeastern North America. They were allowed to return. But two very significant conditions were attached. First, they had to take the oath of allegiance, and second, and perhaps even more important, their settlements had to be dispersed and isolated one from another. In this way, no concentration of French strength in a particular area could arise.

Thus emerged an Acadia fragmented geographically, with French-speaking settlements scattered infrequently along a vast extent of coastline (Figure 1.1). These small groups were effectively cut off from one another by the wilderness or by English-speaking colonization. An uprooted, scattered people, they lived a life of isolation, dependent on harvesting the basic resources of both sea and land.

Almost two centuries elapsed before Antonine Maillet,[2] an Acadian writer, would begin to discover Acadian culture, identity, and landscape.[3] She was the first Acadian writer to develop a massive popular appeal both inside and outside the region. Thériault (1980) describes the first century of their return (1763–1864) as the period of "l'enracinement dans le silence" *(silently re-establishing roots)*[4] and most of the second as the period of gradual development of a sentiment of Acadian identity. Towards the end of this second century, in 1958, Maillet's *Pointe-aux-Coques* was published.[5] While the novel lacks the maturity and range of its author's later creations, it made a significant contribution to Acadian awareness of group identity and community.

Pointe-aux-Coques must be seen in its context, as part of an emerging body of twentieth-century Acadian literature. Since the 1860s, an awareness of belonging to an Acadian community had gradually arisen, but was mostly visible in the political and religious life and in the popular culture of the group. *Pointe-aux-Coques* is a celebration of the life and the place of Acadia. It was a component of the written redefinition of the Acadian culture and identity that was taking place around mid-century and that helped Louis Robichaud become the first Acadian premier of New Brunswick, in 1960.

To the geographer, *Pointe-aux-Coques* has a great deal to say about the Acadian sense of place. The novel portrays a romantic attachment to both local region and village. Indeed, the novel as a whole is romantic. Individualism, love of nature, anti-urbanism, reflections on childhood and on the past, landscapes that depict emotions – all are characteristic themes of romanticism that abound in *Pointe-aux-Coques*. Social conscience and group interests, apart from the formation of the fishermen's cooperative, are relatively minor concerns in the novel. Above all, the story is a celebration of place, of an Acadia largely neglected by a French literature in North America that had been dominated by Québécois writers.

The sea is a central recurring theme. In the Prelude, the reflections of the exiled father focus first and foremost on the sea:

> ... je m'efforçais d'oublier les années et le village de là-bas, et mes agrès de pêche, et la mer ... le fracas des vagues contre la proue, le grondement de la mer au large, le cri des pêcheurs qui s'appellent d'une barque à l'autre ... ces matins de juin où presque tout le village s'ébranlait vers la côte ... les cris sauvages des oiseaux de mer. (17–18)

> *(I tried hard to forget all the years I had spent there, and the village, and my fishing gear, and the sea ... the noise of the waves crashing on the bow, the sounds of the open sea, the shouts of the fishermen calling from one boat to another ... those June mornings when almost the whole village went down to the shore ... the wild cries of the seabirds.)*

To a people whose collective memory is dominated by Le Grand Dérangement, an uprooted people, the roots in the land are also crucial: "Voilà que soudain une vieille solitaire me découvrait l'autre visage de ce peuple enraciné et fidèle: l'attache au terroir" (203) *(There, all of a sudden, an old widow had shown me the other side of this deeply rooted and loyal people: their feeling for the land).*

Besides these attachments to the sea and the land of Acadia, the more specific feeling for the particular village is emphasized many times: ". . . ce petit village, tout entouré d'eau et de prés verts, qui était pour moi toute l'Acadie" (14) (. . . *this little village completely surrounded by water and green meadows, which for me was the whole of Acadia),* and "je reconnus avec émerveillement, en face de la rivière, les trois collines et les vastes prés verts qui se déroulaient jusqu'à la forêt" *(across the river, I recognized with wonder the three hills and the immense green meadows that stretched right to the forest).* These key features in her father's memory of the village are passed on to the heroine long before her arrival in Pointe-aux-Coques, but they remain essential elements of her Acadian landscape, reappearing numerous times in the story.

The village, a cherished haven from a threatening world, both present and past, takes on new significance through Francine's story of the flight from the English two centuries earlier.

Ils étaient quinze hommes – le grand-père de mon grand-père était un de ceux-la – embarrés dans une cave à patates lors du Grand Dérangement. Ils sont restés là-dedans trois jours et trois nuits, espérant toujours voir les Anglais venir les en tirer. Puis, quand ils ont compris qu'on allait les laisser périr comme ça, de faim et de soif, ils se sont mis dans la tête de se faire un chemin de sortie . . .

Mais là, ils craigniont les soldats, ça fait qu'ils s'avont hâtés de prendre le bois . . . . avec rien dans le ventre . . .

Après trois semaines, ils avont débouché à Memramcook, puis ils s'avont installé là. Sur les quinze, il en est mort rien qu'un . . . La faim, voyez-vous, puis les fatigues dans le bois, là-bas de Grand Pré jusqu'à Memramcook.

. . . Le bon Dieu a eu pitié des premiers Acadiens; sans ça, personne serait jamais revenu du trouble qu'on leur a fait! (206–7)

(They were fifteen men – my great-great-grandfather was one of them – shut up in a potato cellar at the time of the Deportation. They stayed there in the cellar three days and three nights, hoping all the time to see the English come and let them out. Then, when they realized they were just going to let them starve to death, they decided to escape . . .

Of course, they were afraid of the soldiers, so they took to the woods right away . . . all with empty stomachs . . .

After three weeks, they came out at Memramcook, and they stayed there and settled. Only one of the fifteen didn't make it . . . died of starvation and exhaustion in the forest . . . it was a long way from Grand Pré to Memramcook.

. . . The good Lord took pity on those first Acadians; if he hadn't, none of them would have ever survived the troubles they'd been through!)

Maillet provides a modern-day rendition of the same story when she has the schoolmistresses become lost in the woods in the snow:

Alors la forêt qui avait fait mirer devant nous, une heure plus tôt, tout son brillant de mousse et de lierre appela soudain ses ombres noires et mystérieuses. La nuit souffla un long vent nord-est à la voix nasillarde. Je sentis la neige me tomber sur le front. Et dans le ciel, soudain, de grands bras sombres se lancèrent des signaux. Il faisait nuit. (126)

(Now the forest, which an hour earlier had been reflecting all the lustre of its mosses and creepers, suddenly began to cast dark and mysterious shadows. The night brought a steady northeast wind, its voice whining. I felt snow falling on my forehead. Up in the sky, great dark limbs sent signals to one another. Night had fallen.)

The uncaring, vast, surrounding forest is the wilderness in which the Acadians have cleared their farm plots and pastures. But the wilderness is never more than a presence, a threat. Acadia is the sea and the farm for Maillet, rather than the forest.

The agricultural tradition is also a strong part of the Acadian sense of place. Maillet ascribes the feeling of Nazarine, the old widow, for her home territory among the inland concessions, a few short miles yet half a world away from Pointe-aux-Coques, to her ancestral roots of more than two centuries earlier in Amboise:

Nazarine n'avait jamais compris la pêche. C'était une petite fille des terres qu'on avait transplantée à dix-sept ans sur un cap rocailleux. Cinquante-trois ans n'avaient pas suffi à lui faire prendre racine à Pointe-aux-Coques. Elle avait germé pendant trop de siècles dans la vallée de la Loire. Il appartient à un Acadien breton ou poitevin de s'embarquer sur l'océan; mais une d'Amboise est fille du terroir, même après deux siècles. (204)

(Nazarine had never understood fishing. She was a young farm girl who had been transplanted at the age of seventeen onto a rocky sea-cape. Fifty-three years had not been long enough for her to put down roots in Pointe-aux-Coques. She had germinated for too many centuries in the Loire Valley. It is second nature for an Acadian from Brittany or Poitou to go to sea; but a girl from Amboise is a daughter of the land, even after two centuries.)

Fishing, however, is the dominant activity in Pointe-aux-Coques. It is much more than a way of earning a living, it is a way of life.

Leurs pères avaient tous pêché. Et cela remontait loin. Plus de deux siècles sur les côtes canadiennes; et là-bas en Bretagne avant la fondation

de la colonie. Sans compter cet exil, ce fameux dérangement de 1755,
cette grande aventure. Les Acadiens avaient connu de quoi, à travers
leur histoire, se rentrer toute la mer dans les veines. (89)

Après quarante ans de pêche, on en vient à connaître tous les recoins et
tous les poissons de la mer. On en vient aussi à les aimer. Un homme
qui a pêché toute sa vie sent qu'il *appartient* une partie de l'eau. (214)

*(Their fathers had all been fishermen. It went back a long way. More than
two centuries on the coasts of Canada, and back in Brittany before the
founding of the colony. Without counting the exile, that famous deportation
in 1755, that great adventure. Throughout their history the Acadians had
always had the sea in their blood.*

*After forty years as a fisherman, you know all there is to know about fishing
and about the sea. You also come to love them both. A man who has fished
all his life feels that part of him belongs on the water.)*

The life of the village has a seasonal rhythm that cannot be hurried.

Et mars vint, avec sa fonte des neiges. Comme l'hiver avait été
particulièrement rude, le printemps s'annonçait long. Le 15 mars déjà,
les routes étaient inondées. Pour un mois, Pointe-aux-Coques verrait ses
quatre voies de sortie barricadées par la neige fondante. Le village, en
cette saison, n'avait qu'à rentrer en lui-même. (129)

*(March arrived, with its melting snows. Since the winter had been espe-
cially tough, it was going to be a long spring. Already on March 15 the
roads were inundated. For a month, Pointe-aux-Coques saw its roads in
and out blocked by the melting snow. During this season the village had to
fall back on its own resources.)*

Saint Pierre, 29 June, is traditionally the first day of strawberry-picking, and
Nazarine will never start before this date. The village picnic, at the end of
August, always comes three weeks after the opening of the lobster season. Social
life is organized to a significant degree around the religious festivals and other
seasonal events.

The novel is above all a statement of the traditional values of the Acadian
group as Maillet interprets them; these values are presented in a manner strongly
reminiscent of the literary romanticism of the early nineteenth century. The
romantic aspect of the work is clearly visible in the five themes mentioned earlier
in the chapter, and which we now turn to.

Individualism in *Pointe-aux-Coques* is very strongly reflected in the father's
intensely personal thoughts expressed in the Prelude:

. . . mon père se mit à me raconter comment l'idée lui était venue, jeune homme, de partir, laisser son village et sa famille et s'en aller en quête de travail dans un pays étranger. Le goût de l'aventure l'avait tenté si fort qu'il avait cédé . . . "je continuais d'aller de ville en ville, d'une usine à une autre. Je n'avais pas de métier et le travail devenait rare . . . Mais je n'avais pas le courage de faire face. Il me semblait que j'étais parti depuis trop longtemps, qu'il serait lâche de me rendre. On se moquerait de mes aventures . . . Je serais un raté; un coureur abandonnant la course, comme tout le monde l'avait prédit. (16–17)

(. . . *my father began to tell me how the idea had come to him, as a young man, to leave his village and his family and to go looking for work in a foreign country. The thirst for adventure was so great that he had given in . . . "I went from town to town, from one factory to another. I didn't have a trade and work was getting hard to find . . . But I didn't have the courage to go back. I felt that I had been away too long, that it would be cowardly to give up. People would make fun of my adventures . . . I would be a failure; a runner dropping out of the race, as everyone had predicted.*)

Numerous other instances can be found, none more striking than the portrayal of grand Dan, the archetype of the rugged individualist who somehow becomes the key figure in the establishment of the fishermen's cooperative.

Love of nature is a theme that is overworked throughout the novel. This is very evident in the passage about the swallows, a standard romantic image:

Les hirondelles cherchaient en silence leurs vieux nids. Et les branches d'érables et de peupliers, saoules de sève capiteuse, pendaient lourdement en couvant leurs bourgeons. C'était la grande attente de mai, où tous les cocons et tous les nids des champs se renouvellent. (160)

(*The swallows searched in silence for their old nests. And the maple and poplar branches, laden with sap, sagged heavily with bursting buds. It was May, the season of great expectancy, when all the cocoons and nests in the fields come back to life.*)

But it recurs frequently elsewhere, most strikingly in this passage: "Ici la nature était plus enjouée. Les branches sèches et les racines pelées damassaient le sol; les feuilles chantaient; et les aigrettes de sapins sentaient bon comme un vent d'été" (176) (*Nature was more joyful here. The dried-out branches and the bare roots patterned the ground; the leaves rustled; and the spruce needles smelled sweet, like a summer breeze*).

Migration to large cities outside the region, often in the United States, posed a clear threat to the Acadian way of life. Maillet's occasional passages of anti-urbanism provide some memorable images, including the vivid "anthill of unhappy people":

Le pays américain n'offrait pas les délices qu'on prétendait. A côté de ses ponts suspendus, de ses théâtres, de ses vastes usines, la ville de lumière artificielle cachait toute une fourmillière de malheureux . . . Pointe-aux-Coques n'était pas misérable. Et quand il le serait, la vaste patrie du capitalisme ne lui offrait pas encore une réponse. (196–97)

(America was not all it was cracked up to be. Besides its suspension bridges, its movie theatres and its huge factories, the city of artificial light hid a whole anthill of unhappy people . . . but there was no misery in Pointe-aux-Coques. And even if there was, the vast dominion of capitalism would still have no answer for it.)

Nevertheless, several of the characters in *Pointe-aux-Coques* have apparently been seduced by the "cities of artificial light."

Reflections on childhood and on the past are a romantic preoccupation. Mlle Cormier's father indulges in such reminiscences:

On regrette le soleil de son enfance avec tous ses rêves et toutes ses joies; on regrette ces pays que l'on a visités dans les croisées des ruisseaux, sur un radeau d'écorce; on regrette cette vie-là, ces amours, ces dix ans. Et cette nostalgie est ce qu'il y a de plus poignant. (16)

(You miss the sunshine of your childhood, with all its dreams and all its joy; you miss those places you floated by along the streams on a wooden raft; you miss that whole life, the things you loved to do during those ten years. Those memories, that's what hurts even more.)

One is reminded here of Muley in John Steinbeck's *The Grapes of Wrath*. Despite the horrors of severe drought and grinding poverty, Muley still identified with the good times of his youth on the farms around Sallisaw, Oklahoma. Maillet's grand Dan also typifies this genre:

Dans notre temps, j'avions ni grosses machines sur les routes, ni radio à la maison, ni que je menions les filles faire des pirouettes dans les salles de danse ou les restaurants. La vie était simple autrefois. Je vivions pauvres, mais contents. Quand Jean reviendra, j'ai espérance que la Pointe aussi reviendra avec lui. Jean, c'est un homme du passé. (119)

(In our day, there were no big machines on the roads, or radios in the homes, and we never went gallivanting around with the girls to dance halls or restaurants. Life was simpler back then. We were poor but happy. When Jean comes back, my hope is that the Point will come back with him too. Jean is a man from the past.)

And it is through Jean, "homme du passé" yet also the new light of Pointe-aux-Coques, that Maillet gives us her most memorable statement of both childhood nostalgia and rejection of the urban life "outside":

> Jean était l'enfant aux yeux avides et croyants, qui avait chéri, comme mon père, un étang de grenouilles. Mais un jour, lui aussi avait découvert soudain les limites de son univers; il s'était aperçu que du centre de l'étang, les quatre rivages lui apparaissaient à la fois. Alors le désir de fuir l'avait tiraillé, comme mon père; le désir de partir à la recherche d'une réponse. Mais cette réponse, il l'avait trouvée chez lui, dans son pays, un matin de juin qu'il s'en allait avec les hommes, jeter les longs filets de corde dans les eaux grises du détroit. Et après ses années de collège, il était revenu dans son village pour pêcher. (158)

> *(Jean had been a wide-eyed innocent kid who, like my father, had marvelled at a pond full of frogs. But one day he too had suddenly discovered the limits of his world; he realized that he could see all four sides of the pond from the centre. He was torn by the desire to get away, just like my father; the desire to go looking for an answer. But he found that answer back home, one June morning when he went out with the men to cast their great nets into the grey waters of the strait. And after his years at college, he had come back to his own village to fish.)*

Landscapes that depict emotions are frequent. The abruptly curtailed lunch in the old cemetery is somewhat Chaplinesque. The schoolmistresses are happily preparing to picnic among the willows and the birches, but when they discover by chance that they are in fact among the early dead of Pointe-aux-Coques, the mood disappears rapidly: "Mais quand nous eûmes découvert, sous un saule, quelques os blancs et deux crânes crevassés, alors nos pains et fromage furent jetés aux oiseaux, et sans nous consulter, nous abandonnâmes aussitôt la place" (177) *(But when we discovered, under a willow tree, a few white bones and two weathered skulls, we threw away our bread and cheese for the birds, and fled without a word to one another).*

The landscape is completely changed by a covering of snow. Winter comes late to Kent County, but in time to assist the mood of the Christmas season: "Il neigeait! . . . Ce jour-là, toute la jeunesse canadienne redevient un petit enfant. La neige possède ce secret de rendre au coeur en un souffle de joie naïve que les années lui ont impitoyablement arrachée" (91) *(It was snowing! That day, all the youths of Canada became little children again. Snow has that ability to make people light-hearted, even those whom the years have treated with pitiless cruelty).*

Christmas is a particularly emotional season in *Pointe-aux-Coques.* Maillet's Acadian Christmas is a classic piece of romantic writing. The words "Tout autour de nous tombaient des chants de Noël mêlés aux gros flocons" (93) *(All around us Christmas carols mingled with the huge snowflakes)* create an atmosphere similar to that of Ann Brontë's poem "Music on Christmas Morning":

> "*Ding, dong! ding, dong!* à l'église pour la Minuit!" hélait de tous bords le clocher en branle. *Ça, bergers, assemblons-nous; allons voir le Messie.* Et les bergers en calotte de poil et en *mackinaw* sortaient de leur Pirogue, de leur Petit Cap, de leur Ile à Jacquot, pour venir adorer. (95–96)

> Et la foule, sur les marches de l'église, avalait, en criant ses voeux de Noël, les gros flocons de ouate blanche qui descendaient doucement de la nuit. Les petits enfants qu'on avait arrachés à leurs rêves promenaient des yeux égarés et éblouis sur ce Pointe-aux-Coques fantastique, qu'ils n'avaient encore jamais vu tout noir. (98)

> *(Ding, dong! Ding, dong! To the church for the midnight Mass!" The church bell rang out in all directions. "Come, you shepherds, come together and worship the Messiah." And the shepherds in their deerskin caps and waterproof capes left their Pirogue, their Petit Cap, their Jacquot Island, to come and worship.)*

> *(And the crowd, exchanging their Christmas greetings on the church steps, swallowed the huge flakes of white cotton wool which floated softly down out of the night. The little children who had been rudely awakened from their dreams gazed in wonder at this fantasy-like Pointe-aux-Coques, which they had never seen before so late at night.)*

All in all, the novel has many things to say to the geographer. *Pointe-aux-Coques* is a hymn to the place of Acadia, "la patrie." But it keeps constantly before us the restlessness just below the surface of a people confined historically to a restricted territory, to a way of life complete enough for some but of limited horizons for others, who will strike out for the States almost at the drop of a hat. Maillet's celebration of Acadian life is a fine source of images and metaphors for a region of considerable historic and geographic significance in the fabric of Canada.

NOTES

1 Elsewhere in this volume (chapter 21), Kobayashi discusses the poetry of Japanese Canadians, who also experienced displacement at the hands of Canadian authorities, during the Second World War in their case.

2 Antonine Maillet is an Acadian born in Bouctouche, New Brunswick, in 1929. She taught school at Richibouctou in the early 1950s, and the setting for *Pointe-aux-Coques* is drawn from these two coastal New Brunswick villages (see Figure 1.1, page 12). She wrote her master's thesis on Gabrielle Roy, and there is a definite parallel between *Pointe-*

aux-Coques and Roy's *La Petite Poule d'Eau*, both of which derive in large part from their authors' postings as teachers to remote settlements, as indeed does Ostenso's *Wild Geese*, discussed elsewhere in the current volume (chapter 18). Maillet now has a wide range of novels, other works, and achievements to her credit. Perhaps best known are the 1971 play *La Sagouine*, which legitimized Acadian French as a written language, and *Pélagie-la-Charrette*, a novel dealing with the return of the Acadians from exile. Her stature in French Canada is now such that she was invited to mediate the televised French-language debate of the three Canadian federal party leaders in October 1988. More recently still, she was appointed chancellor of the University of Moncton, the principal French-language university of Acadia.

3   Maillet thus played a role which Peepre-Bordessa (chapter 2 of this volume) maintains was played by Hugh MacLennan in a Canada-wide context.

4   All translations of French text were done by co-authors Alec Paul and Paul Simpson-Housley.

5   Page references in this chapter are from Antonine Maillet, *Pointe-aux-Coques* (Verviers, Belgium: Nouvelles Editions Marabout, 1980).

References

Thériault, L. 1980. "L'Acadie, 1763–1978: Synthèse historique," in J. Daigle, ed., *Les Acadiens des Maritimes*, 49–94. Moncton: Centre d'études acadiennes.

13

Picturing the Picturesque:
Lucius O'Brien's *Sunrise on the Saguenay*

Ellen Ramsay

Thirty-one years ago, Canada was what can truly be called "a rough country" . . . Now, happily for the modern tourist, all this is changed. Magnificent ocean-ferries ply semi-weekly between the British ports and the principal seaboard cities of the Dominion . . . Steamer, railway, and stagecoach companies vie with each other in providing the readiest, cheapest, and most expeditious means of locomotion. Hotels are numerous and excellent . . . The eight or ten weeks' journey in a timber barque or coal-ballasted brig and merchandise-freighted propeller through the St. Lawrence and Great Lakes to Sarnia or Detroit has become a pleasure tour of at most a fortnight; and the six or twelve months' trip of '49 or '50 is now a pleasant holiday excursion, a profitable way of passing the London "silly season" or the "Long Vacation."
—*Handbook to Canada: a Guide for Travellers and Settlers* (1881)

*T*he Saguenay, the "Great River of Canada" as it was known, was to the nineteenth-century middle-class excursionist what the St. Lawrence River had been for earlier vacationers – a delightful water journey into the heartland of Canada. In the case of the Saguenay, the venture took in the towns from Tadoussac to Chicoutimi, passed Capes Trinity and Eternity, and reached into Lac St. Jean itself (see Figure 1.2, map 3, page 13). With the extension of industrialization along the St. Lawrence and into the tributaries of the St. Maurice and Saguenay, the Lower St. Lawrence region was becoming an extension of Canada's industrial heartland. Yet in addition to the commercial potential of the region in this period, there was sufficient natural beauty to attract a stream of Canadian and overseas excursionists. They came to admire the precipitous hillsides, the chasms and gorges of the blue-capped mountains on the north side of the St. Lawrence. In parts of the south side, they witnessed the less aggressive pastoral charm of towns, churches, streams, convents, and windmills that provided the perfect contrast for the lived experience of the picturesque and sublime.

The accounts, the pictures, and the poetry of the region were also evidence of a profound geographical mapping of the mind onto the landscape in this period. Far from being the idyll depicted in the various discursive and pictorial representations, the Lower St. Lawrence region was fast becoming a locus of activity for the Canadian logging industry. Thus, it is important both to bear in mind the selective interpretation of the landscape by artists of the period and to investigate this representation of the region in pictorial form to gain a better understanding of what the region meant to the nineteenth-century excursionist.

The painting *Sunrise on the Saguenay* of 1880 by Lucius O'Brien, first president of the Royal Canadian Academy, provides an excellent opportunity to study the relationship between the geographical landscape and the full pictorial rendition of the sublime landscape in nineteenth-century Canada. Not only was this painting celebrated in its time as an example of the virtuosity achievable in the pictorial arts, but it was also recognized for its historical position as one of the finest works in the academy's diploma collection. Indeed, it was selected to form part of the nucleus of the academy's collection at the founding of that organization and was granted place of honour over the speaker's podium at the formal opening in 1881. The governor general, senior officials of the Canadian government, Ottawa's society elite, and academicians all toasted the opening of Canada's first national academy and listened to the tunes of "Scotland the Brave" and "Kunstler Leben" beneath O'Brien's scene of the Saguenay.

More was happening here. Despite the picture's prominence and status among Canadian artworks, there was no extended discussion of this painting.

Lucius R. O'Brien, *Sunrise on the Saguenay*, 1880, oil on canvas, 90 x 127 cm, National Gallery of Canada.

This lacuna in the historical discourse must come as a surprise, and yet it is reflective of the rudimentary status of art criticism at the time. It is necessary therefore that we look more deeply into the period, to the physical geography of

The First Exhibition of the Canadian Academy of Arts, *Canadian Illustrated News*, 24 April 1880, National Archives of Canada, C-72968.

the Saguenay, to the lives and times of the painters, and to the expository and literary accounts of the region in order to come closer to what it might mean to picture the picturesque in the nineteenth century.

Raymond Williams has probably provided the most cogent framework for an understanding of the global transformations of town-country relations in the nineteenth century. His renowned *The Country and the City* (Williams 1973) examined how during the nineteenth century the division of labour within a single state became increasingly international (this process had already been visible since the establishment of modern forms of colonial government in the seventeenth century). What had been the relations between villages and towns and then towns and cities became extended to the relations between colonial producers and their local and distant metropolitan markets. Williams makes the point that although we think of landscape painting as a long tradition, as a tradition of painting views that are pleasing to the eye, this convention really only emerged in the late eighteenth century. "Landscape" as a word had no earlier usage than 1602, when it was used to describe topographical landscapes (Williams 1973, 279–87).

For our purposes here, Williams's observations about the globalization of metropolitan relations and the emergence of landscape painting as a convention in roughly the same period may be linked with an analysis of the picturesque tradition. It is no coincidence that landscape painting coincided with the grand tours of a gentrified elite to the various centres of classical antiquity. One would presume some relation therefore between this new international travel and the emergence of the picturesque aesthetic of the eighteenth and nineteenth centuries. Certainly the travels of the Hudson River School of painters from their urban studios in Philadelphia up the Hudson River into the White Mountains (and by the 1880s as far afield as Quebec) must indicate that the picturesque was more than a quest for nice scenery. Here were painters travelling the newly extended rail lines into the industrializing landscape searching for the remaining splendid forests and mountains, and selectively translating them into idyllic scenes of a natural America.

This landscape painting phenomenon was international in dimension. In Australia the discovery and development of the Victoria goldfields in 1850 made possible the patronage of a landscape tradition that provided the foundation for a group of painters known as the Heidelberg School in the 1880s. A similar phenomenon occurred in New Zealand, where landscape art emerged in a popular form among the middle classes. In South Africa the imperial context was still operating and influencing the landscape tradition. Each case serves to illustrate and support Williams's thesis about the internationalization of the division of labour and the concomitant expansion of social relations into this international context through the expansion of imperial trade relations.

The Canadian context for these activities is of particular significance. Here the background and biography of Lucius O'Brien is especially revealing, for his life story and his painterly transformations of the countryside demonstrate the psychological profile of a mind familiar with the environment of nineteenth-century Canada. Lucius O'Brien, as representative of many senior academicians of his day, came to painting through the more commercially viable career of surveying. As a former land and rail surveyor, O'Brien not only had an eye for drawing, but a precise and informed knowledge of geological formations, geographic contours, patterns of vegetation and agricultural growth, the industrial potential of a region, and the impact of transportation on a region. He had, as well, a sharp eye for the geography of industrial conurbations, habitant cottages, small hamlets, and larger towns that dotted the Lower St. Lawrence region. In other words, O'Brien's first professional vocation provided him with all the skills of observation needed for a painter of the landscape.

Lucius Richard O'Brien (1832–99) was an archetypical first-generation Canadian gentleman artist born to an immigrant family who turned his attention to art following a successful career as a surveyor. O'Brien's father, Edward George O'Brien, a half-pay retired British army officer, left his castle in County Clare, Ireland, following the Napoleonic Wars to take up land on one of the preferred land grants given by the colonial government. He and his wife, Mary Sophia (née Gapper), established a farm at Shanty Bay in Simcoe County, oversaw the settlement of the region, and then expanded their property holdings into industrial development in Orillia. With their background, the family was well acquainted with cultural pursuits. Mary O'Brien, not unlike Susanna Moodie, kept lively diary accounts of their settlement in Simcoe County and advanced the arts of poetry and watercolour painting in the region.

The O'Briens raised three sons in the tradition of the young English gentleman. The first son, Lieutenant-Colonel William Edward O'Brien, was called to the bar in 1874, although he later chose to enter farm life and public life with his father. The youngest son, Henry, was also called to the bar in 1861 and is best known as editor of *O'Brien's Division Courts Manual*, the *Canadian Law Journal*, and *Harrison and O'Brien's Digest of Ontario Reports*. Lucius Richard O'Brien, the middle son of the family, prepared for a career in surveying and engineering following his education at Upper Canada College. With the expansion of railway development and settlement during the 1850s, O'Brien charted a successful career as a professional surveyor. In addition to these activities, he managed one of the family's stone quarries in Orillia and held public office as reeve of Orillia in 1859. By 1870 Lucius O'Brien moved permanently to Toronto, where he lived on his savings and investments in a Canadian wine importing business. He took early retirement from business and surveying at the age of forty, as was the custom among gentlemen in nineteenth-century Canada, and turned his leisurely pursuit of painting into a full-time occupation, thus becoming one of the leading artists and patrons of his day.

It was in the context of his acquaintance with Governor General Dufferin (a distant relation of the O'Briens) that Lucius O'Brien came to be painting the Saguenay region in 1879, for it appears that O'Brien accompanied or at least visited the governor general on his vice-regal tour of the region. *Sunrise on the*

Saguenay was one of several paintings that O'Brien produced during three summer trips to Quebec between 1878 and 1880. Although this was not a commissioned painting, it coincided with a series of works for patrons, including *Northern Head of Grand Manan* (1878) for George Brown, *View from the King's Bastion, Quebec* for Windsor Castle, and *Quebec from Point Levis* for the Queen's summer home (Osborne House) on the Isle of Wight. *Sunrise on the Saguenay* is therefore representative of O'Brien's work during the height of his career as a professional artist and holds special significance because of its place in the National Gallery's diploma collection.

O'Brien's painting of Cape Trinity on the Saguenay River captures the geographical site in all its splendour. The work depicts the soaring 450-metre bluffs of granite and gneiss forming the cape, with its three-tiered formation (thus its name Trinity) rising clearly out of the bay. The bluff is one of two promontories flanking the south bank of the Saguenay at this point in the river's course, three-quarters of the way between Lac St. Jean and Tadoussac at the mouth of the river. The other promontory, Cape Eternity, stands on the east side of Eternity Bay. O'Brien's view is therefore painted from within Eternity Bay facing the bluffs and looking almost north, with the rising sun towards the right of the picture. The blue-capped mountains of the Laurentians are seen in the distance. Included in the scene are assorted leisure boats and steamers nestled on the luminous calm of the waters at sunrise. A mist rises from the river, casting a hue over the cliff walls, wrapping the top of the cliffs in mystery.

This picture of the Saguenay is of particular interest for the time period in which it was created. The region had grown tremendously in popularity at the time of this depiction. This was the favourite resort area of the governors general of Canada and of urban trekkers from Quebec City and Toronto, and it was fast becoming a major centre for the commercial excursion trade. Guidebooks dating to the 1850s described three-day excursions from Quebec City down the St. Lawrence to the Saguenay River, then to the Gaspé and up to the St. Maurice River. They gave accounts of trips up the Saguenay River past the two capes and beyond into Lac St. Jean. Travellers were even serviced by holiday hotels along the banks of the river in areas adjacent to the small towns of Tadoussac and Chicoutimi. From the 1870s these travellers were assisted further by the improvement in road networks and partial rail links into the area so that by 1879 tourism had virtually exploded in the region:

> Four times a week in the summer months steamers freighted with holiday-makers and tourists leave Quebec for Tadoussac and Chicoutimi, touching at the various places between these points. To look at the piles of baggage and furniture, the hosts of children and servants, the household gods [*sic*], the dogs, cats and birds, one might think the Canadians were emigrating *en masse,* like the *seigneurs* and their families after the cession of the country to England. But these travellers have a happier destiny than had those who sailed in the Auguste, shipwrecked on Cape

Breton in November, 1762. Murray Bay and its adjoining villages are
the resort of those who want grand scenery, and a quiet country life
with a spice of gaiety. Many families have their own pretty country
houses, but a favourite plan is to take a *habitant's* cottage just as it
stands, and to play at "roughing it" with all the luxuries you care to add
to the ragmatted floors and primitive furniture. Those who want more
excitement find it at the hotels, where in the evening there is always a
dance, a concert, or private theatricals, to wind up a day spent in
bathing, picnicking, boating, driving, trout-fishing, tennis, bowling,
billiards, and a dozen other amusements. It is a merry life and a healthy
one; you live as you please, and do as you please, and nobody says you
nay. (Grant and Fleming 1882)

Yet far from being a picturesque idyll, the Saguenay was on the verge of
becoming one of Quebec's industrial enterprise zones of the late nineteenth
century. The Saguenay River valley, along with the St. Maurice valley, formed
the basis of Canada's logging industry, covering some 260,000 square kilometres
of dense forest. Since the 1860s, the lumber industry had begun to penetrate the
region with sawmills located in Tadoussac, Chicoutimi, and the Lac St. Jean
region. Statistics issued by the Department of Agriculture indicated that since
1850 an estimated $180,000 worth of wood had been exported from this region
to Europe yearly, with a total of 43,289 logs of white pine alone descending the
Saguenay bound for Quebec in the year 1862. Crucial to the further exploitation
of the natural resources in the region was the development of direct rail access
through the heartland of the logging valleys 290 kilometres from Quebec City.
This project occupied rail industrialists from the early 1860s until the route's
completion in the late nineteenth century as they charted through the intermediate mountain ranges. Lumbering was a major Canadian activity, being not only
the principal supply of wood for the British navy but the staple product for
Canada's own industrialization as a primary building material and fuel. In 1879
the Department of Agriculture issued its first handbook on the region. Entitled
*Le Saguenay et le Lac St. Jean: Ressources et Advantages qu'ils offrent aux Colons
et aux Capitalistes,* it promoted the homesteading and industrial advantages of
the area.

Indeed, around the time of Lucius O'Brien's sketching trip along the Saguenay
in preparation for *Sunrise on the Saguenay,* human intervention in the region was
at a high. The federal government's Department of Public Works embarked on a
dredging operation as part of its waterways improvement scheme, and fires
ravaged the valley, destroying stands of pine, denuding many of the mountains,
closing some of the lumber industry, and filling the valley with a choking smoke.
One traveller observed:

There is no rich foliage; forest fires have swept and blackened the hill
tops; a scanty growth of sombre firs and slender birches replaces the

lordly pines that once crowned the heights, and struggles for a foothold along the sides of the ravines and on the ledges of the cliffs, where the naked rock shows through the tops of the trees. (Creighton 1882)

All was not serene and tranquil on the banks and river of the Saguenay in the summer of 1879.

Lucius O'Brien's painting *Sunrise on the Saguenay* must be seen therefore as an indelibly romantic interpretation of the sights and activities of the Saguenay region. The Turneresque borrowings are evident in the selection of subject matter, theme, and execution. O'Brien has selected his subject matter at its most resplendent, before the rising mist of the morning sun. A violet pink hue pervades the work at this moment of dawn; the water rests luminous upon the bay and a hazy light radiates from the partially revealed sun. In the foreground a yacht with several rowboats is safely harboured with two men aboard, two men are quietly rowing on the nearby water, and in the distance a schooner in full sail is silhouetted alongside a steamboat. One is reminded of Turner's *The Fighting Temeraire,* the representation of the past era of sail giving way before the new age of steam. Here one imagines a somewhat more peaceful version of the *Temeraire,* with a gentle co-existence of the two ages displayed respectively in the distance. This then was the ideology of romanticism. The work is an almost perfect pictorial translation of the Reverend William Gilpin's description of the picturesque:

> Mark each floating cloud; its form
> Its varied colour; and what mass of shade
> It gives the scene below, pregnant with change
> Perpetual, from the morning's purple dawn,
> Till the last glimm-'ring ray of russet eve.
> Mark how the sun-beam, steep'd in morning dew,
> Beneath each jutting promontory flings
> A darker shade, while brighten'd with the ray
> Of sultry moon, not yet entirely quench'd
> The evening-shadow less opaquely falls.
>
> (Gilpin 1794)

In almost every respect then, *Sunrise on the Saguenay* is a fitting testimony to the romantic era.

A closer observation of the painting, in conjunction with the archival records of the vicinity, enlightens us to the transformations the artist has made to the geographic site. The most striking studio alterations have been performed on the foreground in order to circumscribe the compositional features of the picturesque formula. In place of the naturally arranged grass, rocks, and bullrushes at the site, O'Brien has arranged a delicate mixture of deciduous foliage, rock, and sandy beach. Structurally this studio artifice serves to attract the eye centrally

Anonymous, *Yacht in Full Sail, in Eternity Bay, P.Q.,* National Photography Collection, National Archives of Canada, PA-8716.

within the composition and within the picture plane. The diagonal branch projecting across the foreground reflection of sunlight counterbalances the monster bluffs in the left middle ground. The centre boulder has been introduced to secure the eye to the left side of the composition beneath the bluffs and to prevent the eye from wandering over the water and across the river to the extreme right. By securing the eye in this way, O'Brien is attempting to strike a balanced composition and to create a sense of the sublime scale of the bluffs in comparison with the small boats and the people in the bay; hence he offers the grandeur and sublimity of nature.

In addition to altering nature's composition for the pictorial effect, O'Brien has also projected Gilpin's prescriptions for picturesque subject matter onto the work. Gilpin rejected industry as a basis for the picturesque in painting, and accordingly O'Brien has tempered any signs of the industry in the valley. The continual stream of boom-tugs described in tourist literature and captured by amateur photographers, the presence of log jams at the height of industrial production in the summer, the dredgers of the Department of Public Works' waterways scheme, the smoke and fire from the conflagrations of that summer are all absent from O'Brien's work. Instead we see the dignified promenade of boats and men upon a restful and perfect scene. The three different kinds of boats are in fact identifiable with the tourist trade. In the foreground there is the popular nineteenth-century wood-burning steam-assisted yacht towing several rowboats. This type of yacht and its full-sail counterpart were commonly used by holiday makers on the Saguenay. The larger schooner in full sail silhouetted in the rising sun is the more exclusive leisure craft of the governor general or some other prominent traveller, and the adjacent steam tug is a regular industrial and tourist boat that plied the river in the summer. These leisure craft, then, are the only signs of modernity in the painting.

To secure further the meaning of the romantic tradition as it was applied in this painting and as it represents a profound geographical mapping of the mind, it is necessary to look more closely at the concrete links between O'Brien's picturing and the aesthetics of the tourist trade in his day. Not surprisingly, given the chronology of the art work, a version of *Sunrise on the Saguenay* was quickly incorporated into the pages of one of Canada's important picturesque travel publications, entitled *Picturesque Canada*. Lucius O'Brien served as the journal's art editor during its brief period of publication and oversaw the illustration of various Canadian scenes within its pages. This publication, centring on a popular middle-class sentiment of the picturesque, echoed similar publications in Britain and throughout the "new worlds." In Britain the new leisure travel into the provinces resulted in publications such as *Picturesque Scenery of Norfolk* (1810–11), *Picturesque Scenery in Sussex* (1821), and *Picturesque Excursions in Devonshire and Cornwall* (1804). As industrial development expanded the transportation networks in the new world, more picturesque publications emerged in the English language: *Picturesque America, Picturesque Australasia,* and *Picturesque Europe.* Each of these publications emphasized the picturesque scenic aspects of the regions under consideration as well as introducing topical concerns about protection of the countryside against the ravages of industry. *Picturesque Canada* was produced for a professional readership in the metropolitan centres of Central Canada, and its editor, George Monro Grant, was a leading reformer in the early social gospel movement. This framework provides us with some basis on which to interpret the picturesque as an aesthetic.

Under Grant's editorial stewardship, *Picturesque Canada* came to embody a conservation philosophy. The romantic yearning for a pre-industrial or pastoral past in Canada had its origins, like the reform movement, in the industrial era. One of the principal tenets of the movement was the belief that, because of the devastation of the land and the accompanying loss of farm land, industrial development could not proceed unchecked. Underlying this concern was a somewhat romantic conception included in the subtitle *The Country As It Was and Is,* suggesting the structural historical alterations that were occurring on the land. The editorial policy set out explicitly to record picturesque scenes associated with a rural past before the ravages of industry.

The primeval beauty of the Old World of Canada, the quaint charm, and the picturesque incidents that gathered round the life of the primitive French and English settlers, are gradually vanishing before the rapid strides of its modern prosperity. It is the design of the authors of PICTURESQUE CANADA to record them permanently here, so that this

volume, presenting an elaborate, faithful and most artistic picture
of "Canada as it is" in this transition period of her history, and a
complete account of the Dominion to the present day, may become a
precious heirloom in the near future of the greatest colony in the Empire. (Grant 1882)

Although the articles in *Picturesque Canada* seldom expressed direct views
on politics, one article on lumbering by Grant and A. Fleming concluded:

Replanting has been suggested to counterbalance the loss (of trees)
caused by fires and reckless cutting. Such a remedy is practically
impossible . . .

One or two measures may be suggested. The Government should,
by a commission of experts and scientific men, take stock of our forest
wealth. This done, the annual increment presented to us by Nature
could be estimated. And then, on no account, should more than this
increment be cut in any year . . . Our form of government makes it
difficult to pass or enforce laws to curb greed. But the call for immediate action is loud . . .

We owe much of our wealth and development to the lumber trade.
It has been one of the greatest instruments of our self-expression during
the past forty years. But the anxieties for a nation's future increase with
increasing wealth and population. Civilized men cannot live in a fool's
Paradise of the present. (Grant and Fleming 1882)

The reference to taking stock of the forest wealth suggests the authors' knowledge of efforts by scientific men such as G.M. Dawson in the documenting of
timber wealth in 1879.

Further features of the picturesque and sublime linked the aesthetic with a
response to the new industrial era. In the absence of the historic association of
the picturesque in Canada (castles, ruins, etc.), writers and artists drew on a
heavily encoded system of references to earlier periods of settlement. The *ancien
régime* was one such period recalled in purely romantic visage. *Picturesque Canada*
included some pictures of devout *habitants*, resilient woodsmen, and physiogno-
mies of characteristic settlers. In the article accompanying O'Brien's illustration
of Cape Trinity, there was an extended description of the rural life and mytholo-
gies of the local settlers, the physical structure of the geography and settlements,
a picturesque description of the region, and historical accounts of the discovery
and human development of the Saguenay (Creighton 1882, 697–740). This,
then, was not a publication for the plebian traveller but a professional presentation of a developed aesthetic for the experienced traveller.

The aesthetic was certainly shared by the passengers of the commercial
tourist trade to the Saguenay, but as Creighton stated clearly in his article on the
Lower St. Lawrence region, "Our way lies not among, though perforce to some

extent with the tourist" (Creighton 1882). Two years after its exhibition at the
Royal Canadian Academy opening, *Sunrise on the Saguenay* was reproduced
under its geographic title *Cape Trinity* within the pages of this picturesque
publication. Apart from changes to accommodate the different medium
(the omission of two birds, the rowboat with two oarsmen and a dinghy, the
recomposition of the foreground, and the omission of the mist), the reproduction of this painting found its place comfortably within the aesthetic of
the publication.

   Given the physical geography of the Saguenay region and the real development of the region for the logging industry, there emerged an elaborate discourse
of the picturesque that prefigures the transformation of the region with a mental
remapping of the land. Whether we examine the expository discourse of the
government's Department of Agriculture, the tourist brochures, or the artistic
and literary discourses of the day, all sources indicate that *Sunrise on the Saguenay*
was the product of a profound psychological remapping of the land into pictorial
form. The Saguenay was hardly the picturesque idyll presented to us in O'Brien's
diploma painting. Rather it was the centre of a public debate on the development
of Canada's wilderness landscape and a battle over the use of natural resources by
contending pressures of industry, agriculture, leisure, and conservation forces.
The painting's pictorial rendition of the region demonstrates the values and
concerns of a painter faced with the transformation of the region and asserts a
harmonious, dignified, and sublime relation between humans, modernity, and

W.J. Redding after Lucius R. O'Brien, *Cape Trinity,* wood engraving, from *Picturesque Canada*
(1882), vol. 2, National Archives of Canada, C-85482.

natural forces. This ability to picture harmony in an age marked by industrial strife, political controversy, and social upheaval is testimony to the romantic yearning that is spawned under conditions of change.

In the international context, *Sunrise on the Saguenay* may be seen as the counterpart to John Constable's work in Britain, to the painting of the Barbizon school in France, and to that of the Hudson River School in the United States. While the work is clearly the product of a specific lived experience in Canadian history, the painting is also the product of greater world forces, those in the internationalization of the division of labour. As the model of city and country in economic and political relationships extended beyond the boundaries of the nation-state into the realm of a world model known as imperialism, we see the concomitant transformation of social and cultural activity around the world. In Canada this emerges in the form of a landscape tradition in the nineteenth century, a tradition premised on the understanding that nature is something to be interpreted and represented in the face of permanent historical alterations to the natural geography. Lucius O'Brien's work emerges as a hallmark of this new era, with *Sunrise on the Saguenay* serving as its insignia at the crossroads of new activity in the arena of industry, tourism, and leisure. Through this painting, we can perhaps better appreciate the profound forces at work upon the human psyche as the individual struggles in the act of creation before an increasingly complex world. Using the existing artistic traditions of his day, Lucius O'Brien renders a scene of tranquillity, balancing all of the forces before him into a pictorial example of the picturesque. It is only through the recalling of archival sources then that we are able to understand precisely how profound an interpretation has been worked in the creation of such a scene and what it may have meant to picture the picturesque in nineteenth-century Canada.

REFERENCES

Creighton, J.G.A. 1882. "The Lower St. Lawrence and the Saguenay." *Picturesque Canada* 2:720.

Gilpin, Reverend William. 1794. *Three Essays: on Picturesque Beauty: on Picturesque Travel; and on Sketching Landscape: to which is added a Poem on Landscape Painting.* London: R. Blamire.

Grant, George, ed. 1882. *Picturesque Canada* 1, inside front cover.

Grant, George, and A. Fleming. 1882. "Lumbering." *Picturesque Canada* 2:237–38.

Reid, Dennis. *Lucius R. O'Brien: Visions of Victorian Canada.* Toronto: Art Gallery of Ontario, 1990.

Williams, Raymond. 1973. *The Country and the City.* New York: Oxford University Press.

14

Revisioning the Roman Catholic Environment: Geographical Attitudes in Gabrielle Roy's *The Cashier*

Jamie S. Scott

Several commentators have noticed how Gabrielle Roy's fiction may be read as a varied, but sustained, effort to locate hospitable places for a French Canadian world within the northern land.[1] For the most part, French Canada is a Roman Catholic world, although the geography of Roy's fiction varies. We have the urban settings of *The Tin Flute*. *Where Nests the Water Hen* offers us a simple life in harmony with nature on a small island in Manitoba. Other works draw upon contrasts between different environments. As barely disguised autobiography, *Street of Riches* and *The Road Past Altamont* explore tensions between childhood in Manitoba and adulthood in Quebec. In a different vein, *The Hidden Mountain* celebrates the inner quest of the artist in terms of geographical variations among the Canadian northlands and the French countryside, Montreal and Paris.

Despite these geographical variations, however, the Roman Catholic world of Roy's oeuvre is characterized by a recurrent theme. Frequently, her writings have been interpreted in terms of a dialectical interplay between things rural and things urban. Ellen Ramsay and Paula Kestelman find similar antimonies in certain Quebec paintings. In Roy's work, this opposition between the country and the city has been understood in terms of innocence and experience, the ideal and the real, male and female, and the contrasting values of rural and urban communities.[2] But different critical vocabularies have led commentators to similar conclusions. Let one commentator speak for all: "It seems as though many of Roy's protagonists – both female and male – need to return to the country prior to death and then back to the city in order to die in an enclosed space, before eternally returning into open nature" (Lewis 1985, 78). Just as Malcolm Lowry condemns the dehumanizing capitalism of urban Vancouver, as Douglas Porteous notes, so in Roy's fiction the enclosed spaces of the urban environment alienate us from ourselves and from one another. But in her revisioning of the Roman

Catholic world of French Canada, Roy also makes it clear that we may recover
an inward sense of personal freedom and an outward sense of human community by returning to the natural environment.

In focusing on *The Cashier*, this paper returns to the opposition of things
rural and things urban, but from a different perspective. Most commentators
interpret the geographical in Roy's fiction in terms of the temporal development
of plot and character. Rhetorical variations in tone and mood are subsumed
under the image of time. While not ignoring temporal questions, this paper
approaches the text as a configuration of geographical points of view. We may
consider point of view as an "evaluative" or "ideological" position, as a "perceptual" or "psychological" position, or as a "literal" or "spatio-temporal" position
of the narrator.[3] These three planes of signification are rarely discrete; the literal,
psychological, and ideological interpenetrate. Whatever the role of tone and
mood in the temporal development of plot and character, the text thus embodies
overlapping and criss-crossing planes of signification. Two advantages result
from our adapting this approach for an analysis of geographical attitudes in *The
Cashier*. First, by distinguishing between author and narrator, we do not reduce
the text's rich perspectivalism to the supposed perspective of a single author.[4]
We gain a more nuanced picture of the relationship between rural and urban
environments. Secondly, we shall discover that Roy's ironic use of the structures
of Roman Catholic ideology offers a framework for mediating, though not
dissolving, contradictory attitudes towards rural and urban environments.

The Cashier consists of three parts of unequal length. In each part, we may
find instances of literal and perceptual attitudes towards geographical objects.
The first part takes place in the city of Montreal. We meet Alexandre Chenevert,
whose name, significantly, as we shall see, means "green oak." He is a teller at
"Branch J of the Savings Bank of the City and Island of Montreal."[5] One of the
most obvious intrusions of the narrator's point of view occurs just after Chenevert
discovers his till is short $100. Exhausted psychologically, Chenevert decides to
quit. But his boss, Monsieur Fontaine, persuades him to pay back the money in
regular pay deductions and to see a doctor about taking a break. The bank will
recover its $100, but Chenevert will have to find extra work to make up the lost
income. The narrator intrudes:

> Perhaps in no other city is spring so springlike as in Montreal. Else-
> where it lacks the overbearing cold, five long months of frost and snow,
> and in most cases, too, the blazing summer which here will follow right
> on winter's heels. Elsewhere it lacks this violence, this brutal harshness
> which, by the contrast they afford, lend springtime in Montreal its
> lovely power.
>   Here are a few, a very few, days of wonder.
>   Perhaps this night alone, and it will be over.

And so it happens that here spring makes people kind.

There is so little spring.

Strange fragile links are forged between men in the city; suddenly their tongues are loosened and their faces grow cheerful. (68)

In tone and mood, these lines bear little or no relation to what is going on in Chenevert's life. While the protagonist of *The Cashier* flounders, the narrator celebrates the human communion forged by the coming of spring to the city. This divergence indicates the journey Chenevert must travel, both inwardly and in outward physical terms.

The first part of *The Cashier* also provides us with instances of Chenevert's perceptual attitudes towards geographical objects. On this plane, we find a greater degree of ambiguity than on the spatio-temporal plane of the narrator's point of view. We learn Chenevert cannot sleep, but in his daydreams he travels the world. In the first few pages we find him in Yugoslavia, Russia, North and South America, India, Italy, Switzerland, France, Germany, Palestine, China, and Japan. In his mind, Chenevert recapitulates the journeys of an archetypal geographer, as he maps out the world in terms of the conflicts and conquests of nations. But Chenevert does not travel in the service of kings and colonists. The ceaseless bombardment of newspaper and radio headlines forces him to the four corners of the world, yet Chenevert is sealed antiseptically within a "little kitchen as clean, white, and dismal as a room in a hospital" (20). Chenevert's "impatient heart set forth somehow to span the globe," but the city demands his presence, as streetcars and car horns herald every coming day (21). Spatial contrasts sum up the ambiguities of Chenevert's life in the city, as he drags "himself from the bank to the North-Western Lunch; from the cafeteria to his cage; from there to the Boulevard St.-Laurent – a tiny little round which demanded more exertion, involved greater fatigue than circling the whole globe" (76–77). Yet walking around the city, Chenevert meets the world's people: "If he did not travel, at least he caught glimpses of other races – the overflow from too densely peopled lands" (77). In another vein, Chenevert briefly imagines escaping to "a deep forest," but the rural and the urban ironically conflate, as he likens the "day's work" to "a barren mountain" (29). "How could he ever climb over it if he could not succeed in sleeping at least for one hour?" (29). Later, relieved at Fontaine's solution to the problem of the missing $100, Chenevert sees the city transformed. But illusory dreams of an unattainable paradise skew his perception:

There remained a strip of light above the ridge of houses, like a sandy beach above the flat roofs and shoddy signs: to be more precise, like the coral island, his Pacific island where, could he only reach it, Alexandre imagined that he might make good his manhood. (67)

Likewise, Chenevert's perception of rural Quebec is distorted. Reading the advertisements for rental cabins, he imagines "simple old Indians passing in single file along this shady forest highway, bows and arrows hanging from their backs" (110).

In the second part of *The Cashier*, the point of view of the narrator and that of the protagonist interpenetrate in a more intricate way. The scene has moved to rural Quebec, north of Montreal, but the picture is complicated by implicit contrasts with the city. Following Fontaine's advice, Chenevert sees a doctor. Dr. Hudon recommends "a change of scene . . . a visit to the country" (106). In the events that follow, variations in tone and mood enable the narrator to reveal variations in the effects of the natural environment upon Chenevert. At first, the cabin he has rented seems too small, the open spaces of the natural environment too intimidating:

> The sun was on its way down; over the most distant vista of the lake it cast a showery glow, sulphur yellow and purple. Elsewhere the sky was suffused with a diminished light just sufficient to illumine the woods which enclosed this wild bit of countryside. Over all reigned a silence that long held Alexandre captive. The peace of the valley smote him like a reproach. Vain was your restlessness, without purpose your anguish, without merit your suffering, all of it a useless sad silence to this spent man. And besides, have you really suffered? nature asked him. (116–17)

Here the narrator speaks through nature to disclose Chenevert's point of view. "He felt that in all the world there was no man more naked" (117). As alienated here as in the city, Chenevert is quick to get rid of his host, the farmer Monsieur Gardeur, the "tender" of the natural environment (119).

Yet the natural environment begins to work a different effect on Chenevert. Nature's intimidation becomes nature's indifference. "In all his life nothing had ever made him feel so alone as this landscape so deeply at peace and foreign, in its way, to his cares as a human being" (119). But the indifference of the natural environment forces Chenevert to revise his attitude towards the city. He begins to see that what he took for solitude in the city was in fact alienation from his own inward self and from others. Alienation thus implies the possibility of urban community. The indifference of nature permits Chenevert to sleep, and he recovers the careless innocence of childhood. There follows "the most beautiful day of his life" (125). Against the backdrop of nature's indifference, Chenevert recognizes that "the most trifling invention . . . here bore witness to man's brotherhood" (129). "Bits of human explanation, wrested from this overwhelming universe, warmed his soul" (129). Inwardly rejuvenated, Chenevert feels a new sense of companionship, a fresh need to share his joy with others. In Montreal he had hated the pesky dog barking in the apartment next door, but when Gardeur's dog visits his cabin, Chenevert confides: "We're always a bit more at our ease when there are two of us" (132). Soon after, he is reconciled with the farmer and his family, who, in their rural innocence, had blamed themselves for being inhospitable, rather than imagining Chenevert impolite and ungrateful for their hospitality. Brought up in the urban environment, Chenevert may never settle in the country. The thought of slaughtering his own meat makes him shudder. At the same time, however, the rural environment represents something more important: "That was not the big point. What mattered was that Lac Vert should exist, and that Alexandre should have seen it with his own eyes. Later on it would always remain his property. To believe in an earthly paradise – that was what he had so deeply needed" (137). This realization enables Chenevert to enter into communion with Gardeur and his family. He is capable of sympathy with his fellow human beings because inwardly he is at peace with himself.

Gardeur's attitude towards the natural environment structurally parallels the attitude of Dr. Hudon towards the urban environment. Both are at home in their different environments. But unlike Dr. Hudon and Gardeur, Chenevert has yet to feel at home in either environment. We have seen how a sense of self-alienation and alienation from others drove Chenevert away from Montreal to rural Quebec. Now he "began to get bored at Lac Vert" (147). He could not live in rural Quebec, centring his "life on meaningless activities – bringing in wood, warming up . . . food, and day after day going through the same tedious drudgery to get water" (148). At the same time, however, this insight reawakens Chenevert's longing for Montreal:

> There, on that evening, Alexandre found the city again. In place of the dusky banks, he perceived the swarm of lights by which cities reveal themselves in the fullness of the night. Homesickness for the crowded nights there, for the intermeshed lives, startled him, more compelling than any longing he had ever felt in all his days, like a longing for eternity. (149)

If time is an image of eternity, here the city becomes an image of the Kingdom of God. Neither the traditional environment of rural Quebec nor the alienating environment of a city satisfies Chenevert's yearning. What he gains from a visit to the country is a renewed sense of community with which to remake the city into a human world. Exposed to the peace and harmony of the natural environment, Chenevert recovers a sense of the oneness of humanity: "In one brief and glorious instant Alexandre had received the revelation that here at Lac Vert men, more even than God Himself, were his constant helpmeets and supports" (144).

Talk of the city as an image of the Kingdom of God brings us to the ideological plane of signification. In the third part of *The Cashier*, the ambiguities arising out of the interplay between the literal and the perceptual planes of signification are finally mediated, though not dissolved, on the ideological plane. "This level is least accessible to formalization, for its analysis relies, to a degree, on intuitive understanding" (Uspensky 1973, 8). The ideological point of view may be that of the author, that of the narrator, that of the protagonist, or some interplay among any or all of these factors in any given text. "The deep compositional structure" of *The Cashier,* however, comes to expression as a revisioning of Roman Catholic attitudes towards rural and urban environments (Uspensky 1973, 8). In the first part of the book, we have seen how the narrator wonders at the communion among people in the city in spring, though Chenevert "knew nothing of it" (69). Rather, the city alienates the teller from himself, from his family, from his friends, and from his customers at the bank. Yet we find Chenevert heading off to work wondering, "Would the Kingdom of God one day be established on earth? Or would it be only in another world that men would no longer do evil to one another?" (30). Later, the North-Western Lunch reminds Chenevert of the Last Judgment, which he imagines in spatial terms: "The crowding into the Valley of Josaphat: all the earth's queues, the patient waiting lines of all the ages, were stretched out, one after the other, doubling back on themselves like mountain roads, a procession to destroy all respect for human life" (42). The attitudes of the narrator and Chenevert interpenetrate in these instances of ideological rhetoric, yet the ideological rhetoric itself suggests the possibility of a mediation between them. This possibility is expressed through the narrator's privileged insight into Dr. Hudon's point of view. The doctor is a figure of care in the city. For Dr. Hudon, Chenevert's "name, indeed, was legion," with all the demoniac associations which that name conjures up from biblical sources:

> Every morning at a set hour he walked down a thousand staircases at once, running from every corner of the city toward bulging streetcars. He crowded into them by the hundreds and thousands. From tram to tram, from street to street, you could see him standing in public conveyances, his hands slipped through leather straps, his arms stretched in a curious likeness to a prisoner at the whipping post. (102)

Reminiscent of the whipping of Christ, this image of life in the city casts commuters as lost souls, and Dr. Hudon as a prophet of salvation. "There came over him a burning desire to save this man – with or against the will of God he knew not" (108).

As we have seen, Dr. Hudon recommends that Chenevert take a vacation in the country. In the second part of *The Cashier,* the ideological rhetoric mediates the ambiguities arising out of the interplay between the narrator's attitude towards the natural environment and that of Chenevert. The fact that on his first night Chenevert sleeps less in the country than in the city indicates that "here God reigned in his most ambiguous aspect" (121). Yet within three days, solitude in nature frees Chenevert "from God and from men" (123). Then he develops a sense of God's presence "seeping through the valley" (126). The natural environment is a sign of divine providence, "a gift from heaven" (128). Spiritually revitalized, Chenevert captures the cultural, natural, and providential dimensions of his world in a phrase: "my cabin, my lake, my God" (130). In the city,

Dr. Hudon had not known whether or not to save Chenevert in the name of God; in the country, Gardeur speaks of the bounty of nature in traditional religious terms: "What I say is, the good Lord piles it on" (135). Chenevert is delighted at the fecundity of nature – fish, moose, berries, fowl, firewood. "The good Lord has been generous to the Canadians," he says (137).

A changed man, Chenevert rides back into the city, filled at once with a sense of rural harmony and a sense of urban melancholy. As the bus approaches Montreal, the figure of a neon Christ confronts him. This figure elicits only regret from Chenevert. In the city, traditional Roman Catholic iconography is indistinguishable from the electric gadgetry of other enterprizing advertizers. On the ideological plane, this statue serves as an ironic and parodic focus for the literal and perceptual ambiguities of attitude towards rural and urban landscapes, to which we have been exposed throughout *The Cashier*. The statue is ironic and parodic because it undermines and yet brings to mind traditional Roman Catholic ideology. For the modern city-dweller, the self-sacrifice of Christ must take on a different meaning. To find this meaning, Chenevert journeyed to rural Quebec. He rediscovers a sense of divine providence in the natural environment and returns regenerated to Montreal. The ideological mediation of literal and perceptual points of view in *The Cashier* thus results in a vision of the city as a place that cares. When he rode out into the country, Chenevert turned his back on the penitentiary and opened his mind to the mighty River Des Prairies. On his return to the city, Chenevert admires the river but thinks also of the inmates of the penitentiary, whose confinement symbolizes the feeling of urban alienation characterizing urban life at its worst. On the one hand, Chenevert is saddened to have to admit "that penitentiaries are perhaps indispensable"; on the other hand, he also finds it sad that on the fringes of the city "a few dust-laden trees struggled for existence" (152). Yet both regrets are cause for hope, not for despair. In part one of *The Cashier*, the narrator describes Chenevert as "a little man in cage number two" (32). By the third part of the novel, Chenevert's cage has become a wicket, and he feels himself "free, unhampered . . . of use to the world" (165). In part one, the North-Western Lunch made Chenevert feel "unnoticed and perhaps even invisible, among all the others, under the eyes of God, Whom he imagined almost always displeased with Alexandre Chenevert" (43). In part three, Chenevert enjoys "the noisy warm atmosphere of the North-Western Lunch" (167). At Christmas the city is full of "man's solicitude" (172). The city even has its own Christmas sounds: "On almost all the streets you could hear the slightly plaintive and powerful grinding of the [snow-blowing] machine which now, in this city, better than the thin tinkling of sleigh bells, represents Christmas in the depth of winter" (174).

This vision of hope is a revisioning of Roman Catholic ideology.[6] In traditional Roman Catholic teaching, divine providence manifests itself in a double revelation. On the one hand, the natural environment is a blessing. We are part of nature, though further blessed by the gifts of free will and reason. These gifts distinguish us from other creatures and give us dominion over them. Gardeur represents this traditional attitude towards the natural environment. Similarly, insofar as Chenevert recovers a sense of human communion in and through his communion with the rural landscape, this ideology embraces his experience, too. On the other hand, divine providence reveals itself in the sacred scriptures. The Bible contains mysteries beyond the achievement of human will and beyond the understanding of human reason, though we are bound in faith to exercise both free will and reason in obedience to biblical mandates. Traditionally, we are all susceptible to the divine revelation in nature, but the Roman Catholic hierarchy serves at once as sole mediator and only authoritative interpreter of the biblical revelation.

Here, *The Cashier* revisions traditional Roman Catholic ideology. His name symbolic of the mercenary attitudes of the Roman Catholic hierarchy, Father Marchand's ecclesiastical authority is ineffectual against Chenevert's perceptions of the rural and urban landscapes. On his deathbed, Chenevert thinks it absurd that divine providence placed human beings in the "terrifying position: love God or lose Him, or rather, love Him because He is to be feared" (187). The heaven of Roman Catholic teaching seems less paradisal than Lac Vert: "What! No more flowers, no more birds with cries as gentle as the rain, no trees!" (198). Inspired by the reality of this natural heaven on earth, Chenevert envisions the city transformed, "now that men had become good neighbours" (199). "Might not Heaven, after all," he wonders, "little by little, come to be on earth?" (199). At the last, this revisioning of Roman Catholic ideology results in Chenevert's imagining his own presence after death in the literal terms of a place on earth. He wants nothing of heaven elsewhere. Rather, "Alexandre went on to consider the place he would continue to occupy on earth . . . something fifteen by eighteen" (207).[7] Perhaps modern science, as epitomized in the figure of Dr. Hudon, is fulfilling the spirit of human communion in the city. Heroin relieves Chenevert's pain; but by making "everything so green," it also bathes the mind's eye in images of natural fertility (209). Chenevert may only have travelled just north of Montreal, but in his imagination he has "roamed the whole country" (212). After his death, "It happens that here or there in the city someone says: . . . Alexandre Chenevert . . ." (217).

NOTES

1 See, for example, McPherson 1959 and, more recently, Lewis 1985.

2 Respectively, see Brown 1956, Ricard 1976, Lewis 1985, and LeGrand 1965.

3 These distinctions conflate those of Boris Uspensky and G.A. Gukovsky. See Uspensky 1973 and Gukovsky 1959.

4 Committing this kind of intentional fallacy is not uncommon in the interdisciplinary study of geography and literature. See, for example, Mallory and Simpson-Housley 1987. In their introduction, the editors invoke Thomas Hardy's critical notion of an author's idiosyncratic mode of regard as a key to the interpretation of texts.

5 The quotation is from the standard English translation of Gabrielle Roy's *Alexandre*

Chenevert, published under the title *The Cashier.* Subsequent citations of the work are from this English edition and are given in parentheses in the text.

6 Gabrielle Roy was familiar with the work of Père Teilhard de Chardin and acknowledged the influence of his ideas on her work. See Bessette 1968, 306. In *The Phenomenon of Man,* for example, de Chardin tries to combine Roman Catholic ideology and evolutionary science to offer an optimistic vision of an ever more complex, but ever more beneficent universe. As creatures of free will and reason, human beings have a special role in this development, in the fulfilment of which all is gathered up in God.

7 For thoughts on death in *The Cashier* from the Roman Catholic ideological point of view, see Murphy 1963.

REFERENCES

Bessette, Gérard. 1968. *Une littérature en ébullition.* Montreal: Editions de Jour.

Brown, Alan. 1956. "Gabrielle Roy and the Temporary Provincial." *Tamarack Review* 1:61–70.

de Chardin, Père Teilhard. 1959. *The Phenomenon of Man.* New York: Harper & Row.

Gukovsky, G.A. 1959. *Realism in Gogol.* Moscow.

LeGrand, Albert. 1965. "Gabrielle Roy ou l'être partagé." *Etudes Françaises* 1:39–65.

Lewis, Paula Gilbert. 1985. "Female Spirals and Male Cages: The Urban Sphere in the Novels of Gabrielle Roy." In Paula Gilbert Lewis, ed., *Traditionalism, Nationalism, and Feminism: Women Writers of Quebec.* Westport: Greenwood Press.

Mallory, W.E., and Paul Simpson-Housley, eds. 1987. *Geography and Literature: A Meeting of the Disciplines.* Syracuse: Syracuse University Press.

McPherson, Hugo. 1959. "The Garden and the Cage: The Achievement of Gabrielle Roy." *Canadian Literature* 1:46–57.

Murphy, John J. 1963. "Visit with Gabrielle Roy." *Thought, Fordham University Quarterly* 38: 447–55.

Ricard, François. 1976. "Gabrielle Roy, 20 ans d'écriture: le cercle enfin uni des hommes." *Liberté* 18:59–78.

Roy, Gabrielle. 1954. *Alexandre Chenevert.* Montreal: Stanké. Translated by Henry Binsse as *The Cashier.* Toronto: McClelland & Stewart, 1955.

Uspensky, Boris. 1973. A *Poetics of Composition.* Berkeley: University of California Press.

15

Monumental Buildings:
Perspectives by Two Montreal Painters

Paula Kestelman

INTRODUCTION

This chapter will address two statements regarding the depiction of monumental buildings in an urban milieu. Dominic Ricciotti (1981, 22) states that the tradition of drawing and painting monumental buildings has, for centuries, been a preoccupation of artists in their "search for the grand." In other words, these paintings are a social commentary on where power lay, and therefore on the nature of the state and the economy. Whether the monumental building was a Versailles or a Manhattan skyscraper, it required wealth to build it and influence for it to be chosen as a subject for painting; the structure itself performed a function, be it economic, administrative, religious, or some mix of these.

Hildegard Binder Johnson (1979, 30–32) states that the public's view of monumental buildings is often dictated to or "framed." The buildings are often seen either as portraits (Johnson 1979, 27) or as solitary subjects dominating the foreground. Adjacent buildings that detract from the grandeur of the monument are either omitted entirely or barely sketched in. Traditionally, paintings and drawings focus on the structure's facade, with special attention given to any sculpture or decoration with which the building may be imbued. The most familiar or attractive perspectives of the monumental building are emphasized. Usually, it is the perspective from street level as a passerby may gaze upward, awe-inspired by the grand structure.

These propositions will be examined in the context of two Montreal paintings selected for discussion, Philip John Bainbrigge's *The Protestant and Catholic Cathedrals of Montreal, Lower Canada from near Mount Molson* (1840) and Adrien Hébert's *Le Château de Ramezay à Montréal* (1930). The paintings present perspectives of monumental buildings in Old Montreal at two distinctive periods in the urban history of the old city core. Old Montreal, site of the first urban settlement of Montreal (1642), has been the subject of many artists' work. Caulfield (chapter 16) discusses Maurice Cullen's residential painting *Old Houses, Montreal* (1909), situated in Old Montreal. Popular images of its narrow streets, and especially of its monumental buildings, have proliferated in the hands of hundreds of artists.

However, the two artists selected for this paper present unusual or non-traditional views of the old city. In particular, they present unconventional views of some of Old Montreal's most historic religious and civic buildings – referred to here as monumental or institutional buildings. The reasons for selecting these unconventional scenes are twofold. First, the artists chose to paint not a single monumental building, but to juxtapose several. Bainbrigge's cathedrals, seen in the far middle ground of the canvas, seem diminutive in relation to the Molson mansion, the windmill, and especially the pastureland in the foreground. Hébert's Château de Ramezay, standing in the near middle ground of the canvas, is dwarfed by Grain Elevator No. 2 in the background, and its dominance is challenged by the presence of several other institutions in the composition.

The second reason for choosing the paintings is that together they document two views of important changes in the urban history of Montreal. The monumental buildings, as the subjects of each canvas, represent both new developments and the continuity of Old Montreal as the historic core of the city. The depiction of adjacent structures and the urban milieu, with which the monuments are interconnected, represents ongoing urban changes typical of historic areas in modern cities. The cross-section of Old Montreal's urban history selected from the paintings documents development of the old city core at two stages: first, during the time of the old city's proximity to and dependence on rural environs, and second, during its peak of modern industrial and urban growth (followed later by the growth of the city's service economy).

The paintings reflect the artists' intimate knowledge of Old Montreal's urban fabric as well as their understanding of the interconnection and competition among urban structures in the fabric. The paintings serve as graphic documents that complement both the street- and house-painting genre, discussed in Caulfield's essay, conveying a sense of neighbourhood and community, and tourist-oriented paintings and etchings, which convey more simplified and even sentimental traditional views of the city.

PHILIP JOHN BAINBRIGGE

Philip John Bainbrigge was stationed with the Royal Engineers in Canada from 1836 to 1842. His extraordinary drafting abilities were utilized in the preparation of special surveys. In the many watercolours he painted while in Canada, he "strived for unusual pictorial effects," often selecting unconventional points of view. His compositions are "forerunners of the advances of late-nineteenth century European art" (Bell 1973, 12). The latter probably refers to what geographers may appreciate as a "regionalist" art (Hart 1982). As such, an artist attempts to convey the uniqueness and special features of a selected paysage.

Bainbrigge's reputation for selecting unorthodox points of view, combined with his draughtsmanship and military training, help to explain the perspective and composition in his rendition of Montreal's two cathedrals. It is a view that records the early connection between city and countryside on Montreal Island, as well as aspects of the economic, social, and religious life of its population.

Most historic paintings (and photographs) focus either on the old city core, the Port of Montreal, or Mount Royal. Paintings that include rural views of the Montreal landscape are rare. Bainbrigge's painting is one of the few graphic records of the early rural, inland landscape of Montreal Island. Bainbrigge selected his vantage point more than one and half kilometres northeast of the old city, near the present-day intersection of Prince Arthur and Colonial streets. His Protestant and Catholic cathedrals of Montreal (the subjects of the painting) stand demurely in the middle ground, whereas an expansive bucolic scene dominates the foreground. The buildings are presented on a narrow strip of land – that is, the old city – and seem to oversee, from afar, the spatially extensive farmland in the foreground. Glimpses of the St. Lawrence River beyond the city are seen distantly in the background.

Bainbrigge's painting with windmill (the oldest monument) and pastureland reminds the viewers that the rich agricultural hinterland was vital to the region's ability to feed its developing population. From Bainbrigge's point of view, as a military surveyor, the abundance of farmland just outside the city was of economic and strategic interest to Great Britain. In fact, by 1825, a mere 20 percent of Montreal Island's population lived within the area of the old city's fortification walls. Most Montrealers lived and worked within the five major faubourgs, or suburbs, that grew outside the city walls and beyond (Marsan 1974, 162). While the suburbs were still semi-rural in character until the mid-nineteenth century, important nodes of industrial and commercial activity evolved within each.

Philip John Bainbrigge, *The Protestant and Catholic Cathedrals of Montreal, Lower Canada, from near Mount Molson,* 1840, watercolour, 15.25 x 25.4 cm. Courtesy National Archives of Canada.

The integration of rural and urban environs in the painting also reflects aspects of the social and religious fabric of Montreal. The twin-towered church building, popularly known as the "Catholic Cathedral," or Cathédrale Notre-Dame, was not, in fact, a cathedral but rather the central parish church for Montreal Island. Also known as "la paroisse," it served the entire French Canadian population on the Island of Montreal from 1722 to the 1860s (when the island was subdivided into smaller parish areas). It was from *la paroisse* that the Sulpician order of priests, who held seigneurial rights for the entire island, centralized their registers and performed most baptism, marriage, and burial ceremonies for both the old city core and the surrounding rural population (Cooper 1969, 22). Bainbrigge, therefore, accurately captured the role of Notre-Dame as it served the "legal and official aspects of church life" for the island parish of Montreal (Cooper 1969, 22). The "grandeur" of the Catholic cathedral is depicted in its central religious-administrative role on the island, rather than by its grand physical stature within a confined urban locale.

The second aspect of the city's social and religious fabric seen in the painting is the parallel development of the French and English communities. The Protestant church and spire, to the left of *la paroisse*, is smaller than the base and towers of the Catholic church. Its size reflects both the smaller English population and the smaller religious influence within its community. Nevertheless, the Protestant cathedral is seen at the same glance as the Catholic church.

The Mount Molson mansion is the secondary subject and fourth monument of the painting. It is depicted as sheltered (or buffered) by trees and a stone fence. Mount Molson was the residence of one of the most powerful financial families in the city. The Molsons were also one of the first families to escape the crowded conditions of the old city to the healthier and more spacious environs north of the city core.[1] The Catholic church is seen bounded by both the English social presence and the financially dominant English community. The spatial separation between the cathedrals on one the hand and between the Catholic cathedral and the English mansion on the other reflects the ongoing socio-economic differences between the French and English communities.

Bainbrigge used four graphic techniques to direct the viewer's eye immediately towards the cathedrals and the old city, even though these buildings are seen as small structures compared to the surrounding rural landscape. These techniques serve to maintain focus on the cathedrals as the primary subjects in the composition. Firstly, the striking vertical and geometric forms of the buildings, combined with the dominant horizontal axis of the old city, act together as a strong visual pull. Vertical and horizontal elements (as linear forms) in a composition often act as the strongest graphic attraction to the viewer. The vertical and horizontal elements are visually dominant and are seen in stark contrast to the gently rolling (curvilinear, rounded) features of the expansive pastureland that include log fences, the windmill, and cattle. Secondly, vertical elements, in a more subtle form, are also seen within the pastureland scene. The softly hewn, weather-worn vertical (cylindrical) forms of the fence posts and windmill are used as a visual motif that repeatedly leads the viewer's eye towards the cathedrals. These vertical elements, seen in both the old city and the pastureland, may also represent the interconnection between the two environs. Thirdly, the warm sunlit colours of the cathedrals and adjacent urban structures visually advance on the canvas, while the cooler, darker green and brown hues of the pastureland visually recede from the viewer's eye. The warm colours act to highlight the buildings seen in the middle ground. Fourthly, the light, warm hues, repeated on the windmill in the left foreground of the composition, act to decrease the perceived – and actual – distance between countryside and city. The diagonal axis of the sail of the windmill, which lazily and subtly points towards the city, is another strong linear element. The sail also helps to draw the middle ground forward, towards the viewer, and acts to interconnect the urban and rural milieus.

The use of light colours as well as of linear and geometric forms becomes a subtle, almost impressionistic means to convey the grandeur of the cathedrals. In the mind's eye, these techniques act to enlarge and enhance the initially perceived small size and diminutive position of the cathedrals compared to the large expanse of farmland.

Bainbrigge's work can also be almost transformed into a surveyor's map; it charts the diversity of features in the area from farmland, to city core, to the river at the horizon. Looking at the composition of features, one can perceive the successive vertical plans or cross-section of the scenery foreground and background. The painting reflects the artist's "advanced" (perhaps "regionalist") landscape style that conveys not merely a formal portrait of a monumental building; the painting also depicts the economic, social, and religious life unique to Old Montreal in the 1840s.

ADRIEN HÉBERT

In Adrien Hébert's 1930 painting *Le Château de Ramezay à Montréal,* the central monumental building – the subject of the composition – is seen in the midst of a diverse and evolving urban milieu. The grandeur of the Château de Ramezay is modestly stated in its position as keystone structure surrounded by several other structures, also monumental buildings. In terms of urban history, as Norcliffe notes in chapter 6 of this volume, this period was the last peak of modern port and industrial activity associated with Old Montreal, from the 1910s to the 1930s.

The view of the Château and its urban milieu is not an entirely usual one. Hébert's view does, however, reflect a French Canadian perspective of the old city core. The painter's vantage point is from a balcony or tall window of Montreal's Hôtel de Ville, looking over the old city below and fronting on the Château. It is a view of the area that was probably popularized by the 1920 photograph reproduced here. The photo presents a sweeping westward view, embracing the entire breadth of the port's magnificent Grain Elevator No. 2, though it is abruptly cropped at the eastern gable of the Château de Ramezay. It

Adrien Hébert, *Le Château de Ramezay à Montréal,* oil on canvas, 69.1 x 59.1 cm, Photographie Musée du Québec. Photo: Patrick Altman.

was an appealing view, perhaps directed towards a wealthy English clientele, who dominated financial, industrial, and central urban development in west-end Montreal, including the banking centre in the west portion of Old Montreal.

By contrast, Hébert presents an eastward view of Old Montreal. East-end Montreal development has been traditionally dominated by the city's French Canadian community. Likewise, the eastern portion of Old Montreal was the historical centre of the Québécois municipal-political dominance of the city. Hébert, therefore, presents a rare view of and a particular social insight into the east-end Montreal milieu. Hébert's view extends well east of the Château de Ramezay. While he omits about half the westward section of the grain elevator,

Photograph of the Château de Ramezay, c. 1920. Courtesy Services d'urbanisme, Ville de Montréal.

the industrial structure is still seen as a celebrated monument in the urban milieu.

With respect to the depiction of monumental buildings, Hébert's Château de Ramezay is (like Bainbrigge's cathedrals) also presented in a diminutive form within the composition. In contrast to the cathedrals, the Château is in reality a low-rise structure; it is not a monumental building in its architectural and physical stature. It is, however, a building of historically monumental importance in Montreal. Historically, the Château has served a succession of vital political, social, and cultural functions in the old city core. Initially, it was built as the French governor's residence, a centre of political activity. Subsequently, it served as a warehouse for the major trading company in the colony; as the first British government house after the conquest of 1760; as an American military headquarters; as the Court of Justice for the city; as offices of Quebec's education ministry; and since the turn of the present century, as a museum (Marsan 1974, 138–39).

With respect to its interconnection with adjacent buildings in the area, the Château may be described as a visual pivot point (rather than a central focus) of the composition. In its middle-ground position, the Château acts as a visual springboard, directing the viewer's eye to surrounding structures: the domed roof of Marché Bonsecours (built in 1842), the silver tower of Chapelle Notre-Dame de Bonsecours (1659), and the turrets of Grain Elevator No. 2 (1911).[2] These monuments encapsulate almost the entire history of Montreal up to that time.

The grandeur of the Château de Ramezay is shared by all structures in the painting and even permeates the entire urban fabric of the scene. The painting captures the many layers of history and urban growth in this part of Old Montreal. By the 1930s, several artists and photographers, including Childe Hassam (*Madison Square Snowstorm*, c. 1909), John Marin (*Movement, Fifth Avenue*, 1912), and Charles Sheeler (*Offices*, 1922), had grappled with the problem of depicting tall buildings or skyscrapers within modern, diverse urban landscapes – buildings that compete for space with parks, historic low-rise structures, and other features at a human scale of construction (Ricciotti 1981).

Hébert used three techniques in approaching the presentation of both the grandeur and the diversity of Old Montreal's urban milieu. Firstly, he achieved a visual balance between low-rise and tall buildings. Although it is the smallest building in the area, the Château de Ramezay, by its placement in the near middle ground of the composition, is the first identifiable building to the viewer. The grain elevator, as the tallest structure and the most imposing, is positioned in the background. The vantage point of the painting from the Hôtel de Ville (unseen on the canvas) suggests the presence of another tall building in the area. Both tall buildings represent the skyward development of the modern city. Secondly, the central position of the Château is diminished as trees obscure most of the building. The dark, cool hues of the trees and shade on the building cause the structure to recede away from the viewer. In addition, the diagonal view onto the Château is a technique that serves both to attract the viewer to the structure and to lead the viewer's eye away from the Château towards the other monumental buildings nearby. Thirdly, even though the grain elevator is seen in the background, its massive structure and lighter, warmer hues bring it forward on the canvas. The sunlit strokes of colour on the Chapelle tower, the Bonsecours dome, and the west gable of the Château are a motif that act to direct attention from each building to the grain elevator.

Hébert's style and composition also address Johnson's (1979) criticism of "framed," or static, portrait-like landscape. The subtle cubist influence contributes a sense of movement to the entire composition. It invites the viewer to explore subjects and forms quickly from several planes and directions. The sense of movement, which represents change and growth of the city, as well as the bustle of human activity, is accomplished by, firstly, the play of shadow and light on all the buildings, but particularly on the Château and adjacent trees; secondly, by the diversity of angular shapes, emphasized in the sunlit roof and gables of the Château, the turrets of the grain elevator, and the Chapelle tower, among other structures; thirdly, by the converging and diverging linear axes of sidewalks and fences along Notre-Dame Street in front of the Château and along the stairways and road that lead to Place Jacques-Cartier to the west (right) of the Château; and fourthly, by the depiction of the people walking towards many destinations in the area.

Hébert used all these graphic techniques – composition, hue, light, and shadow, diversity of geometric linear and angular forms – to present the Château de Ramezay and its surrounding urban milieu as a hub of both early and modern urban development in Old Montreal. A century earlier, Bainbrigge used similar techniques to convey the socio-economic dynamic between urban and rural Montreal, between the two cultures, and between the old city and the innovations brought to the surrounding countryside by the merchant barons.

SUMMARY

Both artists painted views of monumental buildings in Old Montreal as a means to present a personal and unique comment on a larger urban milieu. Bainbrigge and Hébert explored unconventional views of the city, and their paintings offer insights into the economy, society, and power structure of the city. Bainbrigge suggested the co-existence of the city's French and English communities, the interdependence of urban and rural environs, and the emergence of a new class of entrepreneurs. Hébert emphasized the complex of historical identity and modern industrial development within the confines of Old Montreal. The monumental buildings are presented in their social and economic contexts. On the canvas it is their central roles within their environs and within the city that are emphasized, not their central and dominant physical presence. The buildings are seen in context as active components in the urban development of Montreal, rather than as unchanging, grandiose monuments isolated from their surroundings in the city.

NOTES

1 By the 1860s, prestigious residential development, to the northwest of the old city, was well under way. This latter development, in fact, led to the migration of central city core functions to the present-day downtown location northwest of Old Montreal (Hanna 1977).

2 The grain elevator forms a magnificent backdrop on the canvas. It is part of the industrial landscape discussed by Norcliffe in this volume, chapter 6.

REFERENCES

Bell, Michael. 1973. *Painters in a New Land: From Annapolis Royal to the Klondike.* Toronto: McClelland & Stewart.

Cooper, Irwin. 1969. *Montréal, A Brief History.* Montreal: McGill-Queen's University Press.

Hanna, David B. 1977. *The New Town of Montreal.* M.A. thesis, Department of Geography, University of Toronto, Toronto.

Hart, John Fraser. 1982. "The Highest Form of the Geographer's Art." *Annals of the Association of American Geographers* 72:1–29.

Johnson, Hildegard Binder. 1979. "The Framed Landscape." *Landscape* 23, no. 2: 27–32.

Marsan, Jean-Claude. 1974. *Montréal en Evolution, Historique du développement de l'architecture et de l'environnement Montréalaise.* Montreal: Fides.

Québec. Ministère des Affaires Culturelles. 1978. *L'Art du paysage au Québec 1800–1940.* Québec: Musée du Québec .

Ricciotti, Dominic. 1981. "Symbols and Monuments: Images of the Skyscraper in American Art." *Landscape* 25, no. 2: 22-29.

16

Augurs of "Gentrification": City Houses of Four Canadian Painters

Jon Caulfield

ccounts of landscape in Canadian art generally stress painters' treatment of wilderness and rural locales. For example, a recent "iconography of nationhood in Canadian art" centres on the Group of Seven and on various regional natural landscape movements (Osborne 1988). Given the importance of wilderness and rural imagery in Canadian national and regional identity, this emphasis is well placed.

City landscape, too, has been a continuing theme among Canadian painters. In Canada's mercantile urban period, these pictures were most commonly in the topographic or picturesque styles preferred by visiting colonial elites. During the commercial urban era of the mid-nineteenth century, more academic styles were dominant among a growing cadre of immigrant and indigenous artists and their patrons. In industrial/corporate cities of the twentieth century, the urban landscape has embraced a range of contemporary styles.[1] Across these different periods, however, painters' interests have been fairly consistent; they have also been diverse. Canadian urban landscape painting is an enduring record of intimate streetscape and heroic cityscape, commercial downtowns and waterfront industry, noteworthy buildings and popular public locales like open markets.[2]

One common theme among Canadian artists working in cities has been houses. This chapter focuses on the urban houses of four twentieth-century painters, Maurice Cullen, Lawren Harris, Eric Freifeld, and Albert Franck, and argues that a recent rediscovery by middle-class Canadian city-dwellers of old downtown neighbourhoods as places to live is presaged in their work.

CULLEN'S OLD HOUSES, MONTREAL

Shortly after the turn of the century, a break occurred in Canadian painters' manner of depicting city-dwellers' houses. Previously, painted houses were commonly identified by name (*"The Elms"*) or owner's name (*The Jackes Residence*); they were specific houses. Consistent with the title of the Royal Ontario Museum's 1981 exhibit of nineteenth-century Canadian painted houses, *House Proud*, the houses depicted are generally either stately (in the case of houses of the well-to-do) or charming (in the case of more modest houses). They are typically located in bucolic settings at the edge of town or in "park lots" settled by more affluent households – there is usually nothing very urban about them. Among the emerging middle class who created and patronized this work, painted houses appear to have been either icons of material well-being and civility among settlers of a daunting new land, or incidental occasions for a demonstration of painterly taste.

Pictures of the former type (houses as social icons) suggest two matters that touch at the core of bourgeois culture. First, it is vital that persons who, like Canada's emerging nineteenth-century commercial elite, seek to establish bourgeois identity make visible their proprietary status. Second, at the heart of bourgeois everyday life are the ideas of *home* and *family*, "principal achievements of the Bourgeois Age" (J. Lukacs 1970, 624), and an attendant ensemble of values: intimacy, privacy, security, comfort. These social values are embodied in an architectural form, the house, that may be traced to the first bourgeois state, the sixteenth- and seventeenth-century mercantile cities of the Netherlands (Rybczynski 1986, 54). Mikhail Bakhtin has argued that a basic subtext of artistic expression is the degree of proximity, or the social relationship, among the creator, the "hero," and the imagined viewer, towards whom a work is oriented (1973a, 110–11). In early Canada, pictures of houses as heroes seem often to have been oriented towards viewers who required tangible signs of

Unknown artist (Canadian, nineteenth century), *The Jackes Residence, "The Elms," Toronto*, c. 1875, oil on canvas, 61 x 81.3 cm, Art Gallery of Ontario.

prosperity and domesticity in a colony where the apparatus of urbanity was stretched thin. In this context, it is conspicuous both that the figures on the *Jackes Residence*'s lawn are playing croquet, a "leading pastime of the English leisure class" in the late nineteenth century (Reaske 1988, 18), and that they are women engaged in domestic leisure, an appropriate activity for authentic bourgeois females of their era (the males are presumably off at business in the city beyond the trees).

An example of pictures of the latter type (houses as painterly objects) that stands at the close of the nineteenth-century tradition of house painting is James Morrice's *Old Holton House*. Painted in the winter of 1908–1909, this portrait of a venerable Montreal home is unconcerned with bourgeois prosperity or familism but instead is oriented towards viewers who will appreciate its artist's craft: the picture is a pleasant object. Notably, its house is a facade, a two-dimensional surface whose third dimension (its interior) is irrelevant to Morrice's purpose. In the context of Bakhtin's triangle, the picture sets "clear and stable boundaries" among creator, hero, and imagined viewer, with nothing to involve viewers in the house as a social form or in the artist's social perspective towards it (1973b, 69). It is simply an icon of good taste.

Old Houses, Montreal, painted by Maurice Cullen in the same winter, has

James Wilson Morrice, *The Old Holton House, Montreal,* c. 1908, oil on canvas, 61 x 73.6 cm, Montreal Museum of Fine Arts.

Maurice Galbraith Cullen, *Old Houses, Montreal,* c. 1908, oil on canvas, 61.4 x 86.7 cm, Montreal Museum of Fine Arts.

similarities to Morrice's picture. Like *Holton House,* it is a hibernal Montreal streetscape with common decorative elements (snow, horse and carriage, bare trees). But it is quite different from *Holton House* and different, too, from earlier painted houses. It stands at the start of a new approach to city houses among Canadian artists. Cullen's houses are anonymous (we don't know whose they are), ordinary (not notable or especially charming), and clearly city houses (the ground floors are, in fact, shops). And there is life inside these houses; many of the windows are lit. The picture is not just an aesthetic object like *Holton House,* nor a simple icon of bourgeois proprietorship or domesticity, but an example, in a specifically urban setting, of "psychic landscape" (Zemans 1983, 70); it breaks down boundaries between viewer and hero and evokes emotional meaning that city-dwellers are drawn to share in the context of their own urban experience, a feature remarked by a writer who viewed the picture's first showing in 1909: "What could be more captivating than [Cullen's] cold night . . . Happy is he who will know this street strophe and joyous is he who can make it his very own" (Antoniou 1982, 22).

This break in depiction of city houses marked by Cullen was concurrent with two larger changes in Canadian life around the turn of the century. The first concerned painting, whose social base, content, and formal styles altered sharply. A new discursive infrastructure emerged in the patronage of a rapidly growing urban middle class, influencing not only the market for Canadian painting but also "structures of feeling" (Williams 1977, 128–35) in which artists worked. Many painters – for example, the Group of Seven – turned to material that had earlier been outside Canadian art's horizons of expectation (such as Shield landscape) and abandoned previously dominant codes of practice to work in new styles (such as impressionism, fauvism, and cubism).[3] Cullen, in fact, was a key figure in painting's regrouping and in the formation of new "visual ideologies" (Hadjinicolaou 1979, 95–96) in Canadian art. Unlike Morrice, he turned away from prestigious European patronage to stay in Canada, and his work has been characterized as a "first sign" in Canadian painting of a middle-class outlook "not comprador but nationalist" (Lord 1974, 114).

The second change involved Canadian cities, which underwent radical transition around the turn of the century. Urban populations grew quickly, as growth and rationalization of the factory economy were accompanied by a rapid increase in industrial and white-collar labour forces and as the urban fabric was abruptly crowded with new built forms – downtown, the first office towers and large-scale factories; away from the core, middle-class subdivisions and working-class "shack" districts. This shift from the topography of the commercial city to that of the industrial city is reflected in a 1921 review of Lawren Harris's urban landscapes in which Barker Fairley wrote of "a vast gulf between the city's present and its immediate but somehow almost mysterious past" (1921, 276). It was in the new urban environment that anonymous, distinctly urban houses like Cullen's became common in artists' depictions of the city.

HARRIS'S OLD HOUSES, WELLINGTON STREET

At first glance, many of Harris's house pictures appear to have more in common with Morrice's *Holton House* than with Cullen's *Old Houses*. Though nearly always anonymous, ordinary, and clearly city houses, they are not so emotionally compelling as Cullen's; many are simple facades in which uses of light, texture, and plane are clearly conscious exercises in pictorial technique. But what was Harris's intent toward hero and viewer in these pictures? For Morrice, an aesthete, a painting like *Old Holton House* was a "stimulant," a "sensuous form" (Montreal Museum of Fine Arts 1965, 6). Harris, in contrast, was a nationalist and theosophist whose artistic orientation was partly didactic. He wrote that his purpose in his first major house picture, *Old Houses, Wellington Street*, was not only was painterly, to "depict the clear hard sunlight of a Canadian noon in winter," but also had a specific social aspect, "to suggest the spirit of Old York" (Art Gallery of Toronto 1911, 6).

Alone among the Group of Seven, Harris painted extensively in the city, producing pictures that, apart from a few industrial and street scenes, are nearly all house portraits – middle-class houses like Wellington Street's slum cottages, working-class shacks at the city's edge, and occasional houses of the well-to-do, his own social class. What is remarkable is not any one picture (in contrast to Cullen, whose *Old Houses* was his sole painting of city houses), but the sheer volume of Harris's house work. In accounting for his preoccupation with houses, one should note the clues that are found in some of his poems that also feature houses. One describes a dilapidated house in the slums of an industrial city, whose front door Harris took as a sign of hope:

Lawren Harris, *Old Houses, Wellington Street*, 1910, oil on canvas, 63.5 x 76.2 cm.

> In a part of the city that is ever shrouded in sooty
> smoke, and amid huge, hard buildings, hides a gloomy
> house of broken grey rough-cast, like a sickly sin in a
> callous soul. . . .
>
> The windows are bleary with grime, and bulging filthy
> rags plug the broken panes. . . .
>
> But the street door smiles, and even laughs, when the
> hazy sunlight falls on it –
>
> Someone had painted it a bright gay red.
>
> (Harris 1922, 11)

Another describes comfortable houses away from the city, set "in snug villages" and "sleepy valleys":

> Little houses tucked in little yards
> Behind low white fences or bushy green hedges. . . .
> Plump, well-fed, clean little houses
> A big, round rain-barrel by the side door. . . .

And full woodsheds –
Lots of wood for the winter. . . .
Homes for contented folks.
                    (1922, 19–20)

The poems also offer clues to Harris's feelings about cities. He did not like them very much, or at least not industrial cities of the kind that Toronto had become, "pestilential" (1922, 27) places with:

Canals of filth under every street,
Smoke-breathed, din-shrouded,
Seething with blind, driven people
                    (1922, 58)

Who after their day's city work (in an echo of Simmel)
are occupied with themselves and salute one
another grudgingly, or not at all.
They have nothing for their fellows. . . .

                    (1922, 16)

In this context, it is not surprising his "little houses" of "contented folks" are located away from the city.

Harris's viewpoint illustrates the irony of the industrial city. It was the bourgeoisie's creation. Harris's father, for example, was co-founder of a major Toronto manufacturing firm. But the industrial city also displaced the bourgeoisie from their own urban roots. "Bourgeois" ("burger," "burgher," "borghese") *means* "city-dweller" (J. Lukacs 1970, 620). But the industrial city was sorely inhospitable to bourgeois culture, particularly to the values of familism and domesticity, security and comfort, at the core of bourgeois everyday life. Paris solved the problem by banishing industry and its workers to the city's outskirts as Haussmann reconsolidated the downtown as bourgeois terrain. In anglophone society, influenced partly by the views held of women and of family life of eighteenth- and nineteenth-century evangelical movements, the bourgeoisie migrated to suburban "utopias," a diaspora presaged in *The Jackes Residence* (Fishman 1987, 11–12, 35–38). In departing from the heart of the city, the bourgeoisie left behind the physical fabric of their work and leisure life – office buildings and downtown business establishments, theatres and restaurants – which, for the most part, they could continue to use by commuting. But they also left behind their houses and neighbourhoods, the infrastructure of their traditional domestic life, from which they were now alienated.

Thus, old houses, the shells of an ebbing urban culture, were an appropriate image to embody the paradox of the new city and the bourgeoisie's ambivalence towards it. In Toronto, scattered middle-class neighbourhoods did remain, and Harris celebrated these places, where "the spirit of Old York" was still evident, in pictures like *Wellington Street*. His warmest house portraits are of well-to-do city homes, pictures like *Winter Afternoon* in which a house peeks from behind a red picket fence and snow-laden pines as people who are clearly well-to-do pass by on the sidewalks. His attitude towards working-class houses was more ambiguous. Some are portrayed affectionately in lively colours or with smoke of comfy homeyness curling from their chimneys, analogues of the house with the bright red door. Though often dilapidated and inhabited by workers or immigrants rather than by the bourgeoisie, they are places in which Harris finds evidence of domesticity. Others, though, are desolate buildings in barren yards, houses evoked in another poem:

> Are you sad walking down streets,
> Streets hard as steel, repellent, cruel?
> Are you sad seeing people there,
> Outcast from beauty,
> Even afraid of beauty,
> Not knowing?
> Are you sad when you look down city lanes . . . ,
> Dirty, musty garbage-reeking lanes
> Behind the soot-dripped backs of blunt houses,
> Sour yards and slack-sagging fences?
>
> (1922, 57)

In part, what these houses' inhabitants do "not know" is an everyday life of middle-class *home*, domestic security, family intimacy. That, at least, is the view of a bourgeois outsider who finds in the slums of industrial urbanism a disjuncture between the city of the present, where he is a stranger, and the "mysterious," bygone city of his heritage.

FREIFELD'S *ICHABOD*

A concept that may be useful in approaching Canadian city house pictures is the "problematic hero" whose concern is "a search for authentic values in a . . . degraded world" – who exemplifies a formerly implicit basic value that "has lost its connection with the existential conditions" of a group and so now must be explicitly "articulated" (Goldmann 1975, 1; Bakhtin 1973a, 101).

> If the [hero] is unproblematic, then his aims are given to him with immediate obviousness, and the realization of the world constructed by these given aims may involve hindrances and difficulties but never any threat to his interior life. Such a threat arises only when the outside world is no longer adapted to the [hero's] ideas and the ideas become subjective facts – *ideals* – of his soul. (G. Lukacs 1971, 78)

Canadian painted houses of the nineteenth century were unproblematic in this way. They were heroes in whom values of bourgeois urban domesticity were implicit, threatened only by the external hindrances of a colonial environment. But, in the twentieth century, bourgeois urban domestic culture itself has come under complex attack – from modernist design, "[remaking] the home in a new image, stripped of its bourgeois traditions and bereft of easeful intimacy"; from urban *technique*, "subsum[ing] individuality . . . to a set of procedures . . . determined by the technical nature of social engineering" and creating urban environments where "almost nothing can happen . . . which expresses human emotions or feeling"; from the "society of spectacle," a "massive *internal* extension of the capitalist market, the invasion and restructuring of whole areas of free time, private life, leisure, and personal expression" (Rybczynski 1986, 200; Relph 1976, 81; Relph 1981, 104; Clark 1984, 9). One way to read Cullen's and Harris's *Old Houses* is as a first sign of this crisis, a nascent structure of feeling emerging early in the industrial/corporate Canadian urban era in which bourgeois home life can no longer be taken for granted but must be asserted explicitly and hagiologized.

Following Harris, house portraits in styles parallel to his were common in Canadian urban landscape painting of the 1920s, 1930s, and 1940s. The next artist to create a distinct oeuvre in the field did not work until after the Second World War. The exemplar of Eric Freifeld's house pictures, a painting he called his "signature piece" (Duval 1977, 113), is a watercolour of a house in Toronto's Don district titled *Ichabod*, a name that in its biblical context means "what has become of the glory of Israel?" *Ichabod* has been described as "claustrophobic," "suggestive of dark doings," and "inner decay" (Duval 1977, 113, 120), a view that may miss the point. The picture may be read better in the context of Freifeld's comments about a similar painting:

[It] speaks of the lives of the people who lived there and all the associations of those lives. It deals with my response to this old house and the feelings I had when I was alone in it – lives lived, objects identified with personalities, remains of people's lives, romance, the joys and sorrows of a lifetime, nostalgia; a stark awareness that time has passed . . . I had an intimation of love here . . . For a fleeting instant you glimpse the place as it was, filled with life and people and sun and air. (Duval 1977, 161)

It is hard to imagine a more compelling image of the emotional associations of the house in bourgeois society. (Literally, "nostalgia" means "homesickness.") *Ichabod*, a once-grand house whose mansard roof, arched lintels, and gingerbread a nineteenth-century artist might have painted in innocent pride, was by 1950, like Freifeld's other old city houses, only a battered survivor. Like bourgeois urban domesticity itself, it was a residual form of an era past.

Soon after Freifeld painted *Ichabod*, it may have been razed, as hundreds of

Don district houses were in the 1950s and 1960s to make way for downtown commercial expansion, high-rise construction, and public-housing blocks. The postwar decades were another period of rapid population rise and dramatic transition in Canadian cities, as growth-minded governments and a rapacious development industry, under the guise of rational planning, restructured much of the physical fabric of urban life in the new built forms of office and apartment towers, expressways and shopping malls, and suburban subdivisions. Then, in the midst of this maelstrom of boosterism and modernism, technique and spectacle, the patience of those members of the bourgeoisie still clinging to everyday life within the historic city snapped. (Their numbers had, in fact, lately been rising with the first movement of new middle-class resettlers into old downtown neighbourhoods.) In Toronto, developers and politicians seeking to erase such symbolic landmarks of Old York as a romanesque turn-of-the-century city hall, an aging gothic-revival church in the heart of the core, and a monumental neoclassical railroad terminal were confronted by bitter middle-class opposition. But the protesters' angriest efforts were mounted in defence of the city's old streetscapes and houses, places like Harris's *Wellington Street* and like Freifeld's *Ichabod.* Thus, *Ichabod* may have been protected from demolition and still stand, may even have been restored to some semblance of its past glory by a process of intensive renovation, no longer just a painted icon but now an ostentatious, living assertion of the bourgeois city home.

Eric Freifeld, *Ichabod,* 1950, watercolour, 54.6 x 74.9 cm, Yaneff Gallery, Toronto.

FRANCK'S *BACKYARD ON BALDWIN STREET*

Arguably, the period of Canadian city-house portrayal begun by Cullen ended in the work of Albert Franck. Franck was an immigrant painter, perhaps aptly from Holland, the birthplace of the bourgeois house, who, in Toronto, "barked like a dog at . . . urban renewal" (Town 1974, 28). He did most of his house work in the 1960s, immediately foreshadowing the social movement against destruction of the old city, and he became the movement's patron artist. His method was to

Albert Jacques Franck, *Backyard on Baldwin Street,* 1964, oil on canvas, 75.9 x 60.7 cm, permanent collection, Rodman Hall Arts Centre, National Exhibition Centre, St. Catharines, Ont.

wander rear lanes of downtown neighbourhoods seeking likely subjects and sometimes finding that, between the time he decided to paint a house and the time he got to the job, it had been demolished (Fulford 1973). He usually painted not the facades of his heroes but the view from the less formal perspective of their backyards, as in *Backyard on Baldwin Street*.

Like Freifeld's, Franck's houses are battered survivors complete with broken bricks, bent eavestroughs, tattered shingles, scruffy yards. They were characterized by Harold Town:

> Franck painted homes, not houses. They are real and familiar, . . . real through his belief that other homes were like his – warm, social and comfy . . . Albert, the burgher, . . . loved the ritual of home . . . He rigourously excluded quaint details or picaresque touches that might lead to the sentimentalization of his subjects. Franck houses were cathedrals of the ordinary, cocoons of the humdrum, painted as seriously as if they were primal structures. (1974, 28)

And like Freifeld's (in the context of Bakhtin's triangle), Franck's orientation to hero and to imagined viewer is one of intimacy, a relationship arising from a presumption of shared feelings about these old buildings, feelings requiring explicit statement in the degraded world of the rapidly changing postwar Canadian city.

In several respects, the movement against destruction of the old city was successful. Many landmarks of early Toronto were saved from the wrecker's ball, and new zoning and planning ordinances protected old neighbourhoods and houses. In the wake of the movement, the first incursions of middle-class resettlers into old city neighbourhoods became invasive. Middle-class resettlers began moving into downtown districts ubiquitously, a process accelerated by the rapid growth of the city's professional and managerial labour force (and a quickly declining industrial base) and by growing middle-class disillusion with suburbs. One outcome of this pattern has been the displacement of less affluent working-class and immigrant communities, who, it appears, were merely the bourgeoisie's caretakers for their neighbourhoods. Property entrepreneurs, meanwhile, now blocked from demolishing old houses, discovered in them a new form of commodity and began a widespread process of commercial renovation to accommodate mushrooming demand. Perhaps the ultimate irony has been the construction, by a development industry that had only lately wrecked old houses in systematic scores, of batches of brand-new houses meant to *look* like old homes, simulations of bourgeois domestic urbanity.

It was not the city itself that the anglophone bourgeoisie had rejected but rather, influenced by particular threats to their family life and by certain beliefs about proper relations among family members, only the specific form of the industrial city. Now, in the deindustrializing city, the threats of the industrial city are removed. In an era of quickly changing middle-class gender relations, such beliefs have become obsolete. David Ley has observed that "the social geography of the nineteenth-century industrial city may . . . appear to urban scholars of the future as a temporary interlude to a more historically persistent pattern of higher-status segregation adjacent to the downtown" (1984, 201). It appears that, in Canada, this will be the case, a process portended in Franck's house work, and in Cullen's, Harris's, and Freifeld's before him, as the bourgeoisie return to the city of their roots.

NOTES

1 The chapter uses a typology of Canadian urban history based on Stelter 1982 that includes three eras: mercantile, commercial, and industrial/corporate. (Arguably, using Stelter's method for demarking eras, "industrial" and "corporate" cities should not be conflated but treated distinctly.)

2 Other chapters of this book treat themes raised here. Ellen Ramsay (chapter 13) critically examines a well-known nineteenth-century painting of Canadian natural landscape, while Brian Osborne (chapter 3) explores the importance of particular kinds of visual images in Canadian national identity. Specific themes of urban landscape painting are discussed by Paula Kestelman (chapter 15) (monumental buildings) and by Glen Norcliffe (chapter 6) (industrial scenes).

3 This analysis of "discourse" in Canadian painting is based on a model described by Nielsen (1985, 121) that views aesthetic practice in terms of its (1) discursive infrastructures, which include (a) tools and materials of production and (b) an interactional (or social network) base, and (2) norms and codes of creativity, which include (a) horizons of expectation within a field of discourse and (b) discursive forms (such as genres and "styles").

REFERENCES

Antoniou, S. 1982. *Maurice Cullen, 1866–1934.* Kingston: Agnes Etherington Art Centre.

Art Gallery of Toronto. 1911. *Notes on Pictures at the O.S.A. Exhibition.*

Bakhtin, M. 1973a. "Discourse in Life and Discourse in Art." In V.N. Volosinov, ed., *Freudianism: A Marxist Critique,* 93–116. New York: Academic Press.

———. 1973b. *Marxism and the Philosophy of Language.* New York: Seminar Press.

Clark, T.J. 1984. *The Painting Of Modern Life.* Princeton: Princeton University Press.

Duval, P. 1977. *Eric Freifeld.* Toronto: Yaneff Gallery.

Fairley, B. 1921. "Some Canadian Painters: Lawren Harris." *Canadian Forum,* June, 275–78.

Fishman, R. 1987. *Bourgeois Utopias: The Rise and Fall of Suburbia.* New York: Basic Books.

Fulford, R. 1973. "Albert Franck: Toronto's Own Private Artist." *Toronto Star,* 24 March.

Goldmann, L. 1975. *Towards a Sociology of the Novel.* London: Tavistock.

Hadjinicolaou, N. 1979. *Art History and Class Struggle.* London: Pluto Press.

Harris, L. 1922. *Contrasts: A Book of Verse.* Toronto: McClelland & Stewart.

Ley, D. 1984. "Inner-city Revitalization: A Vancouver Case Study." In J. Palen and B. London, eds., *Gentrification, Displacement and Neighbourhood Revitalization,* 186–204. Albany: University of New York Press.

Lord, B. 1974. *The History of Painting in Canada: Toward a People's Art.* Toronto: NC Press.

Lukacs, G. 1971. *The Theory of the Novel.* Cambridge: MIT Press.

Lukacs, J. 1970. "The Bourgeois Interior." *American Scholar* 39, no. 4: 616–30.

Montreal Museum of Fine Arts. 1965. *James Wilson Morrice, 1865–1924.* Montreal: MMFA.

Nielsen, G., et al. "Table ronde: la sociologie contemporaine et ses perspectives critiques." *Sociologie et societés* 17, no. 2: 119–32.

Osborne, B. 1988. "The Iconography of Nationhood in Canadian Art." In D. Cosgrove and S. Daniels, eds., *The Iconography of Landscape,* 162–78. Cambridge: Cambridge University Press.

Reaske, C. 1988. *Croquet.* New York: E.P. Dutton.

Relph, E. 1976. *Place and Placelessness.* London: Pion.

——. 1981. *Rational Landscapes and Humanistic Geography.* London: Croom Helm.

Rybczynski, W. 1986. *Home: A Short History of an Idea.* New York: Viking Press.

Stelter, G. 1982. "The City-Building Process in Canada." In G. Stelter and A. Artibise, eds., *Shaping the Urban Landscape: Aspects of the City-Building Process in Canada,* 1–29. Ottawa: Carleton University Press.

Town, H. 1974. *Albert Franck: Keeper of the Lanes.* Toronto: McClelland & Stewart.

Williams, R. 1977. *Marxism and Literature.* New York: Oxford University Press.

Zemans, J. 1983. "Varley: An Appreciation." In P. Varley, ed., *Frederick H. Varley.* Toronto: Key Porter.

17

Drawing Earth;
Or Representing Region Niagara:
An Approach to Public Geography

Keith J. Tinkler

And Niagara, for thousands of years, will continue to be the Thunder of Waters, whose magnificence no pen can describe, no pencil express; which to be appreciated must be seen in its vast tumultuous waves, as they sweep down the rapids and are hurled into the immense chasm below, and heard in its voice of thunder, which drowns all other voices, and reverberates in one perpetual roar of sound and echo.

—James Hall, Geology of New York (1843)
(comprising the survey of the Fourth Geological District, Albany)

THE CHALLENGE

This essay is my response to an open challenge issued by Meinig in an invited address, "Geography As an Art," to the Institute of British Geographers: "Geography will deserve to be called an art only when a substantial number of geographers become artists" (1983, 325). The magnitude of the problem is neatly encapsulated by my quotation from James Hall, and a contemporary counterpoint was provided in 1986 by an exhibition of works of art inspired by the Niagara Falls held at the Albright Knox Gallery in Buffalo. Frederick Church's monumental painting of Niagara stood out, in both size and quality, but the others represented a very diverse collection of styles and talents. To the riposte that quality in art cannot be determined I have no space to respond, but I refer readers to Houseman 1933 and Rosenberg 1967 on poetry and art respectively. The obvious high-brow moral is that the desire to succeed, to represent, is no guarantee of high-brow success, but the more subtle message is that at the popular level those paintings have served their purposes very adequately, and similar icons serve equally well today. In this century, L.S. Lowry's "quality" has been extensively debated, but his retrospective drew more crowds than the Picasso exhibition. How can we tap this popular and public medium?

I should emphasize that Meinig, when he mentions art, refers to literary productions, not graphic ones, but his reasons for the restriction are nowhere made clear, despite his sensitive discussions on the inner state of an artist, a discussion that is echoed by Wreford Watson (1983) with a similar intensity of feeling. I surmise that Meinig's hesitation in this matter arises from his academic roots: we can all write, after a fashion; thus, a suitable artistic response by an academic geographer might be a literary production of some kind. Even so, Meinig recognizes that the result may not be simply an extension of existing work: "Here we look out on varied and uncertain ground. What might it yield should the geographer try to cultivate it?" (1983, 322).

FOR WHOM WILL WE WORK?

As I have indicated, the real difficulty arises from the audience. Is it to be fellow academics, as Meinig implies, or is it the general public, as Peirce Lewis (1985) suggests in his presidential address (entitled "Beyond Description") to the Association of American Geographers meeting in Detroit? If it is to be an art in the sense of an artistic production (literary or graphic or both), then there can be little doubt that the audience has to be the general public, not a coterie of academics. But then the questions arise, can geographers make themselves into artists, can they produce what is needed, and when and if they succeed, will the result look like geography as we know it? Ellen Ramsay's essay in this volume demonstrates that when a geologist (Lucius O'Brien) reverted to art, the result did not look like geology, and the "geography" was, at least in the image she discusses, wilfully censored!

While I may not have the complete answers to these questions, I can address them. My personal response has two parts. The formal, printed response, found here, discusses some of the theoretical issues at stake in producing a public geography on an artistic basis. The second response, a HyperCard Stack for Macintosh computers on the subject of the Welland Canal, is a sketch (no more), in a medium that has some promise, of how I myself respond to the need to communicate with the public, using the tools I possess. However, this latter is not, and cannot be, a prescription. I define public loosely; my point is that if we are to produce our own work in this genre – poems, novels, films, or other graphics – it must stand on its own feet as art, even if it is driven by an inner logic that is geographical. Whether public geography is the proper term I am not sure, but my intent is that, by whatever means, an implicitly geographical message is conveyed to those not professionally prepared in the field.

AN ARTISTIC MANIFESTO

I believe that geographers can succeed in representing their subject matter artistically if they bring to it personal responses, honest work, and integrity. I choose the word represent advisedly: represent means to "call up by description or portrayal or imagination," to "place a likeness before mind and senses." The imagination can achieve this by whatever means befits the purpose. I also distinguish between subject and subject matter. We certainly shall fail if we try to represent our subject, geography; what we must do is represent our subject matter, the landscape.

My belief that this is possible is an instinctive response to the challenge that Meinig has thrown down. It is in part visceral, subjective, even emotional, but as Lewis remarks, it is not, and must not be, mere "aesthetic self-indulgence." Above all it must be disciplined, a notion I discuss later. I believe this as a professional geographer, trained when the discipline was still unified, though at a time when fragmentation was already a significant threat. My instincts have always resisted fragmentation, although this inclination has rarely been a productive attitude in the modern academic world. I grew up in the English countryside, a fascinating palimpsest of human action on the land, and my primal feelings still take me to field, stream, wood, and wilderness. A sensitivity to the form of the land led me to geomorphology. A love of drawing has always been with me. I draw even when other pressures prevent painting, and I've always used it as a tool in my field work.

Others will react differently, and without doubt their personal responses, and their particular tools, will differ from mine, but it is the integrity of the response that justifies the creative act.

A JUSTIFICATION

Words in a written text create a linear structure, a thread of thought. A temporal narrative is achieved at the expense of spatial structure unless the writer constructs a text with enormous care. A description of space may be achieved by calling up specifically visual imagery and by drawing on a reservoir of the reader's past sensory impressions. On the other hand, pictorial images use two spatial dimensions to represent three, but the narrative content in a picture is very hard to delineate and normally demands a textual knowledge from the viewer equivalent to the reservoir of sensory images demanded by the writer, as art historians make clear.

The two forms are mixed in the general medium of film (e.g., Lewis 1983) and the illustrated book, with various degrees of success. What I propose we do is examine a medium closer to the latter than the former, since it is easier to reflect upon and review a printed image than a celluloid strip. Indeed, what is required ideally includes an interrogative structure – a medium in which the user seeks, and receives, answers to questions posed.

The use of narrative in history has fallen into disuse and disfavour, but Rudwick (1985) has revived it, with both great discipline and great effect, in his account of the Great Devonian Controversy. By maintaining a strict chronology, detailed documentation, and extensive quotation from the original sources, he has constructed an enthralling and revealing account. Like the use of narrative in history, description in geography, the backbone of regional geography so it is said, is frequently disparaged as mere description. Some people say this is a worthless enterprise, and they assert that others say it, but it is hard to find in print a clear statement damning mere description (but see Hart 1982, 27, note

87). Tuan (1989) recalls that the Greek root for the word theory means spectator, which is to imply that theory describes a series of events; following that line
of thought, "mere description" is mere theory. As one who has written theory, I
can say that it is exactly that: a formal description of how certain things come to
be. However that might be, Carl Sauer remarked "that really good regional
geography is finely representational art, and creative art is not circumscribed by
pattern or method" (1956, 298). If it is a matter of having a way with words,
then it is no wonder that some of the greatest regional descriptions are found in
the works of novelists – Thomas Hardy's Wessex being a prime example among
many (Darby 1948). For Region Niagara, let me mention Howard Engel's
Benny Cooperman novels as effective evocations of place. However, recognizing
the excellence of novelists does not solve the problem of writing good regional
descriptions. Indeed, it may be said to exacerbate it because we are not comparing like things. Meritorious as they are, such descriptions do not constitute
geographies, not because they are limited ones, but primarily because they are
the by-products of other central purposes. No, if we want good regional representations, we must produce them ourselves.

The problem with regional description, as it stands at present, is that the
visual approach as a method of representing space is strongly suppressed. The
geographer does try to balance the description by the use of maps and to a lesser
extent the use of photographs. Hardly discernible is the use of the deliberately
drawn image of the landscape, although some entry-level geography texts are
making forays in this direction, for example, Muller and Oberlander's *Physical
Geography Today*. The imbalance is astonishing when we consider that what we
see when we move about is a continual stream of visual images – literally
megabytes of information every minute – yet we try to compress all of them
into, perhaps, a single megabyte of text (that is to say, a book). Is it any wonder
that the gossamer thread weaving a mental image pregnant with meaning so
frequently breaks, and the chain of thought is lost? Cosgrove (1985) has made a
similar point with regard to the neglect of the visual by humanist geographers,
for all that they speak of "images." The journal *Landscape* is an honourable
exception to the charge that the visual is neglected, and several chapters in this
volume rectify that neglect. Relph (1981), for his part, links the decline of the
landscape idea as a visual image in the twentieth century to the corresponding
failure of representational landscape art to interest the art world to a serious
extent. Need I add that these criticisms are directed at the high-brow world?
Landscape paintings still sell in copious quantities, but they are excluded from
serious consideration as "art" by simple semantic subterfuges.

In another paper, Rudwick (1976), prompted by the overwhelming (and
undisputed) use of visual media in geology lectures at that time, demonstrates
that geology in the nineteenth century had to develop a formal visual language of
maps, sections, reconstructions, figured fossils, and landscape drawings in order
to convey the new discipline's message. I have found that in eighteenth-century
writings on the terraqueous globe, regional geological arguments were being

developed through the skilful use of existing maps, measured sections, and imagined views called to mind by prose, an approach that was at once a gedanken experiment in space and time and that depended upon visual imagery (Tinkler 1989). The imagined visual representation was used as a legitimate constructionist argument. Robert Bakewell's diagram of Niagara Falls, which he sent to his father in 1829, is a local and later example (Bakewell 1830; also available in Tinkler 1985, 1987).

Cosgrove (1985) explains how the rediscovery of perspective during the fifteenth-century Tuscan Renaissance enabled the painter to achieve a fine control over man-made spaces that was pleasing to the paying public and introduced science into art. He contrasts this with the position of the contemporary humanist geographer who appeals to the "landscape" idea as the subjective core of an unscientific geography. The laissez-faire attitude of the modern artist (towards subject matter) and the ubiquitous but unselective camera combine in this century to eliminate the imposition on the public of a unified view of the world orchestrated by artists or their paymasters. The North American public is astonishingly ignorant of geography in general, and its sense of space and spatial relations has been all but destroyed (Lewis 1985). Geographers for their part, taken as a general class, try to impose their structured mental images on the world in the form of maps. Like the Renaissance ruler, they organize, partition, and ultimately control geographical space in the mind of the viewer; they too bring science into art, and perhaps they too please their rulers. In one instance they have helped artists, inadvertently: Nicolaides obtained the inspiration for contour drawing, which he introduced to the New York Student's Art League, from maps that he worked with in the First World War (Nicolaides 1941, inside rear dust cover).

RIGOROUS REGIONAL REPRESENTATION

How can regional representation be rigorous, yet subjective and incomplete? A resolution of this conundrum is based on the existence of intellectual discipline. It is a mistake to think that because artists and their emotions are subjective they are undisciplined or unaccountable. An artist is self-critical, perhaps to a fault, with respect to both the content of a picture and its technical production. The public is rarely aware of technical limitations (which is as it should be for public art; everyone must master the tools of the trade), so that the emphasis lies upon the content. The choice an artist makes in subject matter therefore dictates what the public will see, and so one dimension of rigour may be achieved by making choices for the image that are both individually and collectively consistent and comprehensive.

When the image is selected, the intellectual process enters a second phase. How will the image be produced, in a physical sense? Confronted with a landscape, an artist can choose among endless ways of representing it, even in a single media, say pencil. How it will be done will depend on the skills the artist possesses, but more than anything else, at the moment that a mark is made on

the paper, there is selection, elimination, emphasis, and distortion. All are done
without intense deliberation; a fleeting cloudscape, mottling rolling farmlands
with light and shade, wait for no pencil. The unconscious control at the moment
the drawing is made is the force of life's experience. That experience is acquired
in many ways, some deliberate, some not, and the experience should not be
neatly categorized into amateur or professional, artistic or geographical. It is
what Pierre Bonnard had in mind when he said that "drawing is feeling, colour is
an act of reason," an aphorism that rarely makes sense to the non-artist, who
thinks it should be the reverse. See too the instructions that Nicolaides gives on
contour drawing the nude model: "Imagine that your pencil point is touching
the model . . . Develop the absolute conviction that you are touching the model"
(1941, 9). It is probably the same sensation to which Jeans alluded when he
required "an immersion in the meaning of place" to which in the end there "can
only be a personal response" (1979, 211). He is right to part company with
those who would insist that geographical description be replicable, but I am
uncomfortable about endorsing the view that there is an aspect of the essence
of geography (or of art) that lies beyond the grasp of the scientific method,
properly understood. That would seem to circumscribe science unduly, unfairly,
and forever.

Ruskin said, after immersing himself in geology, that "I closed all geological
books, and . . . set myself, so far as I could, to see the Alps in a single, thoughtless
and untheorising manner; but to see them; if it might be thoroughly." Nevertheless, he was fair enough to note too that "the natural tendency of accurate science
is to make the possessor of it look for, and eminently see, the things connected
with his special pieces of knowledge; and as accurate science must be sternly
limited, his sight of nature gets limited accordingly" (1856, 475). Similarly, we
must come to landscape, but there is a final caveat: there can be no completeness, for to stimulate the imagination is the imperative of art.

THE USES AND MEANING OF IMAGERY: ILLUSIONISM

Is it legitimate to be attracted by an image, and if so, what meaning can be
attached to it, what lies behind it? Fortunately, Tuan (1989) has examined the
aesthetics of the surface in a very recent paper. He notes the current disfavour
with which the surface is viewed as a serious philosophy of meaning, and he
categorizes the meanings that may be hidden behind it. For my purposes, there
are two lessons to be derived, one conventional, the other radical.

Firstly, the surface serves as a route to deeper meaning; it can be used to
lead, surprise, even revolt the viewer, whose attention once caught can be led to
other thoughts. The surprise may not be immediate, it may be brought forth by
a secondary image, or by a piece of text, an unexpected juxtaposition.

Secondly, there may be an even more radical interpretation of the surface
aesthetic than even Tuan imagines: perhaps there is nothing beyond it. Perhaps
the surface is all there is, perhaps what lies behind it is an illusion, an impression,
an implication, but one that is impressed from the mind of the viewer. This

contention has the dubious nihilistic flavour of postmodernism (from which I would dissociate myself), but if there is validity in this thought, then the surface takes on a new role, for it must contain all there is to say. Such a view raises the artist to new levels of responsibility, for when he or she selects, designs, and makes a mark, he or she is acting as the censor as well as commentator, as indeed Lucius O'Brien was (see Ramsay, this volume, chapter 13). Although the view is radical, it throws the visual into a new and important light and prevents a shadowy retreat by erstwhile critics into hidden, "deeper," transcendental meanings that only the chosen few can perceive. Test this notion against glossy advertising. It leads you into beliefs the advertiser wishes you to cherish, but in truth, is there anything else but the glossy image? Test it against a landscape. The visual image is first a filter, behind it lies a real landscape, but what lies behind that? Nothing at all except the impress of time, manifest as historical and geographical inertia. Of course, a multitude of socio-economic forces, all "real" but invisible, bear upon the landscape, but you cannot readily take them by the scruff of neck and effect change. You can, however, kick a stone, and you can attempt to explain how it got there. Thus, I claim for landscape a perfectly central role as the only legitimate document. If there is to be a carry-over to the realm of visual art from Bordessa's postmodern analysis of Canadian literature (this volume, chapter 5), which contends that landscape cannot be central because the concept of centrality has lost its meaning, then this would be a position I reject as an artist and a geographer. I don't think it is true, and I don't think it could ever be true.

What Do I Bring You?

I am based within Region Niagara (see Figure 1.2, map 4, page 13), a political entity – a mental convenience, or as Hart will have it "a pedagogical device for organizing and explaining a complex world" (1982, 21). Later he says the region is a "subjective artistic device" (1982, 21). My subject matter, the Welland Canal, neatly bisects the eastern peninsula. It is an artificial substitute for the Niagara River, whose power is readily harnessed, but not so readily bypassed. I represent the canal to you as it would be perceived by a newcomer. Just as I would take you on foot or by car, I draw you along the canal with annotations on the visions I present. I hope that I educate you out of the void and into the canal, and even thread you into the region beyond.

The difficulties in doing this are made easier by the linear structure of the canal. The more general problem lies in the fact that the public is not used to directly assimilating a geographical argument (i.e., one with spatial dimensions), and so the presentation itself must be logically structured, but it must be necessary for the viewer to understand that logic per se, or even to be aware of it.

Needless to say, the spatial scales and the subject matter of the drawings vary greatly, from broad panoramas to local vignettes. I do not rely upon, or ignore, traditional icons: symbols that stand for more in the imagination than the eye can see (for example, Niagara Falls). Their danger is that they emphasize conven-

Figure 17.1
Upper: Entering the canal at Port Weller. *Lower:* Riding high, a saltie without freight proceeds up the canal.

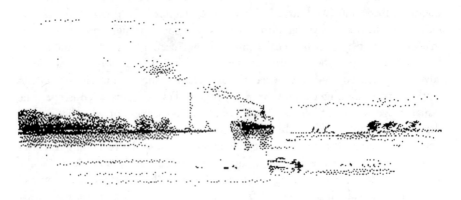

Figure 17.2

Upper: The *Saguenay* passes below the Queen Elizabeth Highway and through the raised Homer Bridge (carrying Highway 81) as it approaches Lock 3. The *Canadian Mariner* emerges from Lock 3. *Middle:* The *Quedoc*, a typical laker, passes beneath the lift bridge for Glendale Avenue. *Lower:* The *Quedoc* waits in early morning mist to enter the flight locks which surmount the Niagara Escarpment.

Figure 17.3
Upper: Squeezing into the lock. *Lower:* Shipbuilding at Port Weller.

tions and generalizations in places where the exception is as important as the rule. It is the danger inherent in seeing only that the prairies are flat. In Relph's (1981) phrase, one must beware of the "average annual landscape" and seek out all the local colour. I have tried both to find the form and to present the processes that synthesize a region. Any landscape is the visible outcome of a massive investment of labour, money, and imagination expended over time; something of that investment must be portrayed.

A HyperCard Stack

The HyperCard Stack is the result of my efforts. HyperCard is an application that comes with all Macintosh computers as part of the system software. It is immensely flexible, for the metaphor is that of a stack of index cards, in which each card contains information in a variety of guises. The HyperCard Stack has a background that may be common to many cards and that can contain graphic images, fields (for text), and buttons that are used to initiate actions, such as moving another card or another stack. The card itself may contain more pictures, text, and buttons, unique to that card. Associated with the entire stack, the backgrounds, the card, and all buttons is a programming language, HyperTalk, used to write scripts controlling the actions chosen by the stack user.

My use of the stack technology utilizes its graphic qualities. Each card has a picture, an image relevant to the canal theme. All these images are from my own drawings or paintings, which were scanned into the Macintosh using an AppleScanner (much like a Xerox machine) under the control of HyperScan, which is software designed to import scanned images directly into a HyperCard Stack. Adjustments to the image can be made during the scanning process by adjusting the area to be scanned and the brightness and contrast. Painting tools provided within HyperCard allow further modifications. The end result is a picture represented by black and white pixels on the computer screen. Needless to say, there is deterioration of the image quality from the original, although I have been surprised at how successful the graphic results have been, given these limitations. In some instances, unpromising drawings in the sketch-book improve on the computer screen!

I have provided each card with a text field giving some background information about the image. The user chooses this otherwise-hidden field by clicking on the picture with the Macintosh mouse; another click removes it from view again. In this stack, text is placed in a card field that is customized for size and placement on the card, thus avoiding the visual boredom that might result from seeing a field in the same place every time. There is no shortage of room in a field, for a scrolling field can be installed if required. Merely as an example, the entire text of this chapter (around 29,000 characters) was placed in a single field, on a single card, at the end of the stack.

Navigation around the stack is designed to be as intuitive as possible. Large, panel-size, hidden buttons on the right and left sides of the background of each card allow the user, by clicking with the mouse, to move to the next or previous

Figure 17.4

Upper: The *Ciudad de Inca* at Welland Dock during the Tall Ship's visit. *Lower:* Leaving the canal at Port Colborne, the Robin Hood flour mill in the background.

card in the stack. Another large hidden button in the centre of the card switches the user to a regional map, which was scanned in from a basemap and then modified with HyperCard's own tools. On this map, transparent buttons overlie place-names, and clicking on a button takes the user to relevant images in the stack. Another button provides access to an inset map (structured in a similar manner) of the Welland Canal within the St. Catharines area. From either map, a button enables a return to the stack at the card last seen. The user thus navigates at will and whim around the images.

Obviously any type of image can be scanned in and utilized in this manner. In the future, similar technology will enable a greater sophistication in the presentation, a finer resolution at the pixel level, larger images, and the incorporation of colour. The stack should be judged in part by the promise it holds as pedagogical tool.

REFERENCES

Bakewell, R., Jr. 1830. "On the Falls of Niagara, and on the Physical Structure of the Adjacent Country." *Loudon's Magazine of Natural History* 3:117–30

Cosgrove, D.E. 1979. "Ruskin and the Geographical Imagination." *Geographical Review* 69: 43–62.

———. 1985. "Prospect, Perspective and the Evolution of the Landscape Idea." *Transactions, Institute of British Geographers*, n.s. 10:45–62.

Darby, H.C. 1948. "The Regional Geography of Thomas Hardy's Wessex." *Geographical Review* 38:426–43.

Engels, H. 1980. *The Suicide Murders.* Toronto: Clarke Irwin.

Hart, J.F. 1982. "The Highest Form of the Geographers Art." *Annals of the Association of American Geographers* 72:1–29.

Houseman, A.E. 1933. "The Name and Nature of Poetry." Cambridge, at the University Press.

Jeans, D.N. 1979. "Some Literary Examples of Humanistic Descriptions of Places." *Australian Geographer* 14:207–14.

Lewis, P. 1983. "Pennsylvania Journey." A television documentary produced for Pennsylvania Public Television Network, produced at Pennsylvania State University, University Park, Pennsylvania, by WPSX-TV.

———. 1985. "Beyond Description." *Annals of the Association of American Geographers* 75: 465–78.

Meinig, D.W., ed. 1979. *The Interpretation of Ordinary Landscapes.* Oxford University Press.

———. 1983. "Geography As an Art." *Transactions, Institute of British Geographers*, n.s. 8:314–28.

Muller, R.A., and T.M. Oberlander. 1984. *Physical Geography Today: Portrait of a Planet.* 3rd ed. New York: Random House.

Nicolaides, K. 1941. *The Natural Way to Draw.* Boston: Houghton-Mifflin.

Relph, E. 1981. *Rational Landscapes and Humanistic Geography.* London: Croom Helm.

Rosenberg, J. 1967. *On Quality in Art.* Princeton, N.J.: Princeton University Press.

Rudwick, M.J.S. 1976. "The Emergence of a Visual Language for Geological Science." *History of Science* 14:149–95.

————. 1985. *The Great Devonian Controversy*. Chicago: Chicago University Press.

Ruskin, J. 1856. *Modern Painters*. Vols. 1–5. London: George Allen.

Sauer, C.O. 1956. "The Education of a Geographer." *Annals of the Association of American Geographers* 46:287–99.

Tinkler, K.J. 1985. *A Short History of Geomorphology*. London: Croom Helm.

————. 1987. "Niagara Falls: The Idea of a History, and the History of an Idea." *Geomorphology* 1:69–85.

————. 1989. "Worlds Apart: Eighteenth Century Writings on Rivers, Lakes and the Terraqueous Globe." In K.J. Tinkler, ed., *History of Geomorphology: From Hutton to Hack*, 37–71. London and Boston: Unwin Hyman.

Tuan, Y.F. 1989. "Surface Phenomena and Aesthetic Experience." *Annals of the Association of American Geographers* 79:233–41.

Watson, Wreford. 1983. "The Soul of Geography." *Transactions, Institute of British Geographers*, n.s. 8:385–99.

18

The Manitoba Landscape of Martha Ostenso's *Wild Geese*

Alec Paul and Paul Simpson-Housley

*I*n this chapter we present a geographical interpretation of *Wild Geese*, a novel set in the Manitoba lakeland of Western Canada around 1920.[1] Martha Ostenso was only twenty-three years old when she produced this remarkable work. It was in stark contrast with the idyllic material popular in Canada at the time, such as the "Anne" stories of Lucy Maud Montgomery discussed in this volume (chapter 11) by Squire. *Wild Geese* has been variously interpreted by literary critics as, among other things, a demonstration of alienation on the agricultural frontier (Harrison 1977); as a study of evil personified in Caleb Gare (Kreisel 1968); as a feminist view of North American rural society (Avery 1988); and as a renunciation of crass commercialism (Mullins 1962). We believe that *Wild Geese* is also of considerable interest to the geographer who studies the treatment of place in literature.

Literary works in many cases deal with the association between people and places, which is a concern of great interest to the geographer. A writer interprets this association through a perceptual filter that is in part personal, derived from his/her own personality and experience, and in part cultural, derived from the values of his/her culture group. Depending upon the precise nature of this filter, the literary treatment of places, landscapes, and regions may be, for example, symbolic, romantic, or realistic. Whatever its dominant characteristic, it can have an important impact on the reader and may convey vivid geographical images. Furthermore, literature may provide useful insights into human spatial behaviour in at a time or place where conventional forms of geographic knowledge were (or are) limited.

Wild Geese is both place-specific and place-less. The novel is set in interlake Manitoba, yet nowhere in the story is Manitoba mentioned. Even Winnipeg appears only as "the city in the south." Publicists have tried to identify the novel with the larger region of the Canadian plains; the descriptive blurb on our paperback version says it is "set on the windswept prairies." But the wind is a key factor only in the fire of the final few pages. And the prairies of Sinclair Ross or W.O. Mitchell are quite unlike the wooded and well-watered area depicted in *Wild Geese*.

Interlake Manitoba lies at the northern farming fringe of the interior plains of North America. Forested as much as farmed, it is generously endowed with lakes, ponds, streams, and marshes. Indeed, the district of Hayland, the "Oeland" of *Wild Geese*, lies only a short distance east of Lake Manitoba, the second largest of the province's so-called Great Lakes (see map 5, Figure 1.2). Bush and woodland are ubiquitous. The land is mostly flat, and in very recent geologic time, it formed the bottom of the vast glacial Lake Agassiz. The waters of this lake drained episodically, so that low ridges marking former beach lines are common. The lacustrine deposits on which today's soils have formed vary in texture and thickness. In some places, till and bedrock are very close to the surface, and soils here may be stony, as on Anton Klovacz's farm in the story.

Ostenso's portrayal of a region where the natural environment is being made over for agricultural use provides much of interest for the geographer. In a brief article in the *Journal of Canadian Fiction*, Lawrence (1976) takes a preliminary look at the layout of Oeland, the district around the Gare farm that is the centre of *Wild Geese*. He talks of the crops, the buildings, the scenery, the relation of the people to the land, in reality and as revealed in the novel, and points out how Ostenso changed the reality where such change was required by the needs of the novel. But Ostenso's treatment of the region goes much further than this. Her descriptions of interlake Manitoba contain a great deal of symbolism that ranges from the conventional and romantic to the starkly realistic. She chronicles the spatial organization of the society, the utilization of natural resources, the limited interactions between ethnic groups, and institutions such as the school and the church. Equally important to the geographer is Ostenso's ability to interpret the landscape through the eyes and feelings of a variety of characters, who respond to it in different ways. Clearly, though, this ability does not extend to the entire cast inhabiting the region, since Ostenso's perceptions are strongly shaped by her own role and personality, especially by the fact of her womanhood and by the cultural reality that she is of the settlers. *Wild Geese* displays only a narrow vision of the natives and "half-breeds," who were and are an important presence in the population.

As Lawrence (1976) implies, when Ostenso lived at Hayland, the region was already a generation removed from the pioneer stage. Geographical isolation, however, remains a dominant theme in *Wild Geese*. The nearest railway is thirty miles from Oeland, and the younger Gare children have never seen a train. The nearest store is ten miles distant, at Yellow Post. A hundred miles away, the big city in the south (Winnipeg) is another world. The geographical isolation is accompanied by an aura of spiritual isolation and human loneliness.

In *Wild Geese*, Lind Archer is the Teacher (always with a capital T), the role that Ostenso herself filled at Hayland for six months. The Teacher is to be in Oeland for only one summer, an observer who knows she will "go back outside." Lind's initial romanticism is made explicit by the view of spring as "a time of intense wonder in the north, after the long, harsh months when the heart is shut out from communion with the earth" (25). When the Teacher visits the Bjarnassons, the air is

> soft and vibrant with the whir of migratory wild fowl. Rain pools filled the ditches along the road, and lay like stained glass in the low sun; the overhanging willows were in full leaf now, the sedges vividly green and as yet unbowed by a single wind. (44)

Lind is sufficiently moved to hold out her hands "as if to gather in the beauty of it from the wide air." Her response reflects the cultural filter of romanticism through which Europeans saw North America in its untamed state.

It takes only a week or two for Lind to start seeing the land as tyrannical, a harsh taskmaster, unforgiving.[2] This perspective results from her meetings with the local settlers, many of whom have depressing tales to relate. Two men have drowned in Bjarnassons' lake. Two of Fusi Aronson's brothers have died in a blizzard. Anton Klovacz, though terminally ill, is struggling to "prove up" his homestead. Lind sees Caleb Gare as hardly human, "a spiritual counterpart of the land, as harsh, as demanding, as tyrannical as the very soil from which he drew his existence" (33).

Nevertheless, the Teacher retains a dualistic response. Oeland is not the bleak, windswept prairie that many critics see as a dominant theme in Western Canadian literature. Lind can still look romantically at this remote northern district, as she does on an evening ride home:

> The air in the wood road was redolent of tree gums. Occasionally a swallow dipped across the light and vanished like the wraith of a bird. As they reached the summit of a ridge halfway between Klovacz's and Sandbo's, Mark and Lind noticed that the sun was just sinking beyond Latt's Slough, drawing a bar of crimson across the long, motionless water. The sprawling shadows of the horses purpled; it seemed as if their hoof beats in the grey dust became softer. Silence had come over the world like a wing. (95)

Lind Archer has lived elsewhere. For Judith, the heroine of the novel, the landscape of Oeland is all she has ever known. Mostly she sees it as the source of her unending drudgery. "The land was here, they were all rooted to it, like the hay, and the grain, and the trees in the bush" (181). There was no escape. After the day's work on the farm, "the body and the brain would be heavy with sleep, and there was nothing to do but throw one's self down like a spent animal, and seek oblivion from thought and feeling" (34). The women in the Gare household, subjugated to Caleb's will, do an "unbelievable amount of work" (209). However, there are many scenes in *Wild Geese* showing Judith in harmony with the earth – a strongly feminine symbol, opposing Caleb's maleness and his determination to dominate the land. Judith has an instinctive feel for the earth, expressed in the passage (53) where she goes to a favourite spot in the bush and lies naked on the damp ground. Caleb never goes into the bush except to spy on people.

The duality in Judith's response to the landscape and her feminine viewpoint are made clear in a memorable passage that describes her looking across "the flat, unsurprising earth." The drudgery of farm life colours her perception of the region, but she has seen enough beauty in it to be aware that somewhere else she can find this beauty, and freedom too:

> Here was the bush land, without magnificence, without primitive redundance of growth: here was the prairie, sparse as an empty platter – no, there was the solitary figure of man upon it, like a meager offering of earth to heaven. Here were the little wood trails and prairie trails that a few men had made on lonely journeyings, and here the crossings where they had met to exchange a word or two. The sky above it all was blue and tremendous, a vast country for proud birds that were ever on the wing, seeking, seeking. And a little delicate wind that was like a woman, Jude thought to herself, but could in a moment become a male giant violating the earth.
>
> She could find the sky and the wind in a more profuse place, where life was like silk, and she belonged there. (112–13)

Judith's dualistic response is androgynous, which is reflected in Ostenso's frequent references to her as Jude, a male name (St. Jude is also the patron saint of lost causes). Her feminine interpretations provide a balance to the masculinity of her role on the Gare farm.

In contrast, Caleb Gare's attitude to the land is always one of antagonism. His surname is an anagram of "rage." He is the male giant violating the earth. He must force the soil to yield the crops that it wants to withhold from him. His greed motivates his cruelty to his family and his ruthless treatment of his neighbours; it places him at odds with nature, and eventually kills him.

Lind, Judith, and Caleb are the most thoroughly developed characters in the story. All three are anglophone. Ostenso's treatment of the various ethnic groups reflects the limited interactions that she, as the Teacher and an outsider, would have had with them. At the time of *Wild Geese*, the northern interlake region was polarized between the native people and the new settlers. There were – and are – many Indian reserves, and natives and Métis probably outnumbered Europeans. Among the settlers, Scandinavians were most numerous. Icelanders had moved here from the rather unsuccessful colony at New Iceland (Vanderhill and Christensen 1963), which was established in 1875 on the west shore of Lake Winnipeg. They appear as the most substantial ethnic group in *Wild Geese*. Others among the settlers are Norwegian, Swedish, Hungarian, and anglophone.

The Bjarnasson family, with their great stone house on the lakeshore, are the most successful Icelanders in *Wild Geese*. They have firmly established themselves in a material sense, but still adhere to many old customs: Caleb Gare's grasping, commercial attitude is foreign to them. Thorvald Thorvaldson, their nearest neighbour, has a "ramshackle farm" and is beholden to the Bjarnassons for many favours (145). Skuli Erickson is a school trustee, along with Caleb Gare, although he speaks only limited English. But the most imposing of the Icelanders is Fusi Aronson, who lives north of Gare's farm and bears Caleb a mortal grudge over the deaths of two of Fusi's brothers. Fusi's fire, spread accidentally to the woodland he has been forced to sell to Caleb, is the cause – along with Caleb's blind desire to save his flax field, the symbol of his senseless greed – of the latter's death in the muskeg that now belongs to Fusi.

The Gares are the only anglophone settler family in *Wild Geese*, but Western Canada had emerged in the late nineteenth century as a society that would be dominated by anglophones and Protestants. Thus, Caleb Gare is a controlling figure in the social institutions of Oeland and the surrounding area. He is the chief trustee of the Oeland school. Hence the Teacher stays with the Gare family; Lind is symptomatic of the imposition from outside of English culture upon Oeland.[3] Caleb is also influential enough in the only church – Protestant, of course – at Yellow Post that Mark Jordan sardonically remarks that Caleb is the church. Caleb is a hard man and a "Christian"; he makes a considerable fuss about the question of whether Anton Klovacz, a Catholic and therefore an infidel, can be buried in the Yellow Post cemetery.

Klovacz is a Hungarian, and his is the only other immigrant family that figures in any major way in *Wild Geese*. They are relatively recent arrivals at Oeland, for Anton "proves up" his homestead only the day before he dies. This recency allows Ostenso to invoke the images of pioneering, placing Mark Jordan on the homestead to carry out basic tasks such as building and clearing. She also has the Klovacz family travel in a covered wagon, the symbol of the westward movement in the United States rather than in Canada, on "a day of high wind, with great canvasses of white cloud sailing across the blue . . . the canvas curtain at the back [of their white-topped wagon] flapping in the wind. The great boundless clouds of midsummer moved over them like a majestic fleet with sails as pure as snow" (151–52).

Ostenso's native people and Métis are stereotypes, shadowy figures only partly drawn, from a society set apart from the settlers. To the farmers, they are "breeds" or "half-breeds," generally encountered in the novel as loafers at Johanneson's store in Yellow Post or as cheap casual labour. The only exception is Malcolm, "Scotch with Cree blood two generations back" (132), who has been Caleb Gare's hired hand for three years. Malcolm, like the migrating wild geese, is an itinerant who lives in harmony with the land.

Movement is a key feature of *Wild Geese*. It is symbolic of the endless "seeking through solitude" (239) that goes on. Lind Archer especially seems to roam freely all over the countryside. As a result, roads and trails figure very prominently in the novel. Elizabeth Marsland (1978) comments that this is typical of prairie fiction, and furthermore that roads in anglophone novels of the

Canadian prairies are not in harmony with their natural surroundings and are used to "represent monotony, fragmentariness, and a sense of imprisonment."

The roads in *Wild Geese* are not like this at all. Nowhere does Ostenso convey any sense of the roads in the Manitoba lakeland forming an arbitrary intrusion upon the landscape. This led Robert Lawrence (1976), in drawing his plan of the area as presented in the novel, to show even the east-west road through Hayland, which is definitely straight and equally definitely part of the rectangular Township-and-Range survey, as curved. Ostenso makes no distinction between the roads of the survey system, which run along the edges of individual farm holdings, and the trails that lead in any or all directions across the farmland. The trails may have been made by the settlers, they may be old Indian trails, or they may follow other routes from times prior to the land survey, as in the case of the road taken by Mark, the boy, and Anton Klovacz's body from Oeland to the Catholic mission twenty miles southeast.

Many important encounters in *Wild Geese* take place on the roads and trails. They are refuges from the imprisoning confines of the farmsteads, especially the Gare farm where "day in and day out, not a soul came; not a soul left it" (34). They cross woodland and prairie, bridge creeks, wind around marshes, lakes, and bluffs, and give fine views from low ridges. Many of the people in *Wild Geese* enjoy travelling along them, and they thus have very positive connotations. Presumably they are also symbolic, representing routes to follow in a search for happiness. An example of this is Malcolm's migration – like that of the wild geese – on horseback from the lumber mills of the south to his trapping grounds in "the land of myriad lakes and rivers" (198) further north. Judith and Sven's happiest times are on the road. The escape to Nykerk Siding on Sven's buggy is Judith's happy ending; the lovemaking that results in her pregnancy occurs in a hollow of woodland by a little bridge along the trail home to Oeland from Yellow Post.

Secret places such as this hollow of woodland and the barn on the Gare farm are associated with the undercurrent of violence that appears occasionally in *Wild Geese*. The violence itself is secretive. Judith and Sven's tryst includes a wrestling sequence that becomes increasingly unrestrained and inflicts cuts and bruises on both of them. When Caleb imprisons Judith in the barn, she throws an axe at him and misses; the scene is played out in a location removed from the rest of the activity on the farm.

The theme of the house as a protection against the elements and a vision of shelter in its varied senses recurs often. Mathias Bjarnasson has built a solid stone house that is an image of himself, "eternal in endurance, eternal in warmth and hospitality of nature" (44). Lind and Mark meet in the cosy little Klovacz house, with the rain pattering on the window pane behind the blind pulled down against the darkness of a wild night. The Gares' eldest son, Martin, dreams of building a substantial new house on the farmstead, a vision Caleb denies.

The woodland and bush are an important counterpart to the farmland. Some of the bush is being cleared – Mark has five acres of "choked birch trees" to clear on the Klovacz' homestead (69) – but much remains in its natural state.

It is an important source of fuel – anticipating the fiery climax to the novel – and of building material – the Gares still live in a log house. The bush also provides wild game, fruits, and berries, and is a source of quiet recreation for those with the intuition to appreciate it.

Other aspects of the natural environment are treated more negatively. The muskeg on Caleb Gare's land is "bottomless and foul. In the heat of summer it gave up sickly vapours in which clouds of mosquitoes rose. Cattle and horses . . . had disappeared beneath its spongy surface" (19). The swamp on the way to Brund's farm has "clumps of floating moss and rank, hair-like grass" and "a suave bleakness" (104). Towards the Catholic mission are miles of "marsh country, flat and dun-coloured with drying reeds" and "without shade," in which Mark and the Klovacz boy see a giant hawk swoop down and back into the sky with a small animal (205).

In this multifaceted environment, farming and the natural landscape are incongruous. The area is clearly not a vacant Eden. There is an abundance of tension resulting from attempts to control nature. The harsh, tyrannical environment is personified in Caleb Gare. He perceives land as a commodity. In his battle for dominance, however, he is the ultimate loser. The muskeg suffocates him and fire consumes his flax. Caleb's end exemplifies a distinctly Canadian theme, the refusal of a hostile environment to yield to human domination. Death by the hazards of nature is a familiar event in Canadian literature (Mitchell 1987). *Wild Geese,* though, is not a story only about Caleb Gare. The female characters appraise the land differently. Both Lind and Judith show themselves to be in harmony with the earth in certain passages in the novel. They find ways to live with the land; while Caleb dies, they survive to continue their quest for happiness.

NOTES

1 *Wild Geese,* by Martha Ostenso, was originally published by Dodd, Mead and Company in 1925. Pagination hereafter refers to the New Canadian Library edition of 1971 published by McClelland & Stewart, Toronto. *Wild Geese* won the Dodd Mead prize for the best first novel by a North American author. Some critics contend that Durkin, Ostenso's supervisor at Columbia University, wrote parts of the work, but if such was the case, the matter was forgotten in view of the novel's immediate success.

2 This theme is pursued by Linda Paul in chapter 7 of this volume.

3 In *La Petite Poule d'Eau,* Gabrielle Roy pursues this theme with gentle irony, placing first a French, then an English schoolteacher in the Manitoba Lakeland school of her novel. In this case, the students are French speaking. Roy's treatment of Canadian landscapes in *The Cashier* is examined by Scott in this volume (chapter 14).

REFERENCES

Avery, H. 1988. "Theories of Prairie Literature and the Woman's Voice." *Canadian Geographer* 32:270–72.

Harrison, R. 1977. *Unnamed Country: The Struggle for a Canadian Prairie Fiction.* Edmonton: University of Alberta Press.

Kreisel, Henry. 1968. "The Prairie: A State of Mind." *Transactions of the Royal Society of Canada,* 4th series, 6:171–80.

Lawrence, R.G. 1976. "The Geography of Martha Ostenso's Wild Geese." *Journal of Canadian Fiction* 16:108–14.

Marsland, E. 1978. "La Chaine Tenue: Roads and Railways in the Prairie Novel." *Canadian Literature* 77:64–72.

Mitchell, K. 1987. "Landscape and Literature." In W. Mallory and P. Simpson-Housley, eds., *Geography and Literature: A Meeting of the Disciplines,* 23–29. Syracuse: Syracuse University Press.

Mullins, S.G. 1962. "Some Remarks on Theme in Martha Ostenso's Wild Geese." *Culture* 23:359–62

Vanderhill, B.G., and D.E. Christensen. 1963. "The Settlement of New Iceland." *Annals of the Association of American Geographers* 53:350–63.

19

Deriving Geographical Information from the Novels of Frederick Philip Grove

O.F.G. Sitwell

$\mathcal{M}$y objective in this chapter is to examine one way in which human geographers can, through an examination of regional novels, deepen their understanding of the places that they study. To this end, I use three of the prairie novels of Frederick Philip Grove as examples of fictional works that are explicitly set in a region recognized by Canadian geographers as having a distinctive character. My approach is not that of a literary critic. Instead, I treat a body of writings as though it were a set of data gathered by the conventional methods of social science. One consequence of this approach is that I must search for an appropriate model, since, insofar as social scientists dedicate themselves to using the methods of science, they simultaneously dedicate themselves to the use of models (Chorley and Haggett 1967). Having said that, however, I must admit immediately that I cannot use the model that I am about to define in the way that I would if I were carrying out a piece of orthodox social science. Rather, I use it as a heuristic device that allows me to be as much like a scientist as a humanist can be. The model in question has a name; it is called *Homo rimans*.[1]

HOMO RIMANS

Rimans is derived from the Latin verb *rimor*, the literal meaning of which is to cleave or to split apart. By extension, it came to mean to pry into, to search for the cause of. *Homo Rimans* is as close as I can get in a single phrase to capturing a particular vision of humankind that has the following characteristics:

- In order both to avoid being chauvinistic with respect to gender and to underline the intent that the model represent people in general, *Homo rimans* is plural – neither he, nor she, but they.
- They are interpreted as being faced with challenges to which they have to respond and problems to which they must find solutions.
- Both challenges and problems exist, within the model, as they are perceived. Consequently, the responses the perceivers make, while always rational from their point of view, may appear to be sub-optimal or even irrational from the point of view of some third party.

- The challenges and problems are categorized as belonging to one of three classes: those set by (1) the physical environment, (2) other people, and (3) the non-material dimension of reality. The last phrase is used as a neutral term designed to discourage the emotions associated with discussions of values in an ideological or religious context. The content of the non-material is established as that which cannot yield consistent measurements, the corollary being that matter does yield consistent measurements. This definition of matter is an empirical one.

  The point that there are different classes of problems is worth emphasizing because it allows more than one explanation for inconsistencies in repeated attempts to measure some object, event, or process. On the one hand, there are people who say that they are not surprised at such an outcome because they believe there is a non-material dimension to the world. We can call such people dogmatic idealists. On the other hand, there are those who attribute discrepancies to the lack of appropriate instruments. They are inspired by the fact that there was a time when we could not measure the behaviour of electrical phenomena because no one had yet invented ammeters, voltameters, and so on. In those days, people could speculate about the cause of the instances of electric charge that were visible in the world around them, but one person's speculation was as good as the next's (or, if it wasn't, there was no way to distinguish what we, having acquired the appropriate instruments, call the better speculations from the poorer ones). Those who assert that one day we will have instruments capable of measuring every form of behaviour, human as well as natural, form the tribe of dogmatic materialists.

  In distinction to these extremes, those who use *Homo rimans* as a guide adopt a pragmatic agnosticism. Nothing more is required.
- Challenges and problems evoke responses that take the form of strategies. This is most obviously the case with respect to the second class of problem mentioned above, that is, other people. They may be perceived as either friends or enemies. The basic strategy used in the case of friends is to converge in space and cooperate in the pursuit of goals. In the case of enemies, the choice is classically between fight and flight (that is, to evict from a specified space by force, or to leave some particular space to be occupied by the enemy).

Equivalent responses can be identified in the case of the other two classes of challenge/problem. In this volume, for example, Porteous (chapter 22) presents Canadians, and beyond them the citizens of the world, with the choice of treating the natural environment as a defeated enemy that can be exploited and abused at will, or as an ally with whom we should live in symbiotic harmony. The different responses of the Maritime settlers and the Swedish peasants to essentially the same choice are identified by Sandberg (chapter 9) as what distinguishes the two groups from one another.

Not the least of the virtues of *Homo rimans*, in the context of this book, is

the fact that the three categories of challenge that are built into the model –
namely, nature, people, and morality – are the same as the three Bordessa uses in
structuring his chapter (chapter 5). It is also legitimate to suggest that there are
echoes of this triad in Scott's identification of three points of view in *The
Cashier:* "the literal, [the] psychological, and [the] ideological" (chapter 14).

REGIONS AND PLACES

Regions have occupied a large place in the methodological controversies that
have given shape to the history of geographic thought (Hartshorne 1939; Minshull
1967). As all North American professional geographers know, we have paid
much less attention to both the word "region" and the ideas inherent in it since
the quantitative revolution than our predecessors did in the decades before 1960
(Johnston 1981). With the aid of historical perspective, we discover that a key
issue in the battles over regionalism (namely, the distinction between the region
as some specific piece of the earth's surface, on the one hand, and the region as a
concept located in people's minds, on the other) rarely appeared in the debates
Hartshorne recorded.

If we concentrate our attention on the concept of region, we can say that
any particular region is an abstraction that is created by some individual in the
course of trying to find the order that we all assume lurks behind the diversity of
the world. Some regions are never given specific names, but are identified under
generic labels such as "the neighbourhood." Most of us can identify, though
perhaps not with great precision, the neighbourhood in which we live, as well as
others, such as those where we work, shop, or travel on holiday.

Because regions begin as private constructs, there need be no agreement as
to the location and extent of any particular one. On the other hand, if people
not only talk about some place but also give it its own name, then, as Robinson
(1973) established in principle, a region as understood by human geographers
has been identified. The prairies of the Canadian West form such a region.

That large region is itself subdivided into two that are distinguished on the
basis of differences in climate, soil, and vegetation. The most commonly used
names for this pair of regions are Palliser's Triangle (or the short-grass region)
and the Park Belt (or parkland). The latter gets its name from the presence of
small groves of poplars that are separated by open expanses of grassland. North-
wards, as winters get longer, the groves of trees become larger and also more
diverse in appearance, as spruce trees make their appearance in them; here, we
are nearing the boreal forest. These distinctions of vegetation, like the soils from
which they spring, are a response to the climatic regimes that prevail in the two
regions. The two regions have in common an alternation of short summers,
better described as warm than hot (though temperatures may rise to uncomfortable heights on individual days), and long winters, marked by the bitterness of
the cold and the ferocity of the blizzards that rage across the open landscape. The
most important distinction between the two climates is provided by the amount
of rain that falls in summer. Not only does relatively little rain fall in Palliser's

Triangle, but the amount that falls in any particular summer varies to a marked degree; all too often the fields are parched by a drought. Worse, dry summers show a tendency to occur in cycles, so that there may be several in near succession. By contrast, in the Park Belt not only does more rain fall on the average, but droughts sufficiently severe to wither the crops are rare.

Within these two regions a myriad of other, smaller ones occur, each of which is known, at least in most cases, only to those who live in them. In many cases the local character of the physical environment of these small regions, which we might distinguish as *districts,* is determined by variations in soil and terrain that are consequences of the great ice age.

As regions become yet smaller, it becomes increasingly common to substitute the word *place* for *region.* In this chapter I have followed that usage.

If, as scholars, we wish to establish the nature of any particular place, and if we do not wish to labour through a summary of the leading characteristics of its physical environment in the way that I have just done, then, as an alternative we could make the following assumption and proceed to the research that is implied in it. The assumption is that a place would be characterized by the responses of those who live in it to the three classes of challenge embodied in the model *Homo rimans.*

There is no doubt that this method involves a degree of subjective judgment. For one thing, it is unlikely that all members of any culture would show exactly the same response to any given challenge. The appropriate response for us, as geographers, would be to treat empirically as belonging to the same class a range of responses shown by the people we are investigating. Again, it is likely that the limits on these ranges will have differing interpretations, but it is in the nature of the social sciences, as well as of the humanities, that such differences should exist and that such judgments should have to be made.

USING *HOMO RIMANS* IN BRIDGING THE GAP BETWEEN LITERATURE AND REGIONAL GEOGRAPHY

In order to show the possibilities inherent in the procedure, as well as to provide initial responses to some of the difficulties that are associated with it, I shall work through a sample exercise. I shall take *Fruits of the Earth* (Grove [1933] 1965) as my primary data source, with supplementary information taken from *Settlers of the Marsh* (Grove [1925] 1966) and *Our Daily Bread* (Grove [1928] 1975).

With occasional deviations made necessary by the desire to make comparative points, I shall deal with the characteristics of the regions in a systematic way, taking each of the major classes of problems in turn.

PROBLEMS AND CHALLENGES SET BY THE PHYSICAL ENVIRONMENT

Each of the novels is set within a physical environment that has its own parameters. In the case of *Fruits of the Earth*, the pioneers who form its protagonists took up land in Manitoba, on the floor of former glacial Lake Agassiz, somewhere between Winnipeg and the boundary with the United States. By the criteria of climate, this region forms part of the Park Belt. As a result, the vegetation "is characterized by a covering of tall grasses, a paucity of shrubs and [surprisingly] an absence of trees except for those along river courses" (Watts 1968, 92). Watts continues: "The absence of trees is to be understood in terms of too much water, not too little. The soil surveys of the area state that before artificial drainage, much of the Red River plain was water saturated for the early part of the summer."

All of these facts are faithfully presented by Grove. Some characteristics are described explicitly, notably the prairie grasses growing on a plain so flat as to allow water to accumulate on its surface after prolonged rain or when the snow melts in spring and, beneath that vegetation, the fertile soil that supports crops of wheat whose volume and quality depend on the weather experienced over the duration of a growing season. Also explicitly described are the efforts made by the authorities to dig "two gigantic [drainage] ditches through the district" (Grove 1965, 16). One additional feature of the region that I did not catalogue above, though the settlers were surely aware of it, is recorded by Grove: the mosquitoes that swarm in myriads during the short summer. Appropriately, too, there is not a drought in the twenty-one years that the action of the novel spans.

The eponymous marsh of the second novel lies some 160 to 180 kilometres northwest of Spalding District, the setting of *Fruits of the Earth*. That distance is great enough to have removed the locale from the Red River plain while still leaving it within the Park Belt, though near its northern frontier with the boreal forest. Here a drought is recorded, but only one. When we turn from climate to soil and vegetation, Grove continues to be our reliable guide. The protagonist of this novel, Niels Lindstedt, homesteads in a district where there is considerable local variation in both these elements of the physical environment, as there is also in the terrain. Grove describes the area thus:

> The southern part of his claim was covered with comparatively small growth . . . To the east, there was much willow; though even there, on a piece of rising ground, ten acres or so of primeval forest remained like an island. West and north of his claim there was sand. Nothing but low, scrubby bush intervened between the claim and the cliff of forest along the creek. (1966, 48)

In *Our Daily Bread* on the other hand, as the novel opens, the crops are withering for lack of rain, and several other droughts are reported in subsequent years. The setting of this novel is "the short grass country of . . . Saskatchewan" (Grove 1975, 4). "Prickly Pear cactus grew in clusters on the bare, rolling hills" (385) near the farm where John Elliot senior, the protagonist of the story, raised his family.

Grove's descriptions may lack the precision of climatic statistics or an ecologist's inventories, but an attentive reading creates images of small-scale regions, defined by their physical environment, with which human geographers would surely be content. On only one point does Grove seem to go astray. "Cattle!" John Elliot said wrathfully. "In short-grass country! Where it takes thirty acres pasturage per head" (1975, 211). Most geographers would look on cattle ranching as being a better choice in such a region than the cultivation of wheat that John Elliot favoured.

Before leaving the topic of the first class of problems, we can note that, at least when the story begins, Abe Spalding deals with them directly. This is because at this time he is not merely a farmer but one who is still using, at least for the most part, a preindustrial technology. By the end of the book, his relations with the environment have become much more indirect. It is not just that he has installed an electric generator so that his cows are now milked by machine, but also that as a prosperous farmer he pays men to do his work for him. He has, in short, joined the great majority of those who live in industrial societies – those who deal with the greatest challenge set by the physical environment (namely, to derive from it the basic necessities of life) by earning or otherwise acquiring the money to buy such necessities.

PROBLEMS AND CHALLENGES SET BY OTHER PEOPLE

An interest in regional structure leads to a consideration of scale. It seems intuitively reasonable to suppose that the strategies people use when dealing with people they know might be different from those they would use in relation to people they only know about, even if both groups of people are accepted as being "us" rather than "them." Observation on the size of the area over which those whom "we" know are dispersed would provide empirical evidence for the size of the "neighbourhood" within which "we" live. In hypothetical terms, it would be possible to envisage a pattern of dispersed rural settlement that was absolutely uniform, so that each individual family on its farm would function as the centre of its own neighbourhood (clearly, the stereotypical nuclear family of the American frontier is implied). In *Fruits of the Earth,* however, we are told that "Nicoll's Corner became the social centre of the settlement" (Grove 1965, 58). The settlement in question was one whose inhabitants banded together to organize and support a particular school district. It was this district that was named after Abe Spalding.

Once the district had acquired a name, it became possible for people to live within it who were on hostile terms with others who lived there without this necessarily affecting the tendency of the local people to think of it as having real existence as their neighbourhood (Robinson 1973).

The issue of the relations between people who know one another has not evoked much interest among geographers. It may be that in this we do little more than reflect our culture, for the contrast between the time, energy, and other resources consciously devoted to dealing with problems of the physical environment and that invested in our relations with other people is striking. What follows is consequently little more than a sketch of the issues involved, as revealed by events in *Fruits of the Earth.*

As we have already noted, the relations between people who have a positive attitude towards one another can be distinguished on the grounds of whether they actually know one another or whether they simply belong to the same culture and thus may make an initial assumption of shared outlook and interests. The experience of Abe Spalding allows us to distinguish three classes of people whom others actually know: in Abe's case, other members of his family, his friends, and those with whom his relations were *formal*, either because he employed or otherwise did business with them or because he had dealings with them through his participation in local government. The relations of the first type can be labelled *intimate*, while those with whom we are friends I shall call *local*. The following excerpt provides an illustration of the former:

> She [his wife, Ruth] was aware that he had begun to look critically at her . . . She was getting stout . . . She knew he disliked stout women. The bed which they had so far shared was becoming uncomfortable . . . A week later he brought that new bedstead home; and henceforth they slept apart. (Grove 1965, 46)

Then there were the people with whom Spalding was on bad terms. These included, at diverse times during the unfolding of the plot, individuals at all three levels of the hierarchy, which one can reasonably call spatial as well as social.

Of the neighbours who were hostile to Abe, only one, Wheeldon, succeeded in defeating him over any issue. It is a truism that the two men were only on bad terms because they lived sufficiently close together to know one another; what is less in danger of being labelled a trite observation is that Wheeldon was able to defeat his rival because of the existence of a system of formal law – a system that at one point Abe fell foul of. In one particular year he failed to pay his property tax, with the result that he was disqualified from voting in local elections. Because we all live within this same system of law, and therefore take it for granted, it rarely occurs to us that this system characterizes the culture in which we live. A science-fictional anthropologist visiting this planet from some remote star, on the other hand, could scarcely fail to include such elements in any planet-wide attempt to classify cultures as well as, in large part, regions.

The Third Class of Problems

In making the point about Wheeldon's use of the law to defeat Abe, I moved to the realm of the non-material dimension of reality. Grove's novels make it easy to show that the ideas for which this phrase is a label do not correspond in any simple way to those things commonly understood as relating to religion. Of traditional religion, which in the Canadian context of the early 1900s we can equate with Christianity, there is scarcely a mention. In *Settlers of the Marsh*, there are literally no references to a church, not even as a building, nor to a minister of religion. In *Fruits of the Earth*, there is a single occasion when "a

Presbyterian minister held divine service at the school. Although Abe was indifferent, he took his family" (Grove 1965, 95). The situation in *Our Daily Bread* is more complex. Biblical phrases echo frequently in the head of John Elliot senior, but on one such occasion we learn that "never had he, in these lines, seen or sought for evidences of verbal revelation; purely theological thought had been unknown to him. He had taken them simply as an expression of the marvel of fruitful propagation" (Grove 1975, 189). But if religion, in the conventional sense, is largely absent, the realm of the non-material is rarely far away. On the first trip made by Abe Spalding to his homestead (about which detailed information is given), he discovers that the prairie over which he is making his way "seemed suddenly a peculiar country, mysteriously endowed with a power of testing temper and character" (Grove 1965, 23). All three novels contain many references along these lines, that is to say, references to some aspect of the physical environment that is endowed with power over the minds of the protagonists.

In this realm, too, there are levels set by the scale of distance over which the values that influence the unfolding story of the Spalding District operate. And as with the challenge provided by other people, there are distinctions to make: in this case, distinctions between explicit and functional values. The former are those that are put into words and may or may not be expressed in people's lives; the latter are the values people show that they hold because they put them into effect in the way they live (Sitwell and Latham 1979). Representative of the former is the whole formal organization of government, ranging in scale from school district to federal state.

We take it for granted that Canadians live within a hierarchy of legally established frameworks whose parameters are those of the local, the provincial, and the national. Hints of the ways in which the lives of individual citizens are affected by these frameworks are found in all three novels. Having already touched on the point, I shall be content here to point out that the story of how Wheeldon did Spalding down illustrates the fact that, while it is possible to distinguish the classes of problems conceptually, in life they are bound together indissolubly. The values that individuals hold affect the strategies they use in their relations with other people – an observation that brings us to a consideration of the role of functional values in establishing the character of a region.

When Ruth Spalding went in secret to find a lawyer who would bring "to justice" the man who had seduced her younger daughter, she was driven by her sense of values. Two of her values in particular are illustrated by the incident: her attitude to her husband (a mixture of fear, awe, and suppressed affection) and her concurrence in the high status awarded in the culture of that time and place to a "good" woman (and concurrence in the condemnation "awarded" one who had "fallen"). The power of sexuality is a theme in all three of these novels, and as such there is little doubt that they provide accurate glimpses into the cultural psyche of a very large, though perhaps difficult-to-define, cultural realm.

On the whole, however, it is another "force" that dominates the lives of

Grove's characters. That force is the power of the market, both in its own right and as mediated by changes in technology. It is this power, as well as all the other elements that characterize the economic relations that exist between individuals in the free-enterprise North American way of life, that is fully displayed in the three novels. For a similar observation made with respect to visual artists, see Norcliffe (this volume, chapter 6).

CONCLUSION

In this chapter I have presented a two-part thesis. The first part contends that if geography is concerned with the character of places, and if places have the character they do because of the ways in which the people who live in them respond to the problems and challenges that they meet, then using a model of human individuals that incorporates the latter assumption will help geographers obtain a more balanced understanding of particular places than many of them have exhibited in the past. The second contends that novels can be used to widen and expand upon the types of information available to human geographers through traditional sources, such as the census and the field survey. To say this is neither to reject those sources, nor to dismiss work based on them as uninteresting. It is to say that there can be more to geography than has been dreamt of in the social science that provided most of us with the terms of reference we have used in our teaching and, even more restrictively, in our research.

Beyond that, however, I want to say that of the essays presented in this collection, the one that expresses most effectively my ambition for *Homo rimans* is that by Kobayashi (chapter 21). She puts her finger on a difficult problem for those geographers who seek to understand what the people who have lived in some place have made of it: namely, the problem "of finding [I would substitute *identifying*] and organizing the information that allows us to tie meaning to context." She also draws attention to vernacular literature "because it is a direct expression of structures of feeling as they occur through everyday life." Finally, "By analysing the poetic act as an expression of structures of feeling, we can approach the emotional realm, so often opaque to cultural analysis." Lacking Kobayashi's gifts in the understanding of poetry, I have never tried to raise my sights above the study of the cultural landscape. I grant freely that the evidence provided by that body of evidence, when one is in pursuit of structures of feelings, is coarse by comparison with that which may be derived from poetry, but I am satisfied that the use of *Homo rimans*, with all their specified qualities, provides a framework for a systematic sifting of a relevant body of evidence, and so goes a long way to dealing with the first difficulty Kobayashi identified above.

NOTES

Author's Note: I wish to thank Ed Jackson for reading drafts of this chapter carefully, and for his many useful comments. He is in no way responsible for any shortcomings it may have.

1 The name *Homo rimans* was suggested to Alan Manzie and myself by Dr. E.C. May of the Department of Classics, the University of Alberta, at the time we were preparing our paper "A Middle Way between the Positivist and Humanist Approaches to Knowledge," *Albertan Geographer,* no. 13 (1977): 57–68. The basic characteristics of the model were first presented in Sitwell and Latham 1979.

REFERENCES

Chorley, R.J., and P. Haggett. 1967. "Models, Paradigms and the New Geography." In R.J. Chorley and P. Haggett, eds., *Models in Geography,* 19–41. London: Methuen.

Grove, F.P. [1933] 1965. *Fruits of the Earth.* Toronto: McClelland & Stewart.

———. [1925] 1966. *Settlers of the Marsh.* Toronto: McClelland & Stewart.

———. [1928] 1975. *Our Daily Bread.* Toronto: McClelland & Stewart.

Hartshorne, R. 1939. *The Nature of Geography: A Critical Survey of Current Thought in the Light of the Past.* Lancaster, Penn.: Association of American Geographers.

Johnston, R.J. 1981. "Paradigms, Revolutions, Schools of Thought, and Anarchy: Reflections on the Recent History of Anglo-American Human Geography." In B.W. Blouet, ed., *The Origins of Academic Geography in the United States,* 303–17. Hamden, Conn.: Shoe String Press.

Minshull, R. 1967. *Regional Geography: Theory and Practice.* Chicago: Aldine.

Robinson, B. S. 1973. "Elizabethan Society and Its Named Places." *Geographical Review* 63:322–33.

Sitwell, O.F.G., and G.R. Latham. 1979. "Behavioural Geography and the Cultural Landscape." *Geografiska Annaler* 61B, no. 2: 51–63.

Watts, F.B. 1968. "Climate, Vegetation, Soil." In J. Warkentin, ed., *Canada: A Geographical Interpretation,* 78–111. Toronto: Methuen, for the Canadian Association of Geographers.

20

"Cloud-Bound": The Western Landscapes of Marmaduke Matthews

Elizabeth Wilton

It was the Group of Seven who drew widespread public attention to the Canadian art scene in the post–First World War era. The Group contributed tremendously to raising the public's awareness (both at home and abroad) of the fine arts, and particularly of painting in Canada. However, the Group's rise to the forefront in the 1920s and the near-mythic tale of their struggle for acceptance overshadowed the work of those painters who had preceded them (Davis 1973; Nasgaar 1984).

In the mid- to late nineteenth century there was a proliferation of art institutions in Canada, especially in Ontario. The men and women who became members of these societies were essentially landscape painters, although some also painted portraits. They were concerned with how best to foster the development of an artistic community and audience in Canada. This group of painters did much of the groundwork for those artists who followed, yet most of them have been taken for granted by Canadian art historians.

These painters, such as R.F. Gagen, J.A. Fraser, Lucius O'Brien, Frederick Verner, F.M. Bell-Smith, T. Mower Martin, and Marmaduke Matthews, helped found artistic organizations, art schools, and permanent houses of exhibition. Some were better known than others. For example, Lucius O'Brien gained public recognition for his work as a Canadian Pacific Railway artist (although many in this group also painted for the CPR) and as the art director for *Picturesque Canada* (Grant and O'Brien 1875). T. Mower Martin received attention for his illustrations for a book entitled *Canada* (Campbell and Martin 1907). However, the painter to whom this paper is devoted, Marmaduke Matthews, gained little public recognition, despite his tireless work to promote the growth of painting and art appreciation in Canada. Matthews was born in England in 1837 and grew up in the town of Fifield, Oxfordshire. He immigrated to Canada in 1860 and in 1867 settled permanently in Toronto, making his living as a painter until his death in 1913.

This paper will pursue an argument that is quite different from the one presented by Ellen Ramsay (this volume, chapter 13). She suggests that the landscape paintings of Lucius O'Brien (a Canadian-born contemporary of Matthews) were in the picturesque genre and often ignored the industrialization that was occurring in Canada during this period. I am, to the contrary, suggesting that a substantial body of the landscape paintings from this period do not ignore industrialization but attempt to wrestle with the tension implicit in it. Some painters, like Matthews, were struggling to represent the relationship between people and the land in the new industrial age.

A particularly insightful theoretical text dealing with this subject is Denis Cosgrove's *Social Formation and Symbolic Landscape* (1984). Cosgrove's approach is especially helpful to Canadian historians seeking an alternative to the Northrop Frye school of Canadian cultural analysis. The "garrison mentality" thesis has served our criticism for decades, providing a framework within which to explore diverse aspects of Canadian experience. However, the concentration on fear of the wilderness as a motivating cultural force has, in modern theoretical discourse, proved progressively less adequate. The time has come to explore the application of new methods, to analyse Canadian culture in a much broader context. We must consider the artist as an individual who is subject to societal pressures and the changes occurring in his or her environment.

This theme of the relationship between humans, nature, and landscape preoccupies Cosgrove's work. He establishes a link between the maturation of landscape painting in the late eighteenth and early nineteenth centuries and the process of industrialization. Although *Social Formation and Symbolic Landscape* is essentially about geographical conceptions of the land, the book offers insight into the tradition of landscape painting. Cosgrove explores the topic of landscape painting because he views the various concepts of the land that emerged over time in different fields (science, culture, economics) as intimately connected. He expounds a convincing theory about landscape painting that applies well to the work of Marmaduke Matthews.

Cosgrove suggests that landscape painting developed hand in hand with the evolution of a new social order. This new order was shaped by the advent of modernization and the corresponding expansion of the industrial capitalist state. Landscape paintings are not objective pictures of the land, Cosgrove asserts, but rather, embody particular ideological "ways of seeing," as John Berger (1973) demonstrated earlier in his work of this title. Cosgrove's approach to landscape painting, when applied to Canada, challenges the Northrop Frye canon. The universal application of the "garrison mentality" theory to Canadian art and literature obscures other equally important forces inspiring this art.

Classical Canadian analysis equates unfamiliarity with fear. In discussing European painting trends, Cosgrove estimates that the decline of landscape painting dates from the late nineteenth century. However, in Canada it is more appropriate to extend the landscape period into the 1920s. This style of painting essentially ended with the work of the Group of Seven, whose heyday in effect corresponded with Canada's "coming of age" during and just after the First World War. Accepting this slight modification, one can better understand the connection between the landscape painting movement and the cultural, political, and economic conditions of the time in Canada.

Cosgrove asserts that landscape painting is a means of appropriating the land. The linear perspective turns nature into the artificial construction of landscape. In landscape painting the individual spectator is more important than the collective experience of the land painted. Human figures cannot be dominant because this would place the subject inside the painting. This is clearly one of the patterns in Matthews's paintings and affirms the validity of applying Cosgrove's theory to Matthews's work. Looking for pattern is one means by which to determine the interests of a particular painter and his or her response to the concerns of the time. The diminutive human figures that appear in many of Matthews's paintings represent his endeavour to situate humans in the new land. These figures are only one of a group of motifs that surface time and time again in his work. Other motifs include mountain scenes, lakes with canoeists, waterfalls, and landscapes with small signs of human industry (be it a barely discernible train or a fisherman). Humans and technology are always inconspicuous elements in Matthews's landscapes. They do not dominate the land.

Many patterns have been discerned by Gaile McGregor in her book *The Wacousta Syndrome: Explorations in the Canadian Landscape* (1985). Although this treatise deals mainly with literature, McGregor devotes a lengthy section to the discussion of nineteenth-century landscape painting in Canada and the United States, recognizing six distinct patterns. She articulates these points with clarity, but her interpretation of what these patterns represent is often unsatisfying. Some of the patterns she identifies are present in Matthews's paintings, and for this reason they are useful in the context of this discussion. McGregor attempts to demonstrate that most landscape paintings of this period portray a sense of claustrophobia and terror in face of the land. In this way, McGregor is very much a part of the traditional approach to Canadian cultural analysis.

The first pattern McGregor recognizes is the presence of human activity in the fore- to middle ground and also the featuring of modes of transportation. She points out that these figures are "dwarfed" in comparison to the surrounding landscape. McGregor asserts that "these features would seem to indicate a desire to dominate the environment symbolically by focussing on the human element, but [there is] a general fear or suspicion that it is the human who is dominated instead. The preoccupation with transportation implies a preoccupation with escape" (1985, 16).

The features McGregor identifies are certainly present in Matthews's paintings. However, it is important to make a distinction between the presence of a human form and the presence of a mode of transportation. Matthews, and all of the CPR artists no doubt, had to include the occasional train in his paintings, since one of his main missions was to advertise the West and so promote tourism along the CPR lines.

Marmaduke Matthews was one of many painters commissioned by William Cornelius Van Horne to work as an artist for the Canadian Pacific Railway. In the literature about the CPR artists, Matthews is never discussed on his own; rather, his name most often appears as an appendage to the names of better-known artists. Yet Matthews was a versatile painter who travelled widely in Canada and the United States. He also returned to Great Britain several times over the course of his lifetime. Although he is best known for his western landscapes, he painted often in Ontario and in different areas of New England.

There are several conflicting accounts regarding the number of years Matthews worked for the CPR. Some sources have suggested two years, others three, and some as many as ten years. Matthews probably had greater artistic control over his non-western paintings, as he would not have been restricted by the dictates of a particular patron.

In Matthews's work, above and beyond the recurring images of powerful landscape, humans, and mode of transportation is the underlying theme of the relationship between humans and nature. All of these levels of analysis are important in evaluating the paintings and the artist and in reaching some conclusion about the period.

Dennis Reid (1979, 6), in commenting on the CPR promoters, says that they "understood the force of images, and they encouraged the associations artists made between their road and the picturesque wonders it opened. Considering that the artists faced considerable pressure to include trains in their landscapes it is verging on the absurd to judge the presence of this particular vehicle as evidence of a preoccupation with escape." Modes of transportation are classically noted as a means to get from one place to another and, in the case of the train, a means both comfortable and fashionable. Could this not be the importance of these motifs?

Matthews's paintings that include trains or hand cars are designed to display the beauty of the mountains and to advertise the CPR. These paintings do not demonstrate fear but rather the possibilities inherent in these landscapes, the grandeur of the mountains, and the ability, by means of the train, to travel through them. The hand car suggests to the viewer that even with something as technologically simple as a hand car, one may travel with relative ease through these mountains. The painting appears on one level to be affirming a faith in technology.

The painting featured in this article is untitled and undated. However, it was clearly painted on one of Matthews's western excursions and therefore may be dated between the years 1888 and 1898. The focus in this particular image is on the railway tracks and the hand car cutting through the mountains. There is a small hut with the door opening on both the new technology and the mountains. Further down the tracks we can just see a man with his back turned to the viewer. The mountains in the background look expansive, not threatening, and frame the central image. The companion painting to this one features a man working the hand car in the distance, and once again Matthews displays the splendour of the Rockies.

Matthews shared an interest in new technology with many artists of the

Marmaduke Matthews, *Railway Scene in the Rockies*, c. 1888, watercolour, 50 x 75 cm. Courtesy Dr. and Mrs. J.M. Goodman.

period. Often his work includes evidence of this interest, suggesting a definite link between landscape painting and the growth of technology. Many of the intellectual societies (like the Royal Canadian Academy) included artists, academics, architects, and designers. Art was also linked to technology through the exhibition places of the new technology, which were most often venues similar to the Toronto Industrial Exhibition. It seems that artists were attempting to work out the relationship between humans, nature, and technology in their paintings. There was also a desire to legitimize art by associating it with more technical disciplines. One can see this very clearly in an essay written by Matthews entitled "Art and Its Uses."

> In this age of broadly diffused education, it has come to be an indispensable requisite that some acquaintance with Fine Art shall be included in the equipment of the scholar. Though no attempt be made to acquire practical skill or power in any branch, the student who omits to learn something of its history, use and applications will be generally esteemed lacking in a very essential item of useful knowledge.[1]

Matthews was himself an inventor and in the latter part of his life devoted much time to this hobby. One of his diaries indicates that he attempted to get a patent for a new bicycle peddle and a collapsing bicycle, among other inventions. He was also interested in steam turbines.

The inclusion of humans in this period of painting is fascinating, particularly because in later Canadian landscapes these figures completely disappear.

This begs the question as to why they were present in this particular period. The human figures served a functional purpose in denoting scale but they have additional importance. McGregor feels that these figures demonstrate two contradictory human feelings: a desire to dominate the landscape and the frustration with and sense of being "dwarfed" by the environment. McGregor's analysis rests on the assumption that in order for humans to be depicted as being comfortable in the natural environment they must be shown in a position of control. This is a dangerous and false assumption. These paintings seem to be portraying, in contrast to McGregor's assertion, humans in harmony with nature.

There are, however, two sides to the analysis of these paintings, neither of which indicates fear. The second aspect has to do with Cosgrove's assertion regarding these figures and with the fact that this practice emerged in a specific historical period. The figures are in a sense "in but not of" the landscape. The figures are viewed from a distance, and they are most often engaged in a task that involves some sort of technology, even if it be a very simple form. Some people are pictured with a fishing rod or a gun or in a boat. This use of technology effectively separates them from the natural environment, reflecting the effect of modern developments on the psyche of these painters.

The fact that humans are depicted in the landscapes denotes Matthews's desire to juxtapose them with nature. He is apparently attempting to work out the relationship between these two entities. Possibly, this deliberate juxtaposition disappears in the work of later painters, particularly in the work of the Group of Seven, because the relationship has been clearly established. Humans and nature are accepted as separate, and land is considered an object. This is certainly a radically different interpretation of the work of the Group of Seven but one that merits attention.

McGregor discusses a further characteristic of nineteenth-century landscape painting: a very low vantage point or perhaps a wall of trees, either of which prevents the spectator from seeing deep into the landscape. This pattern is not present in Matthews's paintings. His works tend to offer substantial vistas to the spectator. In the mountainscapes, one gets the feeling that one is looking as far into the distance as is possible.

An article written by Matthews (1882) for *Rose-Belford's Canadian Monthly* is demonstrative of his personal feelings about the land and about mountain landscapes in particular. Its title, "Cloud-Bound," is in itself revealing. It suggests that in his work Matthews was not concerned with limitations or fear but was striving to attain higher goals and to reach new heights. Matthews saw the mountain as a staircase to the clouds. The article describes an excursion he made while on a sketching trip on the Portland and Ogdensburg Railroad. New England appears to have been one of his favourite places in which to paint. The article describes his walking trip to the summit of Mount Webster by way of Mount Pleasant. Matthews wrote the following about reaching the summit of Mount Pleasant:

The sensation was much the same as I had experienced on other mountain tops, but the scene was unique for all that . . . At this moment, the toils of the ascent were forgotten; or perhaps served only to enhance the gratification experienced; and I felt that I would willingly endure ten times the exertion for such reward; even though, in that lonely spot, I felt strongly my own insignificance, and comparisons with insects actively suggested themselves to my mind. (1880, 288)

This article implies that Matthews had a genuine respect for the natural world, and yes, it made him feel insignificant; but for him this was an extremely gratifying experience. The mountains made Matthews consider his place in the universe and challenged human self-importance. This feeling of insignificance was not, to his mind, daunting but rather verged on a religious experience. Although Matthews was discussing, in this article, his feelings about the White Mountains, one can imagine that he felt the same sort of spiritual attachment to the Rocky Mountains in Canada. No doubt, this was one of the reasons why Matthews painted for so many years along the CPR lines.

The patterns that have been discussed surface in most of Matthews's western and non-western paintings. From merely looking at his paintings, one can begin to understand that there was much more behind them than human fear (or humility) before the grandeur of the landscape. His paintings speak for themselves, if one lets them. They are responses to the land and the society. They are not merely colonial fragments of the mother country's culture.

Matthews was clearly committed to the idea of developing a uniquely Canadian artistic community and fostering the talents of young Canadians. This may be seen in his involvement with the Ontario College of Art and also in the fact that he gave art instruction to students attending St. Alban's School (a boys' school of which his son was headmaster in the 1890s) and Bishop Strachan School (a girls' school). He was obviously very generous with his time and skills and received very little monetary reimbursement, nor any real recognition for his efforts.

Apart from his involvement in the teaching of art and in fostering Canadian art through the Royal Canadian Academy and the Ontario Society of Artists, Matthews was a prolific artist and exhibited his paintings at the art shows at the Toronto Industrial Exhibition, at the shows of the various academies of which he was a member, and in 1893 at the World's Fair in Chicago. This demonstrates that his peers recognized his talent, which makes him an even more important subject for further analysis.[2]

Matthews is only one of a number of painters who have been completely left out of the canon of Canadian art history. His life and work provide an interesting window into this period of painting in Canada and reveal some of the problems with traditional approaches to Canadian cultural analysis. The theoretical method elucidated by Cosgrove in *Social Formation and Symbolic Landscape* allows for a much broader interpretation of these paintings and their meanings. His approach, when applied to Canada, places nineteenth-century artists in the context of time and the changing society within which they lived rather than locking them in isolated conflict with the Canadian wilderness.

NOTES

1 Marmaduke Matthews, *Art and Its Uses* (Marmaduke Matthews Papers, n.d. Trent University Archives).
2 According to J. Russell Harper (1970), Matthews exhibited in Ontario School of Art shows from 1873 to 1910. These shows included the Philadelphia Sesquicentennial Exhibition 1876, the Art Association of Montreal 1880–1910, the Royal Canadian Academy 1880–1911, Toronto Industrial Exhibition 1881–1909, Chicago World's Fair 1893, the Buffalo Pan-American Exposition 1901, and the St. Louis Purchase Exhibition 1904.

REFERENCES

Berger, John. 1973. *Ways of Seeing.* New York: Viking Press.
Campbell, Wilfred, and T. Mower Martin. 1907. *Canada.* London: A. and C. Black.
Cosgrove, Denis E. 1984. *Social Formation and Symbolic Landscape.* London: Croom Helm.
Davis, Ann. 1973. "The Wembley Controversy in Canadian Art." *Canadian Historical Review* 54:48–74.
Frye, Northrop. 1971. *The Bush Garden: Essays on the Canadian Imagination.* Toronto: House of Anansi Press.
Grant, George Munro, ed., and Lucius O'Brien. 1875. *Picturesque Canada: The Country As It Was and Is.* Toronto: Art Publishing Co.
Harper, J. Russell. 1970. *Early Painters and Engravers in Canada.* Toronto: University of Toronto Press.
———. 1978. *Painting in Canada: A History.* 2nd ed. Toronto: University of Toronto Press.
Matthews, Marmaduke. 1882. "Cloud-Bound: An Artist's Experience in the White Mountains of New Hampshire." *Rose-Belford's Canadian Monthly* 5 (July–December): 286–90.
———. n.d. Journal. Wychwood Park Archives, Toronto.
———. n.d. *Art and Its Uses.* Marmaduke Matthews Papers, Trent University Archives, Peterborough, Ont.
McGregor, Gaile. 1985. "A View from the Fort." *The Wacousta Syndrome: Explorations in the Canadian Landscape.* Toronto: University of Toronto Press.
Murray, Joan. 1983–84. "Papers of the Period: Marmaduke Matthews." *Journal of Canadian Studies* 18, no. 4: 172–77.
Nasgaar, Roald. 1984. *The Mystic North: Symbolist Painting in Northern Europe and North America 1890–1940.* Toronto: University of Toronto Press.
Pringle, Allan. 1984. "William Cornelius Van Horne: Art Director, Canadian Pacific Railway." *Journal of Canadian Art History* 8, no. 1: 50–78.
Reid, Dennis. 1973. *A Concise History of Canadian Painting.* Toronto: Oxford University Press.
———. 1979. *Our Own Country Canada: Being an Account of the National Aspirations of the Principal Landscape Artists in Montreal and Toronto 1860–1890.* Ottawa: National Gallery, for the Corporation of Museums of Canada.

21

Structured Feeling: Japanese Canadian Poetry and Landscape

Audrey Kobayashi

𝒱ernacular poetry is one of the most important social activities of the *Issei*,[1] Japanese immigrants who came to Canada during the late nineteenth and early twentieth centuries. The unusually widespread practice of poetry writing is of importance in understanding Issei culture, as it is a conversion of cultural practices in Japan of the late nineteenth century. Perhaps no other popular Japanese literature is as pervasive as that of Japanese poetry composition, particularly in the form of the *haiku*, which has ancient roots and is widely practised by people of all social backgrounds. This has especially been the case since the late nineteenth century, when the practice of poetry writing was adopted throughout Japanese society as part of the transformation of culture that marked the Meiji Period. The social construction of Japanese poetry can be understood from a materialist cultural perspective as the making of tradition and, simultaneously, as the shaping of the terms of everyday life.

As social tradition, poetry is time- and place-specific. Despite the complex symbolism and allusion that define the quality of Japanese poetry, it is almost never thereby abstract but is a circumstantial expression of real human conditions. Time and place are acted out conditionally as poetic meaning, so the context of writing becomes as important as the writing itself. The poems become moments constituted, "brief waves in the life of things" (Blyth 1949, 1). Having meaning and being language, moreover, poetry is shared. It is not a closing in, but an opening out upon the world as it is commonly understood and communicated.

Shared experience is problematic for cultural geographers, both for practical reasons, because of the difficulty of finding and organizing the information that allows us to tie meaning to context, and philosophically, because of the transcendent nature of experience. Even language that explicitly attempts to capture meaning cannot contain its fluid content within a landscape that is always a shifting scene, shared but multidimensional. Ironically, it is this very transcendence – simultaneous oneness, beyond and within, the Zen-inspired objective of inexpressibility – that the haiku attempts to express. This dialectic between transcendence and immanence can be captured linguistically only as the flow of experience – the making past of the present – is communicated. Despite the difficulties of linguistic analysis, then, and in the face of many unsolved philosophical problems, linguistic analysis represents one of the cultural geographer's best hopes for understanding human conditions and geographical change.

This chapter explores creative literature as evocative of those conditions, both in the sense that it expresses structures of feeling by which social experience is organized, and because we can understand the poetic act as a social act that not only expresses, but defines and reinforces the position of the individual within a cultural context. Raymond Williams's (1977) concept of "structures of feeling" provides an interpretive basis for a geography of vernacular literature. Williams's objective was to set literature within a material context and to understand it as both reflecting and constituting changes in the forms of social life. He sought within the literary process that "particular quality of social experience and relationship, historically distinct from other particular qualities, which gives the sense of a generation or of a period" (131). The structure of feeling refers to emergent rather than established social formations, to the point of contact between past (experience) and present (essence). The structure of feeling gives meaning to an event because it exerts pressure on, and sets limits to, human action, which is both the creation and the product of shared culture, immanent and transcendent. The structure of feeling captures, as well as language can, the variable nature of experience. It sets individual experience within the flow of social change and provides a way of knowing the connections, often dark and elusive, that provide evidence of historical conditions.

The notion of structures of feeling provides a number of theoretical entries to an analysis of literary meaning in place. First, it relies upon a notion of culture as, in Williams's terms, a "whole way of life," a constitutive (and material) process whereby people are bound together by structured actions and through which elements of life are strung together in a way that makes sense culturally. Structures are continuous (though variable), meaningful, rooted in place, interrelated, expressive of common knowledge, lived and made living, linkages linked. They are taste, touch, and tone as much as coercion, confinement, and commitment. They need to be communicated in order to be understood, and the means of communication vary in force and ambiguity. Structures are, following Sartre's (1976) notion, rules for living. Literature and art, relying as they do upon form and convention as "significant clues to the recognition of a particular 'structure of feeling'" (Jackson 1989, 39), can be very powerful structural expressions because they heighten the features of shared experience, and so provide guidelines for ways of experiencing.

A structural analysis of literature depends heavily upon setting that literature in context (and, in so doing, giving it structure), not only by linking meaning and experience, but by exposing life along its many dimensions, economic and political as well as aesthetic and sensual, achieving what Williams calls a "sociology of culture" or what Sartre calls simply "history," in the attempt both to overcome reductionism and to give specificity and roundedness to human life. Although Williams was concerned with emergent aspects of historical conditions in order to overcome a "habitual past tense" (128), and he wanted structures of feeling to address those aspects of experience that were not yet rationalized and institutionalized, he failed to emphasize the extent to which those structures are rooted in a past that may be (certainly in the case of Japanese poetry) highly structured and formalized. While the present work strives, therefore, for an understanding of the ways in which the past was converted in the poetry of Japanese Canadians and, therefore, of social change in which "living presence is always, by definition, receding" (128), it also relies heavily upon an analysis of history as social conversion, a past formed into a product that provides much of the raw material through which social change is effected. Vernacular literature, where it is available and where it has gained a significant cultural status, provides that material as a direct expression of structures of feeling as they occur through everyday life.

THE CONTEXT OF VERNACULAR LITERATURE IN MEIJI JAPAN

The "tradition" of vernacular poetry writing, despite its historical precedents, was a social construction of the Meiji Period (1868–1912), a conversion of the past at a time when it could become both a useful ideological tool and a means of aesthetic expression for a population newly awakened to popular education. In this sense, literature underwent a national renaissance, becoming an important part of popular consciousness and appealing to nationalist sentiments. Every Japanese schoolchild at the time was aware that the *Manyoshu* (JCTC 1940), the earliest extant anthology of Japanese poetry, dating from the eighth century, contains poems by both men and women of all classes and backgrounds, from the emperor to the ordinary farmer. The *Kojiki* (Philippi 1967), a foundation mythology, uses poetry to establish the spiritual basis of Japanese nationhood, and thus to link this form of expression with both the ancient and the sacred. Court anthologies were systematically collected from the early tenth century, and poetry writing developed as a refined art among the nobility (McCullough 1985). Its common themes, expressed through allusion and association, particularly relating to the teachings of Zen Buddhism, are deeply embedded in Japanese cultural values and practice, and have been revived throughout history to mould tradition and effect ideology.[2]

The art of haiku, the major contemporary poetic form, developed during the sixteenth century, when it reached its highest standard in the work of Basho. Basho was an itinerant poet who helped both to translate the haiku[3] into its present form and, perhaps more importantly, to establish the social setting in which poetry composition now occurs. Through his travels, he made poetry more widely accessible to Japanese people of all social positions, although for most of them it remained an oral form. He epitomized the revered qualities of the *sensei*, or teacher, surrounded by a "school" of followers who carried on his tradition, emphasizing the shared nature of the poetic act. His most important work, *Oku no hosomichi* (1933), is a travel diary that not only contains some of his most famous poems, but stipulates the context for poetic inspiration by describing the landscapes and settings in which he was moved to verse. So important is his work within the Japanese literary canon that it could be said to codify aesthetic experience, to provide a major element in structuring the human/nature relationship in Japanese culture. This work was widely read and revered by the late nineteenth century, and it provided a kind of template for travellers, including the emigrants who later found the haiku a fitting response to their new experiences in Canada.

It is the social appropriation of literature in the Meiji Period that provides the most important key to understanding the role of poetry in vernacular culture. The Meiji "Restoration" instituted a period of extensive, rapid, and very effective modernization, through which the Japanese government undertook to transform radically its political and economic foundations and, although not as straightforward a task, the cultural conditions of everyday life as well. Seldom, if ever, has a national transformation been undertaken to such specific ends.[4] This transformation depended, however, upon a deep contradiction: while the restructuring of nearly every aspect of Japanese life required fundamental and at times radical shifts in ways of seeing and doing, an effective ideological net, woven of long-established, even ancient, cultural precedents, was widely cast in order to provide the stability in which social change could occur. It was as effective as any manner of coercion in achieving nationalist aims and in establishing the cultural system that is still so important today in maintaining Japan's economic system.

Tradition was in this sense anything but traditional. It was a social construction that drew upon what was deemed noble, right, long-standing, and "Japanese," in the purest sense, in order to define the present by redefining the past, thereby creating a nation along clearly structured lines. At the heart of tradition was the emperor whose restoration represents one of the major ironies of the Meiji Period: over and again, ancient and venerated tradition was mobilized symbolically as a catalyst for modernization and change. Furthermore, one of the key features of the reconstruction of tradition at this time was the adaptation among the common people of practices that had formerly been the domain of the upper classes. This process occurred in the military (Norman 1943), in education (formerly restricted to the titled and wealthy but made universal in the 1870s, with the achievement of 95 percent literacy among school-aged children by the turn of the century [Dore 1964]), and in practices of landowning and marriage (Kobayashi 1992). Befu (1971, 52) calls this tendency the "samuraization" of the common people, who, in all these areas, took on values and practices formerly restricted to the nobility, thus gaining a greater "stake in the system." The venerability of long-standing traditions was used to effect new socio-cultural standards and to maintain an ideological hold on a population that might otherwise prove uncontrollable in the face of radical changes. It was, therefore, simultaneously a cultural anchor weighed in familiar channels to provide the comfort of "tradition" and a means of steering social practice so as to coordinate the actions, experiences, and values of everyday life with a rapidly shifting political economy.

In this context, poetry writing became a pastime of the common people. In 1874 an ancient edict was rescinded and poems written by commoners were accepted at court. In 1882 winners of the annual court-sponsored poetry contest were published in the national newspapers, the entries subsequently numbered in the tens of thousands (Reyes 1983), and poetry writing underwent a renaissance.

Literature in general flourished during the Meiji Period, through an increase in literacy and an expansion of the educational system, through official as well as private sponsorship of intellectual endeavour, and through a vast expansion of the publishing industry that allowed literary works to be widely read. In particular, literary publications flourished at a number of levels, from the vernacular to the very high brow (Okazaki 1955, 57–73). These included popular handbooks on "how to" write poetry, especially the haiku.[5] Such handbooks were available to, and widely read by, the emigrants to Canada, representing a primary source of cultural continuity in what was then viewed as a form of exile.

If achieving universal education was fundamental to the literary expansion, the emphasis placed upon poetry in educational practice was essential to its development as a national pastime. On the one hand, the fact that every schoolchild understood that the writing of poetry by commoners dated back to the time of the *Manyoshu* underscores the strong relationship between poetry and national pride, and the close association between poetic expression and the sense of social belonging. Children were taught not only that writing a poem is a significant social act, but that at certain times – to commemorate a death, at New Year's – it is more significant than at others. The teaching of poetry writing was highly ritualized. Children were taught to chant the 5-7-5 (-7-7) syllabic sequence in much the same way it had been chanted in tenth-century court circles, and the rhythm of this sequence came to be a definitive aspect of Japanese cultural life, an important means of structuring emotional and aesthetic experiences and their appropriate symbolic associations; in other words, the rhythm became a very significant means by which structures of feeling emerged in quotidian terms.

The social nature of the poetic act was further reinforced by the proliferation of poets' "circles." These circles applied the ancient principles of "loyalty and filial piety" (important concepts within the ideological rhetoric of the Meiji Period) to a central figure such as Shiki, the most renowned of nineteenth-century poets, or perhaps a local teacher who gathered together a group of like-minded villagers for occasional poetry-writing excursions or "fireside" readings.

A vernacular tradition so widely followed depended strongly upon fairly rigid formulae, which served the dual function of making poetry writing accessible to people of ordinary talents and, through replication, of reinforcing the very public and shared nature of poetry making, thus rendering it the more valuable as a cultural institution. While such standardization may have reduced its literary value (Ueda 1976, 4), it is in the very lack of originality that vernacular aesthetics (including fashion and some of the performing arts) gain their popular and emotional appeal, and produce the satisfaction of belonging. In this way, a sense of place is both assumed and assured for those who share common understanding and access.

Whereas one reading of the poetic fervour that swept Japan at this time might emphasize the benefits of modernization and education in opening avenues for creative expression, another would recognize that such expressions were also vehicles for the dominant ideology that needed strength and adherence if it was to serve nationalist interests. It would be naive to assume that such interests were always also in the best interests of ordinary people; such were the difficulties of economic change that it is more appropriate to speak in Irokawa's (1985, chap. 7) terms of "Meiji conditions of non-culture." Poetry took on two further dimensions of significance, however, in this respect. First, as a shared emotional outlet, it served to blunt the edge of hardship. There are many examples of poems that romanticize, dramatize, and even glamorize some of the most horrendous human conditions, and that make the endurance of those conditions an indication not of suffering, but of rectitude, just the sort of attitude that would benefit the new nation. Furthermore, Okazaki (1955, 74–85) claims that there was an important correspondence between political aims and public values that set the naturalistic and realist tendencies in the arts of the Meiji Period alongside a political ideology that called for a modernization of indigenous material culture. It was thereby a "moral culture," one that had effects far beyond the simple practice of poetry writing. And within this moral culture, certain attitudes and actions were appropriate to a vision of common interest.

EMIGRATION TO CANADA AND THE CONVERSION OF JAPANESE POETRY

Elsewhere, I have explored the "paradox" that emigration to Canada was an appropriate gesture towards the conditions of modernity imposed within the Meiji political regime (Kobayashi 1983, 1987). In such conditions, there was a conservatism that was deep and traditional – for all that it was recently constituted – and that depended upon a strong attachment to the rural landscape and the dignity of agrarian life. To achieve this life, however, required more resources than the average farming household could muster, and many were forced off the land and into a life of the urban working classes, a life antithetical to the ideals of Meiji tradition. It was in the spirit of continuing a "traditional" life, therefore, that many undertook to emigrate, with the initial intention of working temporarily abroad, in industrial waged labour, in order to achieve the means of returning eventually to village life.

Japanese immigrants to both Canada and the United States established poetry circles, somewhat along the lines of those that had existed in the village setting in Japan. Although the origins of these first groups are obscure, poetry must have been practised very early in Japanese Canadian history, for it appears in published form in the Japanese-language newspapers that were published on Powell Street from the turn of the century. The four forms of popular poems, *tanka* (31-syllables), *haiku* (17 syllables), *senryu* (31-syllable comic poems), and *renga* (linked verse), found expression. Ito (1973) reports formal groups in Seattle prior to the First World War. These groups contributed to magazines, such as *Circle* and *Aji* (taste, flavour, elegance) that circulated through North America. The groups also engaged in correspondence, composing *renga* by mail as in the case of the *Koyukai*, a poetry-writing group organized in British Columbia's Okanagan Valley (Kobayashi 1980). If the experiences of Ujo Nakano (depicted in Ward 1980) and Denbei Kobayashi (pen-name Hosui, depicted in Kobayashi 1980) are typical, the poetry circle was organized around an individual, usually someone who had developed the art before emigrating from Japan and who was recognized as a *sensei*, or teacher, of poetry. The founders and leaders seem to have been exclusively men, although nearly as many women as men made up the membership of the group.

Poetry composition seems to have played three major social roles. First, club members met regularly to socialize, often in a garden, park, or a natural setting that would provide aesthetic inspiration, and to compose poems under the tutelage of the *sensei*. They would also compose and recite poems at parties and other large social gatherings, or on any occasion that provided an opportunity to heighten, and coalesce, the sense of shared experience. This situation differed considerably from that in Japan, where poetry, for all that it carried deep-rooted ideological images, was undertaken as part of a coherent cultural system so that the poetry writers could both enjoy the aesthetic experience and participate in the refinement of the system. In Canada, however, poetry provided emotional sanctuary against the difficulties of immigrant life. This conversion of purpose is reflected in the imagery of the poems, which (as will be demonstrated below) take on a much more specific, immediate sense than indigenous Japanese poetry.

A second social role for poetry was commemorative, most commonly to mark anniversaries of important events or to honour the achievements of a particular *sensei*.[6] Poetry was also used to honour the dead. For example, in 1909 there occurred a disaster in the construction of the Great Northern Railway near New Westminster, British Columbia, where twenty-three Japanese immigrant workers were killed. Some of the haiku and *senryu* sent in memoriam are translated in Ito 1973 (883):

> Graves of Japanese
> Record the strife and struggle
> Of all immigrants.
>
> (Akebono)[7]

> Death followed by death,
> One by one those Meiji days
> Fade in the distance.
>
> (Kojo)

Neither son nor land –
Alone he goes far away
From this empty world.
                    (Koyo)

Mountains and rivers.
Here passing rovers have thrown
Their fading hopes.
                    (Seishi)

Dew or show'ring rain.
Idle the promises
Of this fickle world.
                    (Sadako)

Despite their sombre tone, such lines were an important part of the process of grieving and comforting, of making significant, and of giving substance, meaning, and immortality to ephemeral human ties.

Thirdly, as moral expressions the poems provided a structure of feeling by setting forth the maxims, values, and common terms of experience by which social life was organized. This process not only helped people to adjust to change, but also to maintain the moral values of Japan against the strong forces of change that rocked their lives as immigrants, a project of great concern to the Issei. This was achieved, as in so many other contexts, partly through aesthetics. The experience of aesthetic creation, according to culturally specified norms, was repeated and reinforced through the regular meetings and correspondence of the poets. The carefully chosen venues and the experiences evoked within those landscapes were not "natural" responses to innate landscape beauty; they were constituted responses in which landscape and common company merged to make up an appropriate scene, and in which "Japanese" values were imposed upon a foreign landscape. The language, too, evoked the emotion, the sense of time and seasonality, the wonder of things, the strong tie with the physical landscape, the inevitability of social choice, that reinforced a way of life. An example:

Petals, soft, falling,
Falling pull summer from me
Alone in my garden.
                    (Hosui)[8]

POETRY IN INTERNMENT

Between 1941 and 1949 Japanese Canadians were dispossessed. Uprooted from their homes, stripped of possessions, dignity, human rights, and freedom, they were treated to a variety of abuses and indignities that included relocation, internment, forced labour, deportation (see Figure 1.2, map 2, page 13).[9] It is not surprising that in this situation of intense physical and emotional trauma, of personal and family hardship, which threatened the existence of the Japanese Canadian community, poetry, long recognized as a source of solace, communion, and emotional release, should play a part. Two works are considered here. The first is a collection of poetry and prose reminiscences by Ujo Nakano, recognized as one of Canada's foremost Issei *tanka* poets. If recognized quality removes this work from the realm of the vernacular, it nonetheless expresses well both the experience of uprooting (cf. Maillet, this volume, chapter 12), and the comforting role of poetry. The second example is a collection of poems to mark the third anniversary of the Suhoken Kukai (Strong Friends Poetry Circle), made up of Issei who were interned at Slocan since 1942.[10] This collection, in contrast, stresses the social nature of poetry.

In March 1942 Takeo Nakano was taken from his family at Woodfibre, B.C. –

> Against such a thing as tears
> Resolved
> When taking leave of home.
> Yet at that departure whistle,
> My eyes fill.
>> (Nakano and Nakano 1980, 10)[11]

– to a "relocation centre," converted livestock pens at the Pacific National Exhibition site in Vancouver:

> Reek of manure,
> Stench of livestock,
> And we are herded,
> Milling –
> Jumble of battlefield.
>> (Nakano and Nakano 1980, 13)

thence into forced labour at a work camp in the Yellowhead Pass of the Rocky Mountains:

> Viewed upon arrival
> More so than rumoured,
> Rockies
> Steep snow peaks
> Rise sharply above the roofs.
>> (Nakano and Nakano 1980, 14)

Here, poetry provided an immediate emotional buffer against the trauma of loss and separation. Two weeks after his removal from home, he writes:

My practice of tanka composition was confirmed as part of meeting a still greater need. The near-traumatic separation from my family had meant the sudden removal of important emotional supports, and had necessitated a change in the way I coped with the daily vicissitudes of life. At this time of vulnerability my spirit was malleable, susceptible to any compelling power. As it happened, nature was to be that power. The tanka would serve both to order my perception of nature and to give expression to that perception. (Nakano and Nakano 1980, 20)

Later, in transit to an internment camp in Angler, Ontario, he passed through Greenwood and caught a brief glimpse of his wife and child, who had been confined there and watched from the platform as his train passed through:

> Child by the hand,
> In midsummer swelter,
> Railroad station scene.
> Come to greet me,
> Narrow eyebrows of my wife.

At Angler, although confined behind barbed wire, he again took inspiration from the natural landscape. Recalling an October dawn:

I turned towards the bush beyond the fence. Its ochre had been deepening day by day. The leaves, sprinkled with morning dew, sparkled like a rich brocade. I was conscious of a sadness in the honking of the high flying geese. The wind, which whistled through the fence, was quite chilly. I knew that many emotion-laden tanka would be born of these signs of the deepening of autumn. (Nakano and Nakano 1980, 69)

He joined a haiku club that had been organized by Baisetsu, one of his fellow inmates. The club was

a great success [which] attracted more members as it continued. It survived . . . right up to the closing of that camp at the end of the war. The best haiku written during its existence were collected in an anthology called Tessaku no Seki, "loneliness within the barbed wire fence." We who are fortunate enough to possess a copy hold one page of Japanese Canadian wartime history.

Aside from those days when the haiku club met, many indistinguishable days now followed. (Nakano and Nakano 1980, 70–71)

This *tanka,* written towards the end of Nakano's internment, expresses the adaptive and ameliorative effect of poetry writing:

Summer breeze
Blows soothingly;
In it,
Gradually,
I grow more submissive.

(Nakano and Nakano 1980, 86)

while this one, modelled upon an ancient verse found in the *Kokinshu* (a copy of
which he had with him in the camp), evokes the Japanese landscape as a continuing tie:

Sky.
If I turn around and look,
This moon seems to be the same one
As that of Mount Mikasa
Of Kasuga.

(Nakano and Nakano 1980, 89)

Befitting his position as a well-recognized poet, Nakano's work is personal
and introspective. The Slocan collection, in contrast, proclaims the importance
of companionship in the face of the most trying human circumstances.

The collection was undertaken in the spring of 1945 to commemorate the
third anniversary of the uprooting. Poems were solicited from Issei across the
country. Fifty-four individual haiku were submitted: these are printed at the
beginning of the collection in the order of their receipt. Ten members of the
haiku club presented their work, and there are contributions from the three
haiku *sensei* who travelled to the camp in order to participate by judging the
work and providing written and spoken commentaries. Finally, there is a collection of over a hundred verses on various themes dictated by the three *sensei*.

Although some of the poems are skilfully rendered and contain delicate
metaphors, the allusion running through the collection is neither subtle nor
mysterious. The project was conceived according to the metaphor of the warming spring waters of Slocan Lake "washing away" the hurt and suffering of
uprooting and internment. That three years should be a fitting anniversary is in
keeping with Japanese folk belief concerning the length of time necessary to
overcome trauma. A section describing the purpose of the project states:

Although they cannot forget the days of anxiety on being forcibly
removed to road camps and ghost towns, many Japanese are spiritually
renewed by expressing so skillfully their thoughts of spring when time
and anxiety are washed away in the warming waters.

The renewal effected through the rites of spring is of a very different nature
from that expected in the Japanese village in the normal cycle of the agricultural

year. It seems to have been a highly charged emotional experience, channelled through the structures of feeling that poetry could produce through heightened aesthetic effects. The poems are therefore cathartic, essential elements in going beyond the present. Here are some examples, limited to those written by internees:

> As the waters warm
> Poems celebrate three years
> Of our rustic life.

> After three years
> Green shadows of hills reborn
> From the water's edge.

> Three years to mellow
> In each other's company
> Now we greet the spring.

> Spring water, warming.
> I am happy after three years,
> Sitting at lake's edge.

It is often remarked that Japanese Canadians made the best of the difficult circumstances they faced during the 1940s with the expression *shikata ga nai* (it can't be helped). It is a trite expression, as are most of the poetic expressions in this poetry collection. Originality within bounds was admired of course; it was the basis of respect for the three invited *sensei*. But it was not expected. What was expected was that the structure of feeling that made poetry a cathartic experience should be shared and reinforced, that it should provide a means of coming to terms with difficulty and a tie to a Japanese past now much romanticized as a setting of moral tradition within an inspirational landscape.

CONCLUSION

From their poetry and, more specifically, their practice of poetry, we can learn a great deal of the experiences and the social life of the Issei. By analysing the poetic act as an expression of structures of feeling, we can even approach the emotional realm, so often opaque to cultural analysis. But can we go further, to make statements about human life in general? Recognizing that only empirical research will provide access to the specificity of life that structures of feeling convey, I think the answer is a qualified and cautious yes. Williams, after all, would claim universality for the theoretical status of structures of feeling. On this basis, several concluding points can be made.

First, the analytical concept of structures of feeling provides access to social change, at its edge and from the perspective of those caught up in its flow. The Issei came from a context of rapid social change in Japan and entered a situation of more abrupt and difficult change in Canada. Poetry provided a common thread in both series of transitions.

Secondly, this flow occurs in context, which means two things: that it can be understood as material change, however strongly inspired or imbued with spiritual properties; and that it occurs as the conversion of the past, a process in which the past is constantly re-created, reinterpreted, but never left behind. In both contexts of Meiji Japan and Canada, the meaning of poetry was significantly changed while being reconstituted, and given significance as tradition. To understand the terms of conversion, it is essential to identify the forces of political and economic exigency and to recognize the need to call upon tradition in the face of such pressures.

Thirdly, creativity and emotion are at the root of all experience. However much these features may be stymied, they exist as human potential. Furthermore, they are never in the strict sense individual. They originate univocally (that is, within individual consciousness), but always in a social setting by which they are structured and, through language, given meaning. Japanese poetry no doubt represents a rather extreme example of structured feeling, channelled emotion, and creativity, but it is thereby only a more explicit example of the universally social nature of human experience.

Finally, social change and human experience occur within a landscape, which is itself a social construction, given meaning and feature according to social values which, although not always entirely shared, are to some degree commonly understood and give form to what would otherwise be mere substance (Kobayashi 1989). The relationship with landscape in Japanese Canadian poetry required both a reference, however much idealized, to the landscape of Japan and a reinforcement of the soothing, palliative aspects of the Canadian landscape, selected both to evoke thoughts of Japan and to justify a life in Canada. Japanese Canadian poetry illustrates the universal fact that landscape is everywhere valued, given meaning in moral terms and significance as a social setting in place.

NOTES

1 The word *Issei* means "first generation" and refers to the immigrant generation. Japanese Canadians identify themselves by generation as Issei (first), Nisei (second), Sansei (third), and so on.

2 For general histories of Japanese poetry, see especially Yasuda 1958 and Keene 1976.

3 More properly, it was *haikai renga no hokku* (introductory lines of linked verse). The late nineteenth-century poet Shiki took the first and last syllables of the term to form the word *haiku*, applied retrospectively to Basho's work (Giroux 1974, 15–16).

4 There is a vast literature on the economic and political transition during the Meiji Period. For a general history, Hane 1986 is recommended. For a discussion of changes in everyday life, the most comprehensive works are Yanagida 1957 and Irokawa 1985. For a discussion of ideological constructions, especially the notion of "emperor," see Gluck 1985.

5　A good example of a modern "how-to" book in English is Ichiki 1985. Henderson 1958 undertook an informal survey of literary magazines in 1957 and found no fewer than fifty separate Japanese periodicals devoted exclusively to haiku, and a similar number devoted to *tanka*. Books in Japanese devoted to poetry range in the many thousands, and there are few poetic forms that receive so wide a treatment in English as does the haiku.

6　For example, the author has in her possession a commemorative volume to honour Denbei Kobayashi. It consists of a collection of haiku, hand written in sophisticated calligraphy, collected in a book, and bound in silk.

7　Names given here are the pen-names adopted by individual poets.

8　Unless otherwise specified, translations are by the author. Translation has been undertaken in the knowledge that much is lost, and the difficulties are in some respects insurmountable. There is a controversy among translators concerning whether to attempt a strict translation of both words and syllabic structure or to adopt a freer form more conducive to English usage. The former has been adopted here in the attempt to preserve as far as possible the rhythm, which is as essential to Japanese poetry as the words.

9　There are several accounts of these experiences. For book-length descriptions see Adachi 1976, Ito 1984, or Sunahara 1981. For compelling literary accounts, see Kitagawa and Miki 1985 or Kogawa 1981. For shorter versions, see Berger 1981 or Kobayashi 1987.

10　I am grateful to Mr. Kadota, of Vancouver, for supplying me with a copy of this mimeographed collection. His is the only surviving copy that I know of.

11　This book is based upon a translation of Nakano's 1940s diary and poems written while interned, translated initially by Kasey Oyama and edited by his daughter, Leatrice Nakano.

References

Adachi, Ken. 1976. *The Enemy That Never Was: A History of Japanese Canadians.* Toronto: McClelland & Stewart.

Basho. 1933. *Oku no hosomichi* (The poetical journey in Old Japan). Translated by Isobe Yaichiro. Tokyo: Sankakusha.

Befu, Harumi. 1971. *Japan: An Anthropological Introduction.* Tokyo: Tuttle.

Berger, T.R. 1981. *Fragile Freedoms: Human Rights and Dissent in Canada.* Toronto: Irwin Press.

Blyth, R.H. 1949. *Senryu: Japanese Satirical Verses.* Tokyo: Hokuseido.

———. 1964. *A History of Haiku.* Vols. 1–2. Tokyo: Hokuseido.

Dore, Ronald. 1964. "Education: Japan." In R.E. Ward and D.A. Rustow, eds., *Political Modernization in Japan and Turkey,* 176–204. Princeton, N.J.: Princeton University Press.

Giroux, Joan. 1974. *The Haiku Form.* Rutland, Vt., and Tokyo: Tuttle.

Gluck, Carol. 1985. *Japan's Modern Myths: Ideology in the Late Meiji Period.* Princeton, N.J.: Princeton University Press.

Hane, Mikiso. 1986. *Modern Japan: A Historical Survey.* Boulder, Col., and London, England: Westview Press.

Henderson, Harold G. 1958. *An Introduction to Haiku: An Anthology of Poems and Poets from Basho to Shiki.* Garden City, N.Y.: Doubleday.

Ichiki, Tadao. 1985. *Suggestive Brevity: Haiku into the World.* Kyoto: Biseisha.

Irokawa, Daikichi. 1985. *The Culture of the Meiji Period.* Translated and edited by M.B. Jansen. Princeton, N.J.: Princeton University Press.

Ito, Kazuo. 1973. *Issei: A History of Japanese Immigrants in North America.* Translated by S. Nakamura and J.S. Gerard. Seattle: Executive Committee for the Publication of Issei.

Ito, Roy. 1984. *We Went to War: The Story of Japanese Canadians Who Served during the First and Second World Wars.* Stittsville, Ont.: Canada's Wings.

Jackson, Peter. 1989. *Maps of Meaning.* London: Unwin Hyman.

Japanese Classics Translation Committee (JCTC), eds. 1940. *The Manyoshu* (Ten Thousand Leaves). Tokyo: Nippon Gakujitsu Shinkokai.

Keene, Donald. 1976. *World within Walls: Japanese Literature of the Pre-modern Era 1600–1867.* London: Secker and Warburg.

Kitagawa, Muriel, and R. Miki, eds. 1985. *This Is My Own: Letters to Wes and Other Writings on Japanese Canadians 1941-1948.* Vancouver: Talon Books.

Kobayashi, Audrey. 1980. "Landscape and the Poetic Act: The Role of Haiku Clubs for the Issei." *Landscape* 24, no. l: 42–7.

———. 1983. "Emigration from Kaideima, Japan, 1885–1930." Ph.D. dissertation, University of California, Los Angeles.

———. 1987. "From Tyranny to Justice: The Uprooting of Japanese Canadians after 1941." *Tribune,* 5 June, 28–35.

———. 1989. "A Critique of Dialectical Landscape." In A. Kobayashi and S. Mackenzie, eds., *Remaking Human Geography,* 164–84. London: Unwin Hyman.

———. 1992. "For the Sake of the Children: Japanese/Canadian Mothers/Workers." In A. Kobayashi, ed., *Women, Work and Place.* Montreal: McGill-Queen's University Press.

Kogawa, Joy. 1981. *Obasan.* Toronto: Lester & Orpen Dennys.

McCullough, Helen Craig, trans. 1985. *Kokinwakashu: The First Imperial Anthology of Japanese Poetry.* Stanford: Stanford University Press.

Miner, Earl. 1979. *Japanese Linked Poetry: An Account with Translations of Renga and Haikai Sequences.* Princeton, N.J.: Princeton University Press.

Nakano, T.U., and L. Nakano. 1980. *Within the Barbed Wire Fence: A Japanese Man's Account of His Internment in Canada.* Seattle: University of Seattle Press.

Norman, E. Herbert. 1943. *Soldier and Peasant in Japan: The Origins of Conscription.* New York: International Secretariat of the Institute of Pacific Relations.

Okazaki, Yoshie. 1955. *Japanese Literature in the Meiji Era.* Translated by V.H. Viglielmo. Tokyo: Obunsha.

Philippi, Donald L., trans. 1967. *Kojiki* (Record of ancient matters). Tokyo: University of Tokyo Press.

Reyes, Marie Philomène de los. 1983. *The New Year's Poetry Party at the Imperial Court: Two Decades in Postwar Years, 1960–1979.* Tokyo: Hokuseido.

Rimer, J. Thomas, and Robert E. Morrell. 1975. *Guide to Japanese Poetry.* Boston: G.K. Hall.

Sartre, Jean-Paul. 1976. *Critique of Dialectical Reason.* Translated by Alan Sheridan-Smith and edited by Jonathan Ree. London: New Left Books.

Sunahara, Ann. 1981. *The Politics of Racism: The Uprooting of Japanese Canadians during the Second World War.* Toronto: James Lorimer.

Ueda, Makoto. 1976. *Modern Japanese Haiku: An Anthology.* Toronto: University of Toronto Press.

Ward, W. Peter. 1980. "Afterword." In Nakano and Nakano, *Within the Barbed Wire Fence,* 109–25.

Williams, Raymond. 1977. *Marxism and Literature.* Oxford: Oxford University Press.

Yanagida, Kunio. 1957. *Japanese Manners and Customs in the Meiji Era.* Tokyo: Obunsha.

Yasuda, Kenneth. 1958. *The Japanese Haiku.* Tokyo: Tuttle.

22

A Loving Nature:
Malcolm Lowry in British Columbia

J. Douglas Porteous

$\mathcal{M}$alcolm Lowry is often considered a one-book author, the drunken exiled Briton who wrote *Under the Volcano* (1947), a novel about Mexico, while living on the British Columbia coast. Yet Lowry's post-*Volcano* metafictions evince a deep and loving relationship between the author and British Columbia, while *Volcano* itself reveals a deeply embedded stratum of longing for a home on this northern coastline. Lowry spent much of the years 1940–54 living in a series of squatter's shacks built on the beach at Dollarton, facing industrial Vancouver across Burrard Inlet. To his back, below Seymour Mountain, was what Earle Birney (1987) describes as not a real coastal wilderness but "only second growth with a few big stumps from the slaughtered Douglas firs long gone." But to Lowry, coming from a tamed England, this was very much like wilderness, and, moreover, paradise now.

Always a wanderer, Lowry made his penultimate stand at this point of juncture between an advancing metropolis and a retreating wilderness. In his posthumous *Hear Us O Lord from Heaven Thy Dwelling Place* (*HU* in text page citations) (1969) and *October Ferry to Gabriola* (*OF* in text page citations) (1970), Lowry claims to speak for a wild nature directly assaulted by the city, a most unusual situation in a world where major cities normally operate on wilderness only through an intermediary buffer known as countryside.

Despite shelves full of Lowry criticism, however, very little has been said about Lowry as environmentalist (Porteous 1989a), even though his pronouncements of the 1940s uncannily presage the environmentalist rhetoric that emerged twenty years later. Yet Lowry has important judgments to make on many specific environmental issues (Porteous 1986, 1987, 1990).

Rather than merely reinforcing these earlier analyses, what I wish to do here is to construct a Lowryan environmentalist argument, the kind of general, reasoned statement that Malcolm Lowry might have made had he been sufficiently well organized. Building such an edifice is problematic, for Lowry lived constantly in a personal wilderness of partly finished textual matter and was rarely concerned with the rigorous treatment of abstractions. "It is useless," notes

Grace (1982, 1) "to search for a tightly argued philosophical position in his works."

Yet to the modern environmentalist, Lowry's metafictions are filled with resonances, and "through resonance," as Frye has shown, "a particular statement in a particular context acquires universal significance" (1981, 217). Following this principle, then, and comparing Lowry's statements with later, more sophisticated analyses of the humankind-environment relationship, it is possible to tease out from the often inchoate mass of Lowry's works, both published and unpublished, a series of oft-reiterated themes that together offer a moderately coherent, rather romantic, environmentalist argument. Here, of course, I am operating as the classic Levi-Straussian *bricoleur* (Geertz 1988).

The following argument, then, consists of four related Lowryan propositions with a Canadian coda. The underlying concept is Lowry's preoccupation with the human-environment relationship (see Bordessa, this volume, chapter 5). Living on Bishop Blougram's "dangerous edge of things" between city and wilderness, "sensitive in the extreme, dismayed by man's destruction of the natural world, and deeply enmeshed in the puzzle of man's purpose on earth" (Grace, 1982, xiv), Lowry presents a moral argument that strongly prefigures modern environmentalist thought, is specific to the British Columbia coast, but which may be extrapolated to Canada and the world at large.

HUMANKIND'S DISTANCING FROM NATURE

It was as if they had exchanged sunlight on water for photographs of sunlight on water, cool commotion of blowing grasses and pennyroyal, or reeds and the rippling waters, the soaring love with which they followed migrating birds, for the tragic incidental music that always accompanies documentaries involving blowing grasses, rippling waters, and migrating birds, and soon they would not be able to have told the difference. (*OF*, 191)

In hard winters Lowry was compelled to leave his Dollarton shack for the "mephitic steam heat" of a Vancouver apartment. This transition was accompanied by an abrupt reduction in authentic sensuous pleasure. Despite his fondness for film and radio, Lowry decries these media in order to express the acute loss of the direct apprehension of nature, which is the inevitable result of humankind's heaping up into large electronic cities.

For cities are distant from nature (Tuan 1978). And because Vancouver is no stranger to bears, eagles, and cougars emerging from its adjacent wilderness, we realize that this distancing is mental rather than physical, a product of the growing power of industrialized populations to tame, control, reshape, or even exterminate the natural. We despise that which we control, and we interpose many-layered walls between ourselves and the perceivedly uncontrollable. We harbour a long-standing Judeo-Christian prejudice against wilderness, reinforced by the North American struggle to conquer it. Both Atwood (1972) and McGregor

(1985) tell us that Canadians have traditionally feared the wilderness, huddling so closely within their city garrisons that the Canadian ecumene has come to resemble a slender east-west Chile.

Such a distancing from nature means that wild landscapes can readily be uglified, commodified, or expunged (see also Sandberg, this volume, chapter 9). Nature is expunged simply by building over it. Lowry was deeply dismayed by the expansion of the Vancouver suburbs into the forested Dollarton coastlands. He speculated that "in these last frontiers of the Western world . . . a town has only begun to come of age when industry moved in and trees began to be knocked down and its natural beauty began to disappear," and that this process was analogous to "the popular superstition that one had not reached manhood before acquiring a dose of the clap; the only difference was that clap could be cured" (OF, 226). He suggested that in the atomic age (it was 1949) "people had come to disbelieve in the future so thoroughly that the creation of the permanent, or the excellent, no longer seemed worthwhile" (OF, 227).

Before the suburbs invaded Dollarton, before Lowry's forest became Cates Park, and before Lowry himself returned in sad exile to England, the squatters of Dollarton beach lived far closer to nature than did their city counterparts across Burrard Inlet. Winter storms threatened the very existence of their shacks, cougars were met in the forest, and everyday life included close encounters with trees, birds, animals, tides, currents, and stars. Lowry's visits to the city made him acutely aware of its heightened physical and social artificiality. In contrast, on Dollarton beach, "everything . . . seemed made out of everything else, without the necessity for making any one else suffer for its possession: the roofs were of hand-split cedar shakes, the piles of pine, the boats of cedar and vine-leaved maple. Cypress and fir went up the chimney and the smoke went back to heaven" (HU, 248). Indeed, to Lowry Dollarton was explicitly the Dantean paradiso, its blissful character only enhanced by memories of the Mexican inferno and distant views of the purgatorio of Vancouver.

Commodification of the forest came with suburbia in the form of "view lots" or a few especially shapely trees left amid the slash. The rest was "a suburban dementia . . . of flat ugly houses, the cleared land, stricken and bare, left without a tree to give it shade or privacy or beauty" (HU, 206). Denizens of this "bourgeois horror" were noted for "yapping about the benefits of civilization. How easy it is for people to talk about the benefits of civilization who've never known the far greater benefits of not having anything to do with it at all" (HU, 208) – an extremist view, for Lowry, too, was plugged in to civilization, a Rousseau with a radio as one visitor unkindly put it. And on reflection, Lowry came to the conclusion that "it was not human beings I hated but the ugliness they made in the image of their own ignorant contempt for the earth" (HU, 248).

Discourse on humankind's distancing from the earth and subsequent contempt for it is now more commonplace (Lopez 1986). A wholesale civilized drawing-back from direct experience of unsanitized nature lies at the base of this detachment. According to Evernden (1985) humankind is "the natural alien." O'Neill (1985) states that modern pathological narcissism, commodity eroticism, and neo-individualism together prevent us achieving harmony and kinship with our families, let alone with nation or nature. Reiff (1966) speaks of the "industrialization of selfishness," where quality becomes quantity, where the answer to "what for?" is "more," and where individualist excesses demand the accelerated destruction of natural landscapes. Leiss (1988) notes that this "progress" is driven by greed, envy, indifference to suffering, and a profound confusion between needs and wants. Illich (1973) documents a startling breakdown in conviviality, a quality of community much in evidence, according to Lowry, on Dollarton beach.

In short, citizen consumers appear to have sold their souls for an endless stream of low-grade entertainment. As Lowry so prophetically noted, the media simulacrum is increasingly accepted as the real. In a postmodern world of fragmented pseudo-experiences where "the public," according to Postman (1986, 110), "has been adjusted into incoherence and amused into indifference," and where the notion of the sacred in nature is almost expunged, it is unlikely that citizens will recover any depth of feeling for the wild nature they see on screens in the form of "natural wonders."

According to Postman, and as prophesied by Lowry, screen images have become our culture and the world we view on television seems natural rather than bizarre. Television directs "not only our knowledge of the world, but our knowledge of ways of knowing [our epistemology] as well" (Postman 1986, 79). This world view is infinitely manipulable. Modern "electronic darkrooms" can be used to alter representations of reality at will. Contemporary British Columbia provides an excellent example of this form of visual lying. A 1989 SuperNatural British Columbia advertisement portrays a doe and her fawn on a misty morning in an old-growth Douglas fir forest. But the deer came from a petting zoo, the mist from smoke sprays, and tourists searching the province for old-growth fir forests will find none that are both accessible and large enough to support a deer population (Brown 1989).

Lowry lived on the beach to avoid what he called this "whole false view of life, false comforts constrained by advertisements and monstrous deceptions" (*OF*, 154). He would have been more than wryly amused at Krieger's (1973) article entitled "What's Wrong with Plastic Trees?" and its potential expression in Victoria Inner Harbour in the form of a life-size Douglas fir in bronze.

HUMANKIND'S DESTRUCTION OF NATURE

[A] picture of Progress in the form of Jesus Christ driving a locomotive across a virgin forest. (*OF*, 202)

Leiss (1988, 44) believes that "plastic trees are an expression of our desire to be unencumbered by the claims of other living things in our environment." Lowry, forty years before, glowering across Burrard Inlet at forest company headquarters in Vancouver, was sure that for them nature had become purely an object. In a world of manipulated reality and of immense distancing from nature, it is not surprising that nature is generally seen as a commodity to be used exclusively for the benefit of humankind. The number of Canadian geography courses dealing with "resources" tells the same tale.

Lowry's descriptions of destruction, whether of old carpenters' gothic houses in Vancouver's West End or of trees tumbling down hillsides into Burrard Inlet, are deliberately horrific. He wants us to feel the difference between the two sides of the inlet, as in this poem:

> A marathon of gulls
> A chiming of chickadees
> An ecstasy of swallows
> A tintinnabulation of titmice
> A scapaflow of geese
> A caucus of crows
> An unavoidability of vultures
> A phalacrocorax of capitalists.
>   (Lowry n.d., a)

Unsafe on the far side, we find ourselves dwarfed by the altars of political and corporate greed with no creed except growth, progress, and development, "money being the only language they knew" (OF, 188).

The result is

> a spectacle at first not unpicturesque, of the numerous sawmills relent-
> lessly smoking and champing away like demons, Molochs fed by whole
> mountainsides of forests that never grew again, or by trees that made
> way for grinning regiments of villas in the background of "our expand-
> ing and fair city," mills that shook the very air with their tumult, filling
> the windy air with their sound as of a wailing and gnashing of teeth.
> (HU, 15)

Yet, as in Vancouver today, the visitor is charmed by mountain views, the flight of birds, the changing aspect of the sea, the romanticism of ocean vessels. Lowry's point is that it is only these externalities that made Vancouver's "fero-cious aldermen imagine that it was the city itself that was beautiful" (HU, 16).

It would be tedious to recount post-Lowryan elaborations of his thesis that humankind's primal crime is its usurping of the lordship of the earth and its attempt to assume exclusive title to it. Such attitudes are now commonplace. Here Lowry makes a crucial distinction between earth and world. World, or civilization, is a man-made force intent on subduing, taming, or even replacing earth or nature as understood by animals, aboriginals, and civilization's drop-outs. Dollarton's beach community was indeed finally destroyed by the world, by "civilization, creator of deathscapes, [which] like a dull-witted fire of ugliness and ferocious stupidity . . . has spread all down the opposite bank, blown over the water and crept up upon us . . . along it, murdering the trees and taking down the shacks as it went" (*HU*, 280).

Lowry felt these changes keenly, as excerpts from two poems illustrate:

> Six demons came and cut down three tall trees
> Next to our shack, one windy Saturday
> With neither damn your eyes nor if you please . . .
>
> To cut down all our hopes that lead to heaven
> Like loutish loggers, who to the fire and wind
> Leave nothing but this vicious slash behind . . .
>
> Who'd have no trees at all in their ideal world
> But who with model factories enhance
> Love's [?] green and man and nature's neighbourhood.
>
> (Lowry, n.d., b/c)

Fairly, however, he notes that there were minor benefits to such destruction, including the opening up of new vistas, while "man had not succeeded yet in hacking down the mountains or the stars" (*HU*, 280).

Lowry asserts, rather unconvincingly, that he is not a neo-Luddite, "no enemy per se of the machine," "and that when the author speaks of civilization it is understood that he is not referring to its free institutions, but to its ugliness, its rapacity towards nature, and its destruction of nature and man's natural needs" (Lowry n.d., d). Like Mark Twain before him, Lowry saw civilization as a kind of disease (Crews 1989), its leaders having an urgent desire to destroy nature and become masters of creation. In Myers's words: "When the last [non-human] creature has been accounted for . . . we shall look around and we shall see nothing but each other. Alone at last!" (1988, 37), Lowry's revelatory expression for this consummation is "The Abomination of Desolation sitting in the holy place" (*HU*, 198).

OUR NEED TO LOVE THE EARTH

> *No se puede vivir sin amar*
> (One cannot live without loving)
> —*Under the Volcano*

For to Lowry nature was holy, with Thoreauvian and Wordsworthian intimations of immortality. His chief protagonist is surnamed Wilderness, and Lowry points out that for him, unlike for many Europeans, "the name wilderness is not to be identified with desolation – it is wilderness in the spirit of Hopkins' 'Long live the weeds and the wilderness yet' – in short, the opposite" (Lowry n.d., d).

Modern readers of Greta Erlich, Annie Dillard, Barry Lopez, and the more nature-oriented social scientists and philosophers such as Leiss, Evernden, and O'Neill are beginning to realize that a return to loving the earth – in short, a neo-romantic renaissance – may be the precursor of learning again to love themselves and each other (see also Scott, this volume, chapter 14).

No se puede vivir sin amar runs like a current through *Volcano*, where it refers chiefly to sexual love (eros). In his later work, however, Lowry asserts that physical love is inextricably bound up with love of the earth. "Until I met my wife," murmurs Lowry's alter ego, "I had lived my whole life in darkness." His wife opened up the world of nature as well as her own deep tides and currents, and Lowry's protagonist "often . . . had the feeling that she had some mysterious correspondence with all nature" (*HU*, 249).

Love and nature together have a revitalizing effect on the refugee from civilization. Indeed, the one is manifested through the other. In *The Forest Path to the Spring*, symbols of paradise and rebirth abound; spring is a much-loaded word. The novella climaxes in spring when the unnamed protagonist is going for water to the spring and meets a cougar about to drink. The cougar stands on the path as a symbolic front against the destruction of nature and the consequent profanation of humanity.

For Lowry, the Dollarton beach-dwellers projected active communal love (agape) and were convivial in the Illichean sense. A sense of community and an anarchy of mutual aid were strong. And in this atmosphere of personal and community regard, it seemed natural to extend one's love to the surrounding wildness, whether nature revealed itself as benign, hostile, or indifferent.

Lowry's Dollarton works are awash with lyrical descriptions of animals, plants, the seasons, weather, and the flux and flow of tides. After some time in this setting, Lowry became attuned to nature in all its moods and felt able to recapture "the feeling of something that [civilized] man had lost, of which these shacks and cabins, brave against the elements, were the helpless but stalwart symbol of man's hunger and need for beauty, for the stars and the sunrise" (*HU*, 234).

Rejecting progress as defined by the world, Lowry believed he had progressed in terms of the earth:

> If we had progressed, I thought, it was as if to a region where such words as spring, water, houses, trees, vines, laurels, mountains, wolves, bay, roses, beach, islands, forest, tides, and deer and snow and fire, had realized their true being or had their source: . . . it was as if we were clothed in the kind of reality which before we saw only at a distance . . .
> We were still on earth, still in the same place, but if someone had charged us with the notion that we had gone to heaven and that this were the afterlife we would not have said him nay . . . (*HU*, 284)

It is in this mystical, transcendental mood that Lowry experiences a feeling of oneness with nature that goes beyond love but may be re-expressed in love, a feeling that

> something of vast importance to me had taken place . . . [an] experience associated with light [so that] when years after recalling it I dreamed that my being had been transformed into the inlet itself at sunrise . . . suddenly transilluminated by the sun's light, so that I seemed to contain the reflected sun deeply within my very soul, yet a sun which . . . was in turn transformed into something perfectly simple, like a desire to be a better man, to be capable of more gentleness, understanding, love. (*HU*, 272)

It is notable that wilderness-adventure tourists now deliberately set out to put themselves into situations conducive to such epiphanies (Graber 1976).

LOVE IT OR IT LEAVES YOU

> *Le gusta este jardin que es suyo?*
> *Evite que sus hijos lo destruyan!*
> (Do you like this garden of yours?
> Prevent your children from destroying it!)
> —*Under the Volcano*

This admonitory sign in a Mexican park is horrifically mistranslated by Lowry's Consul as "You like this garden? Why is it yours? We evict those who destroy!" Adam was evicted from Eden, the Consul evicted from both garden and life, Lowry evicted from his Edenic Dollarton (cf. Kobayashi, this volume, chapter 21). Thus, the Consul's mistranslation is more universal than individual, providing a poignant allegory of the human condition.

Earth may be Eden, but there is no reason why earth should be the exclusive domain of a single species that so ignorantly describes itself as *Homo sapiens*. We may be evicted by nuclear winter or by environmental collapse; or, more subtly, by continuing to promote world over earth, we will inevitably evict ourselves from our own souls, the ground of our being.

For Lowry appears to be in complete agreement with Chief Seattle's well-known opinion (quoted in Myers 1988, 37) that "whatever befalls the earth befalls the sons of earth . . . Man did not weave the web of life; he is merely a strand in it. Whatever he does to the web, he does to himself." Lowry, similarly, speaks of the "incommunicability of the feeling [that] man shoots only himself when he shoots [an animal]" (Lowry n.d., e). He speaks of animals' rights and asks "are not nature's rights man's rights in the end?"

Humankind, therefore, should not be too surprised when nature, outraged at the depredations of civilization, withdraws, resists, or takes revenge. The counterpart of the "ferocious destructive ignorance" of the corporate state is the Wendigo, the native peoples' "avenging man-hating spirit of the wilderness"

(*HU*, 245), which drives man to suicide and expresses itself in forest fires, tidal waves, earthquakes, and volcanic eruptions, all of which are well known to British Columbians. Natural hazards, then, from forest fire to greenhouse effect, are nature's reaction to despoliation (cf. Paul and Simpson-Housley, this volume, chapter 18): "Who can be surprised that the very elements, harnessed only for the earth's ruination and man's greed, should turn against man himself?" (*HU*, 241).

This is a judgment matched only by the darkest of ecological doomsayers. It is clearer today that "every power over nature is a power over ourselves" (O'Neill 1985, 152). Yet the tranquillizing of the citizenry has become part of our culture of passivity; we have learned "to be calm in a state of crisis" (O'Neill 1985, 155), waiting quietly for the bang or whimper of the end of the world.

A CANADIAN CODA

Canada, whose heart is England but whose soul is Labrador. (*HU*, 29)

For Lowry, "progress was the enemy, it was not making man more happy or secure. Ruination and vulgarization had become a habit" (*HU*, 205). The heart of the matter was that postwar Canadians had become arrant modernizers, creators of placeless deathscapes, destroyers of the wild earth in pursuit of a profitable world. And the cruel truth was that "Canada's beauty was in its wildness . . . It was the only originality it had" (*OF*, 188).

Lowry's uncompromising denunciation of the British Columbian relationship with environment will earn him few friends:

> Vancouver, Canada, where man, having turned his back on nature, and having no heritage of beauty else, and no faith in a civilization where God has become an American washing machine, or a car he refuses even to drive properly – and not possessing the American élan which arises from a faith in the very art of taming nature herself, because America having run out of a supply of nature to tame is turning on Canada, so that Canada feels herself at bay, while a Canadian might be described as a conservationist divided against himself. (*HU*, 95)

Conservationists divided against ourselves indeed! British Columbia remains the quick-money forestry capital of the world, with a laxity of controls rarely permitted outside the Third World. And Lowry had a word for this primitivism: "We are not styled B.C. for nothing" (*OF*, 171).

Vancouver is Lowry's symbol of capitalistic rapacity. He clearly hopes that the Wendigo will destroy this city, only about sixty years old when he wrote:

> Vancouver is a place of fears
> Her tables have no place for beers
> Her conscience is in sad arrears

Hypocrisy is that which steers
As the rock of gaunt Neurosis nears
From all of which it much appears
My damned ferocious little dears
The fates are working with their shears
She soon could be a place of biers
She soon could be a place of tears
Or, once again, a place of bears
(More happily a place of bears).

(Lowry n.d., f)

Yet, in comparison with his rejection of Europe, his flight from Mexico, and his failure to come to terms with the United States, Lowry regarded British Columbia as a haven. Here he lived a life close to nature, a life that unleashed his creativity.

From this developed a deep love of Canada, which he described as "adolescent, large, loutish, noisy, goodhearted, anxious to please, eternally hopeful, and eternally put upon" (1949). These qualities may have led Lowry to his perhaps prophetic belief that "some final wisdom would arise out of Canada, that would save not only Canada herself but perhaps the world" (*OF*, 202). Here Lowry presages ideas perhaps best expressed in Watson's classic *The Double Hook*, that a period of sterility, death, and emptiness will be replaced by a return to life, fertility, wonder, and community (Grace 1982) – although, as Lowry wryly remarks, "the world never looks as though it's going to be saved in one's own lifetime" (*OF*, 202).

PROFIT VERSUS PROFITEERS

Unnatural acts are overwhelming nature.
—Adam Zimmerman, Chairman,
Noranda Forest Products, 1989

In Lowry's estimation, humankind abuses earth to create a worldly civilization, which is thus held responsible for the destruction of nature. By extension, humankind destroys its own garden of Eden, or paradise, and as a result must suffer the fate of expulsion. In environmentalist terms, Lowry appears a minor prophet, railing at the profiteers across Burrard Inlet. Lowry expressed modern environmental notions long before they became popular, decried the effacement of beauty by ugliness, and anticipated recent philosophical debate by noting that consumer materialism is based on "man's imaginary needs that were in reality his damnation" (Illich 1977; Leiss 1988). He would have laughed uproariously at the recent public relations work of landscape-destroying forest and mining corporations and at the facile deceits practised by the British Columbia government's tourist promotion programs.

Lowry's solution is not a simple-minded "back to nature" movement, nor yet a sentimental mere looking at nature, but an attempt to see nature for its intrinsic dignity and worth, to reinvest nature with the rights we have stripped from it, and to try, at least, to live in greater harmony with natural forces and rhythms. A modest proposal, but one that is now commanding considerable attention from a host of Aquarian conspirators, ecologists, Gaians, and geologians. Lowry envisions a life where wants are more truly in tune with needs, a life where there is time to enjoy the revitalizing effects of nature and love, a life where there is time to stand and stare, and to pursue our school-deadened creativity as an alternative to passive consumerism. As the Consul in *Volcano* realizes, we must make our peace with nature or die.

In July 1989, as I write this, Lowry would have turned eighty. It is also the twentieth anniversary of the landing of an American trash-bearer on the moon. An unidentified talking head informs me that this "giant step for man" means that "we've won immortality for man – we can survive the destruction of the earth" (CBC National News, 19 July 1989). Meanwhile, perhaps encouraged by this nihilist promise, the destruction of landscapes and peoples continues almost unchecked. Few yet understand, with Thoreau, that "in wilderness is the salvation of the world." It might not be too cynical to agree with John Locke that "hell is truth seen too late" and with the El Salvadorean guerilla poet Roque Dalton that

> Environmentalism is the echo
> of the noise
> Of capitalism destroying the earth . . .
> (Porteous 1988)

REFERENCES

Atwood, M. 1972. *Survival.* Toronto: House of Anansi Press.

Birney, E. 1987. Personal communication.

Brown, N. 1989. "Super-Natural Ad Picture Was Faked." *Times Colonist* (Victoria), 27 June 1989, A1.

Crews, F. 1989. "The Parting of the Twains." *New York Review of Books* 36:39–44.

Evernden, N. 1985. *The Natural Alien.* Toronto: University of Toronto Press.

Frye, N. 1981. *The Great Code: The Bible and Literature.* Toronto: Academic Press.

Geertz, C. 1988. *Works and Lives.* Stanford: Stanford University Press.

Graber, L. 1976. *Wilderness As Sacred Space.* Washington, D.C.: Association of American Geographers.

Grace, S. 1982. *The Voyage That Never Ends.* Vancouver: University of British Columbia Press.

Illich, I. 1973. *Tools for Conviviality.* New York: Harper & Row.

———. 1977. *Toward a History of Needs.* New York: Pantheon.

Krieger, M. 1973. "What's Wrong with Plastic Trees?" *Science* 179:446–55.

Leiss, W. 1988. *The Limits to Satisfaction.* Montreal: McGill-Queen's University Press.

Lopez, B. 1986. *Arctic Dreams.* New York: Scribner's.

Lowry, M. 1947. *Under the Volcano*. London: Jonathan Cape.

———. 1949. Review of E. Birney's *Turvey*, *Thunderbird* 5:26.

———. [1961] 1969. *Hear Us O Lord from Heaven Thy Dwelling Place*. London: Penguin.

———. 1970. *October Ferry to Gabriola*. New York: Plume.

———. n.d., a. Poem: "A Marathon of Gulls," Lowry archive, University of British Columbia Special Collections, box 5/26.

———. n.d., b. Poem: "Hypocrite! Oxford Grouper! Yahoo!" box 4/106.

———. n.d., c. Poem: "Save that the Optimistic Ones Are Worse," box 5/95.

———. n.d., d. Typed notes, Lowry to Erskine, re: work in progress, box 32/1, p. 26.

———. n.d., e. typescript short story: "We're All Good Ducks Here," box 32/4, p. 7.

———. n.d., f. Poem: "Noble City Full of Pigeons or Everyone a Hypocrite Including Me," box 5/43.

McGregor, G. 1985. *The Wacousta Syndrome*. Toronto: University of Toronto Press.

Myers, N. 1988. *Gaia: An Atlas of Planet Management*. New York: Doubleday Solidus/ Anchor.

O'Neill, J. 1985. *Five Bodies*. Ithaca, N.Y.: Cornell Universal Press.

Porteous, J.D. 1986. "Inscape: Landscapes of the Mind in the Canadian and Mexican Novels of Malcolm Lowry." *Canadian Geographer* 30:123–31.

———. 1987. "Deathscape: Malcolm Lowry's Topophobic View of the City." *Canadian Geographer* 31:34–43.

———. 1988. *Degrees of Freedom*. Saturna Island, B.C.: Saturnalia, The Saturna Island Thinktank Press.

———. 1989a. "Lowry As Environmentalist." *Malcolm Lowry Review* 23/24:157–59.

———. 1989b. "Landscape of Experience: Malcolm Lowry's British Columbia." In P. Dearden and B. Sadler, eds., *Landscape Aesthetics*. Victoria: Western Geographical Series.

———. 1990. *Landscapes of the Mind: Worlds of Sense and Metaphor*. Toronto: University of Toronto Press.

Postman, N. 1986. *Amusing Ourselves to Death*. London: Penguin.

Reiff, P. 1966. *The Triumph of the Therapeutic: Uses of Faith after Freud*. London: Chatto and Windus.

Tuan, Y-F. 1978. "The City: Its Distance from Nature." *Geographical Review* 68:1–12.

INDEX

Printed in Canada